LOST FROM THE OTTAWA;

The Story of the Journey Back

A Memoir By Pun Plamondon

Published in the United States of America by Plamondon, Inc.
P.O. Box 151, Cloverdale, Michigan 49035

Order on line at www.TRAFFORD.com

Printed in the United States

Front and back cover art by Gary Grimshaw

Bootleg Edition.

10 9 8 7 6 5 4 3 2 1

ISBN.141202265

www.punplamondon.com

DEDICATION:

Spring Cota, my biological mother.

Alice Plamondon, my adopted mother.

Evelyn Whiting, who raised me when the others couldn't.

Patricia Lynn, my wife, who helped salvage my life.

DEDICATION

[illegible] Cole, my biological mother

[illegible] Hamilton, my [illegible] mother

Evely[illegible] Wilson, who raised me with the other [illegible]

[illegible]

ACKNOWLEDGEMENTS

This memoir would not have been possible without the help and support of many people: Lewis Sawaquat, my elder and teacher, who put me on the path to the Ottawa. Gordon Henry, my Ojibway friend, who convinced me this story was worthwhile and the only way to tell it was to write, write, write. The spirit of my Pottawatomi friend and neighbor, Frank Bush. And Kevin Aiken, my cousin, who put me in touch with my biological family.

Sarah Drumm, and her husband Steve, have been involved with this project from the beginning, encouraging, editing and drawing me out--no easy task. Phil Bellfy and Peggy Cunniffe from MNO Press made my work sparkle and snap, I feel, with their final edit. Marilynn Van Dyke and Mark Bonsignore proofread the manuscript, and any grammatical errors are the result of my stubborn insistence. Regrettably, Madelyn Bonsignore passed away after editing the first half of the book. Syd Dulaney and Hank James gave sound story advice and held my hand as I passed the gateway into the world of computers. Steve Losher, Cliff and Sharon Barry, and Tom and Juanita Walsh listened patiently as I read them many chapters.

David Sinclair, Peter Werbe, John Sinclair, and my attorneys Buck Davis and Leonard Weinglass have astute memories of events and times; I relied on them all substantially. Leni Sinclair was most generous with her photographs and Gary Grimshaw executed my cover design masterfully. James Semark, a poet friend from the Artists Workshop days, did a whiz-bang job with my web site. Margaret Saadi Kramer and her husband Wayne have been invaluable as my west coast connection.

The native community of Michigan played a big role in my having found serenity and acceptance. The elders, veterans and storytellers have given freely of themselves; I can only say "megwetch" and hope that as long as the ghost of Pun Plamondon haunts this earth I will be worthy of their friendship.

Likewise, I owe a debt of gratitude to my friends and survivors in our local 12-step program. They've helped me stay sober these 20-odd years and allowed me to be of service to others.

My many friends and neighbors in southwest Michigan have looked out for me and purchased advanced copies of this book as a way of giving financial support.

I will be forever grateful to my lovely wife Patricia who stuck by me through thick and thicker and allowed me to share my life with her. To all I say, "megwetch" (thank you).

Oh! And Neal Akey, who 25 years ago, threatened to sue me if I ever mentioned his name in my book.

DISCLAIMER

I decided when beginning this memoir to remain true to the genre and recreate this story completely from memory. My memories, like most, are composed of what really happened and what I believe really happened. This narrative is not a "report" or "history" or "autobiography" even. It is simply a story of connected events remembered a lifetime after they happened. This is a survivor's story.

I included several appendices to clarify and give comfort to those who need the facts.

The characters in this story are real people, with the exception of Rock-n-Roll Rita, who is a composite of several women I was associated with at one time in my life. Throughout the book I've frequently used initials, aliases, fictitious names, and "*noms de guerre*" to protect the innocent as well as the guilty. Those who are still public figures are referred to by their public names.

If not "true," the story is as close to honest as I've ever been.

Pun Plamondon August, 2004--in the 1836 ceded territories of Michigan.

INTRODUCTION TO THE DETROIT BOOTLEG EDITION

An advantage of self-publishing through a print on demand (POD) publisher is that the author owns the copyright. A disadvantage is that the POD publisher will not accept bookstore returns.

I've decided to independently print my book, in addition to my POD publisher, for sales and personal appearances, to supply distributors, and guarantee bookstore returns. This seems the best way to encourage bookstore placement

Isn't this a great country? I'm bootlegging my own book!

Pun Plamondon, ceded territories, October, 2004.

TABLE OF CONTENTS

Chapter One

INAUSPICIOUS BEGINNINGS...1945-1960

Among the Ottawa of the Great Lakes Basin and beyond there is an ancient tradition still carried out in a handful of old-time Ottawa families.

For a thousand years the tradition has been the same: shortly after the birth of a child, the father gathers the placenta and buries it in the yard near the home, maybe out back near the old oak. This is done so the child will always know where her home is and the spot where she is connected to the earth. Later, when the umbilical cord dries and falls off the baby, the father makes a special leather pouch and places the cord inside. Since the father does not have the close physical connection to the child that the mother has, the father will wear the pouch around his neck or carry it in his pocket so as to build that physical connection. Later, the bag might be hung in the kitchen, in a place where it can be pointed out to the child at critical times, so the child will always know where she belongs.

None of this happened at my birth. Instead, in 1945, I was conceived and born in the State Mental Hospital in Traverse City, Michigan. My father was a 52-year-old half-blood Ottawa suffering from chronic alcoholism. My mother was a 39-year-old mixed-blood Ojibway woman diagnosed with syphilis. And so the circle begins.

*   *   *

Being born in a mental hospital is no big deal if you don't remember it. I don't. I was there several months, according to records, long enough for the nurses and staff to cuddle and coo over me, and call me "Baby Cota," after my mother. Shortly afterward I was christened Lawrence and placed in a foster home, apparently for more than a year. Years later my adopted mother told me that I was in foster care not far from the Plamondon home, and that I had become quite dear to my foster mother.

The Plamondons adopted me when I was 18 months old. My first real memory as a child is of being taken to the Grand Traverse Osteopathic Hospital to be circumcised. I was probably two. I remember being carried as a toddler to a ward with little white cribs, and playing with a toy tractor, then crying hard when my new dad left me there with strangers. I don't remember being cut.

The Plamondons were a white, Catholic, working-class family with roots to the family farm that lead back to French-speaking Quebec. We lived in the back apartment of my dad's small country store. The sign said G&A Grocery--Cold Beer and Wine (George and Alice, my parents' names). When I was five, we moved out of the store and into a house trailer while our new, three-bedroom house was being built on a lot behind the store which was being remodeled and expanded.

Early photos show a smiling brown-faced boy bundled up snug in a brand new snowsuit three sizes too big, the hood cinched down tight against the cold. He's standing in a driveway, in front of a huge pile of snow pushed up by a plow, a trusty Cocker Spaniel at his side.

When I was six we moved into the new house, and my adopted parents had the first of their "own" three children. I remember adults telling me over and over, "You're jealous of your little sister; don't be jealous of your sister." I don't remember being jealous, but surely I was.

In the second grade my parents enrolled me in St. Francis Elementary School, an institution, as I remember it, of torture and torment.

As I got older and my parents' family grew, my mother seemed to live in a constant state of stress. She was perpetually frantic about something--cleaning house, making supper, or getting dressed for church or shopping, caring for my sister, doing laundry or dishes. She seemed to be in a constant frenzy of screeching, scolding, arm yanking and ear pulling.

In preparation for the birth of my second sister, my dad told me I was adopted. Even at eight years old I could tell this revelation distressed him. He told me he had sought advice: some said tell the child, some said don't. He believed that by telling me he was doing the right thing. He said my real parents couldn't keep me, and that God had sent me to my new family as a little baby. He assured me he and my mom loved me very much, as much as their "own" children. He didn't tell me anything about my natural parents, and I didn't think to ask, being so young. It wasn't a big deal anyway, I just wanted to go out and play.

I understood the concept of adoption and realized that the Plamondon family story was not my story. They were not my mother and father, they were my mom and dad. My brother and sister were not my relation. All my aunties and uncles were not of my flesh and blood.

Traverse City sits, like a cherry-red ruby, on the little finger of the "mitten" of Michigan. We lived just 200 yards from East Grand Traverse Bay, where mile after mile of family-owned motels, tourist resorts, and rental cabins crowded cheek by jowl to hug the bay shore and its fine "sugar sand" beaches.

Sometimes as early as May, a group of neighborhood boys and I would swim until prune-toed, so cold our lips turned purple, like a mandrill's ass during mating season. We had a knock-about steel rowboat and a raft built of inner tubes to explore Mitchell Creek, one of several that emptied into the Bay. Behind my house were miles of forests where young boys could hunt monsters or Indians or Korean commies. It was easy to smile.

That forest was my back yard, and I walked every inch of it, with playmates or alone. In my mind this was virgin forest, untrod by humans. I know now the land had been logged off for lumber to rebuild Chicago after the Great Fire and was really only second growth. Still, I could feel the ancient spirits, and felt at home and comfortable there. As time went on and things got more hectic at home, the woods became my sanctuary.

I was ten or so when I got the nickname "Pun." Nicknames were common in our rural neighborhood, all the kids had them. There was "Boner" and "Porky" and "Turd" and "Swindler" and "Crazy Claude." For a while, since many of my playmates couldn't pronounce my last name, I was called "Paladin," after the character in the TV show *Have Gun, Will Travel*. Then I was called Punjab, I don't know why. Finally, the gang settled on "Pun" and it stuck. It means nothing. Actually I liked the name. It didn't have a negative connotation like Boner or Porky and it was original--there was no other like it.

Financially, my family wasn't doing well. The new highway went through and construction closed the family grocery for nearly a year. In addition, the big chain stores, like Kroger and A&P, were becoming popular. Fewer people were shopping the small, independent, mom-and-pop enterprises. The Korean War had just ended, and the country was beginning to move forward. New things were happening, new ideas...plastics. In my eyes my dad seemed to be stuck in an unimaginative, small-town rut.

I was pissed about our poverty. All the people around us seemed to have plenty of money. It was about this time (just after the birth of my second sister) that I started misbehaving in school, and bed wetting too. Adults said I was "hyper-active"--whatever that meant--Ritalin had not yet come on the scene.

I was ten when my brother, the last of my mom and dad's children, was born. The family's financial condition had worsened. Dad kept the store open, but to save money on electricity he would turn on only a few lights, not even the outside sign. The few customers who did stop would come into a dim, gray, dingy store to find shelves as poorly stocked as a Russian grocery, with my dad often nodding-off at the counter.

In those lean times my mom made some of my clothes.

Oh, how I hated that! At a time when kids were beginning to understand fashion and to wear "brands," here I came with my homemade, no-brand coat or shirt.

I remember having to stand on a chair for what seemed like hours while mom pinned and adjusted the garment. I'd fidget. She'd pinch me. "Stand still," she'd snap. I'd slouch. She'd twist my ear. "Stand straight," she'd hiss, then stand back and size up her work. "It isn't straight," she'd heave, yanking me by the arm. "Now stand straight, I'm not going to tell you again." Then it would all start again. I'd wiggle. She'd yank me around. I'd fidget and get stuck by a pin. "Now see what you made me do!" she'd snarl and twist my arm again. I'd start crying. "You stop crying or I'll give you something to cry about," she'd threaten. Tears would fill my eyes; I'd muffle heaving sobs. And on and on it went.

* * *

In our house, Christmas, Easter, First Communion, Confirmation, birthdays and Baptisms were always times for family photos. With mom yanking me around, attacking my hair with a comb, and scolding me to sit still and keep my eyes open, we kids would be lined up on the couch. I see the yellowed Kodak now--me in peppermint striped pajamas holding a new Lincoln Log set, one sister clutching a new doll, the other, a pink plastic tea set still in its cellophane-wrapped box. My little brother is holding up his new teddy bear.

The pictures are always the same: three white, tow-headed kids, perfectly stair-stepped. Then me. Six years older than my nearest sister, I was a skinny, dark-haired, dark-skinned, sullen boy who was obviously not from the same litter. I came to avoid, and still do today, group photo sessions.

It was no better at St. Francis School. I was in trouble almost every day; acting out, cutting-up, talking in class, running in the hall, whatever. Teachers and other adults said I was "seeking attention."

Misbehaving brought punishment both in school and at home. Catholic Corporal Punishment (CCP) was the order of the day. CCP was hammered into my head from the very first day of Catholic school. ALL AUTHORITY COMES FROM GOD. God gave parents authority over children. Parents transfer this authority to teachers. Nuns have compounded authority, not only the authority given by parents to teachers, but additional authority given by God to nuns as His servants.

Once, in the fourth grade, I made Sister Raymond furious. Again I had disrupted her remedial reading class. Maybe by shooting spit balls, rubber bands, or paperclips. Maybe by playing "keep-away" with someone's homework, or passing notes or talking, laughing, pulling a girl's hair or trying to look up her dress. Whatever infraction I had committed that day, Sister Raymond snatched me by the ear and marched me to the front of the classroom. With all the authority vested in her, she ordered me to my knees, facing the class. She paced back and forth behind me, out of my sight. Blam! She hit me on the head with the heavy classroom Bible. Blam! She nailed me again. A few moments later, Blam! She blasted me again. She continued teaching the class. Blam! The kids were so scared and trembling, only the teacher's pet could keep reading. Blam! Class dismissed.

I remember kneeling there scared and humiliated. But, after being blasted on the head by the Word of God half a dozen times, I realized I could take it. She couldn't hurt me. If this was the worse she could do--no problem. I was not afraid of her anymore. Without fear, she had no power over me, which is a good lesson to learn in your pre-teen years.

At home I was forever teasing my oldest sister, making her whine and squeal. If I was told once, I was told a million times: "Leave your sister alone. Don't tease her, don't go in her room, and don't touch her things!"

One day after school my sister and I were in her bedroom. Mom was in the kitchen. I was fooling around, taking my sister's stuff, making her beg to be left alone. While tussling with her I accidentally poked her in the eye with my elbow. She started crying and screaming: "Larry poked me in the eye! Larry poked me in the eye!"

I could hear mom coming, and feel her. The whole house trembled from her rage as she rushed into the room like a sow bear protecting her cub. She was a large woman, as all adults are to a 12 year old. She outweighed me by more than a hundred pounds. She knocked me to the bed, fell on top of me and pinned my hands down as she repeatedly jabbed her finger in my eyes.

For a moment I resisted as she poked and jabbed, over and over. Then I realized I could squint my eyes shut real tight so she couldn't poke my eyes out. I quit resisting and just lay there, defiant. I could stand the pain. She could not hurt me. The threat of pain was no longer a tool she could use to control me. She poked until she got tired, or got her wits about her, and then stopped.

When it was over I had tiny cuts around my eyes and forehead from my mother's fingernails. Then, as she often did, she felt guilty, apologized, hugged me and told me she loved me. She treated the cuts with Unguenteen, a brand name white ointment. I had hundreds of small, moon-shaped, red cuts topped with white grease on brown skin.

My dad's store was just across the driveway from our house. After this eye-popping episode, I went over to the store to hang out with him. As was often the case, one of my friends from the neighborhood was in the store. My friend asked what happened to my face. Thinking fast in front of my dad, I said I was in the woods and got caught in a picker-berry patch.

When we were alone my dad told me that he'd noticed and appreciated that I'd lied to protect my mother. We had a connection, my dad and me. He was low-key, laid back and easy-going, just the opposite of my mom. When I got older we fished and hunted together occasionally.

By the beginning of my teen years, I was a pretty messed up kid. To make things worse, the store was failing. We went on relief, as welfare was called then. I remember being mortified when one of my friends would be at our house for cookies and milk or for supper and mom would serve the watery thin, off-white, powdered milk she got from Government Commodities and shook-up in a large glass mayonnaise jar kept just for that purpose. I so wanted to fit in.

Mom would cut my hair at home to save a-buck-and-a-quarter. She did a terrible job, which my wiggling and fussing didn't help. The result was embarrassing. Nicks and cuts went down to the scalp. My mom used eyebrow pencil to darken in the more obvious gouges. I wanted hair like Elvis; instead, I got a goofy "punk" haircut 30 years before the fad.

I had no-brand clothes, a no-brand haircut, and we

drank no-brand milk. I was adopted, and felt like a no-brand kid. Everybody was something. My classmate Patrick O'Patrick was Irish, Drosdowski was Polish, Perot was French, and "Fenderhead Miller" was English. Who was I? I had dark hair and skin. Why? What was my nationality? In those days I only knew I wasn't a Plamondon.

Betty Anishnabee was dark; she was my classmate and an Ottawa Indian. She, and everyone knew it. It would have been natural for me to identify with her, but, at that time, I didn't know of our tribal connection. She was a nice, sweet girl, quiet and respectful, with good grades and always dressed in well-worn, hand-me-down, Catholic schoolgirl uniforms. Like me, she lived in the country and had a long bus ride to and from school. It was easy to feel superior to her because she was poorer then I was. She was someone I could look down on.

Yet I often identified with the underdog--the kid picked on and ostracized. I remember defending Betty once at our bus stop against some older students who were picking on her. Some former classmates still tell stories where I stood up to bullies and defended the weak and puny.

I was a very confused boy. I never learned how to relate well to others, especially to girls. If I liked a girl, I might walk up to her and pinch her budding boob, or wipe a bugger on her, or slug her in the arm, or kiss her. Yet I could never figure out why I didn't fit in.

* * *

I found alcohol in 1959; I was 14. I'd snatch two or three bottles of beer from my dad's store-cooler and share them with my friends or drink them myself.

* * *

Cool High Life on October evening,
three of us with six.
We chug 'em,
hunch shoulders against the evening chill.
Curse the never changing present,
talk of beer dreams and lives worth remembering.

*   *   *

Beer made me feel good. No matter that I was a no-brand kid, no matter I had a no-brand coat, a no-brand haircut, and drank no-brand milk. No matter I was poor, no matter I didn't have a girlfriend. No matter. Beer made me feel good. I made a promise then and there: whatever I ended up doing as an adult, it would involve drinking. Lots of drinking. In fact, I could not understand why adults didn't drink all the time, since it felt so good.

Many sophomores, juniors and seniors had cars. I had no car, of course, and at 14 no driver's license. If I ever hoped to get out of the house or have a social life, I had to team-up with someone with a car. I knew there were several older students who were drinkers. School legends told of this football hero or that basketball star getting drunk at a party or drinking at lunch hour or even on the team bus as they traveled to games. Some of them had cars.

I hooked up with Bill and Ned, two juniors. "Listen." I said. "The smelt are running. You guys could pick me up Friday night and we could go smelt-fishing."

"Why would we want to do that?" Ned asked.

"Because I got the key to my old man's store." I answered. "We can get some beer and tell our parents we're going smelt fishing. We can stay out all night."

Smelt are an alien species of fish that arrived in the Great Lakes from the Atlantic Ocean when the Welland Canal opened which bypassed Niagara Falls and connected Lake Ontario and Lake Erie. They are a little silvery fish about five to ten inches long. They run in the millions to spawn upstream, just after "ice out" on the many creeks and rivers that empty into the Great Lakes.

I snuck the key to my dad's store. He closed at 10 o'clock. About eleven, my buddies dropped me off at the store and five minutes later returned to pick me up. I threw in a case of beer, a large bag of chips and a pack of Winstons, and we drove off.

We drove around on the sandy two-track roads that wind through the forests of northern Michigan and drank the beer, then went back for more. This time we all went inside. In our drunken, bumbling state, we took two cases of beer, a couple gallons of wine, five pounds of lunch meat, some cheese, potato salad, sweet rolls, a large bag of chips and two cartons of cigarettes.

That was the first time I ever really got drunk. It was also the first time I had a blackout. I remember riding around with my two new "best friends." I remember getting the deer rifle out of the trunk and shooting a five-gallon bucket lit by the cars' headlights. At some point I was no longer conscious. The next thing I knew, I was lying in the bathtub at home with my clothes on, my mother standing over me in her turquoise colored, terry-cloth robe, hair in curlers, screaming at me. I was fourteen.

The next morning my dad called me over to the store. The potato-chip rack lay askew across the isle. Someone had dropped a loaf of bread and stepped on it. The eggs were tipped over in the cooler, and the lunchmeat and cheese had been ransacked. The cigarette rack had been rifled; packs of cigarettes littered the floor.

Tears swam in my dad's eyes. "How could you do this to me?", he said, looking down, shaking his head. For the first time I saw the pain I had caused my dad. I felt his sadness as I looked at his store through his eyes. I moved to start cleaning-up, pushing the blue wire potato chip rack back in place, tears now welling in my eyes too. I wanted to clean the mess up quickly so the sight of it would stop hurting him. Crying, I hugged him, my head on his chest.

My mom wanted to call the cops but my dad talked her out of it. He told me that if my "friends" would come and apologize and pay for the things that were stolen, he would keep it to himself. We'd stolen or damaged more than $100 worth of merchandise. Bill and Ned never did apologize or help pay for the goods; they only laughed and promised to kick my ass if I ever told their names. My dad never did get his money back. I hurt him so.

* * *

Through adoption I had a cousin my age that moved

from Los Angeles with his family to a house only a half-mile from mine. They were rather well off. The father, a barely functioning alcoholic, was pretty much out of the picture. Evelyn, the mother, seemed so glamorous with her pure white hair, attractive figure, and L.A. clothes, the likes of which were not seen on mine or any of my friends' moms. Bill was a good-looking boy, well liked and well adjusted. His sister, Julie, two years younger, was cute, but not much interested in what Bill and I were doing. I wished she would notice me.

On many occasions during this period, my mother would throw me out of the house, as if casting out devils: "...and don't ever come back." Words I loved to hear. My dad would put together what he called a "care package" consisting of eggs, bacon, bread, milk and other foodstuffs and send me up to cousin Bill's. Evelyn would take me in, put the food in the fridge, and make up the spare bed. Bill and I were free to do as we pleased. We even stayed up late to watch *The Tonight Show*, something unheard of in my house. I'd stay a week or two, sometimes three, riding the bus to school with Bill, fooling around after school; everything was fine. Then my dad would call saying mom had calmed down and I should come home. I'd go, knowing it wouldn't last long--my mom's irrationality and my misbehavior would combine to create an electric chaotic tension in the home bound to short circuit.

Alienation from my family was complete, thorough and absolute. I didn't like them. I felt we had nothing in common and I was living on the outside looking in. My dad was cool, but old-fashioned, old school, old-time; he just wasn't with it.

School seemed irrelevant, too. Girls paid no attention to me, or so it seemed. I got along with boys OK. I hated school and would skip for days on end until I was finally caught.

All this led me to the Father Gibault School for Boys in Terra Haute, Indiana, where I was sent when I was 15. I remember a social worker telling my parents and me that, "Boys like Larry need discipline and plenty of it. He'll get it at Gibault." Gibault was a Catholic reform school run by the Brothers of the Holy Cross--who were nothing but Catholic bullies, really. "All authority comes from God" was the guiding principle.

When I was there, in 1960, Gibault was a 3,000-acre hog

and dairy farm in south-central Indiana. There were 120 boys divided into two units: 60 seniors, ages 13-15 and 60 juniors, ages 10-12. The campus consisted of the usual red brick dormitories, a chapel, a school building, an industrial arts building, a separate laundry facility, baseball diamonds, handball courts, a swimming pool, and an exercise field. The Brothers lived in an aged, brick monastery, vine-covered and shaded by ancient oaks.

It wasn't very much different from home or Catholic school. Rules. Rules. Rules. The only real difference was that the brothers hit harder.

Their first method of control was the old "Give Away/Take Away" game. We had rules on the one hand and privileges on the other. If we broke the rules, we lost privileges. Like, if you were a smoker, you could smoke two-and-one-half cigarettes a day. The Prefect was the Brother on duty; he would dole them out. One after lunch. One-half at three-thirty and one after supper. We got our half cigarette by calling "choice" on a fellow smoker earlier in the day. At three-thirty my "choice" partner and I would go to the Prefect, get our smoke, and my partner would break it in half. I had "choice" of the bigger half. We had to smoke standing or sitting around in front of the Prefect. Of course, if you broke a rule you could be taken "off smokes." You might lose your noon smoke, or your three-thirty. Maybe you'd be taken off smokes for a day, a week, or longer.

Then there were movies every Wednesday and Sunday. If you didn't do your homework, or back-sassed a Brother, you could be taken off movies. Occasionally the "off movies" boys would be made to sit in the auditorium where the movie was being shown with their chairs turned around, their backs to the screen. Of course we "off movies" boys would try to sneak peaks at the screen. We'd put our heads down on our knees and try to look upside-down and backward, through the crook in our arm at the screen. And, of course, we always got caught and put off the next week's movie. So it went. I saw about 10 complete movies in the year I was there.

Once my whole family came to visit me while I was there, driving twelve hours straight in the days before interstate highways. I can't say I was glad to see them. They embarrassed me; they looked like such hicks in the '54 Desoto, dad in his new "dungarees," mom in her new print housedress and practical shoes. The whole family was overweight, except for my little brother who was tall and skinny at five.

The visit went so-so. At one point when I was alone with my dad, he asked what I was learning at Gibault. "Not much," I answered, "but at least I'm learning how to fight." My dad looked crestfallen and sad. I understood immediately I'd given an answer he didn't want to hear.

I used the opportunity the visit offered to sneak a couple of packs of Pall Mall's back into the school. Naturally they were found a day or two later and I was taken off smokes and movies for a month and given three "whacks," which I'll get to later.

Gibault had a so-called "candy store." It was really a closet in the school hallway where they stored red licorice, Milk Duds, and dime bags of potato chips. If your parents put money in your account, you could buy goodies on movie night. Again, if you broke the rules you'd be put "off candy-store." Even in those hard economic times, my dad kept money in my account, though I didn't get a chance to spend much since I was very often "off candy-store."

These methods of control were used for common, everyday infractions, like talking in the dorm, talking in the dining hall before the "talking bell" was rung, or talking in the washroom in the morning when sixty teenage boys would rush to pee while slapping down early morning boners to keep our peters from poking through our boxer shorts.

For more serious infractions, like fighting, cursing a Brother, trying to sneak in smokes after a visit, or running away, there was "the paddle." There was nothing fancy about this whipping stick. It was an inch-thick unfinished pine board about three feet long and five inches wide with a crudely cut out handle.

I was soon intimate with this instrument of violence. At mealtime we would line up in the hallway outside the dining hall. Single file, no talking. The Prefect would ring a hand bell and we would file into the dining hall in silence, proceed to our assigned tables and wait for the Prefect to say grace. After grace, the bell would be rung again signaling us to sit down. The bell would be rung once again to tell us we could start eating. Yet another ring of the bell and we could begin talking.

Some days the Prefect would not ring the "talking bell" at all. We'd eat in near silence, sneaking words through hushed whispers, murmurs coming from each table, until a drone filled the room, at which time the Prefect would put everyone "off movie."

I was assigned to a table in the front of the hall, along with five other troublemakers, so the Prefect could keep a close eye on us. On one particular day, we filed in and went to our tables. The bell rang. We said grace. The bell rang. We sat down. Under my breath, without moving my lips so the Prefect, Brother Philip, couldn't see, I said, "Pass the mac and cheese." Sheridan, a boy from Cleveland, and one of only three blacks in the institution, mouthed silently. "You're off mac and cheese." "Set out the god damn mac and cheese," I hissed through unmoving lips. The Prefect was looking away so he didn't see me, but he heard me. "What did you say?" he asked me. "I didn't say nothin'," I responded. "I heard you," he said. *Yeah, but you didn't see me, so you don't really know*, I thought. "What did you say?" he asked again. "Nothin'," I answered.

Brother Philip was a big man, strong, a retired Marine Corp drill sergeant and active bodybuilder, a fifty-five year old hard-ass who shaved all his body hair. He'd have his favorite twelve-year-old junior boy shave his back. Then he'd do strongman poses in front of a full length mirror while his junior boy sat, bare legs dangling over the edge of the bed, with the door of Bro Philip's bedroom wide open at the end of the dorm.

Bro Philip came around the table and stood behind me. The dining hall was still silent, no one was eating; all eyes were on us. "What did you say?" he asked in a calm voice. "Noth...," I began as Bro Philip slapped me across the back of the head. "What did you say?" he asked, his voice beginning to tremble. "Nothing," I insisted. Whap! He smacked me again, harder this time. Again he asked. Again I gave him the same answer. Another smack, this one harder yet. My ears were ringing, blood pounded in my head, my face was hot. He asked again. I responded as before. Whap! Even harder. This went on for several minutes. Excitement was building among the boys. They knew some heavy drama was unfolding that would liven up the dull reform-school day.

Bro Philip sent his favorite wide-eyed junior boy up to

the office to fetch the paddle. He brought me front and center in the dining hall and had me bend over and grab my ankles. He gripped the paddle with both hands, took an appropriate batting stance and let fly. Whack! "Now, what did you say?"

"Nothin', I whimpered, the fires of Nagasaki burning up my butt. "Bend over, grab your ankles," he ordered again.

There was absolute silence in the dining hall; all eyes were riveted to the front, witnessing the confrontation between power and will.

This time he stepped into the swing and let fly a good one. Whack! I was driven to my knees. "What did you say?" he snapped, his composure stretched to the limit. Now I was in control. It cost me dearly, but I pushed him to the edge, which put me in control. Though my eyes filled with tears, they didn't run down my cheek. I was glad of that. "Nothin," I choked out.

Behind me I could feel the boys watching, transfixed. Wanting me to win. Wanting me to show this son-of-a-bitch, just show him, that his power meant nothing to us and that brute force would not break our will.

In the vast wisdom of the Catholic Church, and in the inner sanctum of the administrator's office at Gibault, it had been decided that beating children was good for them and for their education. On the other hand, hitting a child on the ass with a board must be limited to three whacks, remembering the Trinity, I suppose.

Gibault's paddle policy (which had, I assume, the Pope's blessing), gave me the confidence I needed to win this test of wills. Bro Philip had already whacked me twice and I still held hard to the lie. He had one more shot to make me say uncle. I knew I could take it, though I felt like I was going to pass out from time to time as searing pain shot through my backside.

"What. Did. You. Say!?" he raged! Biting off each word as if it were a piece of fresh celery, his face inches from mine, the blue pulsing vein in his forehead looking like a stretch of I-69 on a Rand McNally.

He bent me over again. This time he stepped back about two yards. He took a little hop-step and a jump and hit me with everything he had. My ass exploded. Electric volts of pain shot up my spine and down both legs. I was driven to my knees and slid on that highly polished reform school floor until I thumped against the wall like a duffel bag of dirty sports gear.

I got up and faced him again. My eyes were full of tears, streaks now running down both cheeks.

Once more he asked me. Once more I answered, "nothing'." "Go to your seat," he ordered. He didn't ring the "talking bell" that day.

Brother Philip put me off movies, candy-store and smokes for a month.

As a result of my victory in the open battle of wills, the other boys saw me as one bad motor scooter.

Some of the cute little junior boys, the ones with rounded butts like the girls back home, would send over their deserts with one of the boy waiters, then make Bambi eyes at me when I looked their way. Sheridan would tease, "Ah, Pun's got a girlfriend, Pun's got a girlfriend." For a week I was getting three or four desserts a meal.

One day the Prefect noticed that we had too many desert bowls on our table. He rang the bell for silence. All the waiters took their seats. He inspected all the tables until he found the ones missing dessert bowls--more whacks coming. And so it went. I got 72 such whacks while I was there, not a record by any means, but a respectable number.

I spent exactly a year at Gibault, the maximum length of time allowed in their residential program. I saw my time there as an unique adventure, something to talk about with my friends who's most exciting episodes in life were trips to Disneyland in Hollywood or motel vacations in Florida.

Chapter Two

...LOOKING FOR AN ANGRY FIX...(1960-1965)

I saw the best minds of my generation destroyed by madness,
starving hysterical naked,
dragging themselves through the Negro streets at dawn looking for
an angry fix,
angelheaded hipsters burning for the ancient heavenly connection
to the starry dynamo in the machinery of night...

HOWL--Alan Ginsberg

After a year in Gibault I returned home. Shortly after I found out I was "Indian". The caseworker advising my mom suggested that knowledge about my family origins might dissolve the deep-seated rage of disconnection I was carrying in me. Catholic Child and Family Services, the agency responsible for my adoption and later placement in Father Gibault, prepared a brief report which my mom gave to me on my sixteenth birthday.

According to the report, my father was "Indian," had an honorable discharge from the Army, and had worked as a logger and able-bodied seaman on Great Lakes ore carriers. My mother's family was from Canada, she came to this country as a nine year old and had later been a long-distance telephone operator in the days before dial phones.

THAT WAS IT! Period. That was the extent of the report. There was nothing about my father's tribe, or my mother's. Nothing about syphilis. Nothing about alcoholism. Nothing about the situation of my conception and birth. I was to learn all this much later.

The report didn't change much in my life or the way I thought about myself, others, or the world around me. Knowing that I was "Indian" didn't mean anything since it gave me no direct connection to family or tribe. The only "Indians" I was aware of, besides the "cowboy and Indian" images from the movies or TV, and the two or three who were students at St. Francis, were the drunken Indians that hung out down at the SAIL INN in the "seedy" (my mother's word), slum section of east Front Street in Traverse City. Occasionally the local newspaper would run a story of a fiery car crash killing some Indians out on the Peshawbetown Reservation twenty miles north of Traverse City. What teenager would want to be identified with that? Not that I gave it much thought in any event. I had been raised white, thought of myself as white, and at the time didn't really care.

During my time in Gibault my dad had sold the grocery store and moved three miles into town. One month before my return, he left my mom. Apparently he could no longer take the constant din as she screeched through life in a panic. Eventually he went to California and got a job in a chicken-processing plant in East LA. He sent money home every week with sad letters of desperate loneliness. I remember my mom crying as she got one in which my dad had said, "I kiss pictures of you and the kids every night before I go to bed." Sobbing and daubing her eyes with a Kleenex, her only response was "Isn't that the craziest thing you ever heard?"

I missed my dad, who seemed to be the one stable element in our family. But I also knew I could take advantage of my single parent situation. By now I was six feet tall and 115 pounds, with a harder edge to me after Gibault, and a mean streak that was growing deep and deeper. I made up my mind that my mom would have no control over me.

That summer my cousin Bill broke his neck in a trampoline accident resulting in total paralysis. He nearly died, but after nine months of hospital care he was returned home and eventually graduated from high school. I kept in touch, periodically stopping by just to visit, or going at suppertime to get some free chow. Occasionally I spent three or four days there, as before. I was always welcome and made to feel part of the family. Years later, when I was in BIG trouble, Evelyn and Bill gave support and made me welcome in their home.

That fall my dad returned home by Greyhound after a four-month retreat from married life. I was re-enrolled in St. Francis High. I loathed St. Francis. I hated the strict, narrow, provincial atmosphere. Readin' writin' and 'rithmatic was the extent of the curriculum, it seemed to me. I wanted to go to the public school where all of my other friends went. They had a much broader horizon to look at, I thought, and a much wider selection of opportunities. They had a new modern high school unlike St. Francis's creaky old wood-frame structure built in 1903. They had a swim team, golf team, and ski team. They had the usual football, basketball, track and baseball teams, among others. They had auto shop and wood shop and a big newspaper printed by students at the school on a huge press. They had a debate team and acting class. All of these things interested me.

Nothing interested me at St. Francis except sports. I made quite a name for myself as a trackman and a football and basketball player. I liked the positive attention and probably could have gotten a college scholarship if only I had had the discipline to toe the line. But of course, I was short on discipline. I didn't see that hard work in the present paid off with rewards in the future. I couldn't keep my grades up to remain eligible for sports. Bottom line: I hated school.

I was running with a rough crowd. We were always waiting for a weekend dance or party--hell, a fight would do, anything to break the stagnant boredom of our very ordinary, predictable lives.

Several cliques of teens hung out at the local A&W restaurant. The "gear heads" could always be found underneath the hood of an idling car. The music mavens would gather around their old man's Oldsmobile listening to the AM from some far away place, like Grand Rapids. The whole group snapping their fingers, just on the edge of singing, though few ever did.

My crowd was the drinkin' crowd. Greasers. No, killer grease. We were always on the periphery, shoulders hunched against the social chill, yet fortified with spirits. One night five of us were hanging around--there was "Eggs," a skinny, mousy, sorta greasy dude with zits that looked like eggs cooked sunny-side up. He was from a "broken home" and lived with his mom who worked nights at the cherry plant. Then there was "Bonerack," and also "Rope," so named because his dad tried unsuccessfully to hang himself with one. "Queerbait" was a good-looking seventeen year old who the fags hit on regularly. "Boner" rounded out the crew; a big dumb Hollander, he reminds me today of the former President, Jerry Ford.

One particularly dull evening, a car carrying three uniformed Coast Guardsmen cruised through the A&W parking lot. The Coast Guard has a large air base near Traverse City and friction between the Guard and townies went back generations. We flipped the Guardsmen the finger. They gave us a finger wave back. The six of us jumped in our ride and chased them. We lost them for a bit but then suddenly they were behind us. Good. We pulled into the cherry plant parking lot. They followed and stopped. Everyone got out. Crash! "Bonerack" smashed a beer bottle against the head of a Guardsman, who went running off down the street, blood gushing from between his fingers. A second Guardsman was standing on the curb, his knees bent, ready to jump. I was in front of him, in the street, with a twelve-inch Crescent wrench held at my side. "Queerbait" came up behind the dude and delivered a monstrous two-handed rabbit punch right to the base of his neck. As the Guardsman went down, I took a step forward and swung the wrench. The Crescent caught the dude just on the side of the head, above the ear, making a sound that reminded me of the hard boiled eggs my dad would crack on the side of the kitchen sink as he stood in his Jockey shorts before bed.

The guardsman crumbled to his knees. His two buddies grabbed him and ran for their car. We cursed them, throwing beer bottles and chunks of parking lot pavement as they sped away.

After they left we stood around, cupped our balls in our hands, spit through our teeth and basked in a hot testosterone glow.

Unfortunately, the Guardsmen had gotten our license plate number; two days later we were arrested and charged with assault and battery. I was sixteen. It didn't seem fair. They had chased us. They had followed us into the parking lot. They had gotten out of their car. They had made all the decisions which led to their getting their butts kicked. They should be responsible for their own decisions. If the tables were turned and they had kicked our butts, would they have been charged? Unlikely. We were all given probation and ordered to avoid contact with one another, an injunction we promptly ignored.

When I returned to St. Francis in the fall I was on probation there, too. One month into grade eleven my grades were so bad that I was ineligible to play football. Without football, I saw no reason to be there, so I got myself expelled. The fog of time has clouded my memory--school records say I tore a history book in half and threw it through a window. I don't recall that, but it sounds likely.

One week after my expulsion from St. Francis I paid a visit to the local Marine recruiter. I liked the uniforms. Oh, he was very excited as I told him of my troubles at home and school. "We need tough, feisty young men in the Corps, he said.

On my next appointment he told me the Corps could not use me. "At your young age you have too extensive a police record," he said. I went to the Navy and Army and the first meeting went well. But after they did some checking, the answer was always the same. Too much trouble.

So I said, "Screw it. I don't want no boot camp anyway. I don't want someone in my face yelling. I don't want to take no orders."

I got work on construction crews. Cement work, roofing, carpentry. Over the years I've worked in all the building trades.

I hardly went home. I was crashing at different friends' apartments, shackin' with chicks, and running with riffraff, drunk or hung-over most of the time. I was now seventeen. I had an ever-growing record of arrests, all alcohol-related. I can't say I liked living a lifestyle that resulted in periodic stints in jail, but it seemed better than the life of the "law-abiding" people I saw around me.

In 1963, just after my eighteenth birthday, I received my Induction Physical Notice from the military. The local Draft Board sent fifty-five of us whose numbers were up, including many former classmates, to Detroit by bus for our induction physicals.

Sometime before, having been rejected by all the armed services recruiters, I made up my mind that I would not go in the military under any conditions. I had school friends who served during the "Cuban missile crisis." They said their service amounted to waiting to get nuked by the other side. This less than romantic view of military service supported my anti-military position. I heard about the war in Southeast Asia and something didn't seem right about that either. I didn't understand how invading a poor country, so far away, could be construed as "protecting America." I understand now that my natural inclination to support the underdog and resist authority was at the root of my resistance to military service. Also, by this time I was accustomed to the wild and free life; I knew I would find the strict discipline and direct orders unendurable.

During the written part of the pre-induction testing I made every mistake possible. In the medical history section I marked "yes" to all the diseases and illnesses listed: Scarlet Fever? Yes. Polio? Yes. Leukemia? Yes. Flat footed? Yes. Bed wetter? Yes. Later in the test came: Are you a Communist? Yes. Are you a Conscientious Objector? Yes. Are you a homosexual? Yes. Are you a drug addict? Yes. Do you have a moral or religious aversion to military service? Yes. Have you ever been arrested for a crime? Yes...the one true answer I gave.

The results of the physical exam were a surprise. During the exam I was so hung over that my blood pressure was all out of whack. They kept me an extra twenty-four hours, until my blood pressure went down so they could get a normal reading.

Several months later I got my "1Y" classification, which meant I was "morally or mentally objectionable for military service." That was fine with me, since that was precisely how I felt about the military.

I hooked up with a greaser called "Cube," a gear head

into hot rods. He was always sucking air between his teeth, like "Psstt, psstt." He measured everything, such as engine displacement, in cubic inches: "283 short block" or "350 hemi" or "big block...409." Or, he'd see a woman with big breasts, and sucking air through his teeth, he'd say, "There goes, psstt, psstt, 75 cubes per knocker," or, "Psstt, psstt, her ass is 300 cubes and not one cube more. Psstt, psstt."

His air sucking drove me crazy. But I wanted to get out of town and he was willing to go anywhere, so we took off. He was a year or two older than me with a nice ride. He had the look of "heavy grease:" Levi's slung low, white T-shirt tucked in tight, a thin belt, usually plastic, big black, heavy, "engineer's boots," with a strap and buckle across the instep. And his hair: long, and shiny black, with both sides combed back, meeting perfectly in the center in the back of his head, to form the perfect "ducktail." The top was combed to the center and trained to stand up, creating a palisades pompadour of hair, V shaped, starting in the center of the forehead.

Most of my friends wanted to go to California. "That was where the future was," they said, but I was just contrary enough to not want to go where everybody else was going. I wanted to go east, to New York or Boston or Philly.

The Cube and I drove east and got as far as Reading, Pennsylvania before the money and the "romance of the road" ran out. We rented a flat in the black section of town. Cube got a job in a machine shop; I got work in a bookbindery. He put all his money into a dragster he was building at a speed shop he found across town.

Every Friday I took a two-hour Greyhound ride to the 42nd Street bus terminal in New York, then walked some thirty-five blocks downtown to Greenwich Village. Once I walked to Chinatown, once to The Bowery. I'd just walk, and look in shop windows, too poor and intimidated to go inside any. I'd listen to orators on street corners and weirdoes in the park. I'd go in bars and have a beer, eat pizza by the slice on the street and just keep walking. Occasionally I'd sleep in a phone booth or on the steps going to a basement apartment. I'd stay up all Friday night and Saturday night walking, and drinking in sleazy bars. And more walking, searching, I guess. I'd catch the last bus to Reading on Sunday evening.

I was living and working in Reading when JFK was shot. We were sent home from work early. The big department store downtown had windows draped in purple velvet with JFK's portrait washed in muted light.

I bought a forty-nine Cadillac and headed for Montreal in February. By March I was in Toronto occasionally letting queers fondle me in the public toilets for ten bucks a pop. I got arrested on St. Patrick's Day for drunk and disorderly and called the American Embassy but they were not interested in taking my case.

I returned to TC in the summer of '64 and got work in an auto junkyard, removing batteries from wrecked cars. Once, while drunk, I was arrested for trying to tear down a sign that said "Save Our Republic/Impeach Earl Warren/Sponsored By The John Birch Society." Apparently I was developing a political consciousness since I knew at the time I didn't like "right wingers," and I knew the John Birch Society was a right-wing organization. I have no recollection as to how I came to this political opinion.

When I got out of jail on the Birch Society sign caper I met Moses and Kelly. Moses was a tall, gangly guy with a very long beard and a mouthful of rotted teeth like a row of burnt-out tree stumps. A twenty-three year-old beatnik from New Jersey, Moses had served in the Navy, traveled, and was into books and jazz and folk music. He gave me Jack Kerouac's *On the Road*, and my life was changed forever.

A book! Hell, I hadn't read three books in my eighteen years. I hated books. The only books I knew were "assignments" in school or gifts I got at Christmas instead of the toys I really wanted.

But *On the Road* changed all that. It was about people I wanted to know, adventurous people looking for something new and expansive--searching for something. Whether they met with success or failure was unimportant, as long as their experiences were worth remembering. This was the life I wanted--not the closed-off, narrow-minded, scripted, small town life of my parents and my friends' parents.

My dad used to say "If you could get a job driving a delivery truck for Pepsi-Cola, you'd have it made for life." I couldn't stand even the thought of it. It wasn't that I hated Pepsi, or deliverymen, or even work. I hated the idea that before I was out of my teens I was supposed to get a job and start living the kind of life I saw the adults around me living. No thank you.

I read *On the Road* like a maniac--while walking the streets of Traverse City, while driving, while in a restaurant pounding my thigh with my fist as I read, shouting, "Yes. Yes! YES!" Until I was asked to leave and the wind off the bay blew icicles of possibilities and I knew there was some other life out there.

* * *

Kelly was Moses' friend, a massive 380-pound cat who worked for a time with the carnival. We called him "Carney." The three of us traveled to New Jersey. Moses' parents promised to have his teeth fixed if he'd just move back home and "settle down." Once in Jersey we got jobs as laborers for landscapers and spent the weekends in Greenwich Village, smoking pot or drinking massive quantities of codeine based cough syrup and digging the folk music scene, trying to be part of it.

I returned to TC in the summer of 1965 fancying myself a beatnik, my little wispy beard just starting to come in. I carried around books of poetry, the *I CHING* and *COMMUNIST MANIFESTO*, not to read, though I thumbed through them from time to time, but as symbols of my difference from the ordinary citizen, but I was mostly image with little substance.

Still, I was trying to find something to fit into that wasn't a mold or a straightjacket. I was still trying to find the thing that was real to me. Something in me wanted to do good, to make a difference.

I had heard about the Peace Corps and decided to apply. I got the forms and discovered that an applicant had to have the endorsement of a local public official, clergy, police chief, local judge--someone of that stature.

Asking my parish priest was out of the question. Father Kohler was old school; he didn't understand. He thought I was the Devil incarnate. The chief of police was not a good choice since his officers and I had had many run-ins over the past five years. But, there was Judge Schumer who had sentenced me several times over the last few years. At every sentencing he would lecture me about getting my life in order. "Straighten up and fly right", he kept telling me.

I decided to pay Judge Schumer a visit and ask for his support. I made an appointment and went to see him. When he heard my request he simply said "I'm a Republican. I see no reason why the U.S. should be gallivantin' all around the world trying to help people. We've got plenty of people right here to help. No, I won't sign your application." That was that.

I got work on a Christmas tree farm and earned $1 an hour for a ten-hour day with payment at the end of each day. I rented a room above a pet store and the skid row Rendezvous Bar for $7 a week. Oh, the stench of a pet shop! I'd get drunk every night in the Rendezvous and stagger up the back wooden steps to my room, then go to work in the morning. Day after day.

I had a girlfriend in those days, on and off. Wiseacre was a good, hard working, responsible young woman a couple of years older than me. She must have seen something in me that I didn't see in myself. Wiseacre and I decided to move to Florida. Her dad lived there. Perhaps we'd get married. I wasn't happy with my life and thought maybe Florida would change things.

When we got to Florida I found a job with a land-surveying company and rode long distances in the company truck to the job sites. "Niggers in the back" was the company policy. Every day two or three black guys would scramble into the pick-up bed, even on cold, windy, wet, January mornings. Usually, I road in the cab with the white guys. They thought of me as a white guy and I thought of myself as a white guy. But on occasion I'd scamper into the back and ride with the "boys" just to piss-off the whites. They called me a "Yankee nigger lover" and such. I thought of them as "red-neck nigger haters." I knew no better at the time.

This was the first time I'd been around such racism and I didn't like it. I saw the drinking fountains marked "Colored" and "White." I saw gas stations with inside toilets marked "White" and outhouses marked "Colored." My fundamental sense of fairness and equality was offended. My affinity for the poor and left-out made support for the black civil rights cause easy.

Wiseacre had a job at the local Ford dealership and one

day was reprimanded for addressing an envelope to a black customer as "Mr. Brown." I was in the showroom waiting for Wiseacre to get off work. I heard her boss say, "We don't call niggers 'Mister,'" he said as his fat neck of mushroom flesh bulged over the collar of his white shirt, his pig eyes looked like holes punched in unbaked bread dough.

I rented a house trailer behind Wiseacre's dad's. My drinking episodes became more and more outrageous though I always made it to work on time. Wiseacre broke up with me and asked me leave.

I bought a BSA motorcycle and went to Miami, slept in the public park and killed time in the library with the other bums, hobos and tramps, until the cops rousted us for loitering in a public place. One day I sold tourists enough large coconuts to buy some cheap wine and cheese which I ate at sunset on Miami Beach before getting shooed away by security from the rich and fancy hotels which crowd the shore.

I spent three or four nights at the Jesus Saves Mission. There were two hundred of us packed into a large basement room in downtown Miami. Second-hand church pews were lined up stem to stern. The preacher railed against the evils of drink and made grown men cry remembering the families and self-respect they'd lost. I listened because this was the price to be paid for "a hot and a cot," food and a bed; I had no intention of not drinking, or of finding the Lord. On and on he preached until he got to the savin' part, then he preached some more. For two hours he preached. Finally he said, "God damn-it! No one's going to eat 'til someone gets saved!"

Just then an old wino sitting way in the back got up and started hollering, "I'm saved! I'm saved! The Spirit of the Lord is in me! I've been washed in the blood of the lamb." Scrambling up onto the backs of the pews, wobbling, he balanced there. Then, stepping from pew back to pew back, prancing almost, between the shoulders of the hungry, wrung out men. "I'm drunker 'an a skunk!" He bellowed, teetering. "If the Spirit of the Lord ain't in me, I'd fall on my ass!" He weaved his way to the front of the room, flapping his arms like a flightless penguin to keep his balance. He made it all the way, then jumped down and fell to his knees, bowing real low with his butt in the air and his forehead touching the floor, two pints of Mad Dog 20/20 sticking out of his back pockets. Thank goodness. Dinner, as usual, was a fried bologna sandwich on day-old white bread, no mustard, no Mayo.

I worked day labor in Miami on construction sites. Then I sold the scooter and hitchhiked to St. Augustine, checked out the Old Fort, slept on the beach, and mooched drinks in the gay bars until I was pretty loaded and the old fruits would lean in real close with lavender breath. I did whatever had to be done to survive.

On a whim I hitched up to Charleston, South Carolina--one place seemed as good as the next--catching a ride with an old sissy chewing juicy fruit gum who wanted to polish my knob.

I got to Charleston and rented a room in the old, black section of town where rundown clapboard houses sat side by side high above the street. I got a job with a hardworking black man who ran a salvage business. He'd buy condemned frame buildings and tear them down, salvaging any useful materials. I saw the old fort and the old slave market, in its heyday the largest in the South. "They sold two thousand niggers a day," my boss told me.

When I wasn't working, I hung-out down by the harbor in the sleazy bars which smelled of urine and strong antiseptic.

Three weeks later I rode my thumb to Richmond, getting a ride with a gypsy man whose chrome-trimmed pick-up/camper was decorated with little cloth dangleberry-balls that framed the front and back windshields and rear-view mirror. The seats were covered with long fake fur fabric colored aquamarine, as was the dashboard. Mud flaps with many reflectors completed the magic.

Just across the Virginia line we pulled into a state park which was filled with hundreds of brightly hued pick-ups and campers. There were gypsy camps everywhere. Women in colorful, bright skirts or blue jeans bent over blackened kettles stirring mysterious stews. Children squealed as they raced through the camps. Old men sat in groups, some speaking the ancient Roma tongue, others singing songs accompanied by guitars. Pretty girls and show-off boys made eyes at each other while pretending not to notice each other. I stayed with them nearly a week, playing baseball, swimming, flirting. I slept, like the other teenagers; beneath a large tarp stretched over two picnic tables turned on edge providing a cozy and private space.

I felt comfortable here. I looked somewhat like these people and they accepted me. They didn't think it strange that I was traveling around the South, going from job to job. Perhaps I had Roma blood in me too.

I spent my last night there with Isadore, a skinny sixteen-year-old with black hair the color of a crow's back and a butt not much bigger than a dinner roll. In the light of a candle her eyes sparkled like black hematite. I could have fallen in love but the next day I moved on.

In Richmond I got a flop at the Salvation Army. Manpower, the day labor broker, got me a temp job at Raytheon Corp. Raytheon had a rush contract for electronics cabinets, which were tall, metal affairs that would be filled with electronic components. After a week, I asked the foreman what these were to be used for. "Submarines," he answered. "Piss on it. I ain't building no war machines," I said and walked out.

I don't remember how I came to that political position either. I wasn't a pacifist by any means. But I was aware, through my interests in folk music and news magazines, and through my travels, of the Civil Rights Movement, the Ban the Bomb Movement, the No War Toys Movement, Stop Capital Punishment Movement and the Peace Movement. I didn't seek out or notice these movements because I had high political principles, on the contrary, I was politically ignorant and so had few political principles. I noticed these movements because they stood out, stood against. They did not accept the status quo, but instead, seemed to be going against the tide. This interested me; it was 1964.

I took a Greydog bus to Jersey and hunted up Moses. He was living at home; new false teeth gleaming like the pearly gates of heaven. I got a job working for a land surveyor and spent weekends in the Village drinking large quantities of cough syrup trying to catch that special buzz.

I returned to Traverse City in the summer of '65, when I was twenty. I hadn't seen my family in over five years and was not interested in doing so. But I did see Julie, my crippled cousin Bill's younger sister. She had married a guy named Mike from the University at Miami. Mike was hooked up with SNCC

(Student Nonviolent Coordinating Committee), the most active of the student based civil rights organizations. Through SNCC he had contacts in the AFL/CIO (American Federation of Labor/Congress of Industrial Organizations). He got me a job with them as a union organizer of migrant farm workers.

Building a farm workers union was one of the AFL/CIO's goals and they wanted to accomplish this by seizing the opportunity to organize east of the Mississippi, leaving the west to Caesar Chavez and the United Farm Workers who were organizing in California and Texas. The union recognized, however, that its usual labor organizers-- well-fed men with cigar ashes on their lapels, who looked like gangsters--could not effectively organize migrants who were mostly Chicano's with poor whites and blacks filling out the labor force. So the union hired young folks--college kids--to go into the fields and organize pickers.

We started organizing in Traverse City. In those days, before the advent of tree- shaking machines, thousands of Chicanos would come north every summer to pick cherries. When the harvest was over, they'd move south into Michigan's Saginaw Valley to harvest sugar beets and pickles. Then on to Ohio and Indiana for the tomato harvest. We were close behind. From there it was on to Florida for the tomato, avocado and citrus harvest. We were right there.

There were four of us and Charles Guerrea, a rather serious young cat, and a student at the University of Georgia who was the advance man. When the union big shots in Washington wanted us to organize in a certain area, Charles would do the legwork. He would contact the local Office of Economic Opportunity, Lyndon Johnson's War On Poverty program, to find out how many migrants were in the county and what farms had the best and worst working and living conditions. He'd also inquire into the overall health of the migrants at the local health department and find out if educational and family services were being provided by Catholic Welfare Services or other service organizations.

By the time we organizers came into the area he could tell us where the Republican farms were, where the racist farms were, and whether there was Klan activity in the area. He could tell us too, what health, family and economic issues were facing the migrants. In addition, he had the motels and restaurants scoped out, and knew who the progressive preachers and others were in the community who could help our efforts. Guerrea was good.

My cousin Julie was the only woman on the team. A pretty girl, she was two years younger than me and had gone through St. Francis with her clique of upper-middle class girlfriends, two grades behind me. Her husband, Mike, was our team leader and two years my senior. He put the organizing team together.

The other guy was Clyde, a student at the University of Arkansas and the most militant, Marxist-oriented, argumentative intellectual among us. A little firecracker of a dude, Clyde was quick-witted with off-kilter and unique observations about the society around us.

I was low man on the totem pole, less articulate and experienced than the others, but no less dedicated. I watched and learned.

A year before this, I was sleeping in missions, trading sex for drinks and living hand to mouth. Now I was making $155 a week plus expenses and had a new Chevy to drive. I kept my drinking in check because I admired the people I was working with and didn't want them to see the real me.

The Union was putting big money into this project; we paid our bills with American Express cards. One day Clyde said, as his lip curled revealing a row of uneven teeth, like a picket fence hastily nailed up, "every time we use the card we contribute to the oppression of black people in South Africa, since American Express has stock in South African diamond mines--working class people in America exploit black workers in Africa to satisfy stockholders at American Express." It almost made sense to me, but how did he figure that out I wondered? How did he know these things?

In Kokomo, Indiana, Hunts Ketchup had a huge processing plant and many thousands of acres of tomato fields under contract. At the site of the plant there was also a large labor camp that held fifteen hundred people or more. There was a central cement-block shower-house and toilets. Elsewhere in the camp, only two water spigots, surrounded by a sea of mud, provided water. Housing was shack-type or large tents with the children usually sleeping in the back of pickup trucks. An eight-foot-high fence topped with barbed wire enclosed the twenty acres of camp and plant. A separate gate into the camp was locked at eleven o'clock every night.

Guerrea, our point man, had made contact with Ronaldo, a bilingual Chicano only slightly older than us, who was articulate and highly motivated, and a natural leader among the workers. One evening after a day in the fields, Ronaldo snuck us into the camp, past the armed, white rent-a-cops who manned the gate. Because he was a field foreman, Ronaldo had a shack with a wood floor and a two-burner gas stove. A single 75-watt bulb swung from the ceiling, casting larger-than-life shadows on the grimy walls.

We spent several hours talking with Ronaldo and other foremen. From time to time, Ronaldo would send his children out to fetch another foreman. Soon eight or ten foremen were sitting in that shack, the door wide open to the hot September evening.

We talked of the need for unity, for all pickers to stand together and fight for a better life. We encouraged them to join in the great worldwide movement of workers who were organizing to provide better lives for their wives and children.

The words sounded good and made sense to them, the men explained, but here on the ground in Kokomo, getting caught organizing a union meant not only losing their jobs, but their housing too. With their families and extended families depending on them, organizing for the union was a life and death matter.

We countered that it could and must be done: without risks, nothing will change; without sacrifice, nothing will be gained, we said. We talked of Caesar Chavez and the progress and historic struggle of the United Farm Workers in California. The foremen were duly impressed, but non-committal.

Just then a sedan pulled up to the door. Four thick-necked goons got out. The foremen scattered; the children sat wide-eyed and silent on the cots. We were informed that we were trespassing on private property and were to be escorted to the plant manager's office to await the local police.

The plant manager was a nondescript, cookie cutter white man. He wore a short sleeved, white polyester shirt, tinged yellow from too many washings in the hard water of Kokomo, his clip-on tie stained with last month's tomato soup.

"We've been expecting you," he began. "Our Fremont plant told us you were over there two weeks ago." The Fremont, Ohio plant and camp was a smaller twin to Kokomo. We did well organizing there and didn't get caught.

Mike, always the voice of reason, responded, "You can't arrest us for trespassing...we are guests of these people."

"This is private property and we control who lives on it and who visits on it," the plant manager snapped.

"This is NOT private property," Clyde blurted, his lip curling as his voice rose. "This is corporate property!"

The manager hesitated, rolled his eyes up and to the left, as if looking for a cartoon bubble to tell him what to say next, "We own it. You're trespassing," the manager insisted. The goons flexed their muscles, and felt their holsters snug against their hips.

"Private property is theft"! Clyde snorted.

Just then two sheriff deputies showed up. The manager did not want to press charges, but he did want us escorted off the property and a police report filed. Down the back stairwell we went, the goons pushing us from time to time, trying to provoke us. We kept our cool and got out of there.

We spent another week organizing in the Kokomo area, going out to the tomato fields and talking to individual workers, getting run-off several times. Once a farmer came out with a shotgun to scare us off. We heard that Ronaldo had lost his job and his house and was on his way back to Texas with his family.

When Mike made his report to the Washington Union bigwigs, we were informed that under no circumstance should we get ourselves arrested or beat-up. "We have people for that," we were informed.

From Indiana we moved to Florida: Lakeland, Winterhaven, Frostproof, Okechobee, Belle Glade, and Homestead, organizing tomato pickers mostly.

Okeechobee was a rural slum: the streets dirt, the houses run-down, and the few stores second-rate. White frame buildings, some leaning on poor footings with broken windows and in need of a fresh coat of paint, littered the Florida flatland. You could find no building over one story tall for more than a hundred miles in any direction.

We had contacts in the local Office of Economic Opportunity. A young, all black staff was dedicated and energetic. Together it was decided that we would have a large public meeting. The OEO staff made arrangements with a local black church to have the meeting there and flyers were printed and posted. On the night of the meeting, no one showed up. We scratched our heads and walked in circles in the basement of the church wondering what we did wrong.

I left the church and walked down the muddy street to the local bar, which was a large, four walled military-style tent with a dirt floor, a jukebox, and a plywood bar set up on sawhorses. There were ten or twenty patrons, mostly poor white men and a few blacks. Some nasal hillbilly song was playing on the jukebox. I walked over and pulled the plug. Everyone turned to look. "Listen up everybody!" I shouted. "The Union is in the area organizing farm workers. We need a union!"

A frail older guy with a week's worth of white stubble and the pallor of one who doesn't spend much time in the sun, spoke up. "Yeah", he slurred, "we need a god damn union."

I said, "We need to organize and all stand together so we can demand decent pay for our work. This country needs us to feed them. They won't eat without farm workers."

A toothless old woman spoke through an alcoholic haze, her lips fluttering and flapping said, "We don't need no commie union".

"The growers need you now. Without you, the crop will rot in the fields and the growers will lose millions. You've got 'em by the balls," I continued.

"We got 'em by the balls." The first drunk belched over and over. "We got 'em by the balls."

It went on like this for ten minutes or so. Some didn't look up from their drinks, others staggered to their feet to make some ridiculous statement whether relevant or not, still others let their distaste for the union be known in more subtle ways. Someone bellowed to turn the jukebox back on.

Then it occurred to me that these people weren't farm workers at all. They were just run-of-the-mill, country alcoholics. I plugged the jukebox back in and got out of there.

Several weeks later, in Belle Glade, we tried similar

organizing tactics. But this time we had a fiesta at a local Chicano farm-worker's home. I remember being surprised that a migrant worker would have a regular house with a yard and all. The back yard was decorated with strings of hanging lights. There was plenty of beer. The union paid for a chicken barbeque that simmered for hours in galvanized washtubs purchased new for this special occasion. Several hundred people came and we signed them all up.

From Belle Glade we moved to Homestead in south Florida where we organized tomato and avocado pickers. Mike, who was from Miami, had friends in the area. We were invited to a fund-raising party for the No War Toys Movement in expensive and classy Coconut Grove. I had way too much to drink. I don't remember why the cops came, but they did. And I don't remember what possessed me to do it, but as they were leaving, I jumped on the hood of their car and ripped the windshield wipers off. I was arrested and spent the night in the Dade county jail. Mike bailed me out in the morning, and I was fired.

My time with the union was well spent. I began to understand how society is organized. It isn't just a matter of the strong bullying the weak, the bigger imposing their will on the smaller, nor is it the Will of God that some should be poor while others are rich. It's a matter of all of society being organized to maintain the status quo. The method used is social class division. The ruling class, at the top, makes laws to keep themselves in control. This is true of governments, religions, businesses, institutions and families. The role of schools, family, military and culture is to create mindless citizens who will defend the status quo and maintain the pyramid of power. I would resist.

Chapter Three

TO LIVE OUTSIDE THE LAW YOU MUST BE HONEST… 65-67

--Bob Dylan

I returned to TRAVERSE CITY after getting canned from the union. Carney was living in a "sugar shack" in Kingsley, a one-horse, four-corners town southeast of TC, making maple syrup during the brief season. I crashed on his floor, my sleeping bag sticky and soggy due to the constant sugar-laden steam rising from the huge kettle of boiling sap.

I met runaway Debbie at a crossroads bar in the piney north woods of Michigan. She was barely 18 and had run away from home the year before. She told me her drunken stepfather began feeling her up when she was 16. Soon she was jacking him off. When he forced her to give him a blowjob, she ran away. Her mother was blind and terrified of the obvious truth.

Debbie and I paired up, not out of love, really, but convenience, mutual respect, camaraderie and a need to run, to keep moving--searching for something that felt real, something to believe in.

When sugaring season was over, Carney drew his pay and the three of us headed to Flint in Carney's raggedy old Ford. Carney was from Flint and still had some riffraff connections there. We found a ratty apartment in a house down in the black community. A single mom with three kids lived below us.

At one time Flint was a great bastion of organized labor, and the scene of many united and militant labor actions. Then the union, like the city, began to rot and rust from the inside; now both are only faded, dilapidated dreams of previous working-class glories.

By then Carney had a chick named Trish with him, kind of a pinch faced, whiny girl with a sinus problem. One at a time, we went to Social Services and signed up for welfare. Debbie and Trish claimed to be single moms, Carney and I signed up as unemployed heads of households. For two months we got modest checks and put them together to buy beer and maintain a pad. We went to the bars at night and shot a lot of pool.

As part of the welfare program, we were entitled to government commodities (com'mods) once a month. On the assigned day, we would report at the local community center, sign in, and walk with cardboard boxes to tables loaded with food. There was processed cheese in five-pound bricks--we'd get three or four each; dried beans--we'd come away with five pounds each; multiple cans of peanut butter, boned chicken and beef, lard, boxes of oatmeal, sugar, evaporated milk, and pancake flour. Usually each of us would tote away four or five large cardboard boxes of com'mods.

Once we had our groceries, we'd go door to door in the black community selling the goods for three to five dollars a box. We told the customers they weren't paying for the food but rather for the service of us delivering the food, all quite legal, we said. At the end of the day we'd have 75 dollars or so between us, not bad, but it had to last for a month. In a time when a six-pack of "Bud" was $1.25, cigarettes were 35 cents a pack and gas was 50 cents, this was enough to squeak by on.

We made out for several months, while jumping through welfare hoops, but finally the bureaucracy caught up with us. We were threatened with welfare fraud charges and had to sign documents promising to pay the money back. We signed, but never paid. Presumably, they never did find out about us selling com'mods.

Carney knew a guy named Bob who sold TVs at Sears. Bob would sell TVs and steer customers who needed antennas to us. We installed antennas for a couple of weeks and were making honest money until Carney slipped and fell off the roof of a single story bungalow, landing flat on his back. He had tied one end of a rope around his waist and the other to the brick chimney. Carney's massive bulk ripped the chimney right off the roof. I watched it tumble down as if in slow motion. The upper corner of the chimney hit first with a wood-snapping crunch as it crashed into the roof. Then it rolled and flipped in the air revealing a two-foot gouge in the shingles and plywood, pink insulation showing through. It flipped again in mid-air and hit the eaves, crashing through, breaking roof rafters and ripping off the gutters. Thankfully the irregular pattern of the fall steered the monolith away from Carney.

I scrambled down the roof and surveyed the damage. The roof was fucked, the chimney lay buried in the lawn. Without saying a word we knew exactly what to do. We loaded up our tools and sped off, never to see those people again or return their $25 deposit. "After all," we reasoned, "the rope was worth more than $25." We left the rope tied around the chimney, embedded, as it was, in the lawn.

After that Debbie and I decided to hitchhike to Florida--I don't know why. We didn't need a reason.

Between 1962 and 1966 I was arrested and jailed fourteen times in four States and Canada. One was for "minor consuming alcohol," two for "assault and battery," one each for "leaving the scene of a property damage accident" and "malicious destruction of property," and nine for "drunk and disorderly." At the risk of stating the obvious, let me point out, I had a problem with alcohol.

Despite my full-blown alcoholism, anti-social behavior, and renegade ways, I was a rather likable young man. Through my travels and varied circumstances I'd developed some survival skill that relied on personality and charm. I had a good sense of humor, seemed honest, and was loyal with a certain amount of twisted courage. I was a good conversationalist and was able to speak on a wide range of topics. Most of what I knew came from reading many hundreds of NATIONAL GEOGRAPHIC magazines while doing jail time. I was a hard, if "unreliable" worker who made friends easily and seemed cheerful most of the time.

Chapter Four

MYSTIC KNIGHTS OF THE SEA LODGE HALL--1967

Debbie and I caught a ride outside of Flint that dropped us off at the bus station in downtown Detroit. Everywhere we looked there were young people on the move--college students taking the Greyhound to Florida for spring break, high school kids just out for a good time, soldiers in uniform with duffel bags in tow, and what seemed like hoards of derelict teen-agers dressed in the scruffy fashions of the street, toting knapsacks. It seemed like everyone under thirty in America was going somewhere.

In all my travels, I had never seen anything like this. This was new. There was a spirit in the air--a spirit of freedom--of breaking loose--going new places. And a spirit of resistance and animosity against those who would keep the young from their fated journeys.

We hooked up with Bob and Janet. Janet was a dark-haired Jewish girl from one of the Detroit suburbs. Bob was rather average--an art student at Wayne State, with long, dark hair and a full beard. They seemed like beatniks to me. They had a run-down apartment on Alexandrine, up near the university. We crashed on their floor for a few nights until we "got it together," in the terminology of the times. In those days, there was an openness and willingness to help like-minded travelers. "Peace, Love and Good Vibes" was the order of the day.

We smoked joints mostly; a half an ounce was about $10 then. We read poetry and listened to music and ate brown rice with sea salt while sitting on the floor of the sparsely furnished apartment.

We heard about a demonstration to be held in New York City on April 15, 1967 to protest the war in Vietnam and decided to attend. After loading up with reefer and speed and gassing up Bob's '56 Buick, the four of us hit the road. The speed made us jabberwocky and we chattered and careened through the night. Ideas came like bugs against the windshield--there for a brief second, then cast off into the universe. As the Buick dipped and swayed eastward, one after another, we put forward arguments against the war, educating each other. None of us felt threatened by those villains of our parents' nightmares, the dreaded Communists. The Vietnamese, especially, just didn't seem like a threat. Only people like our parents, brainwashed with fear, believed the hate mongering of tired honkies in Washington, the so-called, "cold warriors," we called them "dinosaurs," an obsolete species.

The draft was unfair, too; if you were married and had a kid, you didn't have to go. I know many who got married and had kids just to avoid the draft, causing the divorce rate to climb. Or, if your daddy had money and could send you to college, you didn't have to go; in those days, college and university education was not as open to people of color and poor people as it is today, which meant that they were more likely to be drafted than middle-class whites. And why, we asked ourselves, were young people the ones dying in the war--let those old farts who started and believed in it go over there and fight. Not only that, but the goddamn leader of South Vietnam was a fascist crook bastard. Why would the United States support such a creep anyway? The Buick roared through the night.

We arrived in New York on April 15, 1967. The entry for that date in the *PEOPLE'S ALMANAC* reads: "The largest antiwar demonstration to date--100,000 by police estimates, 400,000 according to organizers..." Who do you believe?

I don't remember the route of the march, but it was uptown from where I usually spent time in the city. I remember tall, tall buildings, and some occupants emptying wastebasket trash on us from ten, fifteen or sometimes twenty stories up, several times I saw the wastebaskets themselves come hurling down, as if from the battlements of a medieval castle. I even saw a piece of concrete, the size of a waffle iron, crash to the pavement. I remember wide avenues filled with protesters singing and chanting, marching peacefully in rank and file.

Group after group filed by: Veterans Against the War, Clergy Against the War, Teachers Against the War, labor unions, and the War Resistors League. The NAACP and the Urban League marched, too, perhaps partly in response to Dr. Martin Luther King's proposal earlier in the month to unite the civil rights and anti-war movements. King, who supported draft evasion, had called the U.S. government "the greatest purveyor of violence in the world." Added to all these groups was, of course, The New Mobilization to End the War (the Mobe), the principle umbrella organization for many of the participating groups and individuals. This high school dropout had never seen anything like it, or felt anything like the awesome power of what seemed like half a million people, all moving in one direction in spirit and body. My chest swells up recalling this even today.

Though the march through the streets was empowering, the scene on the sidewalk was frightening. They were five people deep with rabid Americans hurling insults, casting aspersions, shouting invectives, screaming epithets and wielding curses. They appeared as jowly, unattractive people with ugly faces and large mouths full of hate and poisonous bile.

I fell in with a group of "American Buddhists Against the War" all wearing saffron robes, baldheads and carrying signs denouncing the "Peace President," Lyndon Johnson. We ended up at the United Nations, I think. I remember being on the wrong side of a chainlink fence when the cops began getting nasty--poking people in the ribs with their batons, whacking them on the back of the legs. I jumped a subway turnstile with a group of protesters and made my way back to the Buick. I committed myself to ending the War, and prayed I would remember that day for the rest of my life.

The trip back to Detroit was uneventful. We did the last of the speed to ward off the terrible, wrung-out feeling of not sleeping for four days. But we knew that sooner or later we had to come down. We crashed and recuperated three days before Bob and Janet asked us to leave.

* * *

Once back in Detroit, it wasn't long before we heard about Plum Street. Modeled on San Francisco's Haight Asbury district, Plum Street was an enclave of hip capitalists making a buck off the latest fad. In the spring of 1967 the fad was Hippies.

Plum Street was a neglected neighborhood that had gone on life-support after the John Lodge Expressway cleaved it in two, separating its eastern part from its Tiger Stadium heart. For blocks around, urban decay took all but a handful of the pre-World War II, two-story frame dwellings, leaving the neighborhood a checkerboard of rundown houses, vacant lots and drab boarded-up retail stores. The Greek grocery on the corner was the only business still open that had any history on Plum Street.

In the spring of 1967 entrepreneurs moved into the area and opened "hip" businesses. Two of these guys, Saul and Marty, took an old frame house and knocked some walls down, put up old barn wood paneling, stocked the place with incense, candles, hash pipes, sandals, posters and beads and called the place a "Head Emporium." "Black Ike" opened a similar joint next door which mostly sold jewelry, earrings and other baubles. Down the street some hippie lesbians opened a boutique selling bellbottoms, paisley skirts, peasant blouses, headbands and other hippie garb. A restaurant with worn wood and brick walls, heavy exposed beams, and whole earth soups and entrees also opened.

An article in *The Detroit Free Press* and follow-up TV coverage soon turned Plum Street into the local "hip scene." All the hippies and hippie wannabees from the surrounding suburbs came to the area followed by all the straight people who came to see the hippies. Within a week, Plum Street, barely three blocks long, became a bustling street happening.

* * *

A nice thing about traveling with long-legged Debbie, besides the fact she was exquisitely fine to look at and an eager, dexterous and adventurous lover, was that she was a street-smart survivor. Debbie knew that for her, as for most young people hitchhiking and living on the street, sex was the only commodity she had to exchange. She saw sex as a tool to be used to better her situation. She never saw herself as a victim of circumstance, but always as a survivor of circumstance. She told me once, "If you're not a survivor, you're just a whore."

* * *

Debbie and I made it over to Plum Street and visited Saul and Marty's "Head Emporium." Debbie scoped out Saul, who was in his thirties, wore horn-rimmed glasses, and had a new beard coming in. Balding front to back, he would comb the hair on the sides to cover his ears. His tie-dyed T-shirt two sizes too small, allowed his oversize belly to peek out below his shirt like a slice of ripe avocado. What must have been five pounds of hippie beads hung around his neck. Ironed and creased bellbottoms with sandals completed the ensemble. His place was packed with customers.

Meanwhile, I made my way down to the "Candle Werks" in the uneven basement, every cubbyhole of which was filled with candles of every imaginable type. There I made conversation with Marty, the co-owner and a short, unassuming cat, who told me, "I'm only in this racket for the money." I told Marty I was an experienced sandal maker from New York's

Greenwich Village, and that he should set me up in a leather shop in his emporium.

I was never a sandal maker in the Village, but I watched one once.

He liked the idea and went upstairs to find Saul. Soon we were all great friends. Not only did Saul and Marty agree to set me up, but they also let Debbie and me sleep in the Emporium until we could get our own place. Later that evening Marty and Debbie took off together. She never came back. Five years later I saw her over by Ann Arbor, stripping in the Anchor Bar.

I figured out how to make sandals in a couple of hours, then went on to belts, bracelets and armbands, zodiac signs, magical pendants, and several styles of wide, fancy belts with hand tooling and shiny metal and colored glass studwork, the "kidney belts" preferred by the old time Harley riders and truck drivers. Saul and Marty made some money, I made a little too. More importantly, I was in the center of the action. I wasn't the action, but I was in the center of it.

* * *

Just next door to the "Head Emporium" was another frame house with three stories and five gables. This building had been rehabbed too--walls knocked down, doorways enlarged and new drywall hung and painted. Black Ike filled half the first floor with baubles and bangles; the other half was a record shop. The second floor was a used clothing boutique. *The Fifth Estate,* one of the first of the "underground" newspapers in the country was being published on the third floor. This weekly paper was a dues-paying member of the Underground Press Syndicate (UPS), a group of papers that supported a national news collection service. These publications were part of the "underground" press, which was not in a practical sense underground at all. Like mainstream papers, they were quite public and aboveboard and, like any newspaper, interested in expanding readership and advertising.

The ideas, world view, politics and culture advocated in the underground press was however, "underground." They went against the established norm, threatened the status quo and advocated positions contrary to our national, state and local governments. In their spirit and "underdog" status, they truly were "underground."

Peter Werbe and Harvey Ovshinsky, the publishers and editors of *The Fifth Estate,* encouraged John Sinclair and Gary Grimshaw, both of whom worked on *The Fifth Estate,* to publish the first issue of *The Detroit Sun* newspaper from the same office. In fact Grimshaw was living in the offices, sleeping, occasionally, on the layout table.

Sinclair came into the Emporium one day hawking the new rag, *The Sun*. He was a tall cat, six-foot-three and several stones over 200 pounds, which isn't important, except that it seems easier for a large person to be charismatic, and Sinclair is. His bushy hair, just getting long, made his head look like a champagne cork. Wire-rimmed glasses seemed to make his face shine. I liked him immediately.

The Sun was a 24-page tabloid bringing together a new cultural content in the highest artistic form. For the first time, I realized that alternative institutions could be created that stood opposed, in form and in content, to those of the establishment.

Sinclair was the editor savant of *The Sun*. He wrote editorials, a column, music reviews and hard news articles. He sold advertising, made deliveries, and helped with layout. All the while he encouraged other young writers to submit work and drew to himself other creative people of many callings.

Grimshaw was the artistic genius of *The Sun*. Quiet, slim, and fine featured, with the delicate, tapered fingers of an artist and long, straight, thick black hair hanging to the middle of his back, Grimshaw was a museum-quality example of a hippie. By this time, he was a nationally known poster artist having produced work for such luminary music spots as The Family Dog and The Filmore in San Francisco, and for Russ Gibb and The Grande Ballroom in Detroit. Grimshaw had worked on the *San Francisco Oracle,* the bearded granduncle of the underground press and one of the first papers to combine new journalism with new expressions of art in the psychedelic form.

The Sun had no rigid, rectangular columns with photos at the top, like tombstones, and countless words turning the page into a gray mist. Instead, it featured hand-lettered headlines and columns that curved and swooped around original artwork. The photos were provided by photographers who were part of the stories they covered, not separate from them. Even the classifieds had hand-drawn graphics. This was liberating stuff to young people who had been raised with strict orders to "stay within the lines," like first graders with new coloring books.

Shortly after I began making sandals at the Emporium, Sinclair and Grimshaw moved to a former dentist's office in a corner building on Warren and the John Lodge service drive near Wayne State University. From a door off the service drive, a flight of stairs led to another door on the second floor. Through it, to the left, was a large room with white glazed tile from floor to ceiling, and a skylight with wire-reinforced glass. This had been the dentist's operating room and was now the kitchen. To the right was the old waiting room, now a music room with a honkin' sound system. To the right of that was a hall that led to six or so examination rooms, ten-by-twelve cubicles that were ideal for an urban commune.

* * *

Saul, from the Emporium, liked the young girls who frequented the business. He was forever leaving for an hour or two with some straight-haired hippie girl. I was still crashing on the floor of the Emporium when Saul made arrangements with Sinclair to rent a cubicle from him. The plan was that Saul would use it during the day for rolling in the hay with his little chickiepoos, and I could stay there at night.

My cubicle, at the end of the hall, overlooked the expressway, which was about fifty feet below street level and maybe one hundred feet from our door. I was there a week or more before anyone even asked me who I was or what I was doing. I just laid back, blended into the background, scoped out the scene, saw where the light shined the brightest, and moved toward it.

Sinclair was the sun that the other planets revolved around at Warren and John Lodge.

The commune was located in a corner building above two storefronts facing Warren and two facing the Lodge. The two Lodge storefronts were the work and performance space of the Detroit Artists Workshop, a collection of artists, writers, poets, musicians, filmmakers, and sculptors. Sinclair and others had founded the Workshop in 1964 as a budding creative community was taking form. Though the Workshop had only a brief life, it had an impressive record of producing music and poetry concerts, art and political posters, and small books of poetry and short stories.

One of the storefronts was open twenty-four hours and was totally trashed. The glass front door had been stolen; no one knew where it had gone. Kids were always hanging around making dope deals or plans to move on, those who stayed dragged in abandoned couches and easy chairs and urine-stained mattresses, one with a large burn in it. The space became a "crash pad" for runaways, and a good place to meet girls who needed a place to stay for the night.

That's how I met "Injun," a sixteen-year-old Mohawk girl who ran away from an abusive family on a reservation in New York State. She stayed with me for several months before telling me she was pregnant and planned to leave. She didn't know where she would go and was rather scared. I told her she could stay with me and raise the baby. She wasn't interested, and one day she was gone. I never asked, and it was never made clear to me if I was the father, though I doubt it.

That same spring, Leni Sinclair, Sinclair's wife, had given birth to Sunny, their first daughter. Besides being a mother, Leni is a masterful photographer and filmmaker--setting up her darkroom in any closet or bathroom she could find. Her archive is an untapped mine of photographs featuring musicians, poets, political activists and cultural events of the time. Originally from East Germany, Leni came to this country in 1962 on a student visa and later applied for and received citizenship.

* * *

About this time, Sinclair and Grimshaw formed Trans-Love Energies, as a "hip" taxi service, believe it or not. The slogan was, "We'll Get You There On Time." Trans-Love Energies (TLE or Trans-Love) attracted a younger type of visionary. Unlike members of the Workshop, who were older, more mature and thoughtful, (though rather inbred and anal-retentive), these newcomers were wild-ass kids, high school-and college- aged, high on life and LSD, open and expansive, bent on seeing a world of possibilities in new ways--don't Bogart the joint.

Quickly TLE evolved into a major urban commune made up of cultural guerrillas and renegades, writers, photographers, filmmakers, poets, poster, graphic, and flim-flam artists, and prophets of a variety of disciplines. Like our predecessor, the Workshop, we began producing concerts and other events at Wayne State. We brought Sun Ra and his fourteen-piece Myth Science Arkestra to Detroit. We brought in The Art Ensemble of Chicago. We produced concerts of the MC5, the folksy SPIKEDRIVERS, and Charles Moore and the Contemporary Jazz Quintet of Detroit.

At the end of May, 1967 TLE organized the first Belle Isle Love-in, modeled on the famous Be-Ins held in San Francisco's Golden Gate Park. The idea was to invite everyone to just come together on this island in the Detroit River and love each other . . .a love-in. We got the MC5 and several other local bands to play for free. We called a press conference, and with the help of the straight media and WABX-FM (one of the first "underground" radio stations in the country) spread the word.

More that ten thousand people showed up. A peaceful day with bikers and Blacks, hippies and straights, queers and the quirky, young and old, suburbanites and city dwellers--it was wonderful. Even though I had taken several hits of acid, my recollections seem to correspond with press reports I read later.

Though the citizens created no real trouble at the Love-In, the cops did. After all, there was open pot smoking, loud rock-n-roll, public use of LSD, nudity and fornication. These, in addition to unity among diverse groups, did not sit well with a police organization that depended on isolation, animosity and separation as a means of control. Because of the Love-In, the attitude of the Detroit Police Department hardened against Sinclair and Trans-Love Energies.

A week later, Grimshaw was working in the Workshop at his drawing table. At that time, TLE had a contract with Russ Gibb, owner of the Grande Ballroom, which was a psychedelic venue similar to the famous San Francisco Filmore. Grimshaw produced all the print advertising for the Grande: posters, handbills, newspaper ads and the like. Grimshaw and I produced the light shows at the Grande and several TLE commune members managed and staffed the head shop. Sinclair booked many of the acts and was, for a time, the manager, of a sort.

On this particularly pleasant, early summer morning in Detroit, Grimshaw was way in the back of the Workshop with the front door wide open. Grimshaw had purchased a kite designed like an American flag--white stars on a blue field on the upper triangle of the kite, with red and white stripes on the bottom. On this patriotic plaything, Grimshaw had drawn an "Egyptian Eye." Below it, in magic marker, he'd written: "Fuck America...Go Fly A Kite." The kite in question was hanging from the ceiling near the back of the Workshop, perhaps forty feet from the front door.

A black-and-white, carrying pure white officers stopped in front, double parked, and, uninvited entered the storefront. Seeing the kite, they arrested Grimshaw on the spot for "willfully displaying an obscene drawing." He was cuffed and hauled away.

* * *

Before becoming a Detroit Recorders Court Judge, Justin Ravitz was part of a band of warrior lawyers who were fighting for poor people against an evermore-repressive police force and political regime. Sinclair contacted him, and he got Grimshaw released that afternoon and demanded a jury trial. Later, at trial, Ravitz was hamstrung by the Judge who would not allow him to argue the obvious First Amendment protections of free speech. Ravitz pushed on, arguing that the police could not have seen the kite from the street, as they had testified. The store was poorly lit, with the only light shining on the drawing table. The early morning sun put the store in deep shadow. No, Ravitz continued, the police stopped and entered the building, not to investigate crime or to serve and protect, as they are sworn to do, but rather to harass and intimidate individuals they found politically or culturally objectionable. It is precisely these tactics, Ravitz argued, that the Detroit Police Department used daily in the minority communities of the city.

When the Judge instructed the jury before deliberation, he insisted the jury not consider the issue of obscenity, since he had ruled it was obscene, but only if Grimshaw posted the kite "willfully."

The jury brought back a conviction. Ravitz immediately filed a appeal which went all the way to the Michigan Supreme Court, where the Chief Justice, G. Mennen "Soapy" Williams reversed the conviction and issued a scathing opinion against the Detroit Police and the presiding Judge.

Despite harassment by the police, Sinclair and TLE became a force in the politics and culture of greater metropolitan Detroit after the success of the Belle Isle Love-In. TLE had earned a certain amount of credibility and became a regular news item in the local media.

Shortly after the kite caper two Chaldean's connected with the Lebanese mob, Tony and Chucky, visited Sinclair with a proposal to place vending machines in our storefront that had been taken over by the street kids. The Chaldean's who controlled the vending machine racket throughout southeast Michigan, were always looking for new outlets and locations for their machines, saw the Workshop as a likely location for pinball, candy and soft drink machines. The Workshop would get a cut of the take with no hassle. Unfortunately, within three days the machines were trashed. Someone carried off the pinball machine, and crowbarred the doors right off the others, stealing the goods as well as the money.

Naturally, Tony and Chucky were pissed. I remember them double-parked on the service drive with their blinkers on, gesticulating wildly as Sinclair stood in the street and hunched his shoulders with his hands out to his sides, a quizzical look on his face.

* * *

One day I noticed in one of the Workshop storefronts that a table, twenty feet long, had been set up and stacks of printed pages had been placed around the entire perimeter of the table. Sinclair and several others were circling the table taking one sheet from each stack as they moved around. They were collating 1,000 copies of a 150-page book titled: *THE STRANGE ODYSSEY OF HOWARD POW,* by Bill Hutton, an Artists Workshop member. I jumped in line and made myself useful; round and round we went. I kept quiet and just listened as Sinclair and his two friends talked jazz, talked poetry, talked writing, talked movies, talked art. After an hour or so, Sinclair's friends left. "Let's do a bump," he said, and laid out some pure crystal amphetamine. We snorted it through a disassembled ballpoint pen and went back to our collating with renewed vigor. Soon I was yakkity yakking about Gypsies and the Union and Greenwich Village. Sinclair was jabbering about Miles Davis's album, *Sketches Of Spain,* who the sidemen and the engineer were, where it was recorded, and what Miles said to the piano player between the first and second takes of such and such a song. We went on for hours, walking and talking, doing a bump now and again, collating *THE STRANGE ODYSSEY OF HOWARD POW.* We've been friends, co-collators, co-founders, co-conspirators and co-defendants ever since.

* * *

The neighborhood around the dentist's office, which was now our commune, was made up mostly of students and recent dropouts from Wayne State, blacks and Chicanos, and a smattering of poor whites. Urban decay was rapidly rotting the neighborhood, as the all-white Detroit Police Department protected the status quo and kept the poor folks in line. Yet everywhere could be felt the energy and passion of those who sought revolutionary social change. Black Nationalists roamed the streets organizing for a mass return to Africa. Other Black Nationalists were advocating the takeover of five southern States and the establishment of the Republic of New Africa. On Wayne's campus, Black Muslims, looking dapper in their suits and red bow ties, sold the Nation of Islam newspaper on street corners, while old-line Communists and Socialists handed out flyers denouncing the United Auto Workers as puppets of the capitalist car companies. The Draft Resisters League counseled young men--kids really--on how to avoid the draft. These were exciting times!

The corner storefront facing Warren Avenue, now

housed The New Mobilization To End The War In Vietnam. The "Mobe" office was always filled with a lot of straight-looking people. The men had short hair and many wore ties. The women were coifed and wore bras and make-up, just like my mom. To me, they looked like plastic people in a plastic world.

I'm sure they had a negative picture of us--endlessly playing "Frisbee" while dodging traffic on the service drive, smokin' dope as speakers balanced in the second floor window blasted out "Sergeant Pepper" or Coltrane or the local boy, Mitch Ryder.

The other storefront facing Warren held the new offices of *The Fifth Estate*. They were nearly hippies, so were easy to get along with.

Naturally, the Mobe and *The Fifth Estate* drew attacks--not from the police as might be expected, but from rabid right-wingers of the Detroit area. A neo-fascist named Lobsinger and his group "Breakthrough" were primarily responsible. Through research others have done, we now know that the Detroit FBI office and it's Special Agent in Charge used Breakthrough as an "independent action squad," like some South American dictators used "Death Squads" to carry out their criminal deeds. The Detroit FBI notified Breakthrough of upcoming demonstrations, helped them set up a filing system for every radical written about in the local papers and gave out addresses of activists so Breakthrough could harass them at home. Breakthrough was essentially a vigilante group that committed acts of terrorism and intimidation with a nod from and tacit support of the Detroit FBI.

It was Breakthrough members who threw beer bottles and chunks of concrete through the second story windows of our commune so often that we finally stopped filing police reports. And it was Breakthrough that firebombed the Mobe and Fifth Estate storefronts, over and over. Even when heavy plywood replaced all the windows, still they firebombed, leaving charred wood and burn marks the shape of large moths at rest. Our living quarters reeked for days with the smell of smoke and gasoline.

Leaving the Mobe and Fifth Estate to the right-wing militia, the Detroit Police focused their attention on the Artists Workshop and John Sinclair. After all, we all smoked reefer, which was illegal--printing a paper and organizing against the war were not.

In 1966, Sinclair and fifty-four others, many of them members of the Artists Workshop, had been arrested in a one-night series of raids for various marijuana charges ranging from sales to possession to conspiracy. The police and media played it as if a major dope ring had been broken-up; in reality, it was a bunch of students, artists and beatniks.

Sinclair was sentenced to six months in the Detroit House of Correction (DeHoCo), the fifty-four others had their charges dropped or were given probation.

Then, just before my arrival in Detroit in April of '67, Sinclair was arrested again for "sale of marijuana" after he gave two joints to an undercover Detroit Police Officer.

Sinclair, rather than "learning his lesson" and going straight, took the fight for realistic weed laws to the street and to anyone who would listen. He began to challenge the law by smoking it publicly and urging others to do the same. This flaunting of the law gave the cops a hard-on for Sinclair and his ilk and made the cops more malevolent then ever in their dealings with us.

*   *   *

When *The Fifth Estate* vacated its Plum Street offices for its storefront on John Lodge and Warren, Sinclair and I decided to open a bookstore in the old Fifth Estate offices on Plum Street. The lease was good for another month. We had ten or fifteen titles published by the Artists Workshop and we were in contact with various other small magazines around the country. Surely they would front us books. In addition, Sinclair had written music reviews for *JAZZ, Sound and Fury, and DOWNBEAT* magazines, and so had some connections in the music magazine biz. We could get stock from them too. Through *The Fifth Estate* and *The Sun* we had contacts with every underground paper in the country. We could get a dozen or so papers on credit; also, Grimshaw had contacts with other poster artists, who could be imposed upon to either donate or advance us some posters and comic books too. Now that we had a place and could get some stock, all we needed was a name.

That came from a writer named Paul Bowles, a not-so-well-known American ex-patriot, self-exiled to Morocco, who was recognized by fellow beatniks as an authority on altered states of consciousness and mild euphorics like reefer and hallucinogens. In one of his books he quoted an ancient Arabic folk saying: "A pipe of kief in the morning will give the strength of one hundred camels in the courtyard."

We called the bookstore "100 Camels" and opened for business. We didn't know it at the time, but Sinclair was under heavy surveillance by the Detroit Police Department. One night after leaving 100 Camels, Sinclair and I were stopped by the police while driving home. Two cop cars pulled us over, with a third carload of plainclothes screeching up right behind. Sinclair started right in: "Why the fuck did you stop us? What law did we break?"

They yanked us out, pushed us around some, called us "fags," and made us lay face down in the gravel parking lot while they ransacked Sinclair's Opel. Sinclair kept at them: "Are we under arrest? Why the fuck did you stop us? What's the charge, motherfucker?" I kept my mouth shut and wished Sinclair would too.

They took the backseat out and threw it aside, along with bundles of *The Fifth Estate* and *The Sun*. In the trunk, all they found, besides several more bundles of papers, was a piece of corkboard with about thirty pairs of custom-made earrings, some with small peacock feathers, others with effigies made of highly polished copper and silver, still others with dangly strips of leather and beads. Sinclair was delivering them to our store to sell, but he forgot to carry them up. The cops thought they were fishing lures. They sat us up in the dimly lit lot and cuffed us behind our backs while they radioed in for any report of stolen fishing lures. An hour or so later, finding nothing and receiving no report on "hot" fishing lures, they let us go.

When the lease ran out, the landlord doubled the rent and we were out of business.

*　　　*　　　*

However, Tony and Chucky, our Chaldean gangster friends, returned with a new business opportunity. Someone in their mob owned an old movie theater, downtown on Woodward, between Cadillac Square and Grand Circus Park. They proposed letting us open it as an "aboveground," after-hours, alcohol-free music nightspot. They would put absolutely no money into the venture, but promised us we'd have no problem getting inspections and city permits, providing we served no alcohol. We agreed and started work on the joint immediately.

As always, the first thing we needed was a name. I recall sitting at the table in our white-tiled kitchen at the commune with Grimshaw and Sinclair. We were talking about old TV shows and Sinclair reminisced about the 1950's *Amos 'n Andy* TV show and how they belonged to a fraternal organization, The Mystic Knights of the Sea. Amos 'n Andy were always going to a "lodge" meeting at "the Mystic Knights of the Sea Lodge Hall."

"We could call it "THE MYSTIC KNIGHTS OF THE SEE LODGE HALL.
The SEE for short!" Sinclair exclaimed.

The old theater had a marquee common in those days, probably "modernized" in the 50's, it extended horizontally from the building, overhanging the sidewalk and boasting no filigrees or curlicues or art of any kind. It was simply a large, pie-shaped structure with fields of white plastic and black channels that held interchangeable letters announcing the "current attractions."

The facade at street level had been redone in smoky blue mirrors. The ticket booth looked like an "isolation booth" on the popular TV quiz shows of the day: well-lit and cramped. On the left was a long, narrow lobby with a concessions bar. Ornate, gilded picture frames, suitable for large movie posters (and part of the original grand architecture), lined the right wall.

The theater had an old proscenium stage that curved out from the front with the movie screen suspended at the curtain line. The only thing remarkable was that all the seats had been removed and a flat floor installed so the place could be used as a roller skating rink. The flat floor was perfect for setting up tables and chairs; scattered elevated platforms provided space for either light-show equipment or designated "VIP" tables.

The plan was to have a club that opened for business at midnight and stayed open 'til four in the morning. The club would not serve alcohol and would be principally dedicated to presentation of "the music." Sinclair felt that we could attract live acts after they finished their gigs at other music venues around town. He postulated that musicians would support a public venue dedicated to presenting the music as its primary reason for existence, rather than the bottom line.

We removed the plastic fields from the marquee so Grimshaw could paint them. Meanwhile he designed and sketched in art on the blue mirror façade, incorporating the mirrors into the artwork in an intricate design of interwoven images and psychedelic visions, to be painted by volunteers.

The mob came through with the inspections and necessary permits, while others in the commune ordered soft drinks, chips and other munchies, scrubbed floors and walls, and replaced hundreds of light bulbs. Grimshaw finished the two panels for the marquee, painting a large red and yellow Egyptian-style eye, outlined in black, with the words THE SEE arched over it. We were open for business.

On opening night, Tony and Chucky showed up in their double-breasted suits and slouch hats and crowded into the ticket booth with Audrey, a young runaway who was a redheaded beauty and recent addition to the commune. Every time fifty or more dollars accumulated in the till, Chucky would snatch it and add it to the bulging roll he kept in his right-front pants pocket. Musically, the night was fantastic. Financially it was a bust. The soft drink and munchie vendors wanted their money; things didn't look good.

The following night was the same: Tony and Chucky pocketed the money as fast as we made it. Apparently, their mob had held them accountable for the loss of the vending machines a month or so previously, and they were determined to get their money back "off the top."

With no money to pay our suppliers or the bands, we folded.

*　　　　　*　　　　　*

Working on the SEE, I met my first wife, Genie. She was a runaway girl of seventeen who had hitched into Detroit from Atlanta. Her dad was a retired Air Force Colonel. "Full Bird

Colonel, Full Bird Colonel," he slurred drunkenly over and over the one time I met him. "You want a revolution?" he blathered over dinner. "I can get you air cover anywhere over the eastern half of the United States," he said, before slumping into his soup.

Genie had been living with Carl, an artist nearly as well known as Grimshaw. Carl was a small-framed, frail-looking kid who had mastered the art of psychedelic lettering--making letters and words drip and spin, causing the eye to shift and see several dimensions at once. Among other things, Carl produced posters for The Grande, the local "psychedelic ballroom."

Genie was a plain yet pretty girl with long brown trusses. She was from Texas and bore the same last name as the president who hailed from that state, so we called her "The Prez."

I had my eye on her for several days before I made my move. I turned on the charm, offered her some speed and reefer, and swept her off her feet, away from Carl and to the commune. At least that's how I remember it.

Chapter Five

"WHO'S GONNA CLEAN UP THIS MESS?" Detroit--Summer, 1967

I'd been in Detroit for two months and hadn't gotten drunk even once. I didn't even want to drink--there was too much going on. Beyond that, The Prez and most of the people in the TLE commune didn't drink, or at least not excessively like my old crew in Traverse City. My new friends felt they were engaged in a great creation. The old culture was dying, eaten away from the inside by its own contradictions and the lies it could no longer sustain. A generation of dynamic young people were redefining the world in their own terms, creating a new culture and value system. The result was a political earthquake, the aftershocks of which are still being felt a generation or more later.

I believed that part of building the new involved rejecting and destroying the old. I came to see alcohol as the drug of choice of the old culture, an acceptable custom in a dying lifestyle. I wanted nothing to do with it.

I had arrived in Detroit in the waning days of The Artists Workshop which was being transformed by a younger generation of visionaries. Of the two Workshop storefronts, street people had claimed one. The other was in better repair, and it's door still locked. The mimeograph machine and reams of paper stolen from Wayne State University were stored there, as were all the books and posters produced by the Workshop. A sculptor and several paint artists still worked there from time to time, but overall, the light was fading.

I was getting rather pissed off at Lobsinger and his band of Breakthrough brown shirts who were firebombing the offices below us and throwing beer bottles and rocks through our second story windows on a regular basis. I felt that if we got to know our neighbors perhaps we could count on them if things got sticky.

I mentioned to Sinclair that I thought we should do a Sweep-In, a general clean-up of the neighborhood. We could get the whole neighborhood out to clean up the alleys, sweep the streets, and talk to each other. We might even put speakers in the windows, get some groceries and have a party.

Sinclair thought it was a good idea; encouraged, I went ahead and organized it.

Once a week, the Detroit Free Press, the more liberal of Detroit's two daily newspapers, ran a column on the front page called *"Action Line!"* It was a consumer advocate sort of thing; they would cut through governmental red tape and overcome obstacles for people who could get no satisfaction through regular channels when dealing with large corporations or institutions. They would intercede for the little guy. They would also perform good deeds for families in dire need--like the poor little girl who wanted to see Mickey Mouse just once before she died of leukemia.

I wrote to *"Action Line!"* and told them of our plan to have a neighborhood Sweep-In. We needed some brooms and shovels; we needed water and trash containers.

Within a couple of weeks, they printed my request and

reported they had made the following arrangements: Public Works would provide a garbage truck, the Fire Department would put a "reducer" on two hydrants and provide four hundred feet of garden hose and Acme Brush and Broom would provide one hundred brooms and detergent. I made the necessary calls and set everything up. The Sweep-In would take place Saturday, July 23rd.

I went banging on doors in the neighborhood, talking up the Sweep-in. The Chicanos, who lived next door to us, on Warren, didn't speak English. I said "Fiesta! Fiesta!" several times and pantomimed sweeping. They gave me an odd look and were polite though noncommittal. The poor whites next door to them--skinny, southern Appalachian folks with red necks and white ribbed chests--didn't know if they would be around or not, though a passel of kids said they would show up. Several Black families on the block showed interest but would wait until Saturday to decide.

Two blocks down, near Trumbell, Wayne Kramer, lead guitarist and driving force in the MC5, had a room in a house with a handful of other hippies. There were always a bunch of musicians hanging around whose participation I could count on.

Down the Service Drive from our place was "The Castle." A three-story monstrosity, The Castle was half a block long and made of cut stone with four turrets overlooking the Service Drive and the John Lodge Expressway. It was full of a parent's worst nightmares: out-of-work musicians, poets who heard voices, coed cuties, dime bag reefer dealers, speed freaks and stone junkies. I could count on their participation as well. Of course the staff and volunteers at the Mobe and Fifth Estate would be at least somewhat eager participants.

With the Sweep-In on Saturday, Emil and I decided to pick up the brooms on Friday morning. Emil was a filmmaker who lived at Trans-Love. He was a funny guy with a full, bushy beard and black, rather stringy hair that hung to his shoulders. He wore short sleeved, cotton, buffalo-plaid shirts tucked into Wrangler jeans hitched up high in the crotch and pulled up taut with a leather belt a foot too long, so that the end would pass through the buckle and dangle like a subway strap from his cinched waist. He could also get this look about him: with his hand to his chin and his fingers rubbing his nose, mustache and beard, he would appear bewildered and bemused as if the occasion required special, concentrated thought.

Emil had a '64 VW bus, the stereotypical "Hippie Van," we drove over to the East Side, off Jefferson, where we found Acme Broom and Brush down by the river in an old waterfront warehouse.

Damn! a hundred brooms is a lot of brooms. They had them boxed. House brooms were five to a box. Push brooms, three to a box with the handles unscrewed. The boxes were four feet long and six inches high. They took up the whole back of the van with several boxes tied on top. Acme Broom and Brush also donated a hundred pounds of heavy duty, concentrated cleaning detergent so we could actually scrub the streets. We signed the bill of lading and split.

We returned to TLE and removed the boxes from the top of the van but left the rest inside since we would be using them the next day. I was excited as I went to sleep with the windows open to the midnight breeze and the city slowing down; all was peaceful.

The next morning I saw Werbe, one of *The Fifth Estate* editors, on the sidewalk outside the paper's offices. "Did you hear about the riots over on 12th and Clairmount?" he asked. I hadn't, so we went inside the paper's office to listen to the radio and watch the TV they had set up.

Overnight seventy-three black folks had been arrested by the Detroit police at a blind pig (an after-hours, unlicensed bar, often located in a private home). The police, employing their usual thuggish ways had raised the ire of the crowd that had gathered to witness the mass arrest. Someone threw a wine bottle, then another one. Shots rang out. The cops took up defensive positions and called for backup. More cops arrived to a rain of bottles and bricks. Tear gas was fired, round after round. People in the neighborhood heard the shots and smelled the tear gas; sirens screeched through the night.

The Tactical Mobil Units or TMUs, of the Detroit Police were a new division, expertly trained and highly mobile with all white cars. They were a high-profile force, specializing in rapid response which guaranteed quick results, the predecessors to today's SWAT teams.

There were a thousand people or more in the street by

the time the TMUs arrived like Cossacks on horseback, trying to push the crowd back. But it was too late. The crowd had power. With bricks and bottles and the occasional pop of pistol shot, they forced the TMU to turn tail and run.

The morning papers had the complete story with pictures. The local TV stations were interrupting regular scheduled programming to cover the ruckus, which was still in progress. The Detroit Police, they were reporting, had lost control on the northwest side. Throughout southeast Michigan, police and sheriff departments were being mobilized. We could see several columns of smoke rising to the northwest, just fifteen blocks away. The Sweep-In was off, supplanted by the current crisis which was a lot more interesting.

By now more people were out and about; word was spreading. Around noon Emil and I decided to take a drive over to 12th and Clairmount, where the riots started, and check things out for ourselves. We hopped in the VW and made our way up Trumbull to Clairmount. A lot of people were on the streets. Cars full of black kids tooted horns, while riders leaned out of car windows to holler encouragement and thrust fists in the air. Groups were gathering in front of barbershops, liquor stores and barbeque joints and returning salutes to passing carloads of revelers.

We turned on Clairmount and the whole scene changed. Bumper-to-bumper traffic crawled along at a snail's pace and cars parked on both sides of the street left barely enough room for traffic.

Clairmount is a residential street of WWII vintage, with brown-brick houses and big front porches. Large oaks and maples shade the street and the postage stamp lawns. Each porch, house after house, was filled with whole families of black folks: grandma in the rocker, mom keeping an eye on things while getting lemonade for neighbor ladies, children riding tri-cycles on the narrow sidewalk that led to the street, staying close. Dad and some of his buddies from the plant, it seemed, were sucking down a few cold Strohs, the beer of choice for loyal Detroiters. House after house, block after block, it was like this. Occasionally knots of teenagers could be seen strolling up and down.

There was no music here; just the sullen stares of the

homeowners, their lives, homes, and families in jeopardy from the fires that raged through businesses just down the block, to say nothing of the all-white police forces of occupation stationed in their neighborhood.

. I was surprised by the number of white couples, with children in the back of their station wagons, who had obviously come from the suburbs to tour 12th and Clairmount. In fact, more than half of the cars contained white folks, which made me uneasy. Suddenly I was ashamed as we found ourselves in a traffic backup with gawkers and rubberneckers, who were apparently insensitive to the lives and suffering of these people.

As we eased down Clairmount toward 12th, we began to see more cops in heavy riot gear: black jumpsuits and boots, dull black helmets and face shields, carrying carbines and pump shotguns and wearing ammo harnesses across their chests. Their tear gas canisters clanked together as they marched in formation.

For a block before 12th, there were no civilian cars parked on the street. Police armored vehicles, TMUs, "black and whites," sheriffs' cars from surrounding counties and various paddy wagons and command vehicles took all available space, narrowing the street to a pinch point.

For the last half of the block, traffic was directed between a gauntlet of cops, badges taped over with black tape so the number couldn't be read. They poked their guns and their white porcine faces through the windows of cars with black occupants to snarl and ask where they lived and their destination. The whites, of course, were just waved through.

As we neared the corner of 12th, Emil got "that look" on his face. His hand went to his chin as he fiddled with his mustache and beard, his lips were pursed as he breathed noisily through his nose. His head listed just seven degrees left, his jaw tilted five clicks past horizontal as he stared through the bug encrusted window of the off-white over aquamarine VW bus.

At 12th, the cops had the intersection blocked; we had to go left or right. With our side windows slid open we had spoken to dozens of cops as we passed through the gauntlet. They all told us to get the hell out of there, and if they saw us again today they'd arrest us. We inched along.

Just as we got to the corner and were turning left, we were stopped. Several cops approached the bus. Sticking his head in and looking around, one of them asked me, "What's in the bag under your feet?" Another cop asked Emil, "What's in all those boxes?"

"Soap," I answered. "Brooms." Emil said. "Hey captain! Check this out," one of the cops called out.

They made us pull over. Cops surrounded us. Ordered from the bus, they made us lie face down on the pavement. One cop stood on my wrist: "So I know where you are." A whole squad attacked the bus. They pulled out the boxes, tore them open and emptied the brooms onto the street. They tore up the floor mats and looked in the ashtray and engine compartment. The captain was focused on the hundred pounds of detergent, discussing it intently with several other officers.

Meanwhile the large crowd of black citizens gathered at the corner began getting agitated. "Hey look! They got the hippies!" I could hear people yell. "Hey hippies! Black Power!" someone else shouted. The crowd was picking up energy, I could feel it. "Hey hippies! Free Love!" someone bellowed from the crowd.

The captain came over to us, his gold shield and insignia on his helmet peeking out from behind the black tape. "Show some ID, boys. You're in big trouble," he said. We handed over our IDs and Emil got that look again. "You boys are going to be charged with possession of explosive making materials," the captain continued.

Emil snapped out of it and began talking real fast "We're students at Wayne; we live on Prentiss. We just came by to see what was going on," he lied. Then I spoke up, "The brooms and detergent were to be used to clean up our neighborhood today." Just then I remembered the bill of lading, "We have a receipt for this stuff," I said. The captain had one of his men escort me to the bus and after some looking, I found the receipt amid the refuse on the floor of the front seat.

Just then a bottle crashed in the middle of the intersection. People started chanting, "Black Power! Black Power." The crowd had grown larger.

The captain looked at my paper--another bottle smashed somewhere close. "Load up your shit and get out of here--if anything comes up, we have your names."

Blam! A block up 12th, the cops were shooting tear gas.

Blam! Another one. The captain and his squad rushed off. Blam! Another one. All the cops were on edge, standing spread-legged, guns at the ready, watching the rooftops.

Emil and I were left with seventy-five brooms scattered around the street; the cops kept the detergent. Quickly I started picking up brooms and throwing them in the bus. Emil got that look for a moment, put his hands on his hips, and then hollered at the cops, "Hey! Who's gonna clean up this mess?"

All the attention was focused up 12th Street. The cops that weren't running in that direction were in defensive positions looking ever so nervous. I threw a dozen or so brooms into the bus and told Emil, "Let's get the hell out of here!" We piled in, and lickety-split, we were gone, leaving the rest of the brooms and a pile of torn cardboard in the street. Out the back, I could see folks from the neighborhood beginning to pick up the brooms. I was near exploding with excitement as we drove away. Emil and I laughed hysterically, slapping our knees and each other on the back. We weren't afraid of the crowd, just the cops.

* * *

When we returned to TLE, radio and TV were reporting that rioting had broken out on the east side and that looting and arson was taking place in isolated parts of the city.

Mayor Cavanaugh took to the airwaves to plead for calm and reassure the public that everything was OK. He announced that surrounding cities and counties had sent forces to Detroit and that the Michigan State Police were in the process of being mobilized and would be in the city by nightfall.

Later that afternoon, I found Sinclair in the Workshop at the mimeograph machine printing up flyers. The headline read; THE FIRST ANNUAL DETROIT LOOT-IN! Then in two-inch letters "GET THE BIG STUFF!" Grimshaw had drawn a cartoon-like graphic that showed hippies and blacks carrying off TVs, couches and refrigerators.

Sinclair printed up about five hundred flyers and he and I took off in the Opel. We drove down Woodward and Cass and some of the cross-streets. Every time we saw a group of people gathered, I'd toss out a handful of flyers, and we'd speed off.

With our work done, we returned to TLE to make ready for the expected Saturday night rumble.

*   *   *

Our building had a flat roof with a three-foot parapet three stories off the ground. There was an access door to the roof in the ceiling of the hallway. I ran an extension cord to the roof and brought up a TV and radio and set them on the chimney. Emil had a pair of field glasses; I took them to the roof too. I went to the Lebanese-owned liquor store to get some snacks for the upcoming evening ruckus, only to find the store closed by order of the mayor and chief of police. When I returned, The Prez, several others and I climbed to the roof and took up our positions.

By now you could see smoke and the pink under-glow of fire toward the east side. The northwest quadrant was fully involved. Cops rode four to a car with the windows down, rifles and shotguns sticking out. Fire engines raced to and fro, the screech and scream of sirens and horns and the acrid smoke of burning asphalt filled the evening air like the groan and stench of hell.

When night came, it got scary. The mayor ordered a dusk-to-dawn curfew. Gas stations were ordered to pump gas only into vehicles, no containers. The only cars on the streets were cops driving slow, lights out, long guns bristled from doors propped open with a foot or a piece of wood wedged near the hinge. Cop cars moved in groups of three, quietly. Every time we saw cops coming, we'd duck down below the parapet, knowing we shouldn't be up there at a time like this.

This was exciting stuff. Nobody liked "the man" the cops. Tonight, "the man" was getting his ass kicked. We wanted to watch.

It was getting worse all the time, or better. Around the clock TV and radio reportage kept our rooftop observation post well informed. It was clear the fires were spreading, especially on the east side. What before had seemed like a localized plume of smoke, now seemed to stretch for ten miles to the north. On the northwest side, the fires were spreading south, a wall of smoke 15 miles long could be seen from our hippie "command center."

Gunfire was sporadic; we'd hear single shots from small arms fired by snipers, followed by outbursts of automatic fire that lasted perhaps five minutes, followed by maybe thirty minutes of calm, if you can call standing in the center of hurricane-fed inferno, with sirens wailing and the streets full of smoke, "calm." Then we'd hear several single rounds from small arms again, followed by bursts and the rat-a-tat-tat of the cops carbines and heavier weapons, then calm again. We came to know the difference between the automatic and semi-automatic fire of the police forces and the single shot "crack" of the snipers.

On the 11 o'clock news Michigan's Governor, George Romney, begged for calm and announced he was mobilizing the National Guard with the first troops arriving the next afternoon. TV had footage of Black citizens, unaware of the curfew, being pulled from their cars. Middle-aged, middle-class blacks were shown being thrown to the ground, kicked and cuffed, generally roughed up and carted off to jail. Rumor had it that Tiger Stadium and the bathhouses on Belle Isle were being used as temporary holding facilities since the police lockups were all full. We stayed on the roof all night, taking speed to keep us on our toes. The electronic media was reporting that the police had given up and withdrawn from large areas on the northwest side and the east side. "No Man's Land," they called it. "Liberated Territory," I called it.

* * *

Sunday, the second full day of rioting, broke hot and humid. By noon the temperature was in the 80s. The stench of burning plastic and tarpaper hung heavily over the neighborhood. The National Guard was yet to be seen. Sinclair and I twisted up some joints and went out driving around in the Opel. The streets were all but empty, with the cops busy at the scenes of looting and burning. We tore up Woodward, blowing through stop signs, disregarding red lights. In Highland Park we drove for miles in the wrong direction on the empty one-way streets. Oh what a feeling! To be in a place where absolutely no law was valid, where government had no control or meaning. This, I realized, was a once-in-a-lifetime experience.

Granted, it was brief and shallow, and came at a terrible cost in life and property, but it was real, and I felt blessed to be a part of it.

At Grand Boulevard we stopped at a corner while another group of drivers cleared a barricade from the street. A car carrying four black cats, all wearing black "doo rags" on their heads pulled up next to us. It was common knowledge on the street that Black Liberation Fighters wore "doo rags" in the "color of the day" to identify themselves and avoid getting shot by other snipers. I was mildly distressed as all four scowled at us. Then the driver started hollering, "Hey! That's Sinclair, 'the king of the hippies!'" referring to the handle with which the local media had tagged Sinclair. The other cats all chimed in, "Cool man, 'king of the hippies!'" Sinclair laughed, gave the "V" for victory sign and held a torpedo joint out the window. The cat in the passenger's seat leaned out, took the joint and said, "Right-on brother--keep your head down." The barricade was removed and we sped off and returned to Trans-Love.

I was upstairs, in our living quarters along with Sinclair, his wife and baby, The Prez, and eight or so other commune members and friends. From the sill of an open window I was sitting watching troop carriers, military jeeps and heavy hardware drive up and down the John Lodge. Suddenly, on the service drive on the northbound side of the Lodge, I noticed six or more "black and whites" moving at a high rate of speed. They squealed around the corner onto Warren and sped across the bridge over the expressway toward our place. At the corner they whipped onto our service drive and screeched to a halt right below me. The first cop out of the car pointed his shotgun at me and hollered, "Stay where you are!" I jumped back and ran down the hall toward the door. Already I could hear the heavy thud of boots on the stairs. I just got the security chain latched when the door opened to the length of the chain. Instantly a rifle barrel came through the crack and simultaneously a butt of a rifle smashed the door at chain level sending splinters and screws flying.

What seemed like twenty or more cops came rushing in, pointing guns at people and knocking some to the floor. I was jacked against the wall with a shotgun jammed under my chin so I was standing on my tiptoes. By now other commune members came out of their cubicles to see what the commotion was about. They were slammed to the floor or held against the wall at gunpoint. Suddenly Sinclair was there holding his infant daughter. "What the fuck are you motherfuckers doing in my house?" he raged. "Shut the fuck up!" the commanding officer snorted. "Get the fuck out of my house!" Sinclair bellowed, his face red, eyes bulging.

I was much taller than God had intended, stretched as I was with the shotgun under my chin. It was pressed so hard there that my tongue was pushed against the roof of my mouth, causing me to salivate and drool copious amounts of spittle out of each side of my mouth.

Sinclair screamed again, "Get the fuck out of my house." I remember wishing he would calm down; *he is going to get us all killed I thought.* "We had a report of a sniper on the roof," the commanding officer said. "There are no snipers on our roof--get out! Get Out!"

Other cops were snooping around, looking in closets and cubicles, tearing tapestries and posters off the walls, flipping over mattresses and generally behaving in a hoggish manner.

Sinclair wouldn't let up. "Get the fuck out of my house!" Then, in a burst of rage he shouted, "Go ahead and shoot me, shoot me! I don't want to live in a place where the cops can bust your door down anytime they want. Shoot me! Here, shoot my daughter, shoot Leni, shoot all of us. You're the ones who will have to answer for it." On and on he raged.

Jesus Christ! I thought, *I wish he'd shut up; he's going to get us all blown away.* Drool was beginning to puddle at my feet. Then, just as suddenly as they came, they left.

A short time later we got a call informing us that Wayne "MC5" Kramer had been arrested. His house on Warren had been raided and he was carried away in chains. It seems he had aroused suspicion by setting up a spotting scope in the big bay window of the second floor master bedroom to keep tabs on the action.

I recall going with Sinclair to a lawyer's office downtown. The massive gothic police headquarters at 1300 Beaubean was surrounded by troops in heavy armored vehicles with 30 and 50-caliber machine guns mounted on tripods. We somehow got Kramer released and settled in for the night's action.

*   *   *

Between June and August of 1967 there were riots in more than 125 cities across America. Parts of Newark, Chicago, New York, Milwaukee, Cambridge, Minneapolis and Detroit had gone up in flames. There were 380,000 troops in Vietnam and though they told us America was winning, the Pentagon reported that 5,008 Americans had died in the war in 1966. Muhammad Ali was arrested for refusing induction into the Army. The Civil Rights Movement, the Anti-War Movement and Hippie culture were sweeping the country like wild fire. With troops in Vietnam and Detroit, could the Empire survive?

*   *   *

Sunday night we stayed at the commune with all the lights out so we wouldn't be seen, but we kept the windows open to hear the battle and watch the light show of tracers and flares. To the east the entire horizon was shrouded in smoke; occasionally, bright flashes would illuminate the underside of the smoke, like fireworks on a cloudy night. To the west, the scene was the same, only closer. The most vivid memory I have of that Sunday night is of the 50-calibers, as they "thumped," "thumped," "thumped" out rounds, every fourth one a "tracer" that looked six feet long as they shot like falling stars across the eerie night illuminating the smoke clouds and occasionally tumbling, end over end, as if in slow motion.

Local news reported that municipal and state police forces, and now the National Guard, were unable to maintain order or quell the disturbance and had been driven from a 144 square block area of the east side with a similar retreat on the west side. President Johnson appeared on TV to plead for calm and the "rule of law" and announced that he was calling out the 101st Airborne, which would arrive the next day, Monday. Mayor Cavanaugh, having toured the riot torn area said "the festival atmosphere" surprised him.

Monday was hot again. I walked down the service drive a mile or so to Grand River Ave. Whole blocks of businesses were smoldering ruins. Abandoned houses and many occupied dwellings were put to the torch, or caught on fire as the conflagration spread. Police and National Guard were stationed every hundred feet or so along both sides of Grand River. Fire crews, guarded by troops crouched behind fire engines, still battled flames up and down the Avenue as far as the eye could see.

On returning to Trans-Love, I found Sinclair and we walked the four blocks over to Trumbell and Forest. We got there just as a crowd had smashed the large windows of the A & P. I saw little black girls in plastic sandals, shorts and tank tops helping grandmas who had hitched up their print dresses, revealing stockings that only went to the knee, and clamored through the broken windows--no one used the doors. Sinclair and I joined the crowd inside. People of all ages and several races were grabbing everything in sight: canned goods, meat, bread, floor wax, packages of rubber bands and tooth paste--it didn't matter; they took it all. These people who had been ripped-off, robbed, scammed, gouged and cheated by A&P were taking back what was theirs. Like a thousand Robin Hoods, they stole from the absentee landlords who had been stealing from them for a lifetime. Sinclair found a 25-pound bag of dog food for "Pharaoh," the commune terrier, and split for home.

Across the street was a Ben Franklin "five and dime." The eight-by-eight foot windows had been smashed and neighborhood residents were flooding the store. I went inside and looked around for something to take. I noticed a "fish eye" mirror in the far corner, used to monitor shoplifters. It was attached high on the wall, next to the ceiling. I climbed up the shelves and ripped it right off the wall, bracket and all.

The Ben Franklin was in an old, single-story, brown-brick building, the kind I remembered from childhood. Inside, in the back of the store, was a balcony, surrounded by a railing with balusters. Three or four desks, presumably those of the bookkeepers and manager occupied the space. A group of cats were up there working on a large, antique safe. Pretty soon they shouted out "Clear the building, we're torchin' it!" People scattered. Thick black smoke filled the store as orange tongues of flame began licking the wall and moving across the ceiling. I took my mirror and cruised home holding it above my head like the championship silver tray at Wimbledon.

For the record, though I won't bore the reader by repeating the familiar details, the commune was raided again that Monday, this time by the National Guard. I have a fuzzy recollection of that raid: I recall looking out the window and seeing a jeep with a 50-caliber mounted in the back that was pointing up at me, and two or three other parked military vehicles on the street below. The sound of many boots stomping up the stairs I will always remember. The door was smashed from the raid the day before and I remember the troops filing right in. "Of course there is no sniper on the roof. We are pacifist hippies," The Prez told them. I don't remember them leaving, but no one got killed or arrested, so good riddance.

Later that day, while playing "frisbee" on the service drive, we noticed fire trucks, police cars, and military vehicles two blocks down on Forest. A couple of us walked down to see what was going on. The 101st Airborne had arrived; rumor had it that they were just back from Vietnam. At the corner of the service drive and Forest sat an old house with a green sign declaring it as a State historic site and explaining that it had been the birthplace of Charles Lindbergh. The sign was splattered with vandal's paint. In white paint, in foot high letters across the front porch someone had scrawled, "LINDBERGH WAS A FASCIST!" Now that historic house was in flames. A fire crew pumped water on the blaze while the 101st watched their backs, M-16s and jeeps with mounted guns at the ready. Since the battle in Detroit had begun, fire crews had been taking rounds from snipers as they tried to bring the blazes under control.

After ten minutes or so, my friends left. I just sat on the curb, watching the action.

A soldier, not as old as I was, walked over and stood above me. "Didn't I see you at another fire today?" He asked in a Georgia drawl. "Nope", I answered, "this is the first fire I've been to since this all started."

"No . . . I think I saw you at another fire," he said, standing with legs spread above me. "Nah," I said, "I just live down there," pointing. Suddenly he ratcheted a round into the chamber of his M-16. "I saw you at another fire today!" he hollered. *Jesus Christ no!* I thought. Instinct drove me to get up and start running straight down the sidewalk toward home. I could feel him aiming at the middle of my back. I wondered if I'd feel the bullet. Then I thought, *I hope I don't die in these pants.* They were full of holes from battery acid I'd spilled while changing the battery in Sinclair's Opel. The soldier never shot; I made it home.

Sinclair, Leni, Grimshaw, Emil, The Prez and others had been talking about leaving the city until this riot blew over. We needed someplace to go. We couldn't go to Cleveland where there were also riots or threats of them. Chicago was the same. In fact, any large urban area was under threat and most of our friends lived in big cities. I suggested we head north to Traverse City and wait out the riots in the sand and sun of Northern Michigan, which we did.

The last image I had of the riots was of three huge Army tanks charging north up the southbound side of the John Lodge at full throttle. Their huge bulk was rocking to and fro as they sped along at nearly 50 mph. Seeing vehicles traveling the wrong way on the expressway was shock enough, but three tanks, each taking up a lane and a half of the highway was beyond anything I could have imagined.

Chapter Six

THE GREAT SLEEPING BEAR...FALL, 1967

We retreated to the Great Sleeping Bear...

...Among the Ottawa whose villages were located on the many rivers that empty into Lake Michigan (Gitchigami), the story is told of the Great Sleeping Bear...

...She lived with her two cubs on the western shore of Gichigami, in the place we now call "Wisconsin." One summer a great fire raged across her homeland, killing many and forcing others to flee their lodges. She and her two cubs were forced right to the very edge of Gitchigami as the fire pressed in. With their hair singed and burning she took the cubs into Gitchigami, placed them on her back, and began swimming to the other side of the great lake.

Halfway there she tired. The cubs had to climb down and swim for themselves. But they were too little and couldn't keep up. The great bear encouraged her children and coaxed them along, but it was no use. She promised the little ones she would wait for them on the shore.

The mother bear reached the shore and lay down to wait for her cubs. Because of her strenuous ordeal she soon fell hard asleep. But the cubs never came. She continued to sleep and the wind blew sand that covered the great bear. And still she waited -- still the wind blew sand.

The cubs sank to the bottom of Gitchigami and two beautiful islands formed. And the wind blew and blew and covered the great sleeping bear, forming a great dune. And the wind continues to blow sand, covering the great bear as she waits for her children. And still she waits and still the sand blows...

Today the two islands are named North and South Manitou (Spirit) Islands and the dunes of the Great Sleeping Bear National Lakeshore stretch some 40 miles along the little finger of the Michigan mitten.

* * *

We camped for a few days then stayed with friends of mine in TC and the surrounding area. To my amazement, and relief, the place I hated, believed dull, and beyond boring, and couldn't wait to get away from, The Prez and Sinclair and my new friends loved and found beautiful. Generally, I was embarrassed of my TC friends, whom I believed to be shallow, country bumpkins. I was astonished and then relieved when others found them interesting. We stayed for three or four days reading the papers every morning to monitor the situation in Detroit and other hot spots around the country.

It was reported that The Detroit Riot left 43 dead (36 black), over 2,000 arrested, 1,700 stores looted by whites as well as blacks, and 5,000 homeless from 1,442 fires.

We returned to Detroit in early August, after the 101st Airborne, the Michigan National Guard, and police forces of the state and surrounding communities had been removed. Only the ever-present Detroit Police remained.

Commissions were formed, studies were done and reports were given, but none of this changed much at the community level. Ultimately, the Detroit Police Department was opened up to hire black and other minorities. But history has shown they can be as criminal, ignorant and arrogant as any white officer.

Soon after our return to Detroit, we were contacted by a black neighborhood community service organization that was connected to the Republic of New Africa. They wanted to use our storefront as a distribution point for free groceries and clothing for homeless victims of the riots. We agreed, of course. I remember driving around Detroit to several makeshift community centers to pick up clothing, canned goods, paper products, and toilet items to be returned to our storefront for distribution.

The destruction of the city was stunning. Block after block of businesses and homes were left in smoldering ruins. The giant chain stores and little mom and pop stores had been put to the torch or caught in the spreading conflagration. Occasionally a home or business would be left standing, untouched amid the rubble, like a lonesome tooth in a vacant mouth.

While they were going on, I saw the riots as a big party--a people's festival and chance to show our ass to the man to shatter the nerves and dreams of the complacent and to piss in the face of long-absent landlords. However, the aftermath was sobering. Seeing citizens--all poor, mostly black--in shock, some wailing by a smoldering pile of bricks, others picking through the rubble for anything of value, a memory perhaps--this gave me pause. Seeing people who had lost their homes and every earthly belonging, some of whom had barely escaped with their lives, made it all real and compelled me to look at the situation through others' eyes.

* * *

I was beginning to live within a world of new beliefs. I believed that American capitalism and imperialism were an evil force in the world--its economic system bloodthirsty, its political system corrupt and poisoned to the core, and its culture, based on greed, selfish individualism and image without substance, to be mind-numbing and deadly--beliefs I still hold today.

At that time I subscribed to the philosophy of "Tune In...Turn On...Drop Out." The concept was easy to grasp: first, "Tune In" to what's going down, where the power lies, who's pulling the strings, what the real deal is; next, "Turn On" using mind-expanding drugs, meditation, spiritual enlightenment, food, music, anything that gets the job done; finally, "Drop Out," get as far away from the dominant culture as possible, grow your own food, make your own music, create your own economy, avoid politics at all costs. (Nevertheless, our commune was more political than most.) Given the conditions of America today, this still sounds reasonable to me.

*   *   *

In the fall of '67 we moved Trans-Love Energies about five blocks to the east, across the Lodge expressway and closer to Wayne State, leaving behind the second floor dentist's office and Workshop storefronts.

We found a white stucco, single story, corner building at Second and Forest that had once been a medical clinic. The 1950's style solid glass front door, with "Pull" stamped on a stylized aluminum handle, opened into a modest sized waiting room. Another door led to a hall, which in turn accessed four small examination rooms. We converted a large room in the basement into the music room, stapling egg cartons to the walls and ceiling to deaden the sound. There were several other small rooms used as bedrooms.

We turned the former waiting room into a small bookstore/newsstand/head shop. Sinclair, Leni and Sunny, their daughter, took a room at the end of the first-floor hall; the Prez and I took one next to them and Sinclair's brother, DS, and his wife, took one across the hall. Grimshaw, and his girlfriend, Judy, took another. Red Headed Audrey took one of the basement rooms, and there were the usual comings and goings of others who stayed awhile, didn't fit-in, or didn't like commune living, and moved on.

DS, with his new bride, had moved to Detroit earlier that summer before the riots, soon after his graduation from

Dartmouth. He had taken a third floor apartment in the old neighborhood, near the dentist's office and fit right in, taking part in all Trans-Love activities. When we moved to Second and Forest he moved in with us. DS is a solid cat, like a Dartmouth rugby player, though he never played. His receding hairline and prematurely graying hair complemented his thoughtful and unassuming demeanor.

We supported ourselves by producing shows at The Grande, the psychedelic ballroom on Joy Road and Grand River. In addition to the income from the small selection of books and newspapers in our waiting room bookstore, we also sold tee shirts and some leather goods. Some of Leni's photos we printed as posters. I clearly remember posters of John Coltrane, Archie Schepp, Sun Ra and Rob Tyner. Subscriptions to *The Sun* and occasional checks for Artists Workshop Press books would arrive in the mail and be added to the kitty. Sinclair would get speaking gigs at high schools or colleges to which I'd tag along at every opportunity. Now and then I picked up some change by doing custom leatherwork.

By this time the MC5 were on fire. The whole band moved to Canfield Avenue, in our new neighborhood, at the same time we did, with Sinclair as their new manager and myself as an occasional part of the road crew. "The 5," as we often called them, opened for Jimi Hendrix in Ford Auditorium and blew the crowd away! We opened for The Who in Toronto and blew the roof off the joint. We opened for Cream at the Grande and brought the place down! We opened for The Grateful Dead in Cobo Hall and brought the band back to our place for joints.

Actually, only Jerry Garcia and a couple of his roadies returned to Trans-Love with us. "The 5" showed up and we stayed up all night twistin' joints: "fire up another one." Garcia and Sinclair were cut from the same cloth. They had both figured out what they wanted to do with their lives early on, which was to smoke dope and listen to music. Both created lives dedicated to that goal: "fire up another one."

They just vibrated that night, Garcia and Sinclair. Garcia was talking about how they were trying to build a community around the music. As "The Dead" got more successful they hoped to fund more community businesses and projects, like creating their own trucking company and sound company and lighting company. Garcia wanted to see hip businesses that could employ hip people so they could put their money into hip projects.

Sinclair could hardly contain himself. "Exactly!", he interrupted, "and we can do that in every aspect of life. We can create our own newspapers, our own bakeries, our own clothing companies! Christ our own universities!"

Garcia was getting hyper now. We all were. We could see it--the alternative, bigger than we ever imagined, shining in the future.

Garcia went on about how some of the Bay Area bands were working together to sponsor this or that project and how they had helped to push Bill Graham (owner of the Filmore and music power-broker) to more progressive positions.

Sinclair, still vibrating like a 220-pound tuning fork, always saw the big picture and couldn't wait to get the floor back in this conversation. "Right!", he said, "we've got to create a complete alternative. It does no good to shake our fist at the honkies and call them names. We've got to show we have something better. We don't even want the parents anyway, we want their kids."

This was pretty heady stuff for me. Here I was smokin' joints with one of my all-time musical heroes and certainly a "Big Star" by any standard, talking about taking over the world. I noticed Garcia was missing the last two fingers on his right hand, up to the second knuckle, and knew he was a working class hero--rich kids generally aren't missing digits, because they don't do the kind of work that costs body parts.

Several weeks later, Janis Joplin with Big Brother And The Holding Company played Detroit, and I made arrangements to interview James Gurley of The Holding Company for our newspaper, *The Sun*. Gurley is a former Detroit boy who spent a lot of time in our part of the city before moving to San Francisco. He was crashing with some of his old friends on Prentiss Street, right in our neighborhood.

The interview was OK; we ran it. But more importantly, I wanted to learn how to interact and be involved with people who had something to say, who had a plan and were on the move. I wanted to find out how people like me, with an oppositional point of view, became significant. If Sinclair and Grimshaw could do it, if Garcia and Gurley could do it, maybe I could too. I wanted to be good at something, anything, but very little interested me. I thought becoming a good interviewer of people I admired would be a way to learn and establish myself; plus, I'd get to hobnob with important people. I did several more interviews over the years, but as with most things, I didn't have the discipline to stick with it and apply serious attention or effort. This was the same thing that had been said about me in grade and high school: I was good in sports but lacked the discipline to reach my full potential. I was smarter than my grades showed, I just didn't apply myself. Here again, I repeated my own history.

* * *

We had settled in at Second and Forest, where everything was running smoothly, and back to normal. Even the firebombs had moved with us. Now we were convinced the right-wingers were after us specifically. As long as we lived above *The Fifth Estate* and Mobe offices there was a question as to whether or not the previous attacks on our home were directed at us or at the politics of our co-tenants.

But now we were a stand-alone unit, there was no ambiguity. The new attacks were directed against us communally, not for our politics, since we professed none, other than opposition to the war and rejection of the dominant culture. These attacks were against our lifestyle, our culture.

They always came at night. The first time, unbeknownst to us, they threw Molotov cocktails onto our flat roof. A passerby must have called it in, suddenly the fire department was at the door, ordering us out and yelling that the roof was on fire. There wasn't much to it, the gravel roof kept the gasoline from igniting the asphalt. The fire department had ladders up and were putting out the hot spots by the time I got up there to see it.

The next time the bombers broke a window in our basement to chuck in a Molotov. This could have been more serious since we kept a five hundred gallon vat of melted wax in the basement as part of our candle making operation--a harebrained idea Sinclair came up with to supply fancy, hand dipped and custom made candles to the many head shops that were springing up across the state.

Through our own quick action the fire was extinguished; we didn't even call the fire department, since they had a reputation of ransacking and trashing personal belongings when called to a fire at a hippy location.

Meanwhile, the Detroit Police kept us on our toes. Our house sat about twenty-five feet off the street with a ribbon of grass along the curb, a four-foot-wide sidewalk and about twenty feet of hard-packed dirt where a lawn once grew. On a regular basis, in the wee hours of the morning, a cop car would pull up over the curb, drive across the sidewalk and park right on the "lawn." They would switch their radio to their outside speaker and turn it up loud. Suddenly, out of a deep sleep, everyone in the house and half the neighborhood would hear the screeching radio traffic of the Detroit Police Department. A person would think they were surrounded by the entire 12th Precinct.

Once, I was reading in the head shop at five in the morning, having gotten into some exceptionally potent speed. I saw a white TMU pull over the curb and up onto the dirt of the lawn and shine its spotlight in all the windows. This was also a common occurrence. At some point I had gotten used to it and wouldn't bother to get up to see what was going on. But on this particular night I was up and dressed and I saw them do it. I ran outside to confront them. "Why the hell are you shining lights in our windows at all hours?" I demanded. "We got a call of a break-in," the cop quipped as he squealed his tires and sped away.

* * *

In late winter of '68, Grimshaw and Judy and The Prez and I drove up to TC for some rest and relaxation. We stayed with friends who had a winterized cottage on the bay. We smoked joints, listened to records and played Monopoly. It was a pleasant interlude. When we returned to Detroit we got back into our routines. Grimshaw doing his art work, Judy cooking brown rice and seaweed, The Prez making arts and crafts to be sold in the head shop. I helped lay out our newspaper, run the mimeograph machine, or sell our paper up on campus. We kept busy.

One night, about three in the morning, I was jarred awake by shouting and a big commotion in the head shop, just down the hall. I put my pants on, no shoes or shirt, and rushed out. Just as I got there, I saw The Prez, Red Haired Audrey and Levine, another commune member, shoving two guys in Army uniforms out the front door, into our vestibule. By the time I got there, the soldiers were in the vestibule and the door was closed and locked. These boys--one black and one white--were drunk. Each held half-full mugs of beer and were raving about getting some of that "Free Love" they had been hearing so much about.

We hollered at them through the door to go home and sleep it off. Suddenly--blast! One of them threw his beer mug through the inner glass door, shattering it. "Fuck it," I said, "I'm going for it," and grabbed a straight-backed chair, with chrome legs and back supports with a vinyl covered seat and back--the kind so many of our parents had during the '50's; I intended to kick some ass.

Damn! Without shoes I cut my feet going through the broken glass. The Prez and Audrey were screaming at me to get back in the house. Levine went to wake the others up.

I cracked the white guy a good one with the chair and turned to deal with the black cat. Shit! He pulled a straight razor from his pocket. I threw the chair at him and dashed for the house. The outside door had locked automatically behind me. He slashed with the razor and caught me on my back shoulder, laying open a five-inch gash, but not very deep. I stepped on the broken glass again and stumbled, giving him a chance to slice me on the shoulder again. Already I could feel the warm blood running down my arm on that cold March morning.

I panicked and turned and ran half-naked down the street. Two blocks away was a 24-hour Shell station; I headed for it. In those days there were attendants who pumped gas for customers. The attendant was filling a car as I ran across the pavement screaming, "Call the police! Call the police!"

I'm aware of the apparent contradiction between calling for the cops when my life is threatened and seeing the cops as the enemy when it wasn't. On the other hand, cops are hired to "protect and serve," and I needed some protection.

I ran inside the station as the pump-jockey pumped, slackjawed at the nozzle. I was hoping to find a wrench or tire iron, anything I could use to crush the black cat's skull.

Clean! The two work bays were absolutely clean. The floor was swept; everything was put away and locked up. Not even a used tire leaned against the wall. Clean. The counters and workbenches were bare, empty. In the far corner I found a valve cover for what looked like a '62 Chevy, straight six, about the size of two metal bread pans fixed end to end. It was greasy but it had the right heft, if I could hold onto it.

I ran outside to face my attackers, not wanting to get caught in a closed space, thinking, *if they're going to kill me at least they'll have to do it in public*. It was about 30 degrees out. The attendant was still at his post, pumping, mouth agape, as the two cats crossed the street onto the well-lit drive of the Shell station.

We faced off, circling. I went for the black cat since he was the biggest threat, trying to hit him in the head or on the arm that held the razor. I missed; the valve cover slipped from my hands and went clattering across the drive.

The white guy rushed me and knocked me down, sat on my chest and gave me a pretty good pounding. I flailed back, but to no effect. These drunken louts were kicking my ass. The black cat came with the razor. Slice. Slice. He grabbed my legs at the knees and held them up to cut the backs of my thighs just below my ass--trying to cut my balls off I suppose. I guess he felt that if he couldn't get any free love, I shouldn't either. Slice. Slice.

I kicked him away but the other guy was still on my chest, pounding my face. I was twisting around on my bare back, trying to kick the cat to keep him at bay. The black cat struck again, grabbing my legs and leveraging me onto my shoulders, he cut twice at my balls with the razor. Slice. Slice. Then somehow he got my legs pinned to the pavement, straddling them. Slice. Slice. He cut the tops of my thighs. Slice. Slice, he did it again. Luckily the white guy's butt was sitting over my hips as he continued to hit me otherwise the razor man would have had direct access to my nuts and I would be singing a different tune today.

It wasn't over yet. The black cat came for my throat and got just a little nick. I grabbed the four-inch blade of the razor with my right hand and tried to break it or wrest it from his grip. I twisted it as I tried to snap it like you would a pencil, one-handed. The blade cut deep into my hand between my thumb and forefinger.

The white guy wasn't slugging me anymore, but was wrestling with my arms, trying to pin them. I wouldn't let go of the razor; I knew if I did, they would kill me.

I'm writing this with an absolutely straight face and honest heart. What happened next is so fantastic as to challenge belief. Yet it is true; were it not, I would be long dead.

We wrestled some more, me holding onto the razor for dear life, the blade going deeper into my palm. Just then, a white, late model, rag-top Mustang pulled into the drive, stopping right beside my head, I remember checking out the hub caps, real close. A big black dude got out, dressed in a three-piece, peach-colored, pinstriped suit and a matching broad-brimmed hat. He wasn't on the job, he was steppin' out.

He pulled out a nickel-plated snub-nosed revolver and said, "Let the kid up." The shiny pistol brought some sense to those drunken maniacs. They got up off me and ran away as my prince on a white horse stood over me with his Excalibur.

"You better get out of here, they may come back", he advised, as he got back in the 'stang and peeled out. Hi Ho Silver Away! I swear to God.

The pump-jockey, having finished his duties with his customer, called the cops who transported me to Detroit General, not waiting for an ambulance.

The cuts, two inches wide and five inches long reminded me of jumbo shrimp after they've been "butterflied" and the mud vein removed. I received nearly 100 stitches but should have received 200. Detroit General is not known for its tidy work. They stitched me every three-quarters of an inch or so; puckers of raw flesh squeezed out between the knots. My hand healed completely. The cuts on my feet and scrapes on my back were the most painful.

Meanwhile, Sinclair was driving around looking for me. DS and Levine walked until dawn searching the streets and alleys of the neighborhood for me. The Prez and Audrey looked for me too, until they got taken in by the police as teenage runaways. When the hospital had finished with me, I called the commune and Levine came and got me in the van.

*   *   *

Two weeks later, Dr. Martin Luther King was killed. I wasn't a follower of Dr. King, not being a pacifist, though I saw his cause as my cause. I leaned more toward Malcolm X, Amiri Baraka (LeRoi Jones) and other Black Nationalist organizations, as well as a new group out of California, The Black Panther Party for Self-Defense.

I felt the only hope for justice for black and poor folks was to take direct action to protect themselves against the racist white police forces of this country.

When Dr. King was killed, the Detroit Police, still reeling from the political firestorm that was unleashed after the '67 riots, clamped down on the city like the Hitler Youth at summer kampen. To my knowledge, not one window was broken, not one fire was set, and not one store was looted. Yet the cops were everywhere; their control was absolute. This was too much. When the police can, at will, shut down an entire city, keep citizens in their homes and stop the life of the city, it amounted to fascism. Sinclair began talking of moving again.

Never financially stable, Trans-Love had fallen on very lean times. With the curfew on for nearly a week, we had no income from the Grande or any of our other hustles. This, in addition to my near-death experience, prompted The Prez and I to leave Detroit.

An acquaintance gave me a 1938 Dodge, set up for desert travel. It had extra wide tires, and 50-gallon water tanks mounted on each running board. A framework of galvanized pipe with exterior grade plywood on top served as a roof over the pickup bed. Canvas sides that could be rolled up or down made the pickup a handy camper. On each door, in block letters, was printed, "Southwestern Archaeological Expedition." My acquaintance was in the import business down along the border with Mexico: he brought in shipments of weed. This was his old business truck.

I put what little money we had into getting the rig in

decent running condition; the next part of the plan called for The Prez and I to scrounge enough money to leave.

Just when we needed him, here came Moses to lead us out of Detroit and into the desert. Moses had done just what his parents had wanted--settled down, got a job, got new teeth, got married, got car payments and house payments, cut his hair, shaved his beard, and went to church every Sunday. Now here he was two years later, running from his wife and all his responsibilities. He had some money, so the three of us left Detroit in early May.

We drove west to Chicago, then south to St. Louis, where we found "the old town" section of the city and met some hippies who sold us a bag of smoke. Then we were off to Texas to visit The Prez's grandma who lived in Vernon, just across the Red River, along the Oklahoma border.

At that time, though we didn't know it, Wilbarger County, Texas, was "dry," no alcohol was sold legally or could even be possessed. One day, Moses and I left The Prez with her grandmother and took the Dodge into the OK state and decided to cop a couple six-packs of Coors, which was not yet available east of the Mississippi. By that time, I had softened my position on alcohol, feeling that I could pick and choose which part of the old culture I wanted to reject or destroy. But I didn't drink like I had several years previously. I didn't get drunk, just copped a glow.

Driving north out of Vernon, just across the river, in Oklahoma, sat two roadside honky-tonks. The one on the west side of the two-lane blacktop was a white bar, a steel- clad, pastel green pole barn structure, the likes of which seemed to be taking over the American landscape. The other one was a black honky-tonk, a dilapidated wood building in desperate need of a coat of paint.

We went to the black establishment, of course, where we sucked down some Lone Star longnecks, played pool and made friends easily with the black clientele. After purchasing two six packs of Coors to go, we headed back to Texas.

This was flat land--for miles and miles, flat. Just over the border, back into Texas, a county sheriff pulled up behind us with his flashing lights on. But pulling over and turning off the engine on this flat road would mean we'd have a hard time getting the Dodge started again. It had a broken starter that went out somewhere in Missouri. It would start easily enough if we parked it on a slight grade and popped the clutch as we got a little roll. We also had a small leak in the radiator that caused the rig to overheat if we weren't moving. Stopping meant we had to turn off the engine or it would overheat.

Meanwhile, the sheriff was right behind us with his lights on. We were only going about 40 miles an hour. A quarter mile ahead I could see a slight rise in the road where a culvert from a drainage ditch passed under it. I told Moses I would try to reach it. Through the back window, he waved at the sheriff, mouthing silently that we were trying to make it to the rise in the road while pointing and gesticulating.

The sheriff couldn't read Moses' lips or sign language. He turned on his siren--we only had 300 yards to go--Moses was making faces, pointing and waving his arms--the sheriff pulled up beside us, lights and siren whirring. I pointed and mouthed, "Just ahead, just ahead."

Unlike Moses, I, on the other hand, could read the sheriff's lips perfectly. He was saying, with a very pissed off look on his face, "PULL OVER NOW!" There was no mistake about it. I only had another 50 yards to go, so I eased over to the gravel shoulder and kept going. Finally I stopped on the down slope of the rise.

The sheriff pulled up behind us and jumped out with his big 12-gauge shotgun as he pumped one into the chamber and ordered us out of the truck while pointing it at my head from ten feet away. He had us spread our legs and place our hands on the back tailgate as he commented about our "sissy sandals." "You boys should get some manly footwear," he said in a lazy Texas drawl.

He kept the shotgun trained on us as he looked in the cab. Finding the Coors, he placed it on the hood of his car and began interrogating us. He wanted our ID and to know where we were coming from and where we were going and where were we staying, the usual questions.

When I told him we were staying with Mrs. Johnson, the Prez's grandmother, he went to his car and got on the radio, nestling the shotgun on the open door of his cruiser while it was pointed at our backs, not twenty feet away.

After ten minutes, he exited the cruiser and informed us that Miss Johnson was a beloved woman in their little town. Since she vouched for us, he was going to let us go. With that he grabbed a six-pack off the hood and threw it in the air. Then, with the fluid movements of a man who had done this sort of thing before, he lifted the shotgun and blew the Coors out of the sky. In the time it took to read this, he grabbed the second six-pack and flung it into the air. Boom! He shot that one too. Then he let us go.

The next day, the three of us left grandma's and headed west into the hill country, then north to Taos, New Mexico. It was well known around the country that Taos was a hippie enclave and a stronghold in the land of the Pueblo Indians.

I don't recall how, but we found a group of twenty or so hippies living in a ranchero a few miles out of town. We moved in. At 9,000 feet, clouds formed right in the living room. One day in the plaza, I met Benjamin, a fifty-year-old Pueblo Indian drunk on his ass. I was sitting on a bench in the plaza; he was sitting beside me, a stranger at the time. Suddenly he leaned over and grabbed my arm. "I have 20 horses," he slurred as he bobbed and weaved beside me. "That's good," I said, trying to ignore him. "You don't believe me!" he said, sounding agitated. "Yes, yes, I believe you," I said, trying to reassure him. Grabbing my arm again he slurred, "I have 100 blankets." "That's wonderful," I replied while sliding away from him on the bench. "You don't believe me!" He charged. "Yes, I believe you," I said. He scooted over next to me. "I have 10 pair of boots!" he blathered. He looked near to passing out, his eyes would close and he'd tip forward, only to catch himself and look around bleary-eyed. "10 pairs of boots, that's great," I said. "You don't believe me!" he said while belching. "I do believe you, I'm happy for you." "I have 20 horses!" he started again.

After ten minutes of this I leaned over to him and said, "Yes. But do you have any peyote?" "I have plenty peyote," he answered. "I don't believe you," I said. He got indignant at that. "I have big jars full," he said, holding up his hands to show the size. "I don't believe you have any peyote," I answered. He grabbed my arm, "Come with me, I'll show you," he promised.

As we walked for two or three blocks through the adobe slums of Taos, Benjamin fell down several times. We reached a small adobe house, that had just two rooms and an outhouse in back. Sitting on the mantel were four institutional-sized mayonnaise jars full of peyote buds, commonly called "buttons." "Do you want to sell any?" I asked.

Peyote is a cactus-like plant that grows in the desert and high valleys of the southwest. They grow close to the ground and produce beautiful flowers out of the rather flat bud. Eating the bud (after removing the dandelion-like fluff from within) produces hallucinations of a spiritual nature and has been used for this purpose by the indigenous people of the area since the Creator first placed them there.

Benjamin sold me two hundred buttons for twenty bucks--ten cents apiece. I hurried back to the ranchero and found Moses and The Prez and we started gobbling peyote. While we were lying around in the back yard, Moses announced he wanted to go back home to his wife in Jersey. He was picking up pieces of twigs and small branches, leaves and dried grass, and leaning them one against the other, creating small, delicately balanced structures as he laid on his side in the May sun eating and gagging on peyote.

The Prez and I told him he should do whatever felt right. Moses continued to build his tiny structures. The Prez and I took a gallon of water and walked out back and up the tall mesa, cleaning and eating peyote as we went. We made love on the mesa top and watched an eagle soar up and down the valley. I saw visions of a turnip-shaped spirit as is customary when eating peyote, while vomiting now and again.

We returned to the ranchero just before dark and to our astonishment saw that Moses had created a vast, intricate structure that covered the whole back yard, which was about the size of a tennis court. Sticks and twigs were balanced and leaning one against the other, intertwined with feathers, gum wrappers, nails, cellophane, as well as other debris. It was vast. It was amazing. Moses was grinning from ear to ear, his face radiant and speech nearly incoherent, still balancing twigs and building his structure to the east, toward the mesa.

Several days later I saw Benjamin in the plaza hunched over and barely able to walk. When he did he limped and hobbled along. His face was puffy and bruised, his nose was completely relocated to under his left eye, and both eyes were blackened, with crusted blood in his ears. He was a mess.

At first he didn't recognize me. Once he did, he told me the peyote he had sold me was not his. The house he had taken me to was not his either, but belonged to his Mexican friend.

We had more than a hundred buttons left, but I saw no reason to give them back since I had paid good money for them, and Benjamin had already paid by getting his ass kicked. No, I'd let well enough alone.

The next day we left for Denver; Moses would take a bus east from there. We hoped to visit The Prez's aunt and uncle and hit them up for money.

We dropped Moses off at the Greyhound, got some money and a footlocker of canned goods from The Prez's aunt and uncle and headed north up the continental divide. In the Wyoming high country on the Shoshone Indian reservation we camped on a high bluff overlooking a deep blue lake. The bare, gravelly ground was hard, so different from the soft, sandy soil and leaf litter that covers the ground in Michigan.

Then on to Yellowstone, where, at sunrise, we met some hippies at "Old Faithful" who gave us a freezer bag full of pot, which moved me to say, "Thank you Lord, there is a God."

We took a week, camping along the way, to get to Glacier National Park, arriving before the park officially opened. We were the only campers at Two Medicine Lake when the ranger showed up, busting through spring snowdrifts with his four-wheel drive. A grizzly just on the other side of the mountain had, he informed us, mauled a biologist. We were to take extreme caution by hoisting our noncanned foodstuffs into a nearby tree.

It snowed that night and we were socked in for three days, the canvas sides of the camper offering comfort from the wind but none from the fear of the bear.

Moving south and west, we camped on the reservation of the Flatheads, so called because they would flatten the heads of their infants by placing them between two boards and cinching the boards tight, at a slight angle, flattening the forehead and giving the skull a pointed look. I imagine it was quite attractive in the day. I know I would have looked twice if I had seen a comely young woman with a flat forehead and pointy-head making eyes at me.

We drove west into Idaho, a land too beautiful for its own good, camping along the Snake River until we were shooed away by forest rangers that were stalking another grizzly that had caused trouble for people. We showered at a private campground at The Devils Bathtub gorge and stole a sign that read "Don't Feed The Bears" which later hung in our bedroom 'til The Prez and I divorced.

Memorial Day, 1968, was spent on the campus of the University of Montana at Missoula with some hippie friends we'd met while watching the Air Force's Flying Blue Angels perform in the deep blue of the Big Sky Country.

After that we headed east, back to Detroit. The only thing remarkable about the rest of the journey was the cloudy, smelly, distasteful water we had to drink at the rest stop outside of Fargo on I- 94.

Chapter Seven

THE FIRST CHURCH OF ZENTA, Ann Arbor--1968

While on our three-month western odyssey, The Prez kept in close contact with Leni and Audrey through letters. I sent Sinclair a postcard now and then.

Meanwhile, during our absence, Sinclair and The MC5 searched Ann Arbor (A^2) for a suitable location to relocate the entire band and so Trans-Love Energies (TLE) could move. A^2 is home to the University of Michigan (UM), and, at that time, a stronghold of rebellion and haven for thousands of freaky hippies dreaming of a new world.

They found "The Hill Street Houses," two run-down, ramshackled Victorians with an old coach house behind them. On the verge of being condemned, these large, three-story structures had breezy porches and slate roofs with several bulky and ornate chimneys standing sentinel over balconies, gables, and beveled glass windows, all in disrepair. Situated on a large lot overrun with unruly vegetation on the fringe of fraternity row, 1510 and 1520 Hill were within walking distance of central campus.

DS negotiated a deal where Trans-Love would buy the complex on a land contract with a payment of $1,500 a month. This was a monumental undertaking that would have been impossible without the financial, musical, and spiritual support of the MC5. They were as committed to creating a new culture and lifestyle as we were, and were willing to put their lives, careers and money on the line for it.

Sinclair suggested starting a church. "That way we don't have to pay property taxes," he reasoned. Sinclair and JC Crawford, The First Prophet of Zenta, established The Church of Zenta with the Hill Street houses serving as monastery, convent and the Zenta See. Smoking marijuana was its first sacrament, and its only dogma was "no dogma." I was on the Board of Directors as the Zenta Nuncio.

In the three months The Prez and I had been gone, the MC5 had become the advance guard of the Midwest rock-and-roll revolution, as well as the financial engine that drove the whole Trans-Love Energies operation. Sinclair managed the band fulltime, negotiating a record deal, booking better gigs, and elevating their business to a professional level.

The MC5 moved into 1510. It housed the five band members, their wives or girlfriends, two or three roadies and their old ladies, as well as several hang-arounds.

TLE personnel made 1520 their home. Some old faces and new ones occupied the second and third floor bedrooms. The Prez and I claimed a cubbyhole in one of the gables of the steeply roofed attic. At one point I counted heads: between the two houses there were thirty-five people, from infants to adults. Together we made up an enclave of cultural assassins right in the heart of the university campus.

On the first floor of 1520, in addition to a large kitchen

and dining room, there were several offices and a side porch converted to a bedroom. There was a major music room with five layers of carpeting on the floor, heavy tapestries on the wall and ceiling, and a great honkin' sound system that could rumble the foundation with its lows and deafen dogs with its highs.

Leni had her photo darkroom set up in the basement, where there was also a large room for newspaper layout with glass topped tables and fluorescent lights underneath, all banged together with 2x4's. Another room held our small press, and several others, small offices.

We'd barely settled in. I hadn't even learned the names and faces of the new people living there when, three days after our arrival, I was arrested on a warrant from Traverse City.

*　　　　　*　　　　　*

I was with Sinclair in his basement office when Audrey entered to tell us the A2 police were upstairs with an arrest warrant for me.

Damn! I thought, *I hadn't been arrested or broken any laws in over a year--except for smoking pot of course. I hadn't even gotten drunk. What could this be about?*

Lieutenant Studebaker and three uniforms were waiting in the front hall. Studebaker was the Community Relations Officer for the A^2 police department. I was told he was on a first-name relationship with many of the activists on campus and had a reputation of being honest, respectful, and generally reasonable. His flattop haircut and Marine Corps demeanor gave the impression of power under control. Several commune members were milling about, wondering what was going down.

Studebaker showed us the warrant. It was for Grimshaw and me. We were both charged with "sale or distribution of marijuana without a license." "Where do I get a license?" I asked innocently.

Sinclair informed Studebaker that Grimshaw didn't live there, then got on the hall phone and called him at his apartment across town.

As the uniforms began to frisk me I argued, "I've never sold pot in my life." As they began to cuff me I resisted slightly, trying to avoid the cuffs. "I've been out of state for months," I insisted. "I want a lawyer--this is bullshit." I protested halfheartedly, feeling I had to put up some resistance for the sake of the onlookers. Unlike Sinclair, I was never very mouthy once I was in the cuffs, preferring to become a model prisoner so as not to call attention to myself.

Suddenly one of the uniforms realized that Sinclair was talking to Grimshaw on the phone. "You're under arrest! You're under arrest!" the cop shouted over and over at Grimshaw over Sinclair's shoulder. "Report to the Ann Arbor Police Department!" he went on. Sinclair held up the receiver and the cop shouted again, "Report to the Ann Arbor Police Department, You're under arrest." Studebaker calmed his boy down, and I was led away, held in an A2 lockup to await transport to TC. I'm told Grimshaw fled to San Francisco that same day, a warrant hanging over his head.

I was certain this was a frame-up. I had never sold or distributed pot in my entire life--oh, I gave away a joint or two here and there, but that's hardly sale or distribution. No, this was a frame, I knew it. At that time, sale or distribution carried a 20-to-life sentence in Michigan. There were ample numbers of people doing that kind of time on these charges; this was nothing to sneeze at.

After transport to TC, I was taken before Judge Schumer, the same asshole that would not sign my recommendation for the Peace Corps some five years earlier. As a District Court Judge, it was his responsibility to arraign me, hold a preliminary exam to establish 'probable cause," and transfer or "bound" my case over to Circuit Court.

However, "Judge" Schumer was really "Justice of the Peace" Schumer. He didn't have the authority to hold preliminary examinations in felony cases. Nevertheless he arraigned me, ignored my pleas for a lawyer, read me the charges, and set bond at $20,000, an impossible amount for me to raise. He set the date for the preliminary exam, and I was returned to the Grand Traverse County Jail.

A week later I was taken before Schumer again. Again I asked for a lawyer. I was told that a Justice of the Peace does not have the authority to appoint attorneys, or even to hold preliminary exams. However, I could sign a waiver of my right to a preliminary exam in District Court, be bound over to Circuit

Court, and have a lawyer appointed and the preliminary exam there.

"No!" I said. "I won't sign anything until I talk to a lawyer." Schumer was losing his patience the way small, powerful white men do when contradicted or back-sassed by a member of the underclass.

"You, Mr. Plamondon, will sit in jail until you sign this waver and are bound over to Circuit court," Schumer snapped. "I won't sign anything until I talk to a lawyer," I insisted. I was returned to jail.

A week later, The Prez and Audrey made the four-hour drive to see me. However, the jailer would not allow the visit since The Prez and I were not married and Audrey was not "personal family." I decided then and there to marry The Prez as soon as I got out.

I sat in jail eighty-four days, straight through the Democratic National Convention in Chicago, listening to developments on newscasts piped into the cellblock of the newly built jail. The MC5 was the only band of national reputation to keep its commitment to play at a "celebration of life" in Grant Park, site of some of the most fierce police violence.

Finally, The Prez and DS found a lawyer and bail bondsman. My bond was reduced to $4,000, a preliminary hearing was scheduled, and I was released after The Prez paid the bondsman $400.

The preliminary was held in District Court in the city office building with blond paneled walls and black accents covering the judge's bench and witness and jury boxes. Recess lighting in the tall ceiling illuminated a streamlined, modern courtroom, with no soul or character, save efficiency.

It all came down to two "roaches." Reefer butts. It seems that the last time Grimshaw and I were in TC--when we stayed with those friends who had a cottage on the bay--we had played monopoly for hours, listened to tunes, and smoked joints. Grimshaw and I each rolled pot from different bags, his and mine.

A young police informant, having been recently busted himself for possession of weed, promised the cops he would gather evidence on all the other pot smokers in the area. He was at the cottage while we were smoking. He testified that he took two roaches out of an ashtray, placed them in the cellophane of a cigarette pack and left the cottage. One roach was Grimshaw's and one roach was mine.

The cellophane pack and its contents were entered into evidence. But wait! There was only one roach in the cellophane.

The state crime lab specialists testified that he had to destroy one of the roaches in order to test it. The other was intact.

The informant testified that he could not tell one from the other.

My lawyer made a motion to dismiss the case based on the fact that the informant was unreliable and it was unclear whose roach was actually being entered into evidence. Nevertheless the judge bound me over to trial, as we knew he would. On the ride home I thought--*for this I'm facing 20 to life? This government is fucked.*

* * *

My political thinking was getting sharper and my attitude more militant--especially since the Detroit riots, the murder of Dr. King, the police riots at the '68 convention, the murder of Black Panthers, the continuing war in Vietnam and the brutal oppression of domestic political opposition against it, and now this phony pot charge.

I was seeing the US government as the primary enemy facing peace-and-freedom loving people across the globe. Not only was the US conducting a vicious, immoral war, they were supporting every right-wing dictator around the world, and fighting against every revolution and struggle for national liberation--from South Africa to South America, from Iran to Puerto Rico. Likewise, the government's support for Israel against the indigenous Palestinians was a replay of America taking over Indian land, as far as I was concerned.

The US was doing everything backwards, it seemed to me. Instead of ousting dictators, they were supporting them. Instead of supporting struggles against colonialism, they were defending colonialism. And Vietnam--Vietnam was successful in kicking out the French and abolishing their colonial rule only to have the Americans invade, divide the country in half, and set up a cavalcade of puppet dictators in the south. Backwards.

In this country, it appeared to me, the ghettos were simply "domestic colonies," a cheap labor force, and when needed, fodder for the machines of war. Violence and injustice was visited on these communities daily by mostly white occupying police forces.

With the recent beatings and arrests of antiwar demonstrators across the country, it was clear to me that the power structure would do whatever it took, including beating, arresting, and even killing its own children, to maintain the status quo.

Yet there were individuals and organizations that were trying to turn the country around. For a year, I had watched the Nation of Islam and marveled at the success they had in organizing former junkies and whores, as well as educated and successful black people, into a political force, locally and nationally.

The Black Panther Party for Self-Defense seemed to be effective in organizing and instilling discipline in street-toughs and ex-cons. Their platform called for black citizens to defend themselves with arms against racist police acting in an unlawful manner. Their tactics of educating their cadre politically and feeding poor children in their neighborhoods seemed to me to be more effective than going to a demonstration every six months, no matter how righteous the cause.

I liked the American Indian Movement, too, though I never thought I could be a member, or even call myself "Indian" since I wasn't full blood and hadn't been raised in the culture and didn't know my tribe.

The view of the white left was less hopeful to a guy like me. Those organizations that weren't old-line communists and socialists, which were as drab and dreary as the Elks club, were mostly student-inspired and student-led. The Students for a Democratic Society dominated the student movement. They worked hard and were oh, so serious, but they seemed to be lacking the vibrant energy of the wider youth movement.

The YIPPIES! were another thing altogether. They were a non-organization with non-leaders and no members. Jerry Rubin and Abbie Hoffman served as willing front men for an organization that existed only when its call to action was trumpeted by the media. They formulated street theater and protests, using the media to educate and carry the message to the uninformed in big cities and small towns across America.

Like Jerry Rubin showing up at the House Internal Affairs Committee (formally the House Un-American Activities Committee) dressed as "The International Revolutionary." With his face painted like an Indian, he wore the black beret of the Black Panthers, black pajamas of the Viet Cong, and armbands representing the people struggling in Asia, Africa and Latin America. He carried an M-16 replica water gun. The obvious message: "I, and the people I represent, are not only as bad as you thought we were, we're worse!" The beauty of it all was that Rubin represented the entire new youth culture, while representing no one. Though neither appointed nor elected, he spoke and acted to express the attitude and aspirations of millions of progressive young people.

Or Abbie Hoffman and his crew tossing out thousands of dollars from the balcony onto the New York Stock Exchange trading floor, while whirring TV cameras captured the bizarre spectacle of salivating, groveling white men scurrying and crawling on hands and knees to scoop-up free money. YIPPIE!

The YIPPIE! model had a certain attraction, but also had its obvious drawbacks. As a non-organization, it was difficult to organize anything practical or long lasting, like a food co-op or medical clinic or free music in the parks. Its "members" were limited to calling for demonstrations, promoting pranks, and performing street theatre--valuable activities, to be sure, but not enough to sustain a movement over the long haul.

* * *

During my eighty-four day incarceration in the Grand Traverse County Jail, I read extensively--underground newspapers mostly, sent in large bundles by The Prez (and approved by the Sheriff) so I could prepare for trial.

In one paper there was an interview with Huey P. Newton, Minister of Defense and cofounder of the Black Panther Party, who was serving a life sentence for killing an Oakland, California policeman during a self-defense shootout. At one point, the interviewer asked Huey what white people could do to support the black liberation struggle. Huey answered, "They can form a White Panther Party."

Of course! I thought, *we can form a White Panther Party utilizing the media and culture the way the YIPPIES! do and organize on the street level as the Black Panthers do.*

Chapter Eight

THE WHITE PANTHER PARTY--1968/69

After my release from jail in Traverse City I returned to Ann Arbor. Within days The Prez and I got married in a local coffeehouse; at least, that's where we signed the papers; there was no ceremony. Neither of us felt that "marriage" had anything to do with love or commitment. The Prez and I, like most of our friends, simply lived together with the unspoken agreement that the situation would continue unless one of the partners decided to change it, i.e. leave. We saw no reason for the state to interfere with the living arrangements between consenting adults. We had learned our lesson, however: if The Prez ever hoped to visit me, or me her, should one of us end up in jail again, we would have to be married. Given the political atmosphere of the time, my rebellious state of mind, and my past, I assumed jail was in our future. So did she. The Mostly Reverend Bob, Head of the Department of Religion and Ethics at the University, officiated over the paper signing and countersigned our marriage license

* * *

Sinclair was a dynamo--still is. If a person wanted to get some business done with him, they had to get into his groove, and keep up! I started traveling to gigs with Sinclair and the MC5. I'd lug equipment with the regular roadies and rock with everyone else during the show, but I went along primarily in order to spend time with Sinclair talking about our present legal difficulties and making some sort of plan for our future survival.

Sinclair still had his sale of marijuana case pending in Detroit. He had been charged with giving two joints to an undercover Detroit Police officer in 1966. Now that my case for "distribution" was added to the mix, we were both facing sentences with a minimum of twenty years and a maximum of life in prison. Sinclair insisted we did not have to go along with this bullshit, but we could challenge the law on every level. Weed was wrongly classified as a narcotic, when in truth it is a benevolent herb. The penalties were cruel and unusual, and local police used pot laws to harass and intimidate activists deemed political or cultural enemies. Sinclair's plan was to go after the law, to get hundreds if not thousands of marijuana users to challenge the law, ridicule the law, resist the law, flaunt the law, and ultimately abolish the law. We agreed to focus and intensify our efforts to reform the weed laws of Michigan and to educate and organize millions of young people in the effort.

After first kicking it around with The Prez, I told Sinclair of the interview I'd read with Huey P. Newton and Huey's call for white folks to form a White Panther Party. My idea was that we should be the ones to do it.

Until this time, Trans Love-Energies, and the Artist's Workshop before it, were hotbeds of apolitical anti-establishment art and culture. We weren't "political activists;" politics did not drive our actions. We were "cultural activists" striving to build a new culture; it was this that inspired our art and actions. All artists should be in conflict with authority, and we were good at it. To be left alone to live our lives differently than those in the dominant culture was all we wanted. Our legal troubles erupted when our lifestyle smashed into their laws.

The government, I felt, was using against us--apolitical hippies, the same tactics they were using against activists in the black, new left, antiwar and civil rights movements. I reasoned that if we educated ourselves politically, we could lead tens of thousands of alienated and disenfranchised young people into a movement that could create a revolution. It seemed to me, at the time, that to survive we would have to respond in a political manner--we would have to organize politically.

Sinclair grasped the idea immediately and articulated an analysis that I only understood intuitively. Like people of color, he explained, hippies were identifiable-through dress, lifestyle, music, and culture, and we were often treated as second class citizens. We could not expect justice in the courts, for instance, or equal opportunity in employment. Not only that, but, as in communities of color, the police often framed and entrapped the leaders and activists in our communities, in an attempt to silence them and effectively get them off the street by draining them of their financial resources and political support. Furthermore-- Sinclair was on a roll-- as a predominantly white minority, hippies, ("white niggers" as we were sometimes called by racists elements), lived in country communes, and in urban ghettos, most on the fringe of Universities; we were in identifiable geographic communities. It wasn't the color of our skin that drew the wrath of the power structure--it was the nature of our culture that led to our treatment as second-class citizens.

Hippies, in the process of building a post-western culture, Sinclair went on, were outside the mainstream, with less of the racists' assumptions, greedy addictions or "divine rights" of the dominant culture. On the contrary, hippies could utilize, embrace, and respect all non-western cultures, reject backward elements of American culture, and build a new and better one.

I suggested that we organize ourselves along the Black Panther model, with a Central Committee (CC), ministers and such. Everything was to come and go from the center; the CC was to direct and control all Party activity. Our organizing model utilized the collective input and decision-making process known as "democratic centralism," in which power, like a spoked wheel, moves to and from the center, rather than in the top down pyramid of western politics.

I began reading what the Black Panthers read: the likes of Mao, Lenin, Ho Chi Minh, Fidel, Nkrumah, and Fanon, as well as anything I could get my hands on regarding the American left.

Sinclair put forward the idea that The White Panther

Party should become the "cultural arm" of the YIP, Youth International Party--The YIPPIES! We agreed to try to recruit into this conspiracy Jerry Rubin and Abbie Hoffman, the front men of that non-organization, as well as their band of artistic saboteurs.

I took on the affectations of a "revolutionary"--machismo and arrogance in a black cycle jacket--with what can now be viewed as comical self-importance. Actually it was another manifestation of the ego-driven acting with which I had made my way through life. In high school I had acted like a jock, then a greaser. Later I acted like a union organizer or a shiftless rambler, and now I acted as I imagined a revolutionary would. I had no underpinnings, no solid place where I felt connected to this universe. It seemed that I was never just myself, was always some character or another in my own private play. I didn't know how to be myself because I spent so much time trying to act like someone else.

But I did like this new role. Now, at least, my relationship to the government was public and clear: I was a revolutionary, a threat to the status quo, and villainous scoundrel to millions of dumbass Americans all hopped up on fear and greed. I finally belonged to something.

Sinclair had visions of ten million hippie rascals infiltrating the very institutions that manipulate and control America and radically transforming them by disseminating information of a revolutionary nature. "Given the right information, people will free themselves," he was fond of saying.

I had visions of column after column of armed hippies, men and women of all shades of color, march-dancing with Sergeant Pepper leading the Corps through the smoldering streets of Washington DC.

* * *

Over the next several weeks, Sinclair wrote the founding documents, got the MC5 on board, and prepared a press release. I began organizing the occupants of our two houses into the core cadre of the party. We had political education (PE) classes every morning where we read and discussed Marxist/Leninist/Maoist thought, as well as poetry, short stories, and plays, all with a revolutionary focus.

I established the position of rotating Officer of the Day, the OD, just as the Black Panthers had done in Oakland. The OD ran the upfront, day-to-day operation of the organization. The OD screened visitors, took messages, scheduled the use of vehicles, answered the phones, arranged appointments and basically gave order to the chaotic scene on Hill Street. Every Party cadre and CC member, with the exception of Sinclair, was expected to take a shift. I did my fair share. Sinclair was exempt because of his exhausting workload and near-constant travel with the MC5.

To my knowledge, we were the only New Left organization in the State that had an office with a phone open 24/7. Few groups even had an office or a phone or an organized way of dealing with day-to-day work and interaction with the community.

Early on we bought White Panther buttons, little tin affairs with a white panther on a purple background. The MC5 threw handfuls of the buttons to the crowd during shows that were interspersed with political raps. Soon we were printing buttons in the thousands. Among the suburban kids of southeast Michigan, having a White Panther button became a status symbol. With the popularity of the MC5 and the button came the attention of more and more kids, many of whom contacted us and wanted to become real White Panthers. Naturally the parents, school authorities, and police were alarmed to see white suburban teenagers wearing white panther pins and carrying Mao's Little Red Book and reading the speeches of Fidel Castro and Malcolm X. The authorities mobilized for a counterattack.

* * *

On September 26, 1968, a short time after my return from eighty-four days in the Traverse City jail, the MC5 signed with Electra Records, and the possibility that our message could reach literally millions of young people became a reality.

Three days after that, militant, homegrown radicals exploded a dynamite bomb at a clandestine CIA office in Ann Arbor, changing my life forever.

I was riding a wired-together '58 BMW shaft-drive

scooter with Rock-n-Roll Rita snuggled-up behind me when we heard the blast.

"That was loud!" she leaned over my back and yelled in my ear.

"We're gittin' outa here!" I yelled back over my shoulder against the wind and the sound of the bike. Rita squeezed me hard and gave the inside of my thigh a sharp pinch, "Dynamite makes me horny," she squealed.

Rock-n-Roll Rita was a dedicated, full-time Party worker and organizer. She was a pert and perky sixteen year-old runaway from Livonia, a working-class Detroit suburb. At the tender age of thirteen she was strung out on poetry and jazz and fearsome ideas about freedom. By fourteen she was sneaking out of her bedroom window, going to clubs, staying out all night in the company of shady, cool characters. At fifteen her parents found her stash of reefer, birth-control pills, Coltrane, and Malcolm, and had her committed to a private mental hospital. She escaped the ward running and never looked back.

I motored the scooter through the University of Michigan autumn evening. The student residential streets, always active, seemed particularly abuzz with much milling about. Back at Hill Street I parked the scooter and Rita and I went inside. Kramer caught me on the steps, just as he was leaving. "What exploded?" he wanted to know. Apparently he heard the blast, like thousands of others, some fifteen blocks away.

"Don't know, maybe a CIA office," I answered. "Cool," Kramer replied and continued down the steps.

Word spread as the shock waves of the explosion rippled throughout the community. People began coming by the house and calling to see if we'd heard the news. "Who knew there was a CIA office in Tree Town?" people wanted to know. "Isn't it against the law for the CIA to operate in the U.S.?" was a common question.

The next day, *The Michigan Daily*, the student-run University paper, and *The Ann Arbor News* carried three-inch headlines about the blast. Statements made by the Chief of Police and the FBI, about who had planted the bomb were meaningless really--they had no suspects; nevertheless, an "antiestablishment group or individual" was felt to be responsible. There was no spokesperson for the CIA. Since no one was injured, the bombing had the support of most of the progressive and radical community.

After a few days the excitement about the bombing ebbed, people returned to their daily routines, and conversations were refocused on the pressing events of the day.

In those days, in Ann Arbor and similar hotbeds across the country, there were demonstrations, street theater, mass leafleting, prayer vigils, and multicultural events happening on a daily basis. The war was the primary focus, though women's rights groups were speaking up, gay people were on the move, and veterans, militant vegetarians, student organizations and minority groups of every description were rising up angry. And new music was driving it all.

In the dead of night on October 16, at the Institute of Science and Technology (IST), on U of M's North Campus, another bomb was detonated. Again there were no injuries, an entrance and little else was destroyed. October 16 is the anniversary of Che Guevarra's death at the hands of Bolivian soldiers who had acted on information gathered by infrared cameras developed at the IST. For years, the IST was involved in research on such high-tech weapons as smart bombs, laser guided bombs, and infrared tracking devices. Headlines honked, but the bombing didn't cause much excitement.

I believe the "antiestablishment group or individual" that carried out the bombing had wished the local and underground press would report, not only the flash and fury of the explosions, but would look deeper at the motives for the bombings. What role, for example, did IST and the university play in maintaining American imperialistic power around the world? What cog in the war machine did the university play? But it didn't happen. Though the underground press talked in general terms about the links between universities and the military, they failed to grasp the opportunity offered by the occasion to make the specific connections.

Sinclair and I met again in late October to finalize the press release and Party Statement and make preparations for the public announcement coming November first. It all sounds much more formal than it actually was. We emphasized the "party" aspect of The White Panther Party and took certain liberties in appointments to ministerial positions. In other words, we made so-and-so a minister of such-and-such without ever talking to them about it. These were friends who had certain talents and whom we assumed, incorrectly in some cases, would want to be part of this new exciting outfit.

We did formalize some things; Sinclair would be the Minister of Information and concentrate on mass education, using the MC5 as the advance guard spearheading our drive to influence the masses of hippies; he would also establish the organizational structure of the Party. The Prez and I would concentrate on organizing Party branches and members, as well as a Party "cadre," a staff of full-time, professional Party activists.

I took the Minister of Defense title and began living a fantasy that brought together Mao, Lenin, Che Guevarra, and Crazy Horse. I admired them all completely. I saw them as self-sacrificing heroes of the oppressed classes, who, through genius and single-minded dedication to their cause, changed the face of history and made the world better for millions of people. Crazy Horse stands alone as an example of unbending principle and courage in the face of an overwhelming shit-storm of white people. I had, and still have, no white heroes, except for the millions of men and women, of all colors, who fought and sacrificed in the Second World War, the war against the fascists.

We named The Prez as "Communications Secretary," reflecting our still somewhat sexist attitude toward women; we would soon learn. The Prez, Leni, Red-Haired Audrey, Rock-n-Roll Rita, and other women within the organization and without, began criticizing us for our chauvinistic behavior. Moreover, the larger women's rights movement was becoming influential throughout New Left and progressive organizations. Soon women were appointed to leadership positions in our organization. A childcare program was established for children of Party members, and male and female alike shared the responsibility for staffing it; they began sharing cooking duties as well. Cleaning the houses was rarely done so division of labor was not an issue there.

It was The Prez's responsibility to communicate CC policy to all branches and organs of the Party--a job she did with dedication and professionalism beyond question. A short time after our founding, she was re-named "Minister of Communications" as a reflection of our advancing understanding of feminist politics.

We named Grimshaw to the office of "Minister of Culture" and Skippy to "Minister of Education." I recruited Skippy away from the Students for a Democratic Society; this, perhaps, was my finest hour.

By this time SDS had splintered into many factions and "affinity groups," like a pine board smashed over and over by an FBI mallet. Prior to joining the Party, Skippy was a member of a faction of SDS who called themselves by various names--The Felch Street Gang, The James Gang, and finally, the Ann Arbor Collective of the Weather Underground, or A^2 Weathermen.

I convinced Skippy that the education of millions of young people through the promotion of revolutionary culture was more effective than taking offensive military action against the government. "If it came down to it, we could do both," I argued.

DS, Sinclair's younger brother, was named Chief of Staff. A chairman and several other ministers were also named, at least temporarily. We set about organizing ourselves and soliciting support from like-minded individuals and organizations.

* * *

In January of '69, Sinclair, the MC5, and their road crew traveled to the East Coast on a promotional tour organized by Electra Records. I flew out to meet the band for a free concert at Bill Graham's Filmore East in New York City.

While there, I hung with Rubin and spent several hours trying to convince him that he and his crew should join forces with us and build a real organization, not just a media image of an organization--a real Youth International Party, with a complete platform and program. He saw the advantages, but was noncommittal and promised to continue talking with us.

For several months I'd been hearing and reading about a group of hard-core militant anarchists from the Lower East Side of New York called the Up Against The Wall Motherfuckers (UAW/MF) and their sister organization W.I.T.C.H. (Women's

International Terrorist Conspiracy from Hell). While in New York I made a point to look them up.

The UAW/MFs were a loose collection of derelict teenage runaways, 20-something street hustling, anarchist thugs, several priestly poets high on LSD, and an unrepentant parolee. The fifteen or so who made up the core of the group lived on the streets of the Lower East Side--in abandoned cars, condemned buildings, or in cardboard structures in vacant lots.

They all coalesced around a guy named Beretta and the slogan "Eat The Rich!" Their political ideology was straightforward: the wealth of the world belongs to everyone. There is enough for everyone; the rich are stealing the wealth of the world--steal it back!

Beretta looked like the movie actor Al Pacino, when Pacino was twenty-four, street tough and wiry. He had greasy hair that hung stringy to his collar and was dressed in a filthy army fatigue jacket, a black turtleneck sweater that had gone six months without being laundered, and Levi's that were shiny from the grit and grime of the streets. On his feet he wore steel-toed Brogans, two sizes too large.

The White Panther Party was not anarchistic; on the contrary, we were hippie communalists or new-age revolutionary socialists. We recognized that some of our closest allies were and would be anarchists. We were open to working with any non-racist organization dedicated to bringing down the government. The UAW/MFs commitment to militant action, opposition to "private property," and general contrariness fit well with our goals and Party slogan--"Total Assault on the Culture!"

When I found them, they were lolling on the stoop, sidewalk, and curb in front of the condemned, boarded-up tenement where they were exercising "squatters rights." They had ripped plywood off the door, scrounged mattresses, couch cushions, car seats, and cardboard to set up living quarters. At night they used flashlights and candles.

For weeks, the sleazy slumlord had been hassling the UAW/MFs, trying to get them out of his building and off his street.

One day, a group of UAW/MFs were hanging out on the stoop of their condemned pad. The slumlord boldly walked up and threw a mayonnaise jar full of battery acid in Pedro's face. Pedro was a 14-year-old Puerto Rican boy, the youngest of the group. New York Fire Rescue took Pedro to the hospital where they treated his second and third degree burns.

The UAW/MFs, like most gangs of rejects from the dominant society, had a tremendous amount of loyalty to each other. Because Pedro was the youngest of the crew, and rather "slow," his comrades had a particularly protective attitude toward him.

A few days later, just before I was to return to Ann Arbor, I was hangin' with Beretta and his posse, who were hustling on the corner. As some panhandled and others waited for an opportunity to boost goods from a delivery van or sell some acid or hot goods, they spotted the grease-ball slumlord sitting on the hood of a car right in front of his tenement, hangin' with his buddy. His white undershirt hiding a black heart and rotted soul.

"You keep an eye on him," Ben said to me as he and his crew scattered, looking for weapons. They found a shipping pallet, tore it apart, and got three good lengths of 2x4s. Several found bricks and a chunk of curbstone concrete. One of the women pulled an ice pick from the folds of her three skirts, Buck knives locked open, a car aerial was snapped off at the base.

They moved quickly, as if Karmic Avengers on a mission from God. They split up and came at him from all directions, walking fast across the street and from up and down the sidewalk. He never saw them coming. They jumped him right on the hood of that car. His buddy cut and ran. They whacked him with 2x4's, several of which broke across his back and head. They cut and stabbed him, going especially for his eyes since Pedro had been partially blinded by the acid attack. They beat him with bricks, whipped him with the car antenna, and chunked him over and over with the concrete curbstone. Then they put the boots to him. They stomped him 'til they were tired, then scattered, leaving the sleaze-bag landlord for dead.

Glad to say goodbye and get out of there, I shook Ben's hand, which was sticky with blood, then jumped on the subway uptown and a bus to the airport. Little did I know that Ben and his crew would come screeching into my life again in the near future.

*   *   *

In April, The White Panther Party announced we would sponsor and host a National Alternative Media Conference in August. Two days later, I was arrested by the Ann Arbor Police for "distributing lewd, lascivious and obscene material to minors with the intent to corrupt the morals of youth."

As well as being a CC member, I was also distribution manager for our paper, THE ANN ARBOR SUN. Every two weeks I delivered the paper to all of our retail outlets in the greater Ann Arbor/Ypsilanti area, shipped the paper to our out-state distributors, and sent off, via Greyhound Bus or airfreight, bundles of papers to our just-budding chapters around the country. As part of my duties as distribution manager, I saw it as my responsibility to get THE SUN into the hands of as many high school students as possible. Over the years, we helped many high school kids start their own papers, usually mimeographed rags of one or two pages with music reviews, editorials against the war, or complaints of how the school administration were dinosaurs and control junkies. When the kids started reporting the names of student "narcs," we usually heard from the authorities.

But getting arrested for "corrupting the morals of youth" was a bit much. Maybe a parent complained and forced action. However, any District Attorney would know this was a First Amendment issue and wouldn't waste their time on it. I believe the local FBI, under the directives in Hoover's Counterintelligence Program, the now famous CoIntelPro, influenced the Ann Arbor Police to arrest me in an attempt to discredit the WPP, the upcoming Alternative Media Conference, and me personally. What would turn off political supporters and conference attendees more than to have one of the principle organizers arrested on a morals charge?

After arraignment I made bond and didn't worry about it.

In June, an "antiestablishment group or individual" placed a bomb under a government car at the ROTC building on Central Campus. The bomb and car exploded, catching the whole building on fire. Headlines beeped, but again, no one seemed to pay much attention. The bombers wished the explosion would have sparked a public debate about why the University, using public money, was involved in training young Americans to conduct genocidal wars around the world that most Americans did not support or at least found questionable. But it didn't happen.

*   *   *

The Prez did a good deal of traveling in the spring and summer of '68. She set up Party chapters in Ohio, New York, Chicago, Milwaukee, Oregon, Berkeley, San Francisco, New Orleans, and Houston, to name a few. I stayed in A2 organizing Party cadre, distributing the *The Sun* and overseeing the repair and restoration of our two big Victorians.

Our organizing tactics were easy to understand. We cast our net wide. Sinclair, the MC5, and the White Panther button attracted mass attention. The mass related to the image. We then filled the image with revolutionary content. This thinned out the mass but it allowed us to identify the core. From the core, exceptional members were identified and asked to become cadre or start local chapters. This method insured that the best rose to the top.

In mid-July of the same year, the Black Panther Party organized and hosted The United Front Against Fascism Conference in Oakland, California, which Rock-n-Roll Rita and I attended. While on the left Coast, we met with WP chapters and supporters in Berkeley, San Francisco, Eugene, and Seattle. Sinclair had a court date toward the end of the month and we assumed we'd return by then.

The fear of fascism in America was quite real, not just the ravings of the paranoid- left. The Houston Plan and the FBI's ColnTelPro agenda can be read by anyone interested in learning firsthand how government agencies conspired to deny American citizens their civil rights. Richard (The Pig Hearted) Nixon contemplated the postponement of presidential elections, wiretapped activists, and propagated fear to undermine fundamental rights of citizens. The BPP was being decimated, their top leadership killed, imprisoned, or forced into exile. The Chicago Seven, whose trial opened millions of eyes to the fascist nature of the right-wing elements of the government, and local police forces with a desire for absolute control, ran roughshod over the rights of young people and people of color. The nation was in turmoil. Only unity among the progressive forces and the fall of the Nixon administration would save us.

The United Front Against Fascism Conference was worthwhile; we connected with important activists from around the country. I met "Preacher," a young dude I'd been reading about in the underground press for several months. He was a leader of a gang out of Chicago called The Young Patriots. They were a white, working-class group, most with roots in Appalachia. Many groups that weren't Old Left, or college debating societies of New Left organizations, were actually street gangs with a political consciousness. Certainly the Young Patriots fit this description, as did The Young Lords (Puerto Rican), the UAW/MF's, the Congolian Maulers, and others.

"Preacher" gave a major address to nearly two thousand people gathered in the Oakland Coliseum. It was something to see him at the podium, a white guy, about twenty-three years old, five-feet-ten, with black beret, black leather scooter jacket with zippers on the sleeves and a drawl thicker than oatmeal. Black Panther outriders, at attention, and looking quite menacing, were stationed in front and at either end of the stage, taking their security jobs quite seriously.

Preacher harangued the crowd, his redneck drawl incongruous given the audience and surroundings. It didn't take long to see where he got his moniker: "They taught me in school that George Washington is a hero," he began "I say he was a bourgeoisie slave owner [applause]...They taught me in school that all people are created equal. Well, in this country, some people are more equal than others...we're fixin' to change that!" [applause]. Vietnam was a rich man's war, he declared, fought by the expendable classes--blacks and poor whites. "We're fixin' to change that!" he chanted [more applause]. The audience caught the rhythm and waited for the next chorus, Preacher went on "My daddy worked in the coal mine until my daddy and the mine wore out, then the coal company abandoned both." The whole audience responded, "WE'RE FIXIN' TO CHANGE THAT!" "They got Hey P Newton in jail!" he shouted. "WE'RE FIXIN' TO CHANGE THAT!" "They got Eldridge Cleaver in exile!" "WE'RE FIXIN' TO CHANGE THAT!" He went on and on, Jesus, it was something to see. As the crowd chanted as one, the first steps toward unity were being taken.

I watched closely as he toned it down, and brought the audience back from the heights created by the call-and-response oratory. He slowed down, "We got pigs murderin' citizens, we got pigs bootstomping our guaranteed Constitutional rights, and we got pigs that are no more than occupying forces in our neighborhoods." A mighty roar came from the audience: "WE'RE FIXIN' TO CHANGE THAT!"

"How do we change it?" he asked rhetorically in a calm voice. "We change it by implementing the report and program that comes out of this conference--The Community Control of Police Initiative!"

The Community Control of Police Initiative was a grassroots organizing campaign sponsored by the BPP designed to pass an initiative that would establish community control of police through a citizens oversight committees, and require police officers to live in the communities they served.

Later during the conference, Bobby Seale, Chairman of the BPP, introduced me to Jorgen, an eager 20-year-old reporter for the Danish daily newspaper, INFORMATION. In addition, Jorgen was the International Secretary of the Danish Left-Wing Socialist Party. He was in this country for three months to write a major piece for his paper on the American Movement in general, and the BPP, in particular. Chairman Seale felt it would be a good angle for him to talk to the hippie inspired White Panthers.

Jorgen was tall like so many Danes of a certain bloodline. He reminded me of the cartoon character "Prince Valiant" with his blond hair, square-cut bangs across his forehead, and a bob cut, just below his ears. We hung out for a day or two and became fast friends.

Several weeks after the conference was over, Jorgen came to Ann Arbor. At the time, I was trying to organize a biker gang from Inkster into new left revolutionaries, armed and on wheels. It was a hard sell. Jorgen was particularly interested in our use of music and culture to attract young people living in a counter-culture lifestyle to a political analysis and action. Having seen our success, he believed it would be a useful tactic in

Denmark and across Europe.

In most of Europe, at that time, the intellectual class and labor unions, whose roots were in the Old Left, dominated radical politics. Stagnant Marxist-Leninist-Stalinists worldviews and political structures could have been summed up in one word, "obsolete." The fact that a new culture was sweeping the western world, a culture driven by the young, with new and creative energy to bring to bear against the greed driven Imperialists, was redefining political thinking. In France, a coalition of students and workers shut down the country and produced weeks of street fighting. The young had force.

* * *

Rita and I, having left Oakland, arrived at our Ann Arbor Headquarters at about 7:30 in the morning on July 28th--just as Sinclair and Leni and Sunny and The Prez and DS and Red-Haired Audrey and other Party members were clambering into vehicles on their way to Detroit for Sinclair's sentencing on his pot charge.

SENTENCING ON HIS POT CHARGE! WHAT SENTENCING? I wondered. I remembered Sinclair had a court date toward the end of the month; I assumed it would be another delay or postponement, or arguing of pretrial motions, like so many other appearances over the past couple of years, and so didn't pay much attention.

I should have. While Rita and I were in California, Sinclair went to court, picked a jury, had a trial, and was convicted--I coulda' fainted.

Sinclair was sentenced to nine and a half to ten years in prison for possession of two joints and carted off to Jackson prison that very morning without being given the right to bond, pending appeal.

I, like most everyone, was in shock. For a moment the lights went out in our world. Darkness and confusion reigned. My best buddy and running partner was now in the hands of my sworn enemy. And I, like everyone else, was powerless to do anything about it, at least in the short term.

DS and Leni pulled the CC together and led the rest of us in designing a campaign strategy and tactics to get Sinclair released.

We formed a defense team made up of Leni and DS; they were in contact with the lawyers and Sinclair in Jackson. The rest of us concentrated on raising money, producing benefit events to raise defense funds, and educating as many people as possible. We all realized that the whole energy of the Party must be directed toward getting Sinclair released. Though The Prez and I continued our political work, our primary organizing focus was to cultivate support for Sinclair's legal battle.

* * *

We held the Alternative Media Conference, as scheduled, at Hawg Tate's farm on Pontiac Trail years before it was bulldozed so that progress could erect a BLOCKBUSTER VIDEO and other obscenities on the land. We had over a hundred attendees, including Big Man, editor of the BPP's official organ, The Black Panther, who presented a workshop. Two Chicano women gave another from the newspaper La Raza. Of course Werbe was there from *The Fifth Estate,* as was Ken Kelley, editor of *THE SUN*. People showed up from New York and Boston and Phoenix and New Orleans, as well as LA, San Francisco, Cleveland, Pittsburgh, and Philly.

We took every opportunity to pitch Sinclair's case, and, by extension, mine, since I was still facing pot charges in Traverse City. We had a complete press package to hand out to conference attendees that explained the history of the case and how marijuana laws were being used around the country to silence and incarcerate political leaders the government found threatening--to say nothing of the thousands of peaceful hippies who were suffering, locked away in jails and prisons, because of obsolete weed laws used as a political tool against practitioners of the new culture. We advocated the position that changing the reefer laws was a grassroots political strategy that would free innocent people from prison--black, white, yellow and red. It would take a weapon away from the pigs and allow us to turn it against them by using it to gain widespread support among the millions of dope smokers in the country. Though response was polite, our audience was not nearly as committed as we were to using pot as a tool against the government.

My friend Abe, the founder and editor of the Chicago Seed, was busted for possession of pot upon entering Michigan on his way to the conference. He posted bond and attended anyway.

As Minister of Defense, it was my responsibility to organize security for the conference. At that time, Washtenaw County was under the control of a well-known, neo-fascist sheriff--the missing link between humans and beasts--Doug Harvey. This same summer ('69), Sheriff Harvey had led the police charge against young people gathering on South University Street, just off UofM Central Campus, that resulted in three days and nights of street fighting. He was notorious for cutting the long hair of the young men he incarcerated. Most liberals and all progressive people hated him.

As security director for the conference, I was not so concerned with a frontal assault from Harvey and his troops--even a dinosaur the likes of Harvey understood that attacking a bunch of news editors and reporters would bring unwanted attention. However, it was well known that Harvey had connections to Breakthrough, the right-wing fascist organization from Detroit, and sympathy for like-minded outfits. I was concerned that the militant right might attack our conference under the protection of Harvey.

I set up armed guards, kids really, at the driveway down by the road. They kept the weapons discreetly tucked in the bushes as they checked credentials of conference attendees. Their main task was to discourage any frontal assault by the armed right. Our command post was up on the hill, on the front lawn, overlooking the field the driveway skirted, and beyond that, Pontiac Trail. Probably only five or eight of us had weapons, all long guns, no pistols. We watched the drive and road for any signs of trouble.

On the second day of the conference a carload of Ann Arbor Police arrived. Security at the drive let them through since they asked in a legal way. I met them at the top of the drive, in the parking lot, with my 12-gauge casually slung over my arm like a bird hunter after a long day afield. Others in the security team stood at a distance, alert.

Conference-goers were rather nervous while eating their cold-cut sandwiches with a pickle and chips. Some of the more timid attendees made plans to leave immediately.

The pigs said they were looking for my friend Abe from Chicago and they wanted me to produce him. "He's not here and you can't look without a warrant," I said very businesslike. The pigs simply turned their car around and left.

Saturday night, after the work of the conference was done for the day, some of us decided to get a few beers to drink at the farm. The Prez and several other people went with me to fetch the grog in the Party-owned VW bug. It was late, and all the beer stores were closed, so I drove to the Flame Bar, at that time a gay bar in downtown Ann Arbor. I parked next to the building in the alley, perhaps fifty yards in from the street, and sent two companions in to get a case of beer. While they were gone, I got out to take a leak. I was standing next to the VW with my back to the open street, pissing against the wall of the building. Suddenly a pig car squealed into the alley and screeched to a stop just behind the VW. I quickly zipped up my pants. "Plamondon, you're under arrest for indecent exposure," the first pig shouted at me. Protesting, I was cuffed and placed in the car. The Prez went near ballistic, and I had to calm her down to keep her from getting popped too. I was taken to an A^2 lockup and made bond in the morning. I speculated that they arrested me in the hopes of disrupting the conference and intimidating the attendees.

It was well known that movement activists were under surveillance by the authorities during this period. Our headquarters, Party members, and vehicles were surveilled more than most. The Michigan State Police Red Squad and FBI did most of the work, though the Sheriff's Department and Ann Arbor Narco's picked up some overtime by watching us. Records show that even the Detroit Police and Navy Intelligence got in on the overtime bandwagon.

Clearly, the VW and anyone driving it were under surveillance. How else would the pigs who'd squealed into the alley and jumped out of their car have known my name without first checking my ID? It was consistent with the harassment I and others in the Party had been receiving at the hands of the local police, and indicative of the police attitude and atmosphere in the country.

Sunday, the last day of the Conference, I was busy with

Skip, grilling chicken for the noon meal, when Red-haired Audrey ran up to inform us that the cops were coming across the field and through the woods to the farm in full battle gear. I ran toward the woods. Crossing over the property line from the neighboring farm and across the field were what must have been seventy-five of them--pigs in a skirmish line, dressed to kill. With the driveway guarded, they had outflanked us. I ran back to the farmhouse to warn everybody to get out of the house, assemble in the front yard, and stay cool--we were surrounded.

As fate would have it, the cop in charge of the operation was Lieutenant Fergy, a childhood chum; we had ridden the school bus together in Traverse City. He was two or three years my senior. I berated Fergy for this police action: "We are peacefully assembled, no laws are being broken here. You have no right to be here," which doesn't mean much when the guy you are talking to has seventy-five heavily-armed men backing him up.

"We have a warrant for Abe," Fergy informed me. "You produce him or we'll search for him." "He's not here," I protested, truthfully. Abe had left the night before when I had gotten busted for peeing in the alley.

By now the pigs had surrounded our group of fifty, or so, milling about on the lawn. After checking some IDs of the men, and not finding Abe, Fergy informed me they would have to search the premises. The bulk of the pigs stayed outside, looking quite stern. I escorted the pigs through the house, which was a rather old, common frame farmhouse, nothing special. A Harley Davidson was parked in the kitchen where it had been for the past six months; the gearbox was on the table and the heads were in the sink. "He's not here." The dining room held a beautiful, antique, round oak table upon which sat a Marshall amp in the preliminary stages of repair. It's back had been removed, and color-coded wires, like neon worms, squirmed from the case. "He's not here." The living room was bare, save for a couple of amp stacks, keyboards, a drum kit, and a paper mache' shark six feet long. "He's not here." On the second floor, the first two bedrooms were open and empty. Fergy and a couple of other cops and I approached the one locked door in the whole damn house. It was Hawg Tate's room, padlocked from the outside with a big brass Yale.

I could see what was fixin' to happen. "Christ he's not in there! Do you think we locked him in?" I pleaded. They just looked at me like I was confused and didn't understand. "Wait! I'll get the key," I begged, "Don't smash his door." "Don't bother," Fergy grunted, "we have a police key." With that, Fergy nodded to a Gomer Pyle pig who promptly kicked the door in. "He's not here." And, like they always do, they left when they were ready. No one arrested, no one hurt, and only one smashed door; I considered that a successful encounter with the pigs. We ate lunch and the conference was over.

* * *

With the help of a Tree Town attorney I pled not guilty and demanded a jury trial on my peeing-in-the-alley case.

The charge was only a misdemeanor, so a "petite" jury was seated; six tried and true citizens took the jury box.

The prosecutor called the arresting officer to the stand and established that the officer and his partner were on routine patrol when they spotted me urinating fifty yards down the alley. This, of course was a lie. With my back to the street in a dark alley behind the VW which was parked next to the building, it would have been impossible for anyone to see what I was doing. Indeed, they screeched into the alley already knowing I was there; why else would they have entered the alley in the first place?

I leaned over to my attorney and told him to go after the lie. He chose another tack. "Officer, was Mr. Plamondon urinating when you got to him?" "No." "How did you know he was urinating?" my lawyer continued, "I could smell it." "How much training in the smelling of urine do you have, Officer?" "None." "Did you get down on your knees, with your nose to the pavement?" "No, I just smelled it."

"Officer, are you circumcised?" The pig squirmed some and glanced at the judge. The court recorder lady smirked. "Yes," the pig answered. "Then you know what a circumcised penis looks like, is that correct?" "Yes." "Can you tell the Jury and the Court, is Mr. Plamondon circumcised?" The pig was starting to sweat a bit and feel uncomfortable. "I didn't see it that close." "But you did see," my lawyer went on. "Could you describe his penis for us, Officer?" Stammering, the pig grunted, "It looked like a tube with skin stretched over it." "Did you inspect Mr. Plamondon's penis to see if it was, in fact, his penis or a "tube with skin stretched over it?" Now I squirmed a bit, embarrassed for the cop; the court recorder was blushing quite red and trying to keep from laughing.

My attorney kept looking at the judge, hoping he would end this farce. He continued. "Officer, is there a city ordinance against passing water through a tube with skin stretched over it?" "Not to my knowledge." "Don't you wish you had checked to see if it was Mr. Plamondon's penis or a "tube with skin stretched over it?" "No."

My lawyer looked at the Judge again, as I slouched in my seat at the defense table, wishing I were invisible. I had visions of my attorney entering my penis as "People's exhibit A" with a red "Evidence" tag tied on. The recorder lady continued to blush crimson and stare at her little gray machine; the pig kept squirming and mopping his brow. The Judge seemed to relish the moment.

"Tell us, Officer, was Mr. Plamondon holding his penis daintily with two fingers or did he have a mighty grip on it with two hands?" Finally the Judge spoke up, "This case is dismissed--defendant had no criminal intent." It was over.

When we weren't in court, we were fighting for Sinclair's release. The District Court and even the Court of Appeals denied Sinclair's release on bond pending appeal. This was unheard of in Michigan jurisprudence and gained us considerable support from the wishy-washy liberals. We continued organizing fundraising benefits, organizing WPP Chapters, printing and distributing The Sun, giving speaking presentations, and making phone calls by the hundreds to important and not-so important people.

* * *

While Chairman Sinclair was in Jackson Prison, a White Panther contingent went to the Woodstock Music Festival to build political support and raise money for his defense.

For me, Woodstock was a four-day out-of-body-experience brought on by the ingestion of several hits of acid (a day), that culminated in the arrest of Leni Sinclair (Sunny was with her Grandmother), The Prez, a Party member from Ohio, and myself.

Arraignments had been made with one of the promoters to give us "all access passes" so we could hobnob with the musicians and their agents and other music biz big-shots and push information about Sinclair's pot case. One of the promoters gave Leni a verbal commitment; we would be able to address the crowd from the stage and pass donation buckets during the concert.

Before leaving Ann Arbor, we had rented a nine-passenger U-Haul van, removed the seats, and loaded it up with camping gear, several folding tables and chairs, T-shirts, posters, booklets, brochures, newspapers, and other goodies to sell and give away at a booth we expected to set up to advertise Sinclair's case.

I don't remember taking my first hit of acid, but I do remember being back stage with Abbie Hoffman marveling at the construction of the stage. Built with what looked like half an acre of plywood framed on a forest of large telephone poles, three stories off the ground and was equipped with an elevator! On the stage proper was another, smaller stage that rotated, rolling on pneumatic lawn tractor wheels so that while one act was performing another was setting up on the back of the stage, behind a curtain. When the first act was over, the stage would rotate and another act was set and ready to go. This small town boy had never seen anything like this before. I was high on LSD-25 and spellbound.

In my altered state, I obsessed over mechanical fasteners, structural connections, and construction principles. I made mental notes: 5/8 lag bolts attaching a 1/4 inch steel bracket holding 4x12 beams that carry 16-2x10s...that sort of thing.

Earlier, Leni had asked me to make the announcement about Sinclair's case from the stage, but I was too spaced out. Abbie, though he was blasted too, had a bigger reputation than I did anyway, so we drafted him to do it. When I walked out to center stage with Abbie and saw 500,000 people stretching from the front, up the hill, and all the way to the horizon, my spirit left my body and hovered high above, floating as I watched the activity below.

Chip Monk was the stage manager. I remember Abbie and I talking to him about the announcement. He gave us one minute before The Who's set was to begin. The Who were already on stage, plugging in their guitars and such when Abbie made a mad dash for the center microphone: "JOHN SINCLAIR IS IN PRISON FOR 10 YEARS FOR DOING WHAT YOU ARE DOING RIGHT NOW...SMOKING JOINTS!" he yelled into the mic. Uninformed about our announcement, Pete Townsend, guitar wizard of The Who, thought Abbie was a lunatic and smashed him in the back of the head with his guitar like a soldier uses a rifle butt to crush the skull of his enemy. Abbie and I beat it out of there, not quite knowing what had just happened. I seemed to be suspended above it all watching.

My next memory is of helping erect a large circus type tent, one of many flown into the backstage area by National Guard helicopters. Abbie and I organized and set up the John Sinclair Memorial Bad Trip Tent for the hundreds of festival goers who were in the throes of a bad acid experience. Inside the tent, I set up dozens of army cots. I remember trying to comfort writhing, disorientated kids but when I spoke, only colors came out of my mouth, shades of orange and red mostly. I was, moreover, still hovering above, watching this all happening to myself and other people.

I remember the clouds opening and rain of biblical proportions as Jimi Hendrix landed by helicopter backstage, and his rushing to one of many trailer/dressing rooms and emerging a short time later. He seemed a smallish sort of cat in his shiny yellow outfit and long scarf. I remember thinking--he looks like a sissy, but he's still my guitar hero and high priest.

Leni, standing in the rain and mud with strands of hair washed over her tired face, was exhausted, crying, and looking like a flood victim or war refugee. She had two, brand new, very shiny, thirty gallon, galvanized garbage cans she wanted me to pass through the crowd to collect money for Sinclair's defense. I could not even look at the cans, they shined so. With my view from above they looked like luminescent beacons in a vast swamp of brown mud speckled with soggy pastel blankets. I hovered above, watching as a guy that looked like me--that was me--told Leni I could not do it. I could not pass the shiny cans through the audience. She begged and pleaded, and her red eyes, with dark bags beneath them, burned holes in my soul, but I could not help. She reminded me of my responsibility to the Party and to the Chairman. I could only say, "Leni, I'm almost not here--I float around."

* * *

When it was over we drove south out of Woodstock. When we hit the New Jersey state line there was a state police roadblock. Cars and vans full of hippies and young people were stopped without probable cause and searched, harassed, and sometimes arrested.

In our case, the pigs ordered us out of the van and began their search. On the dash was my hunting knife with a four-inch blade; we had been camping after all. I was arrested for "possession of a deadly weapon" and a further cursory search of the van was completed. They found some pot and some hash and arrested the rest of my group.

I found this next part suspicious. The U-Haul Corporation had a platform truck at the roadblock; once the four of us were placed in pig cars, they winched the van onto the platform truck and followed us to the Hackensack, New Jersey, County Jail. I had to wonder why U-Haul conveniently had a pickup vehicle on site. I didn't notice other towing services on standby. I suspect the Feds had a description and license of our vehicle and placed the proverbial "All Points Bulletin" to state and local police. I suspect that once our vehicle was spotted, they made arrangements to apprehend us at the next roadblock. Perhaps this is paranoid raving or an attempt at self-aggrandizement--perhaps not.

We were all released from jail with our charges pending. Leni, who was three months pregnant, contacted the Party in Ann Arbor who contacted people at Prentiss Hall Publishing House (which had recently signed a contract with Sinclair for his book GUITAR ARMY); they posted Leni's bond and she returned home. She made some calls and I made bond. I went back to New York City and contacted Abbie and Rubin who got the money together to get The Prez and the young Party member from Ohio out. The Prez, barely two months pregnant, had a miscarriage while incarcerated. I didn't even know she was pregnant--fucking pigs!

*   *   *

Less than a month later, Ken Kelley, who was now Minister of Information for the Party, and I traveled to Chicago to attend an historic meeting of The Young Lords, The Young Patriots, the Black Panther Party, and the White Panther Party. We were to discuss how we could support each other's struggles. Kelley and I were to put forward several fundamental ideas; we could sell and distribute each other's newspapers, exchange personnel from time to time, publicize and support each other's events, vigorously support each other's political prisoners, and arrange to have our legal teams cooperate when feasible.

The headquarters of the Young Lords, where the meeting was held, was a defunct, second-floor bowling alley, above a Mexican restaurant on Rush Street, I believe. The Chicago Red Squad had the building under surveillance, so when the meeting was over each group left at five minute intervals so as not to arouse suspicion. Kelly and I left when told to. We had parked on a side street, off Rush, so our car wouldn't be right in front of the building.

Walking, we made it to the corner, turned right and had just reached our car when a black, unmarked car sped around the corner, jumped the curb and came to a screeching halt just in front of us. Four rip-snortin' pigs jumped out and had me slammed to the ground before I knew what hit me. Kelly was similarly treated. In frisking us they found a pocketknife and a joint on me. Kelly was not charged and was released. I was charged with possession of weed and carrying a concealed weapon. Now I had another 10-20 years hanging over my head--I had the Traverse City weed case, the Hackensack hash and weapons case, and now the Chicago weed and weapons case--would it never end?

Kelley made a call to Abe at The Chicago Seed, the Windy City's only underground newspaper. They put up $1,500 and I was released on bond.

*   *   *

The legal strategy developed by the Central Committee, the legal team, and myself regarding my legal cases, called for postponements or delays by any legal means possible.

Whenever I had a court date, the lawyers filed an avalanche of motions challenging every aspect of the legal process: the process by which evidence had been gathered, the sanity of witnesses, the prejudice of the Judge, and the process by which a jury is picked. We asked for postponements because of work or travel conflicts, illness, anything to put it off until we could get Sinclair out.

All energy and resources remained on Sinclair's appeal. If we could gain a victory in his case we would be in a better position, politically and economically, to fight my mounting legal troubles.

We had a court appearance on October 6th in Hackensack for a preliminary exam on the weapons and hash case. Leni, The Prez, the young cat from Ohio, and I made the trip. The National Lawyers Guild, the most righteous legal outfit in the country, came to our aid. The Guild arranged for a lawyer from New Jersey to represent us during the hearing.

As the proceedings started, the prosecution called its first witness--the arresting officer. The court was informed that the officer had been in a fatal car crash just the week before and was dead. Good! I thought at the time, it serves the son-of-a-bitch right. Today, being somewhat more mature and less angry, I have sympathy for the family and friends of the lost officer. But at the time the son-of-a-bitch was trying to put me and my loved ones in prison. To have love or respect for him then would have been impossible.

The court refused to dismiss the case, even though the principal witness was dead. We returned to Ann Arbor in the wee hours of the morning on the 7th of October, 1969.

Chapter Nine

ONLY MOMENTS TO GO...! 1969/70

DS came bounding down the stairs two-at-a-time, "You've been indicted for the CIA bombing!" he shouted over the clickity-clack of the press, his blue eyes wide in real fear.

I was in the basement of 1520 Hill on the morning of October 7th, printing flyers announcing a benefit poetry reading by nationally known poets Allen Ginsberg and Donald Hall. Our student front organization at the university had secured beautiful and classy Hill Auditorium and this event promised to raise some serious money for Sinclair's legal team, as well as educate large numbers of people about the injustice done to Sinclair at the hands of the legal/political machine of Michigan. With a "headliner" such as Ginsberg, local TV, radio, and print media were eager to do interviews, so we knew our message would carry to the largest possible audience. I was eager to get the material printed so our rather sophisticated media machine could crank into operation.

Hearing the word "indicted," I lunged to turn off the press and stood dumbfounded. DS took a deep breath, trying to calm himself. "I just heard on WABX--a federal grand jury indicted you, Sinclair, and Forest for conspiracy to bomb the CIA office a year ago! You're charged with doing the actual bombing!"

"Indicted? How did I get indicted? Indicted?" I repeated over and over. Flabbergasted, I repeated the question. "Indicted? Who even knew there was a grand jury? I've got to get out of here--they probably have the house surrounded!"

DS and I stood looking at each other. I winced, anticipating the sound of glass shattering, door jambs splintering, expecting, in the next instant, to hear police voices and the smell of tear gas. I involuntarily ducked my head, wincing again, as if I could feel the wind of the near misses and the cartoon sound of bullets ricocheting off the fieldstone walls in the basement of that old dusty Victorian.

The Prez came running down the stairs; she'd already heard the news. "We've got to get you out of here! The kids are here! DS! Go borrow Elsie's car!" DS took off running.

Elsie was Sinclair and DS's mom, who had moved into our Ann Arbor neighborhood to be closer to her grandchildren. She owned a late model Buick and would often lend it to one or the other of her sons.

The Prez talked to me but I could hardly concentrate, expecting in the next breath to hear the nightmarish sound of police boots running overhead, the crackle of radio traffic. "You stay down here," she said. "I'll go get some money and figure out where to take you, now just stay here!" she pleaded again as she dashed off.

"Get me a gun!" I yelled as The Prez disappeared up the steps. I had a nice .38 Special with a four-inch barrel stolen from a pig along with his baton and clear plastic shield during the street fighting in DC the previous summer, when the YIPPIES! had tried to levitate the Pentagon. I flinched again as visions of pig-snouted cops, in riot gear, with guns blazing, filled my head.

I tried to focus on what had gone wrong--how could I be indicted for bombing the CIA? Rock-n-Roll Rita and I were each other's alibi, and she hadn't been indicted. Just what sort of conspiracy was the government building against me? And

Sinclair and Forest? How did they fit into this? Sinclair was in prison and Forest was in the hospital with a shattered leg suffered in a motorcycle accident. I never conspired with either to bomb anything.

I could only believe it was a frame-up. I knew the government had no evidence against me. I had an alibi. Whatever evidence they used to get the indictment must have been fabricated. My mind was in a whirl.

Our old basement was a hunched and rambling space. In addition to offices, print and layout rooms, and Leni's darkroom, there was a laundry room, furnace room and several remote cubbyholes and stashed away corners where mattresses had been laid on the floor for the traveling hippies that would crash at 1520 from time to time. I hid in one of them. I should have told The Prez to get the kids out of the house, I thought as I waited for the inevitable battle to begin.

The Prez returned. "*The Michigan Daily* called--it's on the wire service--they want a quote. Here's $200. I packed your .38 and a box of shells, a Red Book, and some clothes. DS is coming with the Buick, we'll take the back-seat out, he'll pull up to the back door, you run out, lay on the floor and we'll cover you with a blanket."

Cover me with a blanket? That's clever, I thought as I loaded the .38.

The Prez could be an airhead when she wanted to be and was from time to time, especially when she was into her astrology and witchery and other primitive metaphysical practices. But she could also be a strong, decisive, clear-thinking woman; she could take charge and did: that was one of the reasons I loved and admired her.

1520 Hill had a walkout basement that opened to the back of the house and onto a circle drive. DS drove up. I made a dash for the car, dove onto the floor, and was covered with a very thin wool blanket, the kind you might take on a July picnic, Scottish plaid--not really suitable for a scaredy-cat trying to hide from the FBI.

DS took the wheel with The Prez beside him. He whipped out of our drive onto Hill--right turn on Washtenaw--to the Unitarian Church parking lot--left, through the lot, onto the street behind--then a U-turn in a driveway. All of us had used this maneuver in the past to avoid being tailed. DS was certain we were not followed. Then onto the expressway, north out of Ann Arbor. I was calmer now; moving and action helped, though my mind was racing. On we went, with me huddled under the blanket and the Prez giving me instructions, "Don't call the houses. Don't tell anyone who you are. Leave your phone book so the pigs don't get it if you get caught. Don't do ANYTHING! Sit tight 'til we come for you."

The Prez knew a couple of spaced-out Hare Krishna cadets who lived in a commune on a farm, twenty minutes north of town. The Krishnas said I could hide out there, but had to be gone by morning.

I was confined to an upstairs bedroom in the old farmhouse. They didn't want my karma to leave traces in their holy space. I could see the gravel road in both directions from my upstairs window, which helped ease my nerves. If I saw pigs coming, I could at least make a run for it to the woods, the familiar hiding place of my youth. The Prez cut my hair, I shaved my face clean.

By now it was about noon. I kept wondering--Why hadn't I been captured? Why did the Feds release the indictment to the press before they had me in custody? Why did they let me get away? Were they that inept? Or did they have some evil trap I was falling into? Was my flight getting me into something more than I bargained for or could handle? Were they letting me create the kind of scenario that would justify killing me?

DS and The Prez left me at the farm, promising to return after dark and move me to a longer-term hiding spot.

I spent my time fretting over my predicament, realizing that I could give myself up at any time. But it seemed better, since I was still at large, to remain that way. This bombing and conspiracy charge certainly didn't help Sinclair's defense team's efforts to get him released on bond pending his appeal. But on the other hand, it would significantly raise our profile and broaden our support among the Left, who had previously dismissed us as cultural clowns without a serious understanding of the seriousness of a serious revolution. Seriously. Even though, through our newspapers, radio shows, and work with the MC5 we touched and influenced tens of thousands of teenagers on a monthly basis.

For the past seven months, all energy and effort had been directed toward building support for Sinclair. Our lawyers were frazzled; the entire Central Staff of the Party was running on fumes. Our economic situation, as always, was in danger of imminent collapse. Another court case now would put us under for sure. Better I remain underground and become a poster boy of resistance; this might help our CIA case become a cause celebre, which, I must say, held a certain attraction over going to jail.

It was clear to me that "the law" was out to get me. I had the TC pot case (20-life), I had the Hackensack hash case (10-20), I had the CCW and pot case in Chicago (10-20), as well as a misdemeanor for "corrupting the morals of youth" in Ann Arbor which stemmed from distribution of our newspaper. And now this.

A part of me was thrilled. Imagine me, a little 'ole high school dropout from little 'ole Traverse City with the whole fucking FBI looking for me. That had to count for something. I felt like I had arrived, and by extension, The White Panther Party had arrived. I judged an organization's qualifications by the numbers of people it educated and organized, by the revolutionary qualities of its analysis, by who its enemies were, and by the level of harassment and repression directed toward it by the power structure. The wrath of the rabid right-wing government was unleashed against us--we must be doing something right. I was, and am, tremendously proud to have been considered an enemy of the State during those times.

It was after midnight before DS and The Prez returned bringing newspapers and reports of TV and radio coverage. The print media was reporting that there was an unindicted co-conspirator. That could mean only one thing: an informer or snitch of some sort, an agent provocateur even. The Detroit News was reporting that the unindicted co-conspirator was David Valler, known on the streets of Detroit as "President Dave" since he ran for President in 1968.

I remember him as a kind of pimply, stringy-haired hippie, who, besides running for President, an act he took seriously--which made me question his mental stability--made quite a name for himself in the Warren Forest community around Wayne State by blowing up several police cars, a police station, and a draft board. He was the kind of dude people knew by reputation, I knew who he was, but I had never even spoken to him.

I didn't know the details of the conspiracy between the FBI and Valler. But I knew how the scenario worked: The pigs bust some jerk on unrelated charges; in Valler's case, a month or so earlier, he had been arrested by Detroit Police with twenty-five pounds of weed. We knew that; it had been reported in all the papers. It must have been at that time that the pigs started working on him, the way they'd done in a thousand cases before.

Once arrested, the pigs began questioning and harassing Valler, a scared kid, for two or three hours every day for three weeks maybe. I can hear the tough cop now---telling Valler stories about how, when he gets to prison, some big bad bogeyman will buy him and make him his bitch, and he'll spend the next twenty years washing the bogeyman's underwear and getting fucked in the ass, until the bogeyman tires of him and sells him to another bogeyman.

Then the soft cop speaks up, the one with long hair, side-burns and a mustache, wearing bell-bottoms and a paisley shirt, open at the neck. He tells Valler that if he cooperates they can help him, maybe get him sent to a youth prison, or maybe even probation. The would-be stoolie is scared and wants out from under. He'll cooperate, whatever that means.

I could just see it. "So," the tough cop might say to Valler, "isn't it true you talked to Sinclair, Plamondon, and Forest about bombing government buildings?" Valler looks around for assurance, the soft cop nods slightly. "Yes," Valler mumbles. "And isn't it true," the hard cop says while looking at a sheaf of papers, "that you gave Plamondon a quantity of dynamite?" Unsure, Valler stammers, "Yes." Then the soft cop jumps in, "How much dynamite did you give him Dave?" "I don't remember," Valler answers. "Come on Dave, we're trying to help you, was it twenty sticks--thirty sticks?" "Yeah, twenty or thirty," Valler answers hopefully. "Which is it, twenty or thirty, was it thirty, Dave? Did you give him thirty sticks?" the kindly cop asks. "Yes, it was thirty," Valler answers. He's getting the hang of it. "What kind of dynamite was it Dave?" the soft cop asks. "I don't remember," Valler responds. "Was it Hercules powder, 60% nitro, Dave?" the soft cop prods. "Yes, 60% nitro," Valler answers.

Now the tough cop pipes up: "And isn't it true that Plamondon told you he placed a bomb at the CIA office in Ann Arbor?" "Yes," Valler squeaks, wanting to please his captors. The pigs go over it time and again until Valler can't separate truth from fiction. He's in so deep there is no turning back.

According to the newspapers, the government's whole case rested on Valler. We'd deal with him later. Meanwhile I laid low at the Holy Cow Krishna Farm while The Prez and DS briefed me on preparations and protocol of going underground:

First, only under conditions of imminent death or actual arrest was I to call Headquarters. (I broke this rule only once, events will reveal).

Second, I could never, under any circumstances, tell the people hiding me who I was or that I was wanted. (I broke this rule several times, but felt it was necessary given the immediate conditions).

A mail drop was set up with a local attorney who had done some light legal lifting for us in the past and was a committed, personal friend of The Prez's.

I was given a phone number, written vertically, in a column, with a line drawn underneath, as if it were a list of numbers to be added up, so as to defy detection by the pigs if or when I ever got caught. The number was to a pay phone in East Quad, a U of M dorm only three blocks from Headquarters. I could call the number on prearranged dates and times.

We left The Holy Cow Commune and drove all night, arriving in Yellow Springs, Ohio at dawn. DS and The Prez returned to Ann Arbor in the Buick, promising to return after they'd set up some underground connections. I hid out for about ten days with a communist janitor at the local college. I knew him from Detroit where he was a neighborly handyman on the block, fixing broken windows and doors and porches that sagged drunkenly on the old houses of the neighborhood.

Finally, after I spent more than a week resting, reading, and looking for trilobites in a nearby creek bed, The Prez and DS returned with a plan. Trilobites are not generally found in Michigan since the land was scraped, scoured and sculpted by the glaciers and the floods of the melt waters. Ohio was unfamiliar geology, with older, more sedate spirits who moved slowly and were easy to see.

The Prez and DS would take me to Cincinnati where I would catch a plane to San Francisco, take a bus downtown, and call Grimshaw. Grimshaw was to hook me up with people in Berkeley who would transport me to a long-term hiding place. I was to use the name Lou Fife until I made connections with people in San Francisco who could supply me with ID; at this point I had none, leaving my life as Larry "Pun" Plamondon behind me in Tree Town.

It all sounded good as we rode through the night to the Cinci airport, which is actually across the river in Kentucky. After warm hugs from DS, uncertain kisses from The Prez and stern warnings not to call or write the house, they dropped me off at the departure concourse. I was on my own.

I wore short hair with a clean-shaven face, a white shirt with a clip-on tie, permanent press tan slacks and wing-tipped shoes. I felt like a dork and looked like a used appliance salesman who could barely make ends meet.

Everyone in the airport that morning looked like an FBI agent to me--the ticket agents, baggage handlers, the janitor with the mop, the guy in the suit reading a magazine at the newsstand. I noticed two uniformed sheriff deputies at the Hertz counter. I was scared spitless and headed for the bar.

The early morning low-angled sunlight dissolved the blue-green neon of the tavern's interior; combined with the damp chill of air conditioning, the place gave me the feeling of being in a well-lit fish tank. I felt better here--familiar territory. I sat facing the door and sucked down two or three drafts.

My plane was late, I arrived in San Francisco after dark, took the bus to the Greyhound station downtown as instructed, and called Grimshaw from a pay phone at the number given me by DS before he left.

At that time, Grimshaw was the art director and layout/design genius of THE BERKELEY TRIBE. THE TRIBE, like its predecessor, The Berkeley Barb, was in the vanguard of the underground press movement and was a newspaper of national influence. Moreover, it was a bedrock institution of the New Left/counter-culture in Berkeley. The TRIBE was not organizationally connected to the WPP, though we had personal relationships with several of the staff.

You will remember that Grimshaw fled Ann Arbor a year before, on the same "sale-of-reefer" warrant from TC that had cost me eighty-four days in jail. His case, like mine, was still hanging over his head.

The number DS gave me was to a large commercial printing plant, the printer for the TRIBE. It was printing day and Grimshaw babysat the paper through the whole process--checking the colors, the artwork, and a million other details. When the phone rang and I asked for Grimshaw, I could hear the receptionist over the plant loudspeaker system "a Mr. Fife for mister Grimshaw--a Mr. Fife for Mr. Grimshaw--line two." I was certain this phone wasn't tapped.

Grimshaw didn't seem too bent out of shape about my having been charged with the CIA bombing or my being on the lam; his girl friend was not so laid back, however. I spent the night on their couch and awoke to Judy hollerin' "Get him out of here! Now we've got to move again!"

Grimshaw made some calls and then took me to a militant ecologist's house in the Berkeley Hills. The poop on this cat was that he had been blowing up electric transmission towers that belonged to Pacific Gas and Electric, on and off, for several years. He and his woman were kind of edgy too.

I maintained my anonymity for the three or four days I stayed with them--having long discussions about whether socialism, or communism, or anarchy would best preserve the earth--certainly capitalism was on a path of rape and destruction.

I was not in control; I had to do as I was told. I just stayed put until I was instructed to move. The militant ecologist came to me with the next part of the plan. He was to drop me at a certain corner in the Tenderloin District of San Francisco. From there I was to go to a particular address on a particular street, and when I rang the bell, Baretta of the UAW/MF was suppose to greet me with the next piece to the puzzle/plan.

It sounds easy now, but at the time, I was stressed-out. In the week or so that I had been running, the Underground Press was pushing the story, and the mainstream media was featuring it across the country. I acted the stoic, punished revolutionary; yet inside, I trembled in fear of common strangers.

I wasn't so much afraid of getting caught by the police on a chance sighting--that was unlikely, given my recent make-over. What terrified me was being betrayed or left stranded. Or being dropped off on a strange street corner with phony instructions--that would certainly complicate my life and sanity, already balanced on a razor's edge.

But what could I do? Say, "No, I don't like this plan. Come up with another one." Realistically, I had no choices. I was at the mercy of my friends--or my enemies.

The Tenderloin was a low-class, run-down section of San Francisco. The militant ecologist stopped at the corner, gave me the street address, shook my hand, said "Power to the People!" and split.

I felt impending doom. Alone, at night, on the wet streets of San Francisco, I would not have been surprised to see pig cars approaching from every direction, helicopters overhead, shining their giant spotlights on me. I would not have been surprised to feel a jolt, hear a rifle crack, feel myself spinning on the ground, like a balloon released. I would not have been surprised, if, when I rang the bell, the door were opened by a casually dressed agent of the FBI: "You're under arrest."

I walked down the street and found the number, then crossed over and up the stoop steps and rang the bell. "Baretta!" I said as soon as he opened the door. We hugged and he said, "Follow me."

I followed him down a long dirty hall with bags of garbage, backpacks, skateboards, a bike, and ladder littering the way. The first room off the hall was the front parlor, overlooking the street. I could see tapestries on the walls and ceiling and tan paisley bedspreads covering the windows. The room was candle lit and glowed in muted red/orange quartertones that illuminated the huddled shapes on pillows and mattresses Whiffs of reefer and jasmine wafted from the room.

We moved down the hall, past the dining room filled with a drum kit, guitars, and amps; posters of Stalin, Marx, Engle's, Huey P Newton, and wild-haired Albert Einstein stared down from the walls.

Once in the kitchen, Baretta handed me a manila envelope with a draft card, a California driver's license (no picture) and a Social Security card, all in the same name, all unaltered. "Who did you have to kill to get these?" I asked, only half joking. "You don't need to know," Baretta answered. "Are they stolen or manufactured?" I wanted to know. He only scowled at me and nodded his head to the door.

I followed him out the back door and down the steps to a backyard not much bigger than a postage stamp. All the houses on this block had identical back yards, all separated by a six-foot, wooden, Tom Sawyer-type fence. Baretta knew the folks in the house behind him, and had made certain arrangements.

On prepositioned ladders, we climbed into the back yard of the backdoor neighbors and proceeded up their back steps through their back door, down their identical hall, out their front door, down their steps, and into a waiting VW bug. We were out of there, certain we were not followed.

I liked these types of elusive maneuvers--it meant that for a certain amount of time, anyway, I was safe. I knew that as we drove away in the VW, only the people with me knew where I was; I could relax a bit.

Baretta took me to Marin County, just north of San Francisco. He explained that he had talked to The Prez and that arrangements for a long-term hideout were yet to be completed; I would have to lay low in temporary locations for a while longer. I didn't want to hear this--but I had no choice.

Barbara Sabbeth was an Ann Arbor girl who lived with her man in a country house with a gazebo out back, near a creek. She was a poet, musician, and radio personality I knew from back home. I could hide in her gazebo as long as I needed to; the catch was that I must absolutely not let her husband see me. I snuck into the gazebo and kept out of sight.

I spent two nerve-wracking weeks in the gazebo--the November rain seemed endless, and slugs with their slim trails were everywhere. I ate cold canned goods with the tops worried off like a cartoon hobo under a train trestle and spent the rest of my time reading a stack of moldy Good Housekeeping magazines that were stored there. I pondered anxiously day and night about my future. There was still no plausible explanation as to why the Feds released news of my indictment to the press before they had me in custody. I worried that they might somehow be tracking me as I led them to stops on this underground network. God! Where am I going to hide 'til we get it together to fight this case? I kept fretting over and over.

One night, in the pouring rain, I had a visitor. He wore an old-fashioned gabardine overcoat with the collar flipped up. On his head was a gray, cloth hat with furry earflaps hanging down and a fur brim flipped up, the kind of hat you'd expect to see on a North Dakota state trooper in January. I didn't recognize him as I answered his tap on the gazebo's door. I let him in, and we talked for several minutes before he took his hat off--it was Thorazene! This Ann Arbor anarchist and friend from the street had come to take me to a long-term hiding place--the mountains of northern California.

Chapter Ten

BLACK BEAR AND BUFFALO--'69-'70

Black Bear Ranch (BBR) is an intentional community formed in 1968 by a group of Diggers, hippies, beatniks, outlaws, free thinkers, revolutionaries, and visionaries of many descriptions. Located deep in the Salmon Mountains in northern California, on the upper, narrow end of a small hidden valley, with an even smaller valley coming in from the east, it is as remote a place as one can find in the Golden State.

Thorazene and I arrived in the dead of night under a Ramadan moon. I could see frost forming on the rusted metal roofs of several outbuildings and moonlight reflecting off a small mountain stream that skirted a tiny settlement. Thorazene led me up a groaning stairway to the hayloft of an old livery stable, lit with kerosene lamps and kept cozy warm with a little barrel stove.

The hayloft was home to Diane DiPrima, her lover Grant, and, as I recall, two of her small children. Ten years older than I, she seemed like an experienced older sister or worldly aunt. Peace, serenity, humor, and joy surrounded her. Diane was, and is, a woman of stellar reputation as poet, activist, and healer of earth and humans. It has been said that she was the most significant and influential woman of the Beat movement. She founded Poet's Press, which published the work of many new avant-garde writers of the time. She co-founded the New York Poet's Theater. She married black poet LeRoi Jones, now known as Amiri Baraka, gave birth to his daughter, and edited The Floating Bear, a literary newsletter

. Though I had never met her, the year before my coming to BBR, while I was still aboveground, she graciously gave me, through phone conversations, permission to publish a collection of her poems under the title Revolutionary Letters. We sold her book of poems as part of the fundraising effort for Sinclair's legal defense against the Michigan marijuana laws.

Grant, her lover, was a close friend of Thorazene's, both being members of a "anarchist affinity group" (their term) in Ann Arbor who called themselves The Liberty Street Gang.

Thorazene left the next morning to return to Tree Town, and I was left in a new community. Diane and Grant knew about my legal situation; there was one other at the ranch they informed.

I call him "the Whaler." He was one of the original founders of BBR and its de facto leader. He was a bearded, aged, beatnik stevedore from the docks of San Francisco, a twinkly-eyed prankster with connections to the Diggers, a San Francisco group who gleaned, connived, and scrounged food and clothing for the needy--mostly hippies. Diane and I went to visit him in The Big House (TBH), a two-story, rundown frame dwelling, one of millions sold as kits by Sears Roebuck throughout the country until WWII. We told him I was wanted by the Feds but not my real name or the charges against me. Both he and Diane wanted it that way.

The Whaler was always talking history. He told me that Mr. Daggett, who was lieutenant governor of California during the gold rush, had founded BBR. The story goes that Daggett, with the free labor of Chinese coolies, built a twelve-mile road through precarious mountain terrain from the ranch to the nearest town. His hope was that Black Bear would become a small town that would supply the local gold miners who had scattered claims throughout the mountains on streams similar to the one that ran through the ranch. The last mine played out in 1928, and the ranch remained abandoned until elements of The Diggers scraped together the money to buy it in early 1968.

On one side of the dirt road bisecting the ranch was the barn/livery and mountain stream. On the other was the big house and a long-collapsed (earthquake?), white brick post office as well as the old general store, identical to those in Western movies: a long, low building, sitting high above the street, with a wooden sidewalk covered by a tin roof. The general store was in reasonably sound repair and was being used as a children's play palace and school.

Scattered down the valley and up the mountainside were individual homes and hovels, a tepee or two, several hippie-engineered structures made of tin roofing, plywood, and logs. A few camped in tents, one guy lived in the rusting hulk of a '55 Ford station wagon. There were several small conventional cabins with wood-shake roofs. The predominant dwellings were newly built geodesic domes made of plywood and covered in wooden shakes. In all, some sixty people, fifteen of them dirty-faced, snot-nosed, hippie kids, made BBR their home.

I was there only a couple of days when suddenly the children came running down the rutted road shouting, "The pigs are coming! The pigs are coming!"

How could this be? I thought. Outside the ranch, no one but Thorazene and The Prez know I'm here. Without phones or electricity, I knew no one from BB had tipped off the pigs. I ran behind The Big House and up the mountainside, which was covered in mature ponderosa pine. Several hundred yards up the mountain I stopped and found a spot where I could see the road and ranch below through the trees.

Soon three unmarked pig cars appeared on the upper end of the drive just where it came out of the timber. By now twenty or more hippies had come out of The Big House, the children's play palace and several dwellings from up the mountain and down the valley. The three cars stopped just in front of the bar/livery and The Big House.

From a distance I could see eight suits and ties get out of their cars; they were immediately surrounded by the hippie hoard. I thought it odd that they were in suits. I knew they would never catch me dressed like that in this terrain. I also noticed that the hippie hoard was made up mostly of women and children. *Where are the men?* I wondered.

Then I heard--"crunch, crunch, crunch." Then the sound stopped. "Crunch, crunch, crunch." I heard it again. Then it stopped again. Then, "Crunch. Crunch. Crunch." Someone was coming toward me, but higher up the mountain. "Crunch, crunch, crunch." I heard it again.

Of course, I thought, *the plainclothes are only a decoy. The real threat is up here. They probably have the whole ranch surrounded.* As quietly as I could, I moved away from the sound. I found an old burnt-out snag of a ponderosa, broken off about fifty feet up, and scarred by fire, a relic of a previous forest fire or lightening strike. A missing chunk of stump exposed the hollow inside, which was large enough to crawl into. I wormed my way in, hunkered down, and held my breath.

"Crunch, crunch, crunch." Whoever was walking would pass just above me. I waited until the steps began to fade before I hazarded a look. There was "Carolina!"

In the few days I'd been at BBR I had spent some time with him. He was a draft dodger from one of the Carolinas and seemed to be in charge of the garden. He had told me he designed and built the quarter-mile aqueduct at the ranch, which carried water from up the mountain to a large tank behind TBH.

I hailed him and we sat watching the scene below. He told me he had always been an oddball. He hated the people back home who tormented him because of his offbeat ways. At sixteen he had run away from home and walked the entire length of the Appalachian Trail, alone. Then he moved to Mexico and lived with a tribe of Indians for years. Later he showed me photos of an aqueduct two-miles long that he designed and helped build across the desert floor to the Indian village.

He told me the reason I could see no men down below was that most men at the ranch were wanted by the law for one reason or another and made themselves scarce whenever the authorities showed up. We stayed hidden until we saw the pigs mount up and begin backing up the road surrounded by a clutch of hippie chicks who walked along with the cars as they moved, like a funeral cortege walking to a slow dirge.

This seemed odd, too, since the ranch was the only flat ground suitable for turning a vehicle around. Once the cars backed into the forest they would be unable to turn around and so would have to back all the way up the mountain two-track, some three miles to the summit.

Carolina and I waited a suitable time after the pig cars had gone and saw other males beginning to appear before we returned to the drive below where everyone was gathering. Come to find out, the visitors were not pigs at all but local health department officials who wanted to count the number of people and outhouses, check the water quality, and that sort of thing.

The hippie women held their ground however. They insisted that without a warrant or court order, the inspectors were not allowed on the property. In fact, the women would not even let them turn their vehicles around, since leaving the road would require their driving on ranch property.

So the women escorted the cars, as they backed up the drive and into the woods, where they knew the officials would not be able to turn around and so would be forced to drive in reverse the three miles up the mountain to the pass.

I spent my time at BBR fixing and maintaining the aqueduct, as well as digging an outhouse, a most difficult task in the Sierras. I helped build several domes and shot a mule deer or two; on those nights we would poach venison from the back of the ranch pick-up truck. We called it "government beef."

I also built a meat smoker out of an old refrigerator and set it up on the far end of the smaller valley which came in from the east, far enough away so that if bears came for the meat they would be unlikely to encounter humans. Three times a day I'd check on the smoking meat. I still had the .38 Special and while there, would pop off a few rounds just to keep my eye tuned.

One day, as I followed the path through the meadow and into the woods toward the smoker, I saw a massive black bear tip over the smoking fridge full of meat and feast heartily on the venison inside. The bruin was sitting on his haunches with his back to me gobbling the goodies as I ran back to the ranch.

I found John building a dome for his wife and family. He had built two domes, side by side, and connected them with a wide arched hallway. The connector room served as a kitchen, dining and family room. One dome was for the kids to sleep and play in and the other was living and sleeping space for the parents; everyone came together in the middle. Very clever.

John and I returned to the smoker at a fast trot. The bear was still seated, chowing down. Without a moment's hesitation, John took the .38 and walked briskly right up behind the bear, and with the pistol just inches from it's head, blew a hole the size of my fist through the bear's noggin.

We gutted and skinned the bear, hanging the skin in a nearby tree; we dumped the innards down a mine shaft a mile from the ranch. We set up the smoker again, marinated and smoked some of the bear meat and what was left of the venison, and cooked up the rest. The bear meat was too strong and gamy to eat so we ended up tossing the rest down the mine as well, hoping the mountain lions that traversed the area would find it.

Occasionally a ranch resident would "pan" the creek for gold, never finding a nugget the size of a tooth filling, but finding a tad of dust, enough to barter with a dentist over in Etna, thirty miles and three major mountain passes away. He provided dental service in exchange for gold.

I made the trip to Etna once--four adults jammed into the cab of an old Dodge Power Wagon pick-up truck, still branded with the fading paint of the C&O Railroad, the Chessie cat asleep on the door. Another adult, a passel of kids and I huddled in the back for the two-hour drive.

Etna was a beautiful town, old by California standards, dating from the gold rush. There was no LA architecture here, just weathered-wood buildings and storefronts with large, single-pane windows grinning onto wooden sidewalks.

The town had a sizeable Chinese-American population, the offspring of immigrant coolies who built the railroads on desperation pay. There were a goodly number of Chinese restaurants, laundries, food stores and barbershops that looked like they had been there for more than a hundred years.

The Whaler and I went to an old-time saloon with creaking, worn, wooden floors and a massive hand-carved walnut back-bar. The large bevel-edged mirrors gave a faded, shape-shifting reflection where the quicksilver was peeling off the backs. This all came over the mountains by horse and wagon in 1851, according to The Whaler.

I loved being at BBR. I loved the people who were every bit as energetic, creative, and idealistic as my friends and loved ones back in Ann Arbor and Detroit. And, they liked me. I liked my new name: "Robert Lansing Douglas," condensed to the macho, "Lance."

I even had a girlfriend, sort of. She was a sweet little hippie girl from LA, with long straight black hair. She often sat at my feet playing her guitar and singing Joan Baez songs in the soft light of a kerosene lamp in the small, neat cabin she shared with her girlfriend. I could have stayed there forever--the giggling girls, babbling brook, mountain birds at the feeder, afternoon shadows on the wood floor, and the hippie girl who sang so sweetly.

The mountains brought me great comfort, though the spirits there were much younger than the ones I knew in Michigan and I rarely saw them. On one occasion I ate some magic mushrooms and hiked into the mountains where I watched the wind blow the lodge pole pines on the next mountain over. The trees bent, like the bristles on a toothbrush as you pass your thumb over them, in a straight line across the face of the mountain, changing the shade of green as it passed. Each tree became a tuning fork until a great tone rose from the forested rock. A tone separate from the wind and hum of the mountain itself. A tone overwhelming, setting up a vibration that put molecules in motion in every living thing. I stood trembling with energy, in absolute sync with the universe. Then clouds passed, casting shadows on the mountain of giant eagles, saber tooth cats, a family of turtles the size of three townships. I vibrated too, adding my energy to the universe. I felt safe at Black Bear Ranch.

But I was antsy, eager to continue the fight to end the

war, bring down the government of Nixon, and create a new culture. I admired and understood my friends at BBR, and their desire to retreat from the corrupt, decadent, and materialistic world. But someone had to fight, and I wanted to.

I was dying to know what was happening. I wanted to know what was going on with the CIA case, with Sinclair's weed case, with our New Jersey case, and my Chicago case. I wanted to be where the action was. I had been forced underground; I was not there of my own choosing. I could have lived at BBR forever, but I didn't want to. I wanted to return to the struggle in Ann Arbor.

Diane DiPrima told me she had received a message telling me to get to San Francisco and call a certain number in the City to get further instructions. As luck would have it, The Whaler was making a trip to the city to pick up building supplies hustled by the Diggers.

We took the stake-rack Ford and made the city in five hours, The Whaler talking history all the way--the founding of the Longshoremen's Union at the port of San Francisco, the Industrial Workers of the World--The Wobblies--organizing lumberjacks and sawmill workers in the Great Northwest in the early 1900's.

He took me to North Beach, to a hotel above an office supply store. "See that window up there--just to the left of the sign?" He said, pointing out a second-floor window next to a narrow, vertical, six-foot sign which read: SWEDISH AMERICAN HOTEL.

"That's the window Lenny Bruce fell out of the night he shot up while sitting on the window sill. He just passed out and tumbled ass over teacart--couple of cats picked him up and carried him upstairs; he was okay," The Whaler reminisced.

I needed a place to stay for a few days until I could pull everything together so I decided to lie low at the SWEDISH AMERICAN. A single door off the street opened to a stairway leading to a second-floor "lobby," which consisted of a wire cage that held the "front desk" and an old codger who walked with a peg leg. It pleased Allah to give me the same room Lenny stayed in. I sat in the window, reciting Lenny's routines (Father Flanagan's Folly), turning occasionally to pee in the sink to save a trip down the hall.

I called the number I'd been given and reached Detroit Annie, a girl from back home who had moved to Berkeley. She met me at City Lights bookstore, just down the block from where I was staying.

Annie brought news that The Prez was coming to see me. I was elated, being very lonely for The Prez and homefolk. Annie went on with her report very professionally, passing on the message from home as if memorized: in the spring The Prez was going to be part of the Youth International Party (Yippies!) delegation to Hanoi via Stockholm and Moscow. In addition, DS and The Prez were working on a plan to get me to Algeria so I could apply for political asylum. Furthermore, if I could get to Stockholm by Easter I could meet up with The Prez and perhaps go with her to Hanoi, then travel to Algiers from North Vietnam. Annie instructed me to return to BBR and wait for The Prez to come to me.

Annie then passed on the Central Committee analysis of the present conditions: As long as Pun is free, the White Panther Party is in a position of strength. The Party can rally support, amass legal forces, and educate the masses. With Pun underground, the Party is on the offensive.

Likewise, the opposite is true; should Pun be captured, the Party would be on the defensive, responding to the might of the government, an unappealing position.

The unstated conclusion: don't get caught.

My head was spinning. This was big news. I'm still amazed at Annie's ability to remember it all, without notes. The news brought excitement but also frustration since Annie had no answers to the obvious questions--when and how? When will The Prez visit? How will I get to Algeria? Who will help me? When's Easter?

I took comfort in the CC analysis; not only did it seem to be accurate, but knowing that intelligent, capable people were working for me, caring about me--this felt good; I wasn't alone.

I stayed at the hotel several days, going out rarely and drinking a dozen beers a day. The Whaler picked me up and the trip back to BBR was uneventful.

Two weeks later, The Prez showed up. After some desperate lovemaking, The Prez visited with Diane and Grant, then scoped out the scene and people at BB.

As a result of her investigation, The Prez felt I should leave the ranch. She believed that with so many outlaws at BB, surely it would get raided sooner or later. The recent incident with the health department was only a prelude to a larger raid, she thought. "The health department visit was probably only a reconnoiter," she reasoned.

From Grant, she learned that I had been telling various people about who I was, the nature of the charges against me, and that I was running from the FBI. She believed that too many people at BBR knew my story for it to be safe in the long term.

She knew of a commune just over the California border in Oregon. She had a connection there and wanted me to spend the winter in the Oregon Mountains--assuming of course, I could keep my mouth shut.

The Prez had money, so I bought a '38 Dodge pick-up, six-cylinder, flat-head, single-throat carb, four speed with a "grandma" creeper gear, and a three-piece back window. I built a camper out of wood that I covered with tarpaper and a tin roof and we set out. It was late November, 1969.

On the road, The Prez lectured me sternly. "Who all have you told?" she wanted to know.

"I might have told a few people," I answered sheepishly. "I guess I told Carolina, but he's cool. He's a draft dodger, he won't tell anyone."

"That's not the point," she insisted. "You are not only jeopardizing your own freedom, but the freedom of everyone who is hiding you. Who else did you tell?"

"Well, I guess I told The Whaler on our five-hour trip to the city. I probably told the LA hippie girl who sang so sweetly. I might have told John when we went poaching."

"Poaching! You're an idiot,"

"But Prez, I like these people," I said. "They are my friends. I don't want to lie to them. I want to get close. I want to be honest with them. I want them to like me--Pun Plamondon--not some pretend guy from a pretend place. I can't be somebody else."

"Pun, you must," The Prez pleaded. "You can't be honest. Ever, 'til this is all over. Don't you understand? The Feds want to kill you. This is not a joke! The Feds are taking it very, very seriously. You must get real or else you'll be dead--you'll probably get others killed as well."

I hung my head, rounded my back, and hunched my shoulders, while letting my arms droop at my sides. I felt like such a sad sack.

"By the way," The Prez continued, "the Feds put you on the Ten Most Wanted list."

I shivered as a chill passed through me.

"They say you are armed and dangerous and that you used dynamite in the crimes for which you are accused."

This is bad, I thought. The FBI always gets their man. I see how it works: the Feds paint a picture of me as a lunatic militant and place me on the most wanted list, laying the justification for blowing my head off. Scary.

"I'll do whatever you say," I murmured. "Just get me to Algeria." My wind was gone, like a 10-year-old who's fallen from an apple tree, smacking the ground, unable to catch his breath.

Just as quickly, my ego swelled as I basked in the glow of reaching the pinnacle of my renegade career--the Ten Most Wanted list. I felt as if I was certified, certain to go down in history, as if I really was somebody. *I've arrived, I'm officially a threat,* I thought at the time.

The Prez had been making arrangements. She met secretly with Eldridge Cleaver's representative in the Black Panther Party and began laying the groundwork for me getting to Algeria. At that time, Cleaver, Minister of Information of the Black Panther Party, had eluded a massive nationwide manhunt and escaped to Algeria where he was given political asylum.

Eldridge's rep, Kathleen, promised to help and gave The Prez the address and phone number of Eldridge in Algeria. She also gave her the name of a woman in Europe who could get me the proper visa, as well as the name of a contact person in the Algerian government to get in touch with once I got there. Kathleen would notify Eldridge of my possible arrival. She would not, however, in any way help me get out of the USA. Fair enough.

Algeria didn't sound so bad. The Mediterranean--hashish--Arab girls--other liberation fighters from around the world. *This could turn out to be a real adventure,* I thought at the time.

According to The Prez, news from the legal front didn't look good. Money was scarce; the phone was turned off from time to time, as were the lights. Sinclair's appeal and battery of motions were going nowhere. Also, he had been transferred from Jackson, in south central Michigan, the largest walled prison in the world, to Marquette maximum security prison in Michigan's Upper Peninsula, an antique, red limestone monstrosity kept chilled most of the year by the winds off Lake Superior.

Leni had had her second child (Celia Sanchez Mao Sinclair) in January of 1970 while her husband was in Marquette. The seven-hour drive made it difficult for Leni and the defense team to even visit, which was the state's whole point in moving him there.

My legal situation was dire indeed. I was Most Wanted, that couldn't be good, legally speaking. When I went underground, I jumped bond on all my pending cases; the sale of weed case in Traverse City, the possession of hashish and a hunting knife in Hackensack, and possession of reefer and a jackknife in Chicago. Bond had been forfeited in each case.

With our new, higher profile in the media, more support came forward. We were now a national "cause celebre." With the higher profile came more work for the defense team. They now had the task of trying to solicit money and political support for Sinclair's pot case as well as our CIA case. Providing us with an adequate defense seemed, to me, an overwhelming task.

*   *   *

The Prez and I took a leisurely camping trip to Crater Lake in the Dodge camper, avoiding the tourists because of the season. Then we headed for the high plateau in the region of Bend, where the weather was so cold--50 below zero--that the Dodge froze up. We met an old codger who owned a one-stall gas station/garage who let us park the pick-up inside all day to thaw the block slowly. While hanging around the garage we met a comely young woman in her late teens who had dashed in without a coat despite the crunching cold. She bought cigarettes for her sister and mom who shared a house trailer across the lane behind the garage.

The Prez and I returned with the girl only to find the older sister and mother, who still held her trim shape, traipsing around in flimsy nighties and drinking vodka and orange juice, although it was barely ten o'clock in the morning and nearly 20 degrees below outside. The furnace glowed red as it huffed and puffed nonstop.

The three were whores, or so they said, servicing the men from the large plywood plant that dominated the local economy. The women made The Prez uncomfortable with their scanty clothing and their frank discussions about sex and sex for money (including several attempts to recruit her). To be honest, I wished The Prez wasn't there at all, since this opportunity offered the possibility of checking off several fantasies from my life list.

We spent the day drinking vodka and OJ while the youngest girl made eyes at me and openly flirted, parading around in bra and panties. Her older sister, out of habit, I think, offered up some sibling competition by trying to catch my eye. At 3:30, the plant let out and a rough crowd of men began to trickle in. The Prez checked on the Dodge, found it thawed, and dragged me out of there.

We headed west. The Prez had instructions from the Central Committee to visit with Ken Kesey to gain his support in the defense of Sinclair. Sinclair's defense team was putting together a list of prominent authors from across the country and abroad, with the goal of taking out a full-page ad in the New York Times, signed by hundreds of literary notables.

It was after dark when we found Kesey's farm outside Springfield, Oregon, so we crawled off to sleep in the camper. Early the next morning, after we noticed smoke coming from the woodstove chimney, indicating someone was up, we went in and introduced ourselves (I used my alias).

Kesey's house was actually a big renovated barn, nicely done with several bedrooms and a balcony on the second floor, where the hayloft used to be. In addition to the stairway, a heavy manila rope dangled from the roof ridge some 40 feet above allowing one to swing from the balcony to the first floor. I wanted to swing but felt I didn't know Kesey well enough to ask.

The first floor was a large open space with big windows

and lots of light. A red macaw occupied the space over by the windows and wood stove. There was an open living room/dining area, with the kitchen tucked under the balcony in the far corner.

Steven Stills was visiting, so, over breakfast, The Prez and I made our pitch for support of Sinclair's pot case to both Kesey and Stills. Ten years for two joints…outrageous! Everyone agreed.

We talked for a time, and then Kesey and I went out to feed cattle while The Prez stayed with Stills in the warm house. It is always good, when trying to pitch two people, to separate them at some point so as to be able to pitch each one alone. Often it is easier to get a commitment from a lone individual than from someone in the presence of a peer.

From the cattle barn, as opposed to the people barn, Kesey dropped several bales of hay down into an aluminum rowboat, and then we skidded the craft across the frosted grass to a pasture not far away. A small herd of Herefords greeted their breakfast with loud bellows that filled the crisp morning air of the valley. The sun rising over the mountains caused the frost to melt, raising mist to treetop level in the yellow morning light.

Kesey and Stills were eager to get off to a meeting in San Francisco. We ended our visit without a commitment from either but with a promise that our proposal would be considered and that they would get back to us. This usually meant "no," and, in fact, we never heard from them again. We headed for the coast.

Although we had a White Panther Chapter in Eugene, contacting them was out of the question, since they were no doubt under surveillance. The Prez knew of another commune, however, on the coast, at Seal Rock.

* * *

The eight or so hippies that made up the commune at Seal Rock were paired up: boy/girl, boy/girl. We introduced ourselves using aliases and dropped the names of mutual acquaintances and soon fit right in with the group.

Winter on the Oregon coast means wind and rain. We were right on the coast, between Highway 101 and the beach, which was a quarter mile away. It was a chilled and breezy frame house with a Dutch roof and shingle siding. The situation did not allow for them to live off the land so they hustled odd jobs in the area.

The leader of the commune had an agreement with the owner of a local motel just down the coast to paint the exterior as weather permitted. Day after day it rained, preventing us from going to work. We sat around the living room playing Monopoly and blowing smoke rings.

I slept on one couch, The Prez on the other. The pack rats that lived in the attic would visit our Monopoly set, which permanently occupied the coffee table in front of the couches. They stole the tokens. The top hat was missing, as was the car. They took several red hotels and a few green houses. Occasionally they left something in exchange, like a cigarette or a hair barrette. Once they brought us an old-fashioned gartersnap from a woman's girdle.

After what seemed like weeks playing Monopoly while listening to the rain lash our little house, the weather broke. We could start painting the next day.

There was plenty of bright sun, but the wind was stiff and cold off the Pacific. We arrived at the motel and unloaded our equipment--ladders, drop cloths, and such. We planned to scrape dried and blistered paint in the morning, then paint in the afternoon when the weather was expected to warm into the 50s.

As we were easing into the work, as hippies are wont to do, the commune leader suggested I go to the local gas station to get some hot coffee to ease the chill and kill some time. I took the Dodge for the short trip.

The station attendant was an outgoing sort of guy who greeted me with an inane comment about the weather. "Nice to see the sun for a change," he said. "Sure is," I reassured him. "Where you workin'?" he wanted to know. "We're paintin' down at the motel," I answered as I prepared the coffees. "Have you met the FBI agents down there yet?" he wanted to know. "No. Are there FBI agents down there?" I tried to sound calm. "Yeah, the FBI has a field office down there--nice guys--they come in around ten--they're not there every day though," he said while ringing up five coffees in old-fashioned paper cups. He found an oil-stained box and we placed the coffees inside. I paid the man and thanked him, absolutely trembling as I made for my truck.

I flew past the motel, only waving as my four friends stood bewildered in the drive. Once back to the house I told The Prez; we were out of there in three minutes.

"Do you think they were that close, or was it just a coincidence?" I asked as we sped away as fast as the Dodge would take us. "It's hard to say, but it doesn't matter. We've got to get you and this truck off the road." she answered.

The Prez knew of still another Oregon commune just short of the California line, near Cave Junction. We made for it, spending one night camping in the Siuslaw National Forest on the way. The only times I ever felt really safe were while camping, surrounded by trees.

* * *

Sunny Ridge was a commune of some twenty souls who homesteaded an abandoned mining claim snuggled in the Siskiyou Mountains just eighty miles, as a magpie flies, from Black Bear Ranch. (According to their web page, Sunny Ridge Commune members were evicted from their homes by the Feds, the buildings bulldozed, and the earth reclaimed as a National Forest, shortly after I left; Black Bear Ranch is still functioning.)

Sunny Ridge was a well-ordered, clean, and happy clan of dropouts with a tumbling bunch of children that were the charm and sweetness of the commune and the love of all. The Prez and I parked the Dodge behind a clump of manzanita trees, turned on our charm and talked our way in, using our aliases and The Prez mentioning a reference she knew.

We told them we were just passing through and would only be staying a week or two. Nothing was said about my legal situation or the fact that I was underground. We made ourselves useful, The Prez by helping with day care and cooking, while I went off every day with the men folk to cut firewood on federal land in the surrounding mountains.

Sunny Ridge was a sprouting of rough wood buildings darkened by weather, hunkered on a south-facing ridge a hundred yards up a steep drive off the country road. A small stream was dammed a short distance up the mountain creating a reservoir the size of a bathtub. A two-inch pipe and gravity carried water the fifty or so yards to a laundry/bath house outfitted with a sauna, washtubs, and a wood-fired water heater for hot baths. There was no electricity this far up the mountain. The main building was the cook house/dining room/community space, dominated by a massive wood-burning cook stove.

Just across the rock-strewn yard from the cookhouse was another rough but well-made wood structure used as sleeping quarters for childless adults on one side, and all the children of the commune on the other. This was a long, low building, with a stud wall dividing it in two. The Prez and I slept there, sharing a room with M&M and his woman.

During the day, the women, mostly tended to the children. At night, the kids were put to bed by their parents who then went to their own, rough-hewn, apartment type building, just down the path from where the children slept. The childless adults in the other half of the building kept an eye on the children. This seemed to work well; everyone took their responsibility for the children very seriously.

M&M was a rather Rasputin-looking guy with dark stringy hair, a long black beard, and dark eyes, giving him a brooding, troubled look. We became fast friends and spent a lot of time together. In the sauna one night, after eliciting a promise of secrecy, I told him the complete story of my legal predicament.

I noticed, looking back at the time I spent underground, that when I met people I liked, I had a burning desire to tell them the truth about myself, a hankering to be honest, not out of a need for self-aggrandizement, but out of an honest hunger for truthfulness. This is a laudable trait, I suppose, but potentially disastrous when running from the law.

Cave Junction was the nearest little town to the commune. Most of the local storeowners were members of the Illinois Valley Betterment Association, a rancid collection of right-wing bullies and businessmen who hated hippies and everything they stood for. Member stores posted signs in their front windows and doors that read: "HIPPY TRADE NOT SOLICITED OR SERVED." These honkies helped create an atmosphere of fear and terror in the numerous hippie communes springing up in the surrounding mountains.

Sunny Ridge members told horrifying stories of being driven off the road by drunken Republican hooligans, of being cursed and intimidated while on the street, and of being humiliated and verbally assaulted while shopping in local stores.

M&M told me of an incident between some local right wingers and hippies from a nearby commune over the rednecks' repeated burning of a small, pyramid-shaped, meditation structure set on commune property.

Made of plywood, the meditation structure was only large enough for one person. Occasionally someone would meditate there, at other times children played there; most of the time it went unused. One night, local rednecks snuck in and burnt it down. The commune rebuilt it. The rednecks burnt it again. The commune rebuilt again. The rednecks torched it yet a third time. The commune built another, but this time…

This time M&M and another speed-freak hippie lay in wait with shotguns ready. In the dead of night the 'necks parked their Chevy and crept their way through the woods, gasoline can in hand, to the meditation pyramid. Suddenly M&M and his sidekick cut loose on the Chevy. Round after round they pumped into the Bellaire. Birdshot, 00 buckshot, slugs, skeet shot: they shot it all. They blew every piece of glass to smithereens and peppered the body with hundreds of bullet holes. When the shooting stopped, the rednecks beat it to their ride and sprayed gravel for a quarter mile down the two-track, the radiator hissing steam and gas tank leaking like a sieve. They were never heard from again.

This is precisely the type of armed self-defense the White Panther Party was advocating. After all, these hippies were citizens of the United States. Since they could not count on the apparatus of the state to protect them and guarantee their rights, they had every right to take defensive measures. For years, the citizens in the Black, Chicano, Native, and other minority communities faced the same plight and had the same right to armed self-defense, as far as we were concerned.

With my short hair, clean-shaven face, and conservative clothes, I was the natural one to send in to buy needed supplies from the honkie store owners who posted the offending signs. I remember buying small cloth mantels for kerosene lamps from the hardware store and five yards of brown and red paisley print cotton cloth at the dry goods store. I secretly cursed the storeowners and their entire culture, while smiling and nodding politely.

We stayed at Sunny Ridge for two weeks, until it was time for The Prez to return to Ann Arbor. I signed the Dodge over to M&M, and The Prez and I took a bus to Oakland, California. On the trip south, we formalized our plans: The Prez would fly to Stockholm at Easter to attend the International Peace Conference and rendezvous with me there. After a visit of several days, she would fly on to Moscow and meet up with Gumbo and Nancy K, both representatives of the Youth International Party (YIPPIES!).

At that time we were still trying to cement a relationship between the YIPPIES! and the WPP. We wanted the YIPPIES! to be a real organization with officers and offices and a political program rooted in the new culture with the ultimate goal of overthrowing the government. The YIPPIES! non-leaders included Nancy K and Gumbo. They wanted to keep the YIPPIES! as an amorphous, non-organized figment of the media and government's imagination. Yet we were all loyal friends, bound together through struggle, and we remain so today.

For my part, I was to get to Toronto and stay with Gumbo's sister. From her place I was to make contact with The Green Lantern, a young poet who ran a small press that did short runs of exquisite poetry books. I knew him from bygone days in Detroit and the Artists Workshop. He would help me get a passport. But first I had to get to Toronto.

* * *

Once in Oakland, The Prez caught a bus to the San Francisco airport for her flight back home. Our partings seemed like staged and scripted affairs. I would keep a stiff upper lip, showing no emotion, glancing around to see if we were being observed. The Prez would hug and kiss me and remind me to be careful and more security conscious. I would be thinking, How could I best act like a revolutionary? How would Che or Fidel do it? Would they show emotion? Would they acknowledge their fear? I remained stoic, hoping I was playing the role correctly.

This was part of my problem, I realize now. Instead of

being a revolutionary I was trying to act like a revolutionary.

The Prez left me with a kiss, $200, and instructions on picking up more money from a White Panther member who owned a small press in Berkeley and had connections with big-time weed dealers up in the Napa Valley.

As prearranged, I made contact with Detroit Annie again. As might be imagined, she was a Detroit girl who had moved to Berkeley with a small crew six months before. She was a first-rate photographer and had found work with The Berkeley Tribe, the same paper Grimshaw worked for.

She had rented a small apartment, one of six in a modern building up near the University. I stayed there for over a week, jumping at every sound in the hall and commotion on the street. One day, Annie and I went down to Fisherman's Wharf in San Francisco to catch the ferry over to Alcatraz. This was during the Indian occupation of "The Rock" in December of 1969. We stayed overnight, camping and visiting with the occupiers and their supporters.

Though I was "part Indian," I didn't use that as an entrée with Indians since I didn't feel qualified, not being "full-blood," or raised in the culture. I didn't even know how much Indian blood I had or the name of my tribe. I did present myself as a member of the White Panther Party and voiced our uncompromising support for their action. Annie had the foresight to bring several loaves of bread and bricks of surplus commodity cheese, which we left with the occupiers--real support.

This visit was just the sort of unnecessary risk The Prez had been harping at me about. Since the Indians had taken Alcatraz and released increasingly militant statements, it was certain that the Feds had The Rock under heavy surveillance. It was risky going out there, but I felt like I was "counting coup" on the government, tweaking their noses, though they were not aware, that I was. Besides, I believed I looked like a door-to-door evangelist, banging Bibles and bringing souls to the Lord.

When we returned to the apartment, I couldn't go in. A great gripping paranoia swept over me and I refused to enter the building. Annie went first and checked it out. She convinced me that it was not only a safe place, but the only place I had to go. I had to either enter the building, or walk the streets. I spent several nerve-wracking days cowering in the apartment, talking myself through the fear.

A few days later, the money from the Napa weed dealers came through. I had nearly $500 and no reason to remain in Berkeley. I knew that for my own peace of mind I had to get to the country; I needed some trees, my old reliable security blanket.

I decided to return to Black Bear; with any luck, I could spend New Year's there with the LA hippie girl. But I needed a gun. I had traded the .38 Special to The Whaler for a 30-30 lever action carbine. I thought that since I was living in the mountains, a rifle made more sense than a handgun. When I left Oregon I had not only signed the truck over to M&M but gave him the carbine as well. Now I was without a piece. I firmly believed in righteous self-defense. I told my wife and others who knew of my situation that if the pigs came to arrest me in a legal fashion, I would go peacefully, but if they sent an assassin, or surrounded me and just started shooting, I'd shoot back.

Detroit Annie had an attorney friend who owned a legally-registered P38, semi-auto, 9mm handgun. He gave it to Annie to give to me until I went back east on my way to Europe, then Annie was to get it back to him.

We took Annie's old VW bug with no starter or back window, or, we were to find out later, brake lights, and set out for northern California with the pistol stashed under the passenger seat. We made it to Yreka just fine, but were turned around by the Highway Patrol at a roadblock because the passes to the west were snowed shut. There would be no getting to BBR for several days. We decided to return to Berkeley.

We spent New Year's Eve in a cheap motel outside of Weed and New Year's Day hiking Mount Shasta. We left Shasta around noon heading south on I-5. While passing through steep mountains covered in massive pines, we were pulled over by the highway patrol.

Even though we had no starter, Annie turned off the bug; a move I believed to be stupid at the time. A single patrolman in a snappy uniform approached. The 9mm was within easy reach, just under my seat.

After the usual request for driver's license, registration, and proof of insurance, and after asking for my ID, the pig informed us we had no brake lights. I still had the California driver's license, Social Security card and student ID from UC Berkeley that I'd received from Beretta three months earlier. (Oddly enough, California driver's licenses did not have photo ID in 1970.)

I kept thinking; *the 9mm is under the seat. I should shoot this son-of-a-bitch.* I kept my eyes open and mouth shut as I watched the scene go down.

The patrolman and Annie retreated to the cop car leaving me with a lump in my throat and the pistol under the seat.

Soon Annie and the pig returned. She was carrying a brand-new ticket for operating an unsafe vehicle. Annie got in and the cop stuck his head in the window. "How come I smell marijuana in here?" he wanted to know.

My heart sank, then rocketed to my throat, I thought I might puke.

"Do you have any marijuana in there?" he asked.

Before I could answer Annie pulled a baggie, half full of pot, out of the breast pocket of her wool, black-and-red-plaid shirt. "Only this," she answered, handing him the baggie--another move I thought quite stupid.

The oinker came around to my side of the bug. "Do you have any?" he said as he leaned in the car. *I should grab this guy by the head and blow his brains out,* I thought. "No, I don't smoke," I answered.

He returned to the driver's side and had Annie get out. Then he cuffed her hands behind her back and led her to the back seat of his car. *I better shoot this motherfucker!* I thought as I watched them through the rear view mirror and the missing back window. *Maybe I could make a run for it,* I supposed.

Instead, I left the gun under the seat and went back to the cop car too, and got in the front seat with the officer, putting on the air of innocent confidence.

He looked at me, then at Annie. "If I search that car, will I find anything in there that will surprise me?" he wanted to know.

"There's a pistol in there," Annie blurted out--another move I thought really stupid at the time.

That got the officer's attention. "Where will I find this

pistol?" he went on. "Under the passenger seat," she answered cooperatively. Another stupid move. I thought, *I should have shot him--it's too late now.*

"You stay here," he ordered and went to fish the 9mm out from under the seat. He brought the weapon back, took the magazine out, wedged it in his belt and placed the gun on the dash.

"Is that a registered pistol?" he wanted to know. "Yes." Annie responded, "It's registered to my friend," she went on, giving the owner's name. The very professional officer got on the radio and called in the make and model and serial number of the piece.

After what seemed like an hour, the radio crackled and the patrolman was informed that the gun was duly registered and quite legal.

"Why do you have this gun?" the officer wanted to know. "I was raped recently," she responded. "My attorney gave me his gun until I could get my own," she went on--a very good answer I thought at the time, though I didn't know if it was true or not.

He kept us there for another hour, quizzing us, looking through our car and backpacks. Finally he told me to take Annie's car back to Berkeley, Annie would be taken to jail in Weed where she would make bond and be home by the next day, he said.

I could barely believe I was walking away from this! Without a starter, the bug would not start, so I got the officer and Annie to give me a push by hand. It was a strain to contain my laughter--here I was on the Ten Most Wanted list, getting a push-start from a California highway Patrolman and his prisoner!

The bug fired up easily. I gave a wave and was on my way, pounding the wheel over and over with my palm and exclaiming, "I don't believe it! I don't believe!"

I was only down the road a few miles when I noticed the flashing red lights of the cop car behind me. I was certain the jig was up. I figured he must have received a radio dispatch informing him I was a wanted fugitive. Or perhaps Annie broke down and told him who I was in order to save her own bacon--she had been crying and very upset in the back of the pig car as I had driven away. I pulled to the side but left the bug running. The cop pulled in behind me and walked to my vehicle. He had the 9mm! "This is a legally registered firearm," he began. "If I turn this in I'll have reams of paperwork. You take the weapon. Just keep it visible on the seat so it isn't concealed--you'll be fine," he said while handing me the handgun and the magazine! In addition, he passed the keys to Annie's apartment to me and I was gone again.

I drove the four hours back to Berkeley tossed between a state of over-the-top elation and absolute terror. On the one hand I had apparently escaped the clutches of the law; yet, on the other, I was afraid of getting stopped again. If the pigs found the gun I wasn't sure I could talk my way out of it a second time. Annie could still spill the beans. More likely, however, they would receive some new information that would tip them off. If this happened, I could not expect the pigs to be as reasonable, polite, and professional as the one who had stopped us, especially knowing I was armed. I kept the pedal to the metal and made Berkeley after dark.

Annie made it home by suppertime the next day. After the near bust in northern California, I was too nervous to stay at Annie's. She made arrangements for me to stay in a friend's school bus parked at a repair shop in a light industrial section of Oakland. The bus was one of twenty or so hippie-owned vehicles parked in a lot beside the shop, which was surrounded by a rusting and sagging cyclone fence topped with three strands of broken barbed wire.

I spent nights in the bus--sneaking into the fenced lot after dark, careful not to be seen since Oakland had just passed an ordinance forbidding anyone to live in a vehicle on any street or private property. I would sneak out before daylight, walk the streets, go to the university, the library, or down to the port of Oakland, just to kill time until nightfall; then I'd sneak back into the bus. This went on for a week, until it was time for me to start making my way to Stockholm to meet up with The Prez.

Annie borrowed a car and drove me to the airport in Eugene to catch a plane to Buffalo where I expected to cross the border into Canada. I felt the San Francisco airport was too "hot," and at a smaller one there would be less chance of surveillance.

As I waited for my flight in the airport bar in Eugene, I sucked down a few cold beers while watching Richard "The Pig Hearted" give the State of the Union address. It was the third Tuesday in January, 1970.

Chapter Eleven

CANADA TO EUROPE 1970

My flight out of Eugene was without incident. Upon landing in Buffalo I took a Yellow Cab to downtown Niagara Street and got a room in a $10-a-week transient hotel above a sub shop. This section of the city was made up of cheap hotels, boarded-up storefronts with apartments above, alkie-bars, strip-joints, pawn shops, and the like.

I stayed in my room mostly, coming out once a day to buy a "grinder" (as subs were called in that part of the country) from the shop below. Sometimes I'd buy a TIME magazine, New York Times, or Penthouse from the newsstand across the street, and a 12 pack of beer from the liquor store down the block. The rest of the time I spent in my room reading by the light of a bare bulb dangling by a three-foot cord from a 12-foot ceiling--or sleeping--or pleasuring myself by hand several times a day. Once or twice, I went out late at night to one of the nearby bars to have a few drinks and some human contact. It was easy to strike up a conversation with the working girls that frequented the place. Unfortunately I had no money for such indulgences, though I desperately wanted some warm human contact--a woman to hold through the night and to wake-up with in the morning.

It seems to me, from my personal experience and from what others have told me, that living underground is similar to being a soldier, police officer, fireman, ambulance driver, or prisoner: long periods of crushing, overwhelming boredom are followed by short periods of intense stress, which are followed by boredom, then stress, on and on, over and over.

I spent more than a month in that room in Buffalo--just killing time until I was told it was okay to get to Canada. I had no visitors, though I called the pay phone in East Quad and talked to The Prez or DS or Audrey every Thursday at 7 pm.

Finally I was told I was expected in Canada. The plan seemed easy; I had been across the border dozens of times over the years and anticipated no problems. Once across I was to call Gumbo's sister, who was expecting me; I would be safe with her.

I packed my duffel and counted my money; I had $80. Having left the 9mm with Detroit Annie in Berkeley, I was weaponless; besides, taking one across the border was out of the question. I made my way to the Greyhound station and caught a bus to Toronto.

The fare was $13. We crossed the Peace Bridge and pulled into Canadian Immigration. An Immigration Officer boarded and walked slowly down the aisle, glancing at each passenger. He walked right past me. *So far, so good,* I thought as he reached the back.

During this period, thousands of young men were

fleeing to Canada to avoid the draft and service in the murderous war in Vietnam, so Canadian and U.S. Immigration were on "high alert."

The overwhelming majority of these young men of conscience were fine, upstanding, even courageous boys who had fled the U.S. with the help of their family or church. Others were not so fortunate and suffered as families were split, father against son. It takes courage to stand alone when the whole nation, including one's own family are confused by "duty" to a government which is based on lies.

"Where were you born?" The Immigration man standing above me wanted to know.

"Boston," I answered. I had one flimsy piece of ID, a tattered library card from Boston College. Since I had plans to get a passport in Canada, it made sense to leave my California ID for others to use.

"Where are you going?" The officer asked.

"Toronto." I answered with all the confidence I could muster.

"How long will you be staying?"

"Two or three weeks."

"Are you employed?"

"No. I'm a student." The questions were coming faster now, I was beginning to sweat.

"Who will you be staying with?'

"My girlfriend," I stammered, faltering

"What's your girlfriend's address?"

This is not good, I thought, *to be singled out this way...*I couldn't remember her address or phone number. I mumbled something; it was clear I was unraveling.

"How much money do you have?"

"About $65." I answered.

"That's not enough money for a two-week stay in Canada, please follow me." He led me off the bus.

I grabbed my gear and followed. I was led into a small office and waited while the officer called the Royal Canadian Mounted Police. They were there within minutes. They placed me in their car, then transported me across the bridge and deposited me at the U.S. border in front of the U.S. Immigration Office. A U.S. Immigration Officer invited me inside.

The room had glazed yellow wall tiles, the color of baby shit, a well-worn wooden counter layered with umpteen coats of green paint, one for each new administration I assume, and the hard echo of a large room with no soft surfaces, the tell tale signs of a state bureaucracy or institution.

The Immigration man wanted some ID. I handed over my folded, faded and flimsy library card from Boston College. I told him I was a student there and a U.S. citizen. I told him that I had been robbed a few nights before in Buffalo and my wallet with my entire ID was stolen. I told him the library card was in my shirt pocket so the thief didn't get it. I told him Canadian Immigration would not let me in the country because I didn't have enough money for the length of time I intended to stay. I told him I was just trying to see my girl in Toronto.

He asked if I had filed a police report about the robbery with the Buffalo Police. I told him no.

He told me to sit on a long gray wooden bench. He tapped on a computer, the first one I'd actually seen. He'd tap for a bit, scratch his head--hunt and peck, tap, wait--tap some more and wait, scratch his head, and then do it all again.

For more than an hour I sat and watched expectantly, believing that at any minute New York State Troopers, with their Smoky Bear hats, and gray breeches tucked into high-top black leather boots, would enter and place me under arrest. My only escape would be running out the door, jumping the railing and landing on the ice flows that choked the river some thirty feet below, then hopping from flow to flow until I made it to the Canadian side, where I would have to scale the concrete flood wall, like a rock climber, thirty feet to freedom. But then I thought better of it.

Luckily, I wasn't arrested. After what seemed like the longest time, the Immigration man simply leaned over the counter and told me I could go.

I walked out under the long shed roof of the US Immigration depot just as a Greyhound Bus with "Buffalo" displayed in its destination port was passing through the lane--I hailed it and got a ride back to downtown Buffalo.

Now I was desperate. I had to get to Toronto--the whole plan hinged on it. I decided to fly. I took a bus to the Buffalo airport, bought a ticket ($39, I seem to recall) and caught the flight.

There was no ramp for disembarking from this puddle-jumping airline, just a steep stairway rolled to the plane and a long walk across the tarmac to the terminal. At the terminal there were two doors, one marked "Canadian Citizens," the other marked "All Others."

I went for "Canadian Citizens." The Immigration guy seemed bored as he leaned on his podium-like desk and asked where I was born. "Toronto," I answered as I walked past. "Go ahead," he responded. I was in.

A quick call to Gumbo's sister, and she was there within an hour. She was an average looking young woman, a year or two my junior. She had the whole basement apartment in a stately old mansion in the York section of the city, not far from the Royal Ontario Museum where she worked. She kept pretty much to herself; we never really connected or spent time talking, I suppose it was safer that way.

When Thursday night rolled around, I called the pay phone in East Quad back at the U of M at the prearranged time and talked to Rock-n-Roll Rita. I informed her that I had made it to Canada and was taking steps to secure a Canadian passport. So far I was on schedule and was planning to meet up with The Prez in Stockholm at the International Peace Conference a day or two after Easter. Rita told me DS would be coming to see me shortly and bringing me some more money.

The Prez and DS raised money for me by face-to-face solicitation of individual donors. There were a handful of professors at the U who could be counted on to cough up a couple hundred bucks from time to time. Then there were some nationally-known musicians and entertainment types who would support my effort to avoid capture by the Nixon/Mitchell/Hoover triumvirate. There were also the weed dealers; they came through more than once when DS put the touch on them.

The Prez had connections on a national level. She solicited funds from Jane Fonda and other movie stars, musicians with national reputations, and a young woman whose daddy was an international tire magnate, among others.

* * *

Meanwhile I contacted The Green Lantern, the Toronto poet and printer I had corresponded with while I was active in The Artists Workshop and 100 Camels Bookstore in Detroit. He was 25, like me, and had a second-floor apartment in a two-family house in a quiet neighborhood not far from the University of Toronto. His wife and young son completed the perfect model of a progressive, well-educated, young Canadian family.

He put me in touch with the Front de Liberation du Quebec (FLQ) those stubborn French-speaking Canadians who want Quebec to be an independent country. Over the years these militant separatists put up armed resistance to the dominant English-speaking government of Canada.

I made friends with Father Brule, a French-speaking priest and longtime chaplain to the outlawed FLQ. He felt we were both fighting the same enemy--the cultural imperialists of the US and Canada. He instructed me on how to obtain the proper application forms for a passport.

Having seen the wanted poster issued by the FBI, I knew they were looking for a dude with prominent scars near the right eye and eyebrow, among other scars noted under "identifying marks." I used Cover Girl make-up to hide the scars on my face, and eyebrow pencil to fill in the scar in my right eyebrow. I had my passport picture taken at a sleazy little photo shop in Toronto's Chinatown. The photo showed a neat and tidy young man in a white shirt with a clip-on tie--say "cheese."

I picked up the appropriate forms at the post office and Father Brule helped me fill them out. He signed them, stating that he had known me all my life, that he had baptized me and my father, and that our family was an upstanding, hardworking Canadian Catholic family. He signed my photo swearing I was Duke DuBois.

With my Chinatown photo, I filed the papers and two weeks later was notified by post to pick up my passport at government offices in downtown Toronto. I remember it well. It was a bright, cold, and windy day in early March. I believed that if I were going to get popped in Canada, it would probably be at this time, while picking up my passport. If they were onto me, I could be walking into a trap. Despite my grave apprehension, I got in line, and when my number was called, I went up to the window and got my passport, as simple as that.

DS arrived during this time bringing three hundred dollars. He briefed me on the legal situation. Nothing had changed really. The Central Committee still believed that all Party energy and resources must continue to be directed toward getting Chairman Sinclair out of prison, and I concurred. The Party and our supporters were making slow but steady headway in educating the people of Michigan to the injustice done Sinclair and others in a similar situation--ten years for two joints--come on!

DS reiterated the need to keep the CIA bombing case "on the back burner," to keep it low profile. For one thing it would be difficult to make the argument that Sinclair was just a hippie with some pot and the victim of overzealous police and courts while simultaneously having to defend a charge of conspiracy to blowup a CIA office. We had to keep these two issues separate, DS explained. Additionally, our financial, physical, and legal resources were maxed out; to add the CIA case to the mix now would overwhelm us and destroy the Party.

He informed me that The Prez had made significant contacts through Kathleen Cleaver and that arrangements could be made for me to receive political asylum in Algeria. DS urged me to do this in the strongest, yet loving, terms. He told me he wanted me somewhere safe, where he didn't have to worry about me getting shot by the pigs. He argued that if I got asylum in Algeria, I could write and be a voice of a midwestern boy with a counter-American view of the world, a valuable asset in the battle for media influence and control.

"You would be safe, Pun--for a year or two or more--until we were ready to deal with the CIA case," I remember him pleading.

I liked the idea. I knew that moving from place to place, crossing borders and immigration and all that involved, was a scenario for my capture. Algeria, moreover, sounded very romantic.

I needed vaccinations for malaria, yellow fever, sleeping sickness, and several other African diseases, so I traveled to Windsor, Canada, just across the river that formed the border between Detroit and Canada. This allowed several Central

Committee members to slip into Canada and meet with me before I went overseas.

I rented a room in the once-fancy and ornate jewel of downtown Windsor, The Windsor House Hotel. What was once a Grand Lady, replete with velvet trimmings and diamond chandeliers, was showing her age and years of wear. When I was there, she was no more than an aging bar hag with sagging breasts, bad teeth, a hardened liver, and run down shoes.

I did an extensive interview with Kelley and Righteous Rudnick, both White Panther members. Kelley was a CC member, the former editor and publisher of the Ann Arbor Argus and, later SunDance, both underground papers with influence and inspiration beyond their short lives. Righteous Rudnick was a musicologist, writer, masterful radio guru, and stone heroin junkie with influence and inspiration beyond his short life. I never took kindly to junkies, with the exception of Rudnick who was so extraordinary in his enthusiasms and media genius that I tried to overlook his use of "death drugs," as we called all "hard" drugs. Over the years, I pleaded with him to stay away from smack. I threatened, cajoled, gave him the "cold shoulder," prayed for him, and, in his last dying year, avoided him.

Upon reading the interview now, some thirty-three years later, I am struck by the shallowness of my answers and seemingly brainwashed responses. It's embarrassing. This isn't to say my responses weren't solid political answers based on a "correct analysis and understanding of the international political conditions of the time." Just as the last sentence has no spirit or heart to it, so too, I was without a spirit. I was forever trying to mimic or act in the spirit of Crazy Horse or Ho Chi Minh rather than in the spirit of Pun Plamondon.

What I understand now but could not have known then, is that I had no center at the time; I wasn't comfortable with myself since I didn't know who I was. I was still a no brand kid.

The vaccinations came off without a hitch. I took a flight from Toronto to Montreal, then from Montreal to Stockholm. It was Easter Sunday, 1970.

* * *

While on my two-hour layover in Montreal I called Jorgen, the Danish cat I had met at the United Front Against Fascism Conference in Oakland less than a year before. He was glad to hear from me and promised to meet me when I landed in Stockholm.

* * *

Jorgen was the International Secretary of the Danish Left-Wing Socialist Party, one of thirteen political parties with seats in the Danish Parliament. He was also a "features writer" for the major Copenhagen daily INFORMATION. At twenty-one, he had already established himself within the Danish left as a dynamic young Dane.

Jorgen traveled from his home in Copenhagen to meet me in Stockholm as I got off the bus from the airport. We slept on the floor of his friend's apartment for a night or two until The Prez arrived. Then The Prez and I got an antique room in a cute little family-owned hotel with a brass-wire-cage-elevator just big enough for two people to squeeze into. All the works of the elevator were exposed, the pulleys, cables, wheels, counterweights--so quaint.

We told them we were newlyweds. It was $8 a night with breakfast delivered by the matronly wife in her apron, hair in a bun. She rolled in a silver cart with a silver serving platter and fancy cover. Removing the cover with a flourish she revealed a beautifully glazed omelet that looked to be half a meter long, surrounded by little round potatoes, baby sausages, thin slices of orange and sprigs of parsley.

The International Peace Conference was held in a great, modern, sweeping building in the heart of old Stockholm; delegations from all over the world were present. Though we didn't attend the formal conference much, we did stop by several times--enough to notice that there were plenty of opportunities to hear boring speeches along with a few brilliant ones.

Away from the conference, we spent time with individual members of various delegations. We had polite tea with the North Koreans at their hotel suite. The Angolans provided Nehi orange and grape soda at their single hotel room.

Most of our time however, was spent with the North Vietnamese delegation.

Han, a young man my age, who was not more than 4'10" tall had an endearing manner and was up-to-date on contemporary western culture. He asked if the Doors or the Jefferson Airplane had new albums out and if we'd seen the movie Easy Rider. He spoke eight languages and was on leave from his regular job as an interpreter at the Paris Peace Talks. The "Talks" had been underway since 1968, the foregone conclusion of which the United States would drag out until the last helicopter lifted off the US embassy in Saigon on April 30, 1975.

The Prez and I spent a loving and lovely week together in Stockholm--then she was back on a plane, this time to Moscow, enroute to Hanoi. She traveled with Nancy K and Gumbo, both of whom had established themselves as able, articulate activists, creative organizers, and liberated hippie women every bit as media-savvy and politically inspired as their male partners--Jerry Rubin and Stu Albert. Rubin and Nancy K were YIPPIE! founders and organizers out of New York--Gumbo and Albert worked out of Berkeley and had stellar credentials as YIPPIE! activists.

While in Moscow, the three women dressed in black silk pajamas and conical straw hats, the uniform of the Viet Cong, and picketed in front of the United States Embassy--in Moscow! The international media picked up the story (with photos) of the three American women just before they were hustled off by Russian Secret Police and sternly scolded. They were kept under surveillance until their flight for Hanoi several days later. I was never more proud of my loyal wife than I was when she poked the Russians and the Americans in the nose for the entire world to see. Picketing in Moscow, unheard of!

This was a time of discovering new possibilities, of taking risks, and of challenging old limits. Most of us grew-up in a world of "can't and don't." Those who do not accept the conventional restrictions, who thumb their noses and show their ass to the old order, these people become saboteurs of the status quo and sow the seeds of the new culture. These women called international attention to the cause of world peace, and showed others they could do the same by challenging the old order, both

Russian and American. They saw the possibility, they took the risk, and they get my kudos.

After the International Peace Conference, I returned by train to Copenhagen with Jorgen. He lived with his father in one of the older suburbs of Copenhagen, in a small, well-kept house we might call a "cottage." With its thatched roof and quaint garden, it was like living in a fairy tale. I relaxed for the first time in several months. I stayed in the upstairs guest bedroom in a goose-feather bed with a down quilt so deep and thick it was like returning to the womb.

Just down the street from Jorgen's house, at the four corners, sat an old rusting German "pillbox" gun emplacement, a reminder of the German occupation during WWII. Jorgen's father, a man in his 60's when I knew him, was somewhat of a national hero for his role in the Danish resistance. I was in the company of quality men.

A week later, Jorgen arranged for me to give presentations at several universities in the Nordic countries, for money. We traveled by train (during which we partied with the hundreds of young people who used the rails) to Ahus, Denmark to meet with university students. Jorgen acted as my translator. I was introduced as Duke DuBois, YIPPIE! organizer.

Then twenty-four hours by train to Uppsula, Sweden, and the university there, where student groups had organized a conference on liberation struggles around the world. There were movies, speakers, poets, graphic artists, and dance troupes. The African National Congress was represented, as were groups from Angola and Mozambique. The Eritreans, who were fighting for independence from Ethiopia, were represented, as were the Tupamaros guerrillas from South America. The Vietnamese, of course, were there, as was someone from the Irish Republican Army and a Palestinian spokesman.

It was at this conference that I met up with Matti. At thirty she was an attractive, petite black woman with short-cropped hair. Born in Trinidad, raised in France, and educated at the Sorbonne, she worked for the United Nations. She was a friend of Kathleen Cleaver, who had given The Prez Matti's number in Stockholm with instructions on how to contact her. Matti was instrumental in my getting to Algeria. She arranged for the Algerian Ambassador in Sweden to secure my visa, and then Matti gave me the name of a contact person in Algiers, who was an American woman working for the Algerian government as a translator in the Ministry of Information. Without Matti, it would have taken longer and been much more difficult to obtain my visa. Five years later, I heard that she was accused of being a CIA agent. I find this unlikely since she knew of my legal status and what I was charged with. Had she been an agent, she could have secretly turned me in without blowing her cover.

Also at this time I met Eva, a tall, skinny, pretty young woman whose mother was the Danish Ambassador to Czechoslovakia. We had a fling. For a week we lived the high life at her mother's estate in Copenhagen, smoking hash, eating caviar and crackers, and making love in odd places--the butlers pantry, wine cellar, library, the upstairs hall and the back garden. I liked her very much, but then I missed The Prez very much, and I was lonesome for home. In my emotional condition, Eva's affection and tenderness seemed quite exquisite, making me wonder if she was the only woman in the world who could bring me such comfort.

She wished for me to go with her to Czechoslovakia later in the spring and live with her in the Ambassador's mansion in Prague. I was tempted to do so--I knew I would be safe there, and I did care for her--but life in any part of the Soviet Union seemed dull and boring--gray people living in a gray world. I declined. I often wonder where my life would have taken me had I gone to Prague with Eva.

Later, Matti hooked me up with some black American supporters of the Black Panther Party who were quietly living in exile in Sweden while avoiding criminal charges of one sort or another in the States. Five of us rented a Volvo and set out for a meeting of international supporters of the BPP held in Frankfurt, Germany. The plan was that I would fly out of Frankfurt to Rome and then on to Algeria. I said goodbye to Jorgen and promised to call once I got to Algeria.

Suspecting that the meeting in Frankfurt would be infiltrated by either the CIA, the FBI, the German Secret Police, INTERPOL, and/or other intelligence services, I made only a brief appearance--just long enough to give me time to meet someone, anyone, who would provide me a place to stay for a few days. As it turned out, I met Wolff, a German militant who worked as an editor for a major German publishing house. I told him I was a Canadian lefty on my way to Algeria, and he let me stay with him. Wolff took me to several "cell" meetings where the topic was political education of the cell. I was impressed at the dedication and discipline of these young militants, who were studying economic theory and the mass psychology of fascism. I interviewed several German activists on cassette tapes, which I intended to have published in our newspaper.

* * *

I arrived at Rome International Airport late on a Sunday evening--flights left for Algeria on Sunday, Tuesday, and Friday. Since I didn't want to pass through Italian customs and immigration, I was restricted to the international section of the airport for a day and half while waiting for the next flight to Algiers.

Italy did not seem to be as laid back and peaceful as the Nordic countries, or even Germany. This was doubtless because it was dealing with a highly organized and militant movement made up of outlaw groups responsible for kidnappings of financial and government officials, bank robberies, shoot-outs, and bombings. Italy responded as any government would--with more and harsher police force.

It is the goal of militant, radical organizers to push the government to greater and greater forms of police oppression, which, they believe, will spur the masses to more and more militant action as they resist the ever-increasing oppression from the state, until resistance from the people is greater than the force of the state, that is, until they bring the system down. What this theory seemed to translate to at the moment was the presence everywhere in the Rome airport of pigs dressed in black jumpsuits and carrying machine guns and the other paraphernalia of a police state.

Until this time, my drinking had been quite under control. I got loaded a few times with Jorgen and his father, but always in a responsible manner. With a day and a half until my flight, too nervous to eat, and with a wheelbarrow full of Lira (having exchanged my German Marks and Danish Krona), I spent my time drinking.

I woke up, having passed out across a row of seats just five meters from a wall of glass that curved for what seemed like half a kilometer along the front of the building. Through my hangover haze I saw a "Black Maria" or "Paddy Wagon" come screeching to a stop just in front of me, at the curb on the other side of the glass wall. "POLICIA" was printed in gold letters one meter high across the side of the van. (Paddy Wagons were originally called "Patty Wagons" since they were used to pick up drunks, mostly Irishmen, off the streets of New York City.)

Quickly the back door of the wagon flew open. Men in black jump suits, with machine-guns and helmets, scurried from the vehicle. In less than a minute they were in a formation of twenty, running double-time toward the main entrance just fifty meters away.

My stomach sank. Oh damn! They're coming for me, I thought. I sat up quickly, only to discover I'd pissed myself--from my waist to my knees, front and back; even my shirt tails were soaked. Then the pigs were in the building, running down the concourse in my direction, still in formation, machine guns held across their chests.

I sat in my hangover haze clutching my backpack in my lap trying to hide my wet pants and trying to focus my mind on what to do. My greatest fear was that these Italian pigs would capture me. Photos would be taken and splashed across the front pages of newspapers back home, showing me with pissed pants, looking like an outlaw ridden to ground while bareback on a well-lathered pinto.

The running phalanx of pigs was upon me in an instant and blew right past me as I sat on the urine-soaked Naugahyde wondering what to do.

The Policia, it turned out, were only changing shifts. Further down the concourse, I could see them double-time up to another assembled squad, stop, and salute. The other squad then double-timed right past me, out the door, and into the truck, which sped away, the whole incident took less then two minutes.

Hung over and humiliated, I made my way to the men's room holding my suitcase in front of my crotch and the duffel so it covered my ass. Once in the stall I took off the wet pants (no underwear) and shirt and put on some dirty yet dry clothes. I ditched the wet clothes in the trash on the way out, went to a clothing store in the airport's international section, and purchased new khakis and a white shirt to go with my clip-on tie. I went back to the lavatory, washed up as well as I could and changed into new clothes and was ready to board my flight to Algeria.

Chapter Twelve

ALGERIA 1970

The plane to Algeria was a four-engine prop job. I hadn't ridden in one of those since 1961, when I returned to Traverse City from Father Gibault reform school. I was sixteen at that time. I would spend my twenty-fifth birthday in Africa.

Once in the air, as was usual on international flights, stewardesses pushed a cart down the aisle of the plane selling cartons of cigarettes, bottles of liquor, and sundry other items which were duty-free when purchased while in international air space. Later they passed out declaration forms so passengers could declare the property they were bringing into the country. This declaration form was to cause me considerable grief when I was preparing to leave Algeria.

Getting into Algeria was hassle free; my passport and visa were in order, though there was the usual language barrier.

During the time of my stay, Algeria's Revolutionary Government had enacted laws making Arabic the official national language, replacing French. The French, who had come to Algeria in 1830, had, like most white, European imperialists, not only raped and pillaged the country and its people, but imposed its own language on the populace as well. Eight years before my visit, a war of national liberation had finally succeeded in kicking the colonizers out. Now the names of streets and government agencies were being changed, as were official and quasi-official documents and publications such as deeds, marriage licenses, schoolbooks, and maps.

Luckily for me, most Algerians in the capital, Algiers, were still speaking French. I carried an "English to French" dictionary that I would fumble through, while butchering words, trampling phrases, and torturing listeners.

My instructions from Matti were to contact a certain woman at the Algerian Ministry of Information, whose phone number I had, she would give me further instructions.

Once off the plane and through the rather small terminal, I took a cab to the Ministry, showing the driver the address scribbled on a scrap of paper. The ride into the capitol city was startling. Along the wide expressway-like boulevard, hundreds of women in black or blue robes with veils covering their faces led donkeys loaded with bundles of firewood, large earthen jars filled with water, or baskets of oranges or artichokes. That's when it hit me--this is a Third World country--poor. Having seen poverty only in "the west," I was ill-prepared for the scope of underdevelopment I was to witness in Algeria.

Once at the Ministry I paid the driver with "dinars," having exchanged my lira at the airport in Rome. However, I was not allowed into the Ministry building; armed soldiers stopped me at the door. Even without my dictionary I could understand "Arretez!" spoken by a soldier who held his hand in front of him, palm out. The question, "Rendezvous?" (Appointment?") needed no translation when asked by a man in a uniform, holding a gun. When I answered "no," the guards replied, in French, "On n`entre pas." (Do not enter) and, pointing down the steps "Retournez."

I used my dictionary to noodle out how to ask people where a pay phone was. (There were no pay phones on street corners or gas stations, hell; there were very few gas stations. No pay phones in restaurants or bars--very few bars, and those found only in the European quarter of the city, none in the Arab quarter, the Kasbah.) I asked several people before I understood that pay phones were at the Centre Bureau de Poste (Central Post Office), located near the grand park, close by the ancient Port of Saaid, in the heart of Algiers. I made my way there, lugging my suitcase and backpack.

I called the woman at the Ministry--she told me to find a hotel near the Kasbah and to contact her again after I settled in.

I found a cheap hotel ($3 a night) overlooking the port on the Boulevard de Che Guevara. Boulevard de Che Guevara! Imagine my shock! The world was upside down! I was now in a country that honored and memorialized the very people my government vilified and cast as without a single human quality. This government had the same heroes I did. What a feeling!

Che Guevara--probably the greatest international revolutionary of the time. As a young man of Argentinean nationality, he became a doctor and then a revolutionary. Exiled to Mexico by the military junta of Argentina, he hooked up with Fidel Castro and eighty-two other Cubans for a planned "invasion" of Cuba. The "invasion" was a disaster; of the eighty-three, only thirteen made it alive to the Sierra Madre Mountains. These thirteen, Che among them, went on to lead the first and only successful armed revolution in the entire western hemisphere against a strongman dictator who was supported by the United States. Anyone with an ounce of sense knows that thirteen people don't make a revolution without the support of the masses of people. Viva Fidel. Viva Che!

Che believed that he had a responsibility to support any struggle anywhere in the world where people take up arms against oppression--anywhere people fight for national liberation and self-determination.

After Cuba, Che followed his beliefs to Angola, and some say Mozambique, fighting in liberation struggles in the heartland of Africa. He went on then to Bolivia to take up arms in the life-and-death struggle of the Indians and peasants of that country for freedom, justice, and peace. Bolivian soldiers killed

Che in October of 1967 with help from the U.S. which provided fly-over pictures of the Bolivian jungle taken by heat sensitive cameras, that tracked Che's troop movements by the heat emitted from their campfires. (The Institute of Science and Technology at the University of Michigan was bombed, in October of '68 in response to its involvement in war research and to commemorate the anniversary of Che's death.)

The boulevard de Che Guevara! It sounded so sweet--it blew my mind, I felt like shouting!

I called Eldridge Cleaver and introduced myself. He picked me up in his car at one of the many sidewalk cafes popular in this part of the world due to the warm Mediterranean climate. I'd admired him for several years, having read his book SOUL ON ICE and some articles he'd written for RAMPARTS, magazine and having known about his work with the Black Panther Party. In addition, the BPP had been the model and inspiration for the White Panther Party, which held all Black Panther personnel and personalities in the highest esteem.

He was rather standoffish at first, not knowing me or anything much about me. He reckoned Kathleen had mentioned someone like me to him, but he didn't really know what the deal was. The next day he picked me up again and was somewhat more forthcoming and easygoing. I assumed he'd made a call and had done some checking.

He would pick me up nearly every morning. I think he liked having me around; I was someone he could brag and show off to. Once he took me sightseeing, pointing out many mosques and the embassies of Cuba and North Vietnam. Then on to the offices of the Palestinian Liberation Origination (PLO) and The Popular Front for the Liberation of Palestine (PFLP), as well as to the offices of freedom fighters from Angola and Mozambique and other liberation headquarters of countries around the world. I visited them all eventually, alone or with Eldridge, collecting pamphlets, papers, reports, and posters outlining the nature of the various struggles.

One day Eldridge took me out to his house, a nice, small villa east of Algiers not far from the Mediterranean. The first thing I noticed was a loaded AK 47 propped near the front door.

We usually went up to the University of Algiers however, in the European quarter, and flirted with the girls.

Eldridge had quite a following of young women and some men who wanted to associate with this famous American revolutionary and author. I tagged along like a country bumpkin cousin. I didn't mind though; I enjoyed and felt comfortable playing second fiddle--always have.

It was at the university that I met Fatima, a young Palestinian woman born in Palestine, raised in France, and now a student at the University of Algiers. Everything about her mesmerized me--her charming and melodious broken English, her dark eyes and long lashes, her soft and smooth skin, the color of extra virgin olive oil, her face, as smooth as a new olive, and her hair, thick and black as a ripe olive. Her undying love for Palestine and dedication to the cause of her people also completely captivated my soul. I would have crawled through a kilometer of broken glass and sewage for her had she asked. I so wanted to get in her pants--and be able to say I had made love on three continents; but alas, it was not to be.

I spent as much time as possible with Fatima, but she had classes and a circle of friends and other commitments. I saw her ten times or so in the two weeks I was there. We would sit in the park near the harbor--she'd tell me of her neighborhood in Paris and of the family home in Palestine. She would talk to me, too, about her parents and all her cousins. It was during these discussions with Fatima about family and land that I realized I was unconnected to anything. Not family or land. I could live anywhere since I had no roots anywhere. This saddened me; I had never felt so alone in the world. We also talked of history and the future. Fatima was studying languages and hoped to be a leader someday of the Palestinian state.

My relationship with Fatima was different than those I had with western women. I didn't talk with a foul mouth. I didn't talk of sex and drugs and rock-n-roll. She inspired different thoughts. My only future, I believed, was to stay alive and take part in a great worldwide revolution for justice. The last time I saw her she let me hold her hand, but blushed, turned away, and held her headscarf across her face when I tried to kiss her cheek.

The rest of my time I spent walking in the shadowed, narrow alleys and streets of the Kasbah and the open-air market. This huge market, located in the same spot since Mohammed walked the Earth, seemed to stretch for miles. Every manner of foodstuff, spices, and herbs was laid out on canvas in front of row after row of square tents without walls. There was livestock, too, and tents full of radios. It seemed like acre upon acre of tents were selling brassieres and flip-flop sandals which had been strung around the roof edge of the tents and were catching the breeze off the Mediterranean like a million windsocks.

Large cloth signs were stretched across boulevards and streets proclaiming, "U.S. IMPERIALISTS OUT OF SOUTHEAST ASIA," complete with a picture of a skinny and decrepit "Uncle Sam" in striped trousers and top hat getting kicked in the butt by a Viet Cong caricature.

Algiers is an ancient city, yet, like Detroit or any major Western city, there were large sections with closed and abandoned storefronts. Unlike Detroit, however, the Revolutionary Government had found creative uses for them. In the empty windows, the Algerians would set up educational displays in an attempt to educate the poor and largely illiterate population and to address issues facing the nation. One storefront, for example, would have an exhibit promoting literacy with photos of smiling children reading and information on how to join the literacy campaign. In another would be a display presented by the Red Crescent Society, the Arab world's counterpart to the Red Cross, extolling citizens to give blood to support the Palestinian freedom fighters. Yet another would have a photo essay depicting battle scenes and village life in Vietnam.

One that impressed me very much addressed the ongoing problem of blindness. It seems there is a little fly that lays its eggs in the eyes of infants. When the eggs hatch the larvae eat the eye or otherwise causes blindness in the child. I saw numerous storefront displays demonstrating the life cycle of this fly and dealing with prophylactic measures for preventing this type of blindness, the correct method for washing the eyes and the proper solution to use.

One day while walking in the Kasbah I came to the attention of a group of young Arabic-speaking boys, six or eight of whom began pestering me for money, holding out their small, dirty hands, panhandling I assumed. I still had some coins from Norway, Denmark and Sweden as well as some change from

Germany and Italy. Hoping to get rid of the boys I doled out the change, a few coins to each boy, but they wouldn't leave; they kept following me, attracting more children as we moved through the market and business district of the quarter.

Finally I noticed a movie theater showing some kind of fantastical flick made in India featuring dragons and flying carpets, blue giants, men in bloomers, and women in gauzy pajamas. I paid my admission and went inside hoping to avoid the children. Though I didn't have a clue about the details, I did recognize the classic storyline; the villain was vanquished, the hero won the girl and saved the village.

Two hours later, upon leaving the theater, I was greeted by a group of thirty or more begging, clutching, pestering kids wanting more money. I tried to shoo them away but to no avail. An elderly man in a rather dirty robe came to my aid, chasing the boys off while scolding them. He then turned to me and shooed me away too, speaking in Arabic and giving me hell.

My biggest problem while in Algiers, besides being a stranger in a strange land and lonesome for home and the touch of loved ones, was having to eat every day. The language barrier was so intimidating to me that I would only eat one meal a day so as to minimize the trauma of trying to communicate. Usually I ate gyros purchased from street venders--a delicious pita-bread sandwich with goat, chicken and beef, some sautéed vegetables on top with yogurt spooned on. But a steady diet of gyros was rather thin for daily fare, so I decided to go to a cheap, sit-down restaurant and order the most expensive item on the menu. Since I was only eating one meal a day this seemed reasonable.

I found a little hole-in-the-wall place, long and narrow, with the kitchen in the back and six to eight small tables up front. I picked a table near the back. A young Arab waiter appeared dressed in black shoes, black trousers, and a white shirt with a black bow tie; a serving towel was folded neatly over his arm. He handed me a menu. "Steak Tartar" was the most expensive item on the it. I recognized the word "steak" but had never heard of the dish and didn't have a clue what "tartar" was.

The waiter, who spoke French, took my order and returned moments later pushing a cart draped with a tablecloth on which was set a bowl covered by another one inverted over it. He pushed the cart up to my table, uncovered the bowl, and placed the empty top bowl in front of me. The bottom bowl contained a mound of hamburger--ground beef. With a theatrical flourish the waiter picked up a silver serving fork and spoon and began to work the scoop of raw meat. He broke a raw egg into the meat and continued to stir, then added several pinches of chives and some spices. He continued to stir and pat and prod the lump of rawness with dexterity and practiced grace. He then slid the concoction from the mixing bowl onto the serving bowl in front of me--a few more pats and taps, some fresh ground pepper, a slice of ripe avocado to one side and a slice of orange to the other, a sprig of parsley, and it was done--voila!

He stood back with his towel over his arm, looking quite pleased with himself and waiting. I looked at the reddish brown blob of raw flesh with yellow marbling flecked with green, then I looked at the waiter. I thought maybe he was going to touch a match to it or something, perhaps he would ignite it and a great whoosh of flame would go up giving off the smell of cooked meat. But no, he just stood there nodding and saying something over and over in French that ended in "monsieur."

Finally I realized he was not going to cook this thing. I shuddered. With trepidation I jabbed a forkful. Up came a clump of raw meat, raw egg and a big booger of egg white snot dangling down coated with pepper and chives. I put my fork down, laid ten dinars on the table, and got up and left. I decided to stick with the gyros. I also decided I could not live here, it was all too alien--I wanted to go home.

If I had had a friend with me, someone to share the experience with and talk to, it might have been different. As it was, I was lonesome. I saw Eldridge three or four hours a day, but frankly I was getting rather tired of his bragging--the important people he was going to see at this or that embassy, the important people he was going to have dinner with, the important people who were coming to his house, or this or that General or Party Secretary or Minister he knew.

My contact in the Ministry of Information took me to dinner a time or two. One afternoon we went to her apartment in the European quarter for lunch. The apartment building was unremarkable--white stucco with a red tile roof, maybe five stories tall. What was remarkable was the elevator system. In each car, just above the panel containing the buttons designating floor levels, was a coin box like the ones at the mall, on a mechanical riding horses for children--25 cents a ride. My host explained that the coin boxes were a security device, a remnant of colonial times. In order to make the elevator work, a token had to be deposited. The tokens were free and only made available to tenants of the building. Since the tenants were always Europeans, the tokens functioned to keep the Arabs out. The coin boxes were now disabled but remained as a reminder of French apartheid.

My contact from the Ministry explained that political asylum was no big deal. I had to register with the police and the Ministry of Internal Affairs. I would have to support myself and stay out of trouble. That was it, but I could not expect the White Panther Party to support me long-term and finding a job seemed out of the question; I felt it unlikely I would stay in Algiers long.

On my twenty-fifth birthday I trekked to the Central Post Office to call home, collect. I got DS on the phone. After enthusiastic pleasantries, DS informed me that he was working on a deal whereby I could turn myself in to the Feds if they promised a reasonable bond. I was thrilled! I wanted to go home.

DS explained that this would take time though, and that I should just sit tight until the deal was solid. Though I didn't tell him so, I knew then and there that I was going home immediately.

As romantic, exciting, enlightening, and revolutionary as Algiers was, I was completely out of my element. There were no hippies, no rock-n-roll. Oh, the young people did dance to some kind of western music up in the clubs in the European quarter, but one could hardly call it rock-n-roll and it was just barely dancing. There was no junk food, or FM radio, no avant guarde art scene, no pot. Oh, old men would sit for hours in sidewalk cafes in the Kasbah, in the early morning sun, nibbling hashish and drinking green mint tea from small glasses. But I was not of that culture and would never fit in.

I called Jorgen in Denmark and informed him of my intention of returning to the states. He encouraged me to return via Copenhagen by May 1st so I could participate in the May Day march.

The last time I saw Eldridge in Algiers, I whined about feeling like a fish out of water and being "dreadfully homesick for rock-n-roll, dope, and sex in the streets." I borrowed $250 from him, promising to repay it "when the revolution comes." He seemed glad to be shed of me. I suppose I was impinging on his time, if not cramping his style.

I had to pass through Algerian Customs to board my flight, a TWA jet to Copenhagen via Switzerland. Upon opening my suitcase the Custom Agent found my two tape recorders and dozens of cassettes. He questioned me by saying two words, several times, most likely: "La papier jaune, papier jaune" I couldn't work my dictionary fast enough to understand what he was saying, though I understood there was a problem.

Soon another agent joined him. Then they both pestered me, asking over and over: "La d`eclaration en douane papier! Papier de d`eclaration!" I began to worry I might miss my plane. By listening very closely and thumbing through the dictionary I realized they wanted me to show my customs declaration paper to show I brought the tapes and players into the country. Without the paper I was expected to pay a duty or tariff of some sort for taking the cassette machines out of the country. They paid no attention to the mounds of books and pamphlets, posters and cassette tapes gathered from the many embassies and liberation offices I visited. Meanwhile I could see my plane sitting on the tarmac, portable steps still in place, the engines revving.

"I have no money...no dinar, no dinar," I kept saying. A supervisor was called, a stern man in a gold encrusted hat and a military uniform with the air and stature of a general. The general said slowly in heavily accented English, "Declaration paper."

I looked quizzically, like a puppy trying to understand its master.

"Declaration paper! Declaration paper!" he repeated as he waved the yellow sheet in front of my face. It was just like the yellow sheet I was given on the plane before I arrived in Algiers.

"No declaration paper." I responded

"Non d`eclaration papier?" He looked shocked.

I explained as best I could that I assumed I only had to declare items I purchased on the plane. Since I purchased nothing, I declared nothing.

"Non, non, non," he said as only a French speaker can.

Meanwhile the ground crew scurried under the plane obviously making ready to depart.

"No declaration--you must pay duty."

"No money, no dinar," I said putting on the most pitiful expression. "Home to see ma ma," I said, nearly frantic.

Then the strangest thing happened. He asked me what kind of work I did. I told him I was a house painter.

"Go! Go!" he said, pointing the way.

I quickly stuffed everything back into my suitcase, slammed the top down and bolted for the door, my suitcase under my arm. Two attendants were waiting at the base of the stairs, ready to wheel it away as I ran up two steps at a time.

Chapter Thirteen

USA VIA DENMARK...SPRING 1970

I was unable to contain my excitement at the prospect of going home. I didn't have a plan, but I knew I could hide out once I got there. I realized too that there was a good chance I would get captured or killed. I accepted this as the risk of going home.

I had never wanted to go underground. Unlike the Weathermen and other clandestine groups that planned a strategy for going underground, even looked forward to it, I had no desire or intention of leaving my community and leading the subterranean life--until that fateful day in October of 1969 when my indictment was announced over the radio.

I don't now, and never have, regretted my decision to flee the law. The options were straightforward--get arrested, on what I knew to be framed-up charges, and go to jail while hoping for reasonable bond, which was very unlikely, or, flee the indictment and stay free until the Party was in a better position to fight the case. I chose the later, half-grudgingly.

* * *

I arrived in the Danish capital in the last days of April. The parks and streets were full of smiling, fair-haired folks. Danes take to the out-of-doors when the sun warms the earth and the air smells sweet with green growth and the sound of songbirds. Winter is harsh--spring is the reward.

The whole nation seemed to be smiling, at ease with one another and the world, familiar as family. Most of the population is made up of Nordic Danes, who have fair skin and hair and a common history and origin going back a thousand years in that ancient land. Like a village, there was a common unity, a common culture that created a level of familiarity and comfort in the citizens.

This is lacking in the States. Our nation is made up of many cultures, but we feel most comfortable with our own. We will never have the village experience in the States except in our small intimate communities. When I recognized this, I realized I was not comfortable in any culture. I had no genetic community, no culture of origin that I identified with. I loathed the white dominant culture of America I was raised in, and I was not comfortable in Arab culture. Though it was pleasant, I was not a Dane and would never connect to the ancient earth and the culture that grew from it. I was a man without a culture and so without a center, without a place to stand connected to the earth and any of its people. I felt like a no-brand kid again.

This is why the hippie movement attracted so many young Americans, including myself. We were alienated and disenfranchised from the culture we were raised in and saw an opportunity to create a new culture. A culture, which could leave behind the dastardly sins of the old. A lifestyle not based on racism and greed, not based on arrogant might and mindless obedience, not based on class, wealth, and selfish individualism, not based on endless consumption. We believed we could build a new culture that could change all that. It's too early to tell the results of our efforts.

* * *

A warm rain washed the cobbled streets clean and brought out the crocuses, paper-whites, daffodils and the first shoots of tulips on the morning of the May Day celebration. The May Day tradition has a long and colorful history across Europe and the communist's countries. A worker's holiday with parades, picnics, speeches and celebrations. It was even celebrated here in the states for a time. It was Nixon that had May 1st officially renamed "Law Day."

It was also Nixon who, the night before, on April 30th, had announced the widening of the war in Vietnam by the "incursion" of US forces into Cambodia. The populous seemed stunned and incredulous that Nixon would expand the murderous conflict while The Paris Peace Talks were in progress and it was obvious to the whole world that America would not win the war.

In Copenhagen, ten thousand marchers gathered in a large park. Since it was May Day, all the labor organizations and their auxiliaries were present, proclaiming solidarity with working people the world over, and with the people of Vietnam in particular. It seemed to me the atmosphere was more that of a circus parade than a demonstration. There were jugglers, mimes, and fire-eaters, and thousands of people with drums, horns, and whistles creating a tremendous din. Street theater groups performed along the marchers' route, and even a puppet theater found an audience. Families walked together as dads pushed strollers and licked ice cream. One guy held a sign that said, "THE END IS NEAR," in Danish.

Going up a slight rise in the street allowed me to look forward and back to get a good view at the size of the crowd. The march stretched for a kilometer or more in each direction, a river of people with banners, placards and flags. As the march took us through the working-class section of the city, people lined the sidewalks and cheered. Block after block of multistoried apartment buildings--what we call "projects"--

sprouted red flags from windows, punctuated occasionally by the anarchists' black banner. Whole buildings resembled red poppies with flecks of black flags like seeds. People hung from windows and blew horns or beat on pots and pans. It was something to see.

The route of the march was designed to keep the crowd on the far bank of the river, across from the American embassy. As we neared an intersection and a bridge, Jorgen sidled up to me: "stay close," he said, "the dragon is loose."

At the intersection, where the bridge crossed the river, ruffians among the marchers turned right to march over the bridge. This was a younger, more rambunctious crowd than the main group of marchers. They were all dressed in gloves, heavy boots, and either football or motorcycle helmets; some wore gas masks and hockey pads. From somewhere long, wooden poles were produced. Hand-to-hand and shoulder-to-shoulder, people gripped the poles holding them chest high. This line of marchers became the front line. Placed end to end, the poles stretched across the entire width of the street. Slowly the front line began to move across the bridge holding the poles in front, chest high.

Splitting off from the main body of marchers, who continued to parade toward their peaceful destination, a renegade column of two thousand or so, followed the group who were crossing the river. As the front line moved forward they began to stomp their feet in a measured marching cadence. Soon the entire crowd was marching and stomping in unison as it progressed at a slow, steady pace.

Though Jorgen and I had joined this alternative column, Jorgen insisted we stay to the back of the crowd. Once over the bridge the column turned left, and we could see the US Embassy five blocks down. The street in front of the embassy was blocked with city buses parked nose to tail. In front of the buses were a hundred or more Copenhagen cops in formation and in full riot gear, waiting for orders. In front of them was a skirmish line, four deep, with officers spread out so they could use their batons. In front of this skirmish line, facing the marchers, was a solid line, from curb to curb, of Danish police kneeling on one knee behind plastic shields held side by side across the street, creating a solid wall of clear acrylic two meters high.

The column, stomping a slow beat, continued toward

the Embassy. At an intersection our human river of two thousand split when the right half of the front line, still carrying poles, turned down a side street and began jogging toward the next intersection. We watched them jog away from us as we continued straight.

At the next intersection, we looked down the side street and saw our other column moving parallel to us toward the embassy. A great roar rose from the two columns of stomping, marching Danes.

One block from the line of cops and plastic shields, the lead marchers picked up the pace to a slow jog, continuing to stomp in time while holding the wooden poles chest high in front of them as they ran. The mass behind them began jogging too. It was like seeing a human avalanche building momentum as it approached an immovable object with gathering speed.

Fifty meters from the line of kneeling police, the front line broke into a full gallop; a thousand marchers behind them began running too.

The first line crashed headlong into the line of kneeling cops with a sickening clash of wood and plastic and tooth and bone. The wooden poles, and the marchers holding them, took out the first two rows of cops creating a tangled mass of people and shields, helmets and placards. The next tier of cops got in some free licks with their batons as marchers lay wriggling on the ground. When another surge of marchers crashed into the mass of cops the whole scene became a violent madhouse, like a medieval battle.

Jorgen and I made our way around to the other side of the embassy. Here the cops' skirmish line held. There was no fighting, but evidence of a recent rumble lay scattered on the street--helmets and gloves, flag poles and signs, several sneakers and a crutch. A few walking wounded held rags to head wounds or clutched their ribs as medics tended them.

We returned to the front of the building and found a rumble in full swing. Marchers were flailing back at police with flagpoles and sign handles; others were trying to rescue those caught by the cops. One guy with long, red hair and beard, wearing a Viking helmet (metal, with two horns) was wielding a wooden staff against three Danish police officers with shields and batons. They cowered before his onslaught, holding up their shields and backing away in the face of Thors' son's fury.

Jorgen noticed a long line of cop cars on the other side of the river--reinforcements, apparently. We slipped away with a small group of demonstrators and went to the nearby Pan Am building and kicked in all the windows at sidewalk level to show our rage at American imperialism and the widening of the war.

Two days later I was on a flight to Toronto.

Chapter Fourteen

BACK IN THE USA---Summer 1970

As soon as I stepped off the plane in Toronto, I saw the headline: GUARDSMEN KILL FOUR AT KENT STATE! It was May 4, 1970.

When Nixon widened the war by invading Cambodia, people around the world reacted with anger and stunned disbelief. The incursion seemed the epitome of spiteful arrogance and contempt for life on the part of the Nixon administration. The whole world knew the US would not win the war in Vietnam. It was just a matter of time before America abandoned its murderous folly and left that part of the world to the people who lived there.

In this country, student leaders and others called for strikes and mass action on campuses and workplaces across the land.

I contacted The Green Lantern again. At this time he was on the Board of Directors of the Rochdale Housing Cooperative, owners of an urban skyscraper housing co-operative near the University of Toronto. He was surprised to see me, to say the least, though he finagled me a bare, unfurnished apartment on an upper floor where I felt relatively safe. Only The Green Lantern and Jorgen knew I was back in North America. He was absolutely trustworthy, especially since he was a co-conspirator on the procurement of a fraudulent passport. He had an interest in my safety.

The Prez didn't know I was back, nor did DS, Leni, Rock-n-Roll Rita, or the lawyers, nobody. I had to make my own plans and use my own resources to pull this off. I laid low for a week or more, plotting my return, rarely going out except to buy peanut butter, bread and beer. At a head shop I bought a copy of every underground newspaper in stock. I wanted to catch up--get a feel for the pulse of the counter-culture. I returned to the empty apartment and read every paper cover to cover.

It was apparent that resistance to the war had significantly increased in the eight months I'd been underground. The culture of resistance and peace movement had infiltrated and influenced every small town and big city across the nation, and more citizens than ever were taking matters into their own hand to show their disgust with the government. Militants bombed government installations, Catholic priests and pacifists blocked munitions trains, more young men fled to Canada. On the 14th of May, two black students at Jackson State College, in Mississippi, were killed when police fired into their dormitory during a night of strike and antiwar demonstrations. The country was in turmoil. The power structure was killing its own children and imprisoning its own priests in what appeared to be a last deadly grasp at continued control. Nixon, Attorney General Mitchell, and FBI Director Hoover were proving themselves to be the dinosaur pigs we'd been describing them as.

*　　　　　*　　　　　*

Without a revolutionary party there can be no revolution: This is fundamental Leninism. Without a revolutionary party, the movement will focus on a single issue, failing to articulate the interconnectedness of the issue to the many others that face the people; rarely is it radical and almost never militant.

The need for a vanguard party to lead the mass movement was, and still is, apparent. I never envisioned the WPP as the party to lead the revolution; though I did believe we were the only ones qualified to lead the youth and counter-culture wing of a larger revolutionary party, which never materialized.

During the Vietnam era, ending the war was the single major issue galvanizing the movement. Yet similar movements centered on the issues of civil rights, women, Labor, gays, and the environment, among others, are all interrelated and, taken in total, involve the interests of the majority of Americans--the American Bolsheviks.

War is only a symptom. The root of the problem, the radicis, is greed and the need to exploit wage workers under the capitalist/imperialist system. Ending the war did not solve the underlying problem. As natural resources become scarcer, as countries compete for trade, as workers are pitted against each other in the wage-market, the power structure resorts to violence to exploit raw materials and control markets, the beasts of war crouch on the sideline, eager to support the power structure. After all, America was founded on land and natural resources stolen from the First Nations and the initial wealth of the country was created by slaves, this was done under the guiding principle of "might makes right," and "Manifest Destiny."

*　　　　　*　　　　　*

In one of the underground newspapers, I found a half-page ad announcing a large outdoor music festival to be held in Bowling Green, Ohio. Scheduled to play was a band called The UP!, a group of young musicians Sinclair had been grooming as another White Panther band before his incarceration; DS was their manager, so I knew he'd be there. Party personnel would also be on hand staffing the literature table and selling T-shirts and other items. I was so lonely and lonesome, so very homesick, that I felt I just had to see them. With The Prez still in Hanoi, I hoped to see Rock-n-Roll Rita or another Party sweetheart who might be inclined to share vigorous sex with me, believing these might be my last days of freedom or even life.

*　　　　　*　　　　　*

Author,
Feb. 1947,
22 months,
Traverse City,
Michigan.

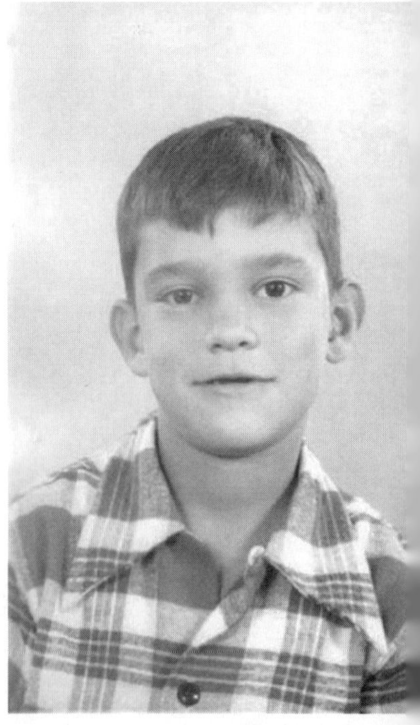

Author,
6 years old, 1951,
Traverse City,
Michigan.

Author,
16 years old,
Traverse City,
Michigan.

Author, Ann Arbor West Park, 1968 (photo Leni Sinclair) .

Detroit Artists Workshop / Trans-Love Energies, 1967 (riots) – New Mobilization to End the War and Fifth Estate office in storefronts. (photo Leni Sinclair).

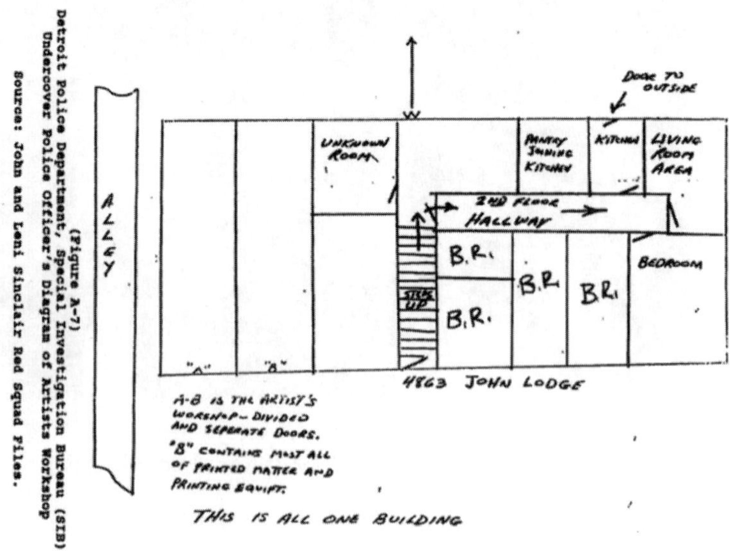

Red Squad floor plan of Trans Love Energies commune.

Leni Sinclair, Ann Arbor, 1971
(L. Sinclair archive).

Cheeseburger,
Ann Arbor
People's Ballroom,
1969
(photo L. Sinclair)

Grimshaw, Detroit, 1971
(photo
L. Sinclair)

Author with Black Panthers Masi Hewitt and Sam Napier 1969
(photo L. Sinclair)

Sunny, Skippy and Alan Ginsberg, Ann Arbor, 1969 (photo L. Sinclair)

Author, Underground Media Conference, Ann Arbor, 1969. (photo L. Sinclair)

The Prez and author, Underground Media Conference
Ann Arbor, 1969. (photo L. Sinclair)

Sinclair and Red Haired Audrey, Ann Arbor, 1969.
(photo L. Sinclair)

Emil, 1967, Johnny's Restaurant, Detroit. (photo L. Sinclair)

Author, 1969, Detroit Rock n Roll Revival (photo Charles Harbutt /Plamondon archive)

Werbe with unknown Panthers, Federal Building, Detroit 1969 .
(photo L. Sinclair)

Forest, Detroit
White Panther Captain,
1969,
(photo L. Sinclair)

Author, underground, Berkeley, California, 1970 (photo Detroit Annie/Plamondon archive)

CIA Trial Defense Team, Detroit, 1970, L-R, Back Row: Pat Roberts, Liz Gaines, Ken Mogil. Third Row: William Kunstler, Leonard Weinglass. Second Row: The Prez, Neal Fink, Ken Kelly. Front Row: D. Taube, DS, Buck Davis. (photo L. Sinclair)

Author, underground, San Francisco, California, 1970. (photo Detroit Annie/Plamondon Archive)

Buck Davis, 1970, lead attorney White Panther Party / Rainbow People's Party, Detroit law offices. (photo L. Sinclair)

DS, law offices, Detroit, 1970 (photo L. Sinclair)

Sinclair, The Prez and author, at press conference
upon author's release from prison, July 1972.
(photo L. Sinclair)

Fenton, Ann Arbor, 1971 (photo L. Sinclair)

Lewis Sawaquat in 1836 ceded territories of Michigan, 1986. (photo L. Chambers)

The Author, Mosquito Ranch in the 1836
ceded territories of Michigan, 2004. (photo Tom Walsh)

While still in Canada I went through my suitcase and took out all the posters, books, and pamphlets I'd collected during my visits to embassies and offices of various national liberation fronts while in Algiers. Certainly Communist posters and written material calling for the defeat of US imperialism would catch the eye of any customs or immigration agent checking me out as I tried to re-enter the States.

I left the printed material with The Green Lantern with the understanding that I would reclaim it "when the revolution comes." I kept my two tape recorders and several dozen cassette tapes of interviews with revolutionaries I'd conducted during my travels. I felt it unlikely a border agent would listen to my tapes.

When I left Toronto The Green Lantern made me promise to destroy the passport he helped procure for me just two months earlier. He was afraid the passport would be traced to the Quebecois, Father Brule', and ultimately to him, should I get captured. I promised.

I took a train to Detroit and entered the country without incident, not even having to show my passport, which I burned outside the station upon my arrival. I couldn't stay in Detroit; the FBI field office would certainly have circulated my picture to local police who would be expecting me to show up in my old haunts. A safer bet would be a short bus ride to Toledo and a $15-a-week flop in a rundown hotel near the Greyhound station while I waited for the Bowling Green concert.

Still convinced that the FBI was out to kill me, I needed a gun. I made my way around the small area of rundown Toledo with down-and-out businesses--the usual strip-joints and seedy bars found in parts of a city in decay. A certain strip club had a particularly sinister smell and smoky air about it, a dark shadowy joint with hillbilly songs playing on the jukebox. I got good vibes when I entered.

I hung out for a few hours in the morning, nursing a beer, then a couple of hours in the afternoon sipping a beer, then from eleven in the evening until closing. I maintained this pattern over several days, flirting with the strippers and waitresses, calling the bartender by his first name, and engaging in conversations with other patrons. It didn't take long before I was considered a regular. I struck up a conversation with

Wayne, another regular. Though a young man, he had the thin, vexed, and harrowed look of an ex-convict, he had a pallid complexion; a night person who saw the sun rarely. I let him know I needed a handgun.

Later that night he brought me nickel-plated, two-shot .38 derringer, like the ones old-time gamblers kept up their sleeves. "It's only 25 bucks," he said, scanning the room as he laid the piece on the table in the back booth.

"Christ, I can't use that," I said. "I couldn't hit the mirror from here with that two inch barrel."

"Twenty-five bucks, take it or leave it--there's ten bullets too," he said, looking over his shoulder.

The derringer was not much bigger than a pack of cigarettes. I held it under the table and checked it out closely, then gave Wayne the money.

At that time I carried a used, slim and trim, imitation leather attaché case. I loaded the palm pistol and placed it inside the brief case.

Our business finished, Wayne and I went to the bar to have a beer. Leaning over halfway, I lightly dropped the briefcase six inches above the floor…BLAM!

A shot rang out! No one knew where it had come from. The top of the bar splintered as the bullet struck it on its trajectory to the ceiling. The bartender ran crouching from behind the bar and out the back door; several others followed him or scurried under tables.

Wayne and I hit the floor with the others. On my knees I saw my briefcase with the whole corner blown out; a whiff of smoke, like a cartoon picture, was wafting from it. I could smell burnt gunpowder and smoldering papers from its oxygen-starved interior.

The slight jolt as the attaché hit the floor must have jarred the hammer on the loaded derringer, causing it to fire.

In the momentary confusion, I grabbed my still smoldering case and hightailed it out of there. I took a circuitous route back to my flop and hid out, trembling. When it was time to go, I ditched the attaché, and stuffed the derringer in my pocket, and took an early morning bus to Bowling Green.

I spent a few hours killing time in several restaurants waiting for the festival to get into gear so I could blend in with the crowd. At midmorning I went to the field where the gathering was to be held. The place was ready, the stage was built, stagehands were scurrying to hook up the PA and lighting systems. Several bands were milling around with more arriving all the time. Excitement was building in anticipation of the noon opening.

I mingled with several dozen people in front of the stage, watching the final setup. Just then DS walked in front of the stage laying a heavy electrical cable along the ground. I stepped in front of him. "Hi DS!" I said showing an exuberant grin. For a split second he didn't recognize me. Then his eyes got big and he went ashen. "Pun! What the fuck are you doing here?" I could see his shoulders droop and his chest cave slightly as if taking on yet another weighty load.

"You can't be here! You've gotta leave--we're under constant surveillance--I've got to get you out of here." DS spun on his heels and began to walk away, and then he turned and came back. "Put some sunglasses on for Christ's sake," he said, then turned and walked away.

I thought he would be glad to see me. But he was terribly alarmed and frightened. I got the first inkling that I might have messed up bad.

Within five minutes Rock-n-Roll Rita had sidled up next to me and whispered, "Come with me, Pun."

I followed as she walked out of the festival grounds, across a four-lane boulevard to a pizza and beer establishment. We went in and I ordered a beer. Rita stayed outside to see if we were followed; we weren't.

Not yet being twenty-one, she ordered coffee. "Pun, DS said you really screwed up. We can't deal with you right now. John's case is going up on appeal, the phones are turned off, we don't have any money. Why did you come back?"

I felt bad. Running underground alone, with my fear and loneliness, I gave no consideration to the effect my actions had on my loved ones and supporters. This was not the first time my impetuous behavior had caused others grief. I felt like the time I stole beer out of my dad's store--it seemed like a good idea at the time, but confronted with the aftermath, I knew it was wrong.

"Why did you come back?" Rita pleaded.

"I was lonesome and missed everybody." As soon as I said it I realized how selfish and lame my statement was. "DS is supposed to be hooking up a deal so I can turn myself in," I said, hoping this would have some effect.

"The lawyers are working on that, it's not a big priority, and all the lawyers' time is put on John's appeal. You were safe there, why did you come back? We don't even have a place for you to stay. Why did you come back?" she repeated in disbelief.

There was a band out of Toledo on the festival bill called THE KRAAK! They were White Panther supporters, though not Party members. Rita had instructions to take me back to Toledo where I was to stay at the KRAAK! house until I was retrieved early in the morning after the festival was over.

We were there in an hour, smoking several joints along the way. This was the first pot I'd had in several months; the high brought on a wave of paranoia that made it nearly impossible for me to function.

My terror--or the pot--had affected my sight. Everything appeared as if I were looking in the wrong end of a pair of binoculars: small and very far away. The Bic lighter I held in my hand seemed no bigger than a vitamin capsule.

The KRAAK! house was empty; everyone was at the festival. Though Rita had to return to the festival, she spent more than an hour trying to calm me down.

Once Rita was gone, my paranoia knew no bounds. I sat on the couch alone, the derringer pointed at the door, expecting my worst nightmare to become real as I stared at the TV that looked to be a hundred yards away and no bigger than a picture on a driver's license.

Well after midnight several carloads of KRAAKS! rolled in with DS and Rita and Skippy. My paranoia had lessened but the music and commotion of several dozen people in the house threatened to put me over the edge again.

Rita and Skippy got me in a van and we headed north into Michigan. Once moving, my paranoia subsided. The ability to see into the distance made all the difference. They brought with them some groceries, a tent, sleeping bag, radio, flashlight, and other camping gear. I was going to be spending some time camping in the woods; this gave me comfort.

*   *   *

One of the principles taken from Mao Tse-Tong and adopted by the Black Panther and White Panther parties was the principle of "criticism/self criticism." We believed that by continually reviewing and analyzing our political work, as individuals and as an organization, we could recognize our failures and shortcomings and take measures to correct them. We vigorously criticized each other's political work, as well as our own. All Party members in whatever branch or chapter, at whatever level of leadership, accepted this principle and practiced it without mercy.

It was particularly painful to listen to Rita and Skippy scold and criticize me on our two-hour trip to my hiding place in Michigan. They reminded me of the many self-righteous harangues I gave at weekly Party meetings denouncing "bourgeois individualism, bourgeois adventurism," and "romantic notions of revolution." According to them, I was forever stressing the need for "collective decision making, collective leadership, and collective action." By returning to the States as I did, they said, I had broken every principle I had so eloquently articulated as Minister of Defense.

I could only hang my head, agree, and wonder what The Prez would say when she returned from Hanoi.

They took me to the Grass Lake State Game and Recreation Area near Jackson. Since it was only mid-May there were few campers and no ranger on duty in the vast acreage of forests, lakes, and marsh. We found a secluded spot and set up camp.

Before they left, Rita and Skippy gave me my orders: I was to stay in the tent--STAY IN THE TENT! I was not to be seen by anyone. ANYONE! I could go out to relieve myself; otherwise I was to STAY IN THE TENT! Skippy left me a 12-gauge shotgun and a box of shells. I still had the derringer and carried it unloaded in my back pack.

They promised to return before my food and water ran out. I stayed there a week, reading all day, doing just as I had been instructed.

Skippy returned with The Prez, who was just back from Hanoi. She surprised me by simply saying, "You disappointed everyone--everyone who helped get you to Algiers, just everyone."

"I'm sorry, I wasn't thinking," was pretty thin gruel, but was all I could offer.

Skippy and Prez had news. Sinclair's hearing on the right to bond pending appeal was soon to go before the Michigan Court of Appeals. The case law and court precedent gave us reason to believe that we would win and that Sinclair would be released on bond.

More importantly, to me at least, was the news that they had found a permanent place for me to hide. It was in the farthest reaches of Michigan's upper peninsula, in the wild and sparsely populated Keweenaw.

They explained that negotiations were only just about ready to begin with the Feds regarding my turning myself in. The Feds said they were interested in discussing it, that's as far as it went they said.

The Prez stressed that the longer I remained underground, the better position I was in to bargain. The Feds would not make a deal if they believed they were close on my trail. Only if they had no idea where I was would they be interested in dealing.

Unfortunately, unbeknownst to any Party members, the Feds were already aware I was back in the States. They had infiltrated an informer into the Party, Dennis Marnell. He had taken up with The Prez and was sleeping with her every night while living with her at headquarters. He knew I was back, but no one told him where, thank God. He passed this information on to his handlers.

Skip and The Prez moved me from Grass Lake farther north to the Pigeon River Area in northern Lower Michigan while final preparations were made for my trip to the Keweenaw.

Two weeks after my move, while at my camp in the Pigeon River, I was visited by The Prez and Stu arriving in a rental car, while Skippy and Forest showed up in a VW hippie van. Stu and The Prez were there for a visit, Skippy and Forest to take me to the Keweenaw.

Stu gave me a serious tongue-lashing in front of the others. Though he was not a Party member, he was a friend and a man I held in high esteem, still do. Today I realize The Prez and the Party had brought in Stu to talk some sense into me, to get me to lie low and take all this more seriously.

He criticized my entire attitude and demeanor. He pointed out that in interviews I'd given and articles I'd written while underground, I came across as a "swashbuckling outlaw without a care in the world." Rather than use my notoriety to put forward a coherent analysis and plan of action, he said, I used the media opportunities I had to call the FBI "a bunch of faggots," to threaten and taunt them "like a fifth-grader thumbing his nose to the bullies who are half a block away."

Everything he was saying was true, I see that now. At the time, I countered by saying I was exhibiting "revolutionary arrogance in the face of overwhelming odds." I told him I hoped to excite young people to rebellion. I hoped to show that extreme action was survivable, that the consequences were not as bad as living with the status quo. I wanted kids to take militant action, to cross the line--go beyond the point of no return, as I had.

*　　　　*　　　　*

Everyone spent the night at my camp. The guys slept in my tent. The Prez and I took to the mattress in the van. Little did I know that it was to be the last time I was to feel a woman's touch or sleep in freedom for more than two-and-a-half years.

By noon we had broken camp. Skippy showed me the weapons he'd brought: two 30 caliber, semi-auto, M1 carbines, a 12-gauge pump shotgun and several hundred rounds of ammunition; these were added to the 12-gauge and the derringer I already had. I put the derringer in the glove compartment, and we stashed the long guns under the camping gear. After stoic hugs and kisses, with bravado I had learned from habit, we said goodbye.

The Prez and Stu headed south, back to the ongoing struggle to end the war, to free Sinclair and other political prisoners, to support national liberation struggles around the world, to speak truth to power, to protect the earth, to build a new culture in the smoldering shell of the old, to resist the government, to join the ranks of the lowest, to sing, to dance and walk sideways, smashing and making love while getting higher and higher. I loved the fight; it was the only thing worth living for.

*   *   *

Skippy, Forest, and I motored the van westward to Wolverine where we picked up a case of beer and jumped on I-75 heading north toward the Mackinac Bridge connecting Michigan's two peninsulas. Forest was driving, Skippy was in the back, I was riding shotgun and sucking down cold beers. It was now nearing the end of July and already the humidity given up by the big lake was making life miserable. We sped along with all the windows open, trying to get some cooling relief.

Near Indian River, having drunk mass quantities of beer, I had to pee. Forest pulled up an exit ramp and stopped 50 yards short of the cross-road at the top of the exit. At the top of the ramp was a Texaco gas station; the attendant was on the drive rinsing it down with a garden hose.

Once stopped, I got out to relieve myself. The floor of the front seat was littered with empty beer cans, potato chip bags, and candy bar wrappers--the usual flotsam of a road trip. While I was taking a leak, Forest leaned over, picked up the empty beer cans and tossed them out the open door into the ditch, to our everlasting shame. I was still peeing when the guy at the gas station started hollering at us.

Apparently he had seen the beer cans being tossed. We were too far away to hear exactly what he was yelling, but I could make out words like "litterbugs--sons-of-bitches--throw it--own yard."

When finished with my business I went over and picked up a few of the cans and waved them over my head to show the guy we were picking them up. Back in the van with my handful of cans, we proceeded up the ramp, across the road and down the entry ramp on the other side. As we passed the gas station we saw the attendant leaning in the window of a Michigan State Police car talking to the driver.

Within a minute, the cop was behind us, lights flashing. "What are we going to do? Should we shoot the pig? Should I run?" I asked as Skippy maneuvered one of the shotguns out from under the camping gear. "Sit tight," Forest urged, "We've done nothing wrong, just sit tight."

We held our collective breaths as the officer approached the van and requested our IDs. Skippy and Forest had standard

Michigan driver's licenses and draft cards. I had a draft card and social security card the Party secured for me in the name of George Edward Taft III, who lived at 1336 N. Halstead in Chicago, a fictitious name and address. I had the derringer between my legs, hoping it wouldn't go off unexpectedly.

The cop returned after spending several minutes at his car with our IDs. He was quite pleasant. Returning our papers he said, "You boys can go back and pick up the trash on that exit ramp, or, you can follow me to the barracks and we'll take that van apart, bolt by bolt."

We followed him as he made a U-turn to the southbound side of the expressway. We walked the several hundred yards of the exit ramp picking up all manner of trash left by ignorant honkies and even stupider hippies like us.

* * *

Three hours later we were across the bridge, and an hour west of St. Ignace near Naubinway on Highway 2, a two-lane state road and one of the two east/west corridors in the Upper Peninsula.

Though it was heavy, traffic moved at 60 as we passed a boarded-up, crossroads gas station and noticed a county sheriff's car parked out back, in a clump of trees, as if hiding.

I watched in the side mirror as the sheriff's car pulled into traffic with some six cars between us. I kept glancing in the mirror as I tried to wake up Skippy who was now sleeping in the back.

Forest was at the wheel shouting, "Skippy, wake-up! Wake-up!" as he glanced in the mirror, then shouted, "The pig passed a car, the pig passed a car--he's after us."

My stomach rose in my throat. In my side mirror, I saw the sheriff's car squirt in and out, dodging the oncoming traffic--now he was four cars behind us--now three.

With Forest and me yelling, Skippy was beginning to come around. "Wake-up! Wake-up! The shit's coming down--the pigs are on us!" we shouted.

Now the sheriff was two cars behind--now one.

"Do we shoot it out? Do we shoot it out?" I kept screaming as Forest glanced in the mirror and kept up with the flow of traffic. Skippy rubbed his eyes and tried to get his bearings.

"Should we shoot him? Should we shoot the son-of-a-bitch?" I kept asking. Skippy, only half awake now, was hollering, "How many of them--where are they?"

Forest, with one eye on the mirror exclaimed, "He passed, he passed, he's right behind us! We've gotta pull over--he's right behind us!"

"Should we shoot him? Should we shoot him?" I yelled.

His lights and siren came on adding to the confusion of the moment.

"Get me the carbine! The carbine!" I yelled as Skippy rummaged under the camping gear with the long guns. I had the derringer in my hand but didn't know what to do with it.

"Don't shoot him! Don't shoot! No shooting!" Forest yelled as he eased off the gas and onto the shoulder. "Maybe he's not after us, let's see what he wants."

We pulled to a stop, and Forest quickly exited our vehicle to go back and talk to the deputy with his driver's license and vehicle registration in hand.

Skippy was just inserting a thirty round banana clip into a carbine that was tangled in tent-stakes and tarps when I glanced in the side mirror and saw Forest face down on the hood of the sheriff's car, his hands cuffed behind his back; the Deputy standing over him with a pistol to his head.

"He's got Forest! He's got Forest!" I yelled.

Skippy looked out the back window just as a State Police car came screaming from the other direction. The driver locked up the breaks, put the car into a four-wheel skid across the lane of oncoming traffic while throwing gravel and burning rubber, coming to a stop just twenty yards in front of us.

Skippy was hollering, "What do we do? What do we do?"

"I don't know! I don't know! I don't FUCKING know!" was all I could say.

In a flash, the state cop was out of his car and up the bank beside the road thirty feet from me and slightly above the van. He had an M1 carbine and a banana clip of his own.

I looked in the mirror; Forest was still spread-eagle over the hood of the car. The deputy was holding a massive chrome plated revolver in Forest's ear while talking over the external loudspeaker on the roof of his car.

"Exit the rust-colored van," he repeated several times. "Exit with your hands up."

I had the derringer in my hand. I looked at the cop next to me, up the bank. He had his carbine pointed dead at me.

"I'm getting out, I'm giving up," I told Skippy as I put the derringer in the glove box. "What are you going to do?"

"I'm getting out too," he said.

I shoved both hands out the sliding window to show I wasn't armed. I hollered to the cop that there was someone in the back and they were coming out too. I was afraid that if Skippy suddenly slid open the side door the cop would spook and start blazing away at us.

The cop was closer now, 15 feet, I could see him shaking. He had me reach out the side window and open the sliding door from the outside. He made Skippy get out and lie in the ditch while he cuffed him as he kept the carbine trained on me.

In the mirror I saw the deputy move Forest and lay him face down in the ditch. The state cop approached, telling me to keep my hands in sight. He quaked as he jammed the barrel of the carbine against my head and opened the door of the van very slowly. Once out, he leaned me against the van and patted me down while repeatedly jabbing the barrel of the carbine just under my ear. In his fear and trembling I was afraid he was going to shoot me by accident.

More cop cars began arriving; there was scurrying as we three prisoners were placed in separate cars.

I made a stubborn attempt to maintain my cover as George Edward Taft III. I told the pigs I was a hitchhiker and didn't even know those jerks. I was still clean-cut, unlike Skippy and Forest who looked like hippies, so this could be a plausible story. The state cop with me was on the radio talking with his sergeant. The trooper was instructed to look for identifying scars near my right eye. I still wore cover Girl make-up to hide the scars. The trooper radioed back that he saw no scars near my right eye. His apparent uncertainty gave me the faintest glimmer of hope that I might be able to talk my way out of this. I insisted I was a student on summer break and had never been in trouble before, "not even a parking ticket." The radio squealed again and the officer was told to look for scars on my top left forearm. He found four diagonal scars about three inches long, the result of a broken beer bottle fight in a slum bar in Reading, PA, in 1963.

I knew it was over. A great sigh gushed from my throat and it seemed my chest shrank as the stress left me. I was captured, but not killed. I knew the media attention given my arrest would make it difficult for the FBI to kill me now without questions being asked. I knew I was safe, if no longer free.

Chapter Fifteen

TOE TO TOE WITH THE NIXON MOB--1970

"Send lawyers, guns and money
The shit has hit the fan"

--Warren Zevon

From my basement cell in the old, red limestone jail I saw the Northern Lights and took it as a "sign" of good or ill, I didn't know which.[1]

[1] For the next thirty months I was held in country jails and federal prisons. My knowledge of events was necessarily acquired after the fact, and restricted considerably. I read and signed every motion, memorandum of law, and filing by the defense. I studied every motion and argument made by the prosecution. I was knowledgeable about the details of the case but unable to participate directly in its preparation or in other aspects of the defense, a torture in itself. The story of the CIA case and its consequences deserves its own book, to be written at another time.

After our arrest the three of us were separated and held in the Mackinac County Jail at St. Ignace. Later the FBI transported me to Detroit where I was immediately arraigned and formally charged with conspiracy and bombing government property. Then I was taken to the seventh floor maximum-security section of the Wayne County Jail (WCJ) where I was to spend the next eleven months.

Skippy and Forest were charged with "harboring a fugitive." Skippy went into the legal grinding system and ended up in prison in Minnesota, doing one to five. Forest (my co-defendant in the CIA case) and I cooled our heels in the WCJ. Sinclair was in Jackson and later in Marquette Prison.

The White Panther Party called a press conference to address my capture. The Prez and several others spoke for the Party. National Yippie! figure Abbie Hoffman was there to show support. The Party line on the case was this: we, like thousands of other Americans, were victims of a government conspiracy to stifle dissent, to discredit and silence political and cultural leaders found objectionable, and to create an atmosphere of fear and dread in the nation. Fear and dread was essential to the evil triumvirate of Nixon/Mitchell/Hoover and their wicked designs on the Constitution.

The press conference, like most in the past, was an exercise in militant rhetoric, which is an understatement. At one point Abbie jumped to his feet, pulled a bayonet from its sheath and threw the knife into the table. "Twang!" the handle vibrated as the blade stuck in the tabletop. "The arrest of Pun Plamondon will be avenged!" Abbie shouted from behind dark glasses, his hair flying--great footage for the cameras, but the prosecutor used the incident as justification for demanding $100,000 bond.

After several days in the Wayne County Jail, Buck Davis paid me a visit. He introduced himself as from the Detroit Office of the National Lawyers Guild (NLG). He mentioned that White Panther Party Central Committee members DS, Fenton, and Kelley had just returned from New York, having enlisted the services of William Kunstler and Lenny Weinglass, two "heavyweight" movement lawyers and NLG members who had conducted a successful defense of The Chicago Seven just months before.

Everyone had heard of "The Guild," as it was often

called. Back in the thirties the Guild helped organize the United Auto Workers and the Congress of Industrial Organizations. They helped prosecute Nazis at Nuremberg, and were one of the non-governmental organizations selected by the U.S. to represent the American government in the founding of the United Nations.

During the McCarthy era, Guild lawyers defended the Rosenbergs, as well as blacklisted Hollywood personalities and hundreds of innocent victims during the anti-communist hysteria.

More recently, Guild members had represented the families of murdered civil rights workers Schwerner, Chaney and Goodman, who had been killed by southern law enforcement and members of the Ku Klux Klan during the bloodiest times of the civil rights struggle.

At the time they took our CIA case, Guild lawyers had been defending members of the Black Panther Party, the American Indian Movement, the Weathermen, the Puerto Rican independence movement, as well as draft resisters and, the now famous trial of the Chicago Seven anti-war activists. Who will ever forget the picture of Bobby Seale chained and gagged in Judge Hoffman's courtroom?

Inwardly, I gave a great sigh of relief when I heard the Guild would take our case. I felt like we had the best in the country. My sighting of the Aurora Borealis and now retaining Guild lawyers seemed to indicate a positive trend.

Buck Davis was an unknown quantity. Just twenty-seven and only a couple of years out of Harvard Law School, he'd never tried a case in court. In fact, he told me later, that upon graduation from Harvard he had never been in a courtroom or even a lawyer's office.

Throughout the sixties Lenny Weinglass built his national reputation as an advocate for political dissidents. He defended Anthony Russo in the Pentagon Papers case and, just months before taking our case, had participated in the brilliant defense of the Chicago Seven. During the Chicago trial he had been cited for contempt twenty times.

William Kunstler was noted for defending black power advocate Stokely Carmichael, antiwar priest Daniel Berrigan, and BPP Chairman Bobby Seale as well as the Chicago Seven.

During the Chicago trial Kunstler was cited for contempt by Judge Hoffman 22 times.

A day after my first meeting with Buck, deputies escorted me to the visiting booth. There, on the other side of the bulletproof glass, were Weinglass and Kunstler, who were on the way to the airport, having conducted meetings with Buck and other defense team members. We touched hands on the glass as we talked guardedly over the telephone. I was overjoyed that these guys were on the team. They promised to return within a week to hold a proper meeting of attorneys and defendants.

The White Panther Party had a most impressive defense team. The "heavyweights" were backed up by a column of Detroit and Ann Arbor attorneys who were invaluable as researchers, strategists, and advisors. These attorneys and law students were in the trenches, on the front line in the fight against neo-fascism in the guise of the Nixon mob. They deserve a much greater tribute than is possible here.

Buck informed me that he had prepared a motion seeking reduction of my $100,000 bond, but given my fugitive flight to avoid prosecution and Abbie's trick with the bayonet, he held little hope it would be granted.

About this time my sister visited me. The last time I had seen her, or anyone in my adopted family, she was thirteen years old. Now she was twenty and on her way to Germany to continue her university studies. She opened the door to reconnection with my family, though that would not happen for several years, until I was released from prison.

Meanwhile, The WPP engaged in a fearless and thorough inventory of our theory and practice. We had internal discussions about changing the Party name, with Sinclair writing from Jackson and me from Wayne County Jail. We criticized ourselves publicly, in our newspaper, as individuals and as a Party. I wrote a long, self-critical piece pointing out my adventuresome behavior and romantic desire to make armed revolution without the support of the broad masses of the people.

As a Party and as individuals we toned down our militant rhetoric. We abandoned all national organizing and focused on our local base of support in an effort to create liberated territory and institutions and organizations to stand against those of the power structure. We changed our public image from one of leather-jacketed militants to a less threatening one of leather-jacketed community organizers. This strategy not only reflected the broader changing political scene and the need for us to garner support from a wider base, but also aided our defense efforts by accentuating the positive and downplaying our militancy.

The entire Party took part in the discussion regarding the name change. Early on, consensus had been reached on the need to change the name; the debate to determine the new name took a little longer.

For some time I had felt the name and image of the white panther was limiting. In the beginning we felt it was important to make a bold, public statement in support of The Black Panther Party; what better way to do this than to model their name, organizational structure, and political line? This also reflected my belief that people of color in general, and black folks in particular, would be the leading force for revolution in this country.

As time went on I came to believe the White Panthers looked like tag-alongs, a white-tip on the tail of a black panther, unable to articulate its own vision. The "White Panther" metaphor, carried to its logical conclusion, meant the White Panther Party was for white people exclusively--nothing could be farther from the truth.

Sinclair was in prison during the Woodstock Music Festival and was blown away by the size and scope of the gathering. He was convinced that the Woodstock gathering was a major manifestation of the new culture that was emerging among young and progressive people across the nation. He felt we should change the name to "Woodstock People's Party" to commemorate that historic event and identify ourselves with the progressive aspects of the culture featured at Woodstock.

Having been at Woodstock, I was less impressed. I felt the name would be dated soon and did not believe it offered a positive image of what we were about. After all, Woodstock was a capitalist venture that was ill-prepared to deal with the consequences of its own advertising. It was a great cultural event, but not one I'd want as the image for a revolutionary party--I couldn't forget the rain and mud, the five of us getting arrested and The Prez's miscarriage.

Others of us argued for "The Rainbow People's Party." The rainbow reflected the multi-ethnic and multi-cultural make-up of our organization and the new culture. The rainbow is the symbol of beautiful calm after the cleansing storm. The rainbow arches over all. According to the myth, it leads to a pot of Columbian gold. A rainbow brings good luck--to say nothing of seeing a double rainbow. All of its associations were positive.

Through letters and visits with our wives, Sinclair and I put our ideas forward. The Central Committee and Party cadre continued the discussions. Eventually a consensus was reached; we became The Rainbow People's Party (RPP).

The Detroit Chapter of the new Rainbow People's Party opened a "trial house" in Detroit to serve as headquarters and office and meeting place for our upcoming CIA trial. Various political and cultural icons stayed there during visits to help raise money or build political support.

As our court date neared, Sinclair was transferred from Jackson prison to the Wayne County Jail. Weinglass, Kunstler, and Buck visited the three of us as a group, the first time I'd seen Sinclair in a year and a half. Kunstler swept the room for "bugs" using a special watch that was suppose to "beep" when in the proximity of electronic listening devices. None of us trusted the device, so critical defense communications were scrawled on yellow legal pads.

The government built their whole case on David Valler. According to Valler's affidavit, he supplied me with a quantity of dynamite and supposedly talked to me about my bombing of the CIA office. This was an absolute lie. I don't remember ever speaking to Valler, and he certainly never gave me any explosives. I knew it was a frame-up.

Sinclair's chances didn't look bad. Valler was supposed to have talked to him about bombing buildings; however, before the bombings, while we still lived in Detroit, Sinclair had had an outright phobia about Valler. He thought Valler was literally crazy and avoided him at all costs. It was impossible to believe that he would ever talk to Valler about destruction of government property by use of explosives.

Forest's situation was somewhat stickier. As a resident

and longtime activist in Detroit, Forest had more opportunity to be involved with Valler, which might allow the government to make a conspiracy case against Forest. Our defense would be based on discrediting Valler and showing how the government conspired against us to bring these charges. We were confident and eager to go to trial.

Damon Keith was to be our judge. Appointed in 1967, he was one of only a handful of black judges sitting on the federal bench. His short tenure made it difficult to "read" him through his record, though others on the team assured me he would be fair and fearless.

Our first public hearing was on our pretrial motions, held in the federal courthouse in Detroit. Earlier, the defense team had decided that confrontational tactics, such as those used in the Chicago Seven trial, would not be useful in our endeavor. Our judge was considered "liberal" compared to the senile and reactionary Judge Hoffman in Chicago. Hoffman was a pawn of the government, Keith was not. There would be no outbursts from us in response to any outrageous rulings and no theatrics to capture media attention. We were going to fight this case on basis of "the law."

On our hearing date the courtroom was packed. Party members and supporters took up two-thirds of the available seats. The press, law students, lawyers and the public filled the remaining high-ceilinged, federal space.

As we three defendants entered the courtroom, all our supporters rose in unison and stood silently until we were seated. This indicated to the prosecution that we were an organized and disciplined group capable of keeping our supporters in line. We knew the judge would hear about this display of disciplined support and take notice. Sinclair told me thirty years later that the sight of all those people standing in the courtroom as we entered was the most exquisite and powerful of his career. I only barely remember it.

The defense filed a battery of motions, most of which the judge denied. One of our motions requested that the judge make available to us the place, date, and time of birth of each member of the jury panel so The Prez could calculate their individual astrological charts and a collective chart for the jury as a whole. We argued that this was essential for us to get a fair trial. The

Prez had been casting astrological charts for years and had quite a reputation. She wrote a column in *THE SUN* and had cast charts for the Detroit Tigers, Pistons and Red Wings, as well as many rock bands including The MC5 and the entire White Panther Central Committee. The judge denied our motion.

We filed a motion requesting a psychiatric examination of Valler. At the time Valler was serving a seven to ten year sentence for possession of marijuana and a two to five year sentence on a state bombing charge. In interviews he had done with local media, Valler had stated that he doubted his own sanity. In another he proclaimed he had taken more than three hundred trips on LSD. In one of the state prosecutions, Valler's defense attorney had requested a sanity hearing, and the state court had ordered Valler to submit to a forensic examination. Yet Keith denied our motion, which was a setback.

Believing we were victims of a government conspiracy, we filed a motion requesting that Judge Keith dismiss the indictment on the grounds that it targeted our political activities as leaders of a radical political party and that the indictment violated our First Amendment rights of association and free speech. This motion was denied, as we knew it would be.

We filed a motion challenging jury selection and showed that young people, our peers, were systematically excluded from jury service. This caught the judge's attention and he ordered a full hearing on the issue.

We argued that jury pools were chosen from voter registration lists. The list used to pick the pool were only updated every three years, leaving young, newly registered voters, off the jury list for three years. Additionally, young people were, by and large, alienated from the government and the political process, and so were not inclined to register. Also, given the highly mobile lifestyle of millions of young people, their inclusion on jury pools is highly unlikely. We showed that although the population of potential jurors aged 21-29 was nearly 18%, the jurors from this age group who were qualified for actual service by the court's screening system was only 9%. We argued that young people in America constituted a separate class and accommodations must be made to include them in the political and legal process.

Keith gave this motion a full public hearing. We called

Julian Bond, a former leader of the Student Non-Violent Coordinating Committee (SNCC), and then a Georgia state legislator, to testify. At one point Judge Keith asked Bond whether, as a black man, he would prefer to be tried by twelve black jurors over the age of forty or by twelve white jurors under twenty-five. This had to be a tough question for this well-known civil-rights leader. Bond testified that the ages of the jurors would be more important to him than their race, and that he would rather be tried by twelve white jurors under twenty-five than twelve black jurors over forty.

We called noted poet Allen Ginsberg and State Representative Jackie Vaughn III, a black progressive politician from Detroit, to testify as to the unique nature and make-up of this new "youth class."

Judge Keith was troubled by the disparities pointed out in our motion. He wanted to address and correct these disparities but said he just didn't know how. Kunstler rose to address the court. "Your Honor," he said, "the government has no problem with finding young men, eighteen to twenty-five to send to Vietnam, and certainly it can find a way for young people, eighteen to twenty-nine to sit on juries." Still, motion denied.

On October 5, 1970, we filed a motion for disclosure of electronic surveillance. It was common knowledge that the government was wiretapping radicals and anti-war activists during this time. In numerous political trials around the country, motions seeking disclosure of electronic wiretapping similar to ours had been filed. The government simply responded by saying it knew of no wiretapping, and that was the end of the matter.

In response to our motion, the prosecution and defense entered into a stipulation. The prosecution represented to the court that it had no knowledge of any electronic surveillance of the defendants, and that the local office of the FBI was also unaware of any electronic eavesdropping. The US Attorney's Office also stated that it had asked the Justice Department to conduct an inquiry of the FBI in Washington in order to check for any record of having wiretapped us. The prosecution further stipulated that it would turn over to us any electronic surveillance that might come to its attention.

Two months later, in December, the stipulation produced results. Attorney General John Mitchell had filed a sworn affidavit stating:

> Defendant Plamondon has participated in conversations which were overheard by government agents who were monitoring wiretaps which were being employed to gather intelligence information deemed necessary to protect the nation from attempts of domestic organizations to attack and subvert the existing structure of government.

What's this? The government admits to wiretapping me! Why? What did they hope to gain by acknowledging their taps of me? Did they perhaps want to enter the tapes as evidence? Though this was unlikely, maybe they were inept and the right hand didn't know what the left hand was doing. This was bewildering. First the government let me slip away when the indictment was handed down; now they admitted wiretapping me when they didn't have to. What was going on? Why?

Keith ordered a full hearing. The government argued, in a fully-cited brief and supporting memorandum, prepared and signed by then Assistant Attorney General William Rehnquist, that, even though a prior judicial warrant had not been obtained, the authorization of the Attorney General, as representative of the President, was sufficient to make the surveillance legal, regardless of the warrant requirements of the Fourth Amendment. Further, the United States Attorney instructed Judge Keith that any determination to ignore the provisions of the Fourth Amendment was solely a matter of Presidential concern and the courts should not question the decision of the Executive branch.

What? We looked at each other around the defense table--did we hear correctly? Does the government contend, as the prosecutor seems to be saying, that the United States Attorney General, as agent of the President, has the constitutional power, in the interest of national security, to authorize electronic surveillance of any citizen without a court-issued warrant? The defense team immediately filed a motion seeking to compel the prosecution to turn over the wiretaps or drop the case, as per the agreed-upon stipulation and any number of legal precedents and court rulings.

The Nixon administration responded by putting forward what came to be known as "The Mitchell Doctrine." This amounted to the nullification of the Fourth Amendment of the Constitution, which guarantees Americans the right to be free in their homes and communications from unreasonable searches and seizures.

Judge Keith did not accept the government's argument. In a tersely worded ruling he stated:

> In the instant case the Government argues that the President, acting through the Attorney General, has the inherent Constitutional power: (1) to authorize without judicial warrant, electronic surveillance in national security cases; and (2) to determine unilaterally whether a given situation is a matter within the scope of national security. The Court is unable to accept this proposition. We are a country of laws and not of men.

Judge Keith concluded by ruling that:

> In the opinion of this Court, the position of the Attorney General is untenable... Such power held by one individual was never contemplated by the framers of our Constitution and cannot be tolerated today... This Court hereby ORDERS that the Government make full disclosure to defendant Plamondon of his monitored conversations.

That should have been the end of it. The government prosecutors would give the defense team the tapes of the taps, or transcripts of the tapes, and we'd move on to the trial stage. Instead the government refused to release the transcripts of the wiretaps and appealed Keith's ruling to the Court of Appeals by actually suing Judge Keith. This was a rare move in American jurisprudence and hence the official caption of the case is US -v- US District Court; the government hoped to force Keith to reverse his ruling.

By moving to appeal before our trial even took place, the Nixon administration revealed that its true motive in bringing these flimsy charges against us was not principally to get a conviction in our case, which was clearly unlikely, but to subvert the constitutional protections of the Fourth Amendment and to use our case as a vehicle for their nefarious plot.

The government's appeal of Judge Keith's ruling, before our trial even took place, was unanticipated by the defense team. The attorneys swung into action. Buck prepared a motion challenging the Executive's right to appeal in this case. Bill Bender of the Constitutional Litigation Clinic (CLC) at Rutgers Law School was pressed into service to write the motion challenging the government's assertion that the President had an "inherent right" to wiretap citizens at will, under the ruse of "national security," without the checks and balances of judicial oversight.

The tactical defense plan called for Kunstler to fly from New Jersey to Cincinnati with the Constitutional Litigation Clinic brief and meet Buck with the second brief. The two documents and supporting memoranda would be presented together. Kunstler would present oral arguments in the afternoon before the Court of Appeals in Cinci.

On I-71, just south of Columbus, Ohio, Buck's car hit a patch of black ice, slid sideways into the median, flipped and rolled several times and came to rest on its top. Buck's briefcase shattered, cutting off his ear and scattering the brief for a quarter-mile on I-71.

Kunstler, after arriving in Cincinnati, heard of Buck's accident, rented a car, drove to Columbus, and walked up and down the expressway retrieving Buck's brief and legal memoranda. The pages were smeared, wet and soggy. After a brief visit with Buck in the hospital, Kunstler set out to find a dry-cleaning establishment. He found one and hired them to dry the pages on a heated machine used to press pants; the brief and memoranda were restored. With Buck in the hospital undergoing surgery to reattach his ear, Kunstler made the oral argument by himself, brilliantly.

The brief and oral argument presented by the Executive branch was remarkably revealing. Under the direction of then Assistant Attorney General, William Rehnquist, the government attorney put forward arguments dredged from old English law last heard in the fifteenth, sixteenth, and seventeenth centuries by British monarchs who claimed "inherent power" to take any action deemed necessary by them to protect the nation.

The Court of Appeals would have none of it. Chief Judge Edwards, writing for the majority, noted the irony of this argument:

> It is strange, indeed, that in this case the traditional power of sovereigns like King George III should be invoked in behalf of an American President to defeat one of the fundamental freedoms for which the founders of this country overthrew King George's reign.

Judge Edwards, in blunt language rarely found in judicial opinions, called this an "argument in terrorem," which "suggests that constitutional government is too weak to survive in a difficult world and urges worried judges and worried citizens to return to acceptance of the security of "sovereign' power."

Further, Judge Edwards wrote:

> The government has not pointed to, and we do not find, one written phrase in the Constitution, in statutory law, or in the case law of the United States, which exempts the President, The Attorney General, or federal law enforcement from the restrictions of the Fourth Amendment in the case at hand.

The Court of Appeals ordered the government to turn over transcripts of the tapes to the defense. Again we assumed this would be done and the case would proceed to trial.

However, the Nixon administration announced that it intended to take this case to the US Supreme Court in hopes of a sympathetic hearing and definitive ruling in the government's favor.

After our Appeals Court victory Buck paid me a visit in the WCJ. Upon my arrest in the Upper Peninsula of Michigan I was charged with "possession of false selective service cards (draft cards), with intent to use as false identification." Buck reasoned that since the wiretap issue was going to the Supreme Court, it could be well over two years before we went to trial in the CIA case; it had already been eleven months since my arrest. There was no reason for me to sit in the overcrowded and obsolete WCJ until trial, he said.

Buck suggested I plead guilty to possession of false selective service cards so I could be sentenced in federal court and transferred to federal prison where I would do easier time. The draft card charge carried a one to five year sentence. Buck felt he could get the Judge to sentence me to just enough time to keep me in prison until the Supreme Court decided the wiretap issue and the CIA trial began or the case was dismissed.

It didn't take long for me to agree to Buck's offer. I would have done nearly anything to get out of the hellhole that is the WCJ. My time had been spent in maximum security--a seven by ten-foot cell. I kept myself busy reading and doing push-ups, yet the prolonged incarceration with minimal human contact was taking a toll on my mental and emotional well-being.

Buck made the arrangements and I was transferred to the Western District of Michigan and housed in the Kent County Jail (KCJ) in Grand Rapids, where once again I was placed in maximum security. "Max" in KCJ was much better than in Detroit. There were only four maximum-security prisoners; we each had our own cell and the cell doors were left open during the day. We were locked up at night. The rest of the time we played cards or dominoes on the floor, walked up and down the catwalk, or read.

I was in Kent County for less than a week when a fellow prisoner, a "trustee," sidled up to the bars on the other side of the catwalk. He explained to me that cleaning the visiting room after visiting hours was one of his jobs. He said if I wanted something smuggled into the jail it could be left in the visiting room and he could get it back to my cell hidden under the dust mop he used for cleaning.

Humm, I thought, *some reefer would be nice.* On her next visit I instructed The Prez to tape three joints to the underside of the metal ledge on the other side of the bulletproof glass in the visiting cubicle. After visiting hours were over, the trustee pushed his industrial-sized dust mop back to the cellblock. He upended the mop and there were the three joints. I gave the trustee one and kept two for myself. At night, locked in my cell, I puffed the weed--nice.

On the next visiting day The Prez followed the same routine, taping the joints to the underside of the metal ledge. Two hours later the trustee came back pushing his trusty mop.

Shadrack, Trickshot, and I were sitting on the floor playing dominoes. The usual banter accompanied our game. Slap! Is the sound dominoes make when forcefully slammed to the floor during a vigorous game. Slap! "Five and five is ten and five is fifteen." I said. Slap! "Ten and your fifteen is twenty-five and you're out of sixes--you'll be goin' to the bone yard, motherfucker," Shadrack responded. Trickshot played, and, after drawing a six/three and slapping it down, I countered, "Twelve and three is fifteen, and now you're out of sixes, go to the bone yard you puke eatin' dawg."

The trustee, on the other side of the bars, began talking to me in a rather loud whisper. "I couldn't find it. It's not there," he said while looking up and down the catwalk. "Bullshit!" I hissed, keeping my whisper low, suspecting the catwalk was bugged. "I saw her tape it there, just like last time." "I couldn't find it. Where is it? It's not there," the trustee insisted. I knew the jig was up and turned and walked away, back to the dominoes game--I knew the goon squad would be coming.

Meanwhile Shadrack and Trickshot were keeping up a steady stream of domino jargon. "Find a stump to fit your rump and I'll domino you 'til your butt-hole jumps," was one of Shadrack's favorite sayings.

Two hours later the goon squad arrived, removed the four of us from the block, ransacked our cells and found no contraband. When leaving, the captain of the guard informed me I was charged with conspiracy to possess marijuana. "Gee," I said, "What are you going to do? Arrest me? Throw me in jail?" "You wife is charged too," the captain said.

Needless to say the defense team was rather perturbed at my indiscretion and would not put any effort into this Mickey Mouse case. They found a court-appointed lawyer for me and left me to my own devices.

I was arraigned and a date for the preliminary exam was set. At the preliminary it was revealed the whole thing was a set up. The trustee was acting on behalf of the sheriff's department; they had entrapped me. During our loud whispering conversation the trustee was recording our talk on a mini tape recorder, no bigger than a pack of Marlboro's kept in his shirt pocket.

During the preliminary exam the prosecution played the tape recording, although I don't know why. The trustee could be heard clearly saying, "I can't find it--where is it?" and other leading questions. My voice came across as only a mumble, no clear words. What was clear was Shadrack's boisterous chatter in the background and the slap of bones on the floor. "Go to the bone yard motherfucker!" and "When your mamma was pregnant she shoulda' swallowed a brick and smashed your head in--now who's the best domino player? Whooo's the best?" Shadrack went on and on.

The judge and court personnel smiled at the apparent ineptitude of the police and prosecution. Nevertheless The Prez and I were bound over for trial. My court-appointed lawyer arranged a plea bargain. I would plead guilty to attempted possession of marijuana and get sentenced to six months. In return the charges against The Prez would be dropped. I took the deal, especially since I was going to be locked up for more than six months anyway.

Shortly afterward I was taken before Judge Fox in Federal District Court in Grand Rapids, where I pled guilty to the draft card charges. I was sentenced to twenty-eight to thirty-six months in prison, long enough to keep me behind bars until the Supreme Court decision on the wiretap issue.

I was transported to the Federal penitentiary at Terra Haute, Indiana--"The Hut," as it was called by the cons in the system. I remembered my last visit to Terra Haute, when I was in Father Gibault School for Boys. I'd made a circle; I hoped it didn't end here.

After several days in "quarantine" I was taken to the warden's office. He was just another white guy doing his job. I was escorted to a chair before his desk. He looked up from my file. "We've got two kinds of time here, Plamondon--easy time and hard time. What can I put you down for?" he said while touching the lead of his #2 pencil to his tongue. "Easy time," I said.

There are three classifications for federal prisoners: minimum, medium and maximum. Regulations say that minimum security prisoners, when leaving the prison must be accompanied by one armed guard. Medium security prisoners, when going outside the walls, must be in leg irons and handcuffs and accompanied by an armed guard. Maximum-security prisoners must be accompanied by two armed guards and wear full irons: leg irons, belly chains, and handcuffs.

I was assigned to the construction and maintenance crew. Because of my pending cases, I was classified as a maximum-security prisoner. At that time they were enlarging the "yard," building a new wall around the perimeter of the joint. Every morning I reported to my work assignment, but was relieved of my work detail and sent back to my cellblock since building the wall technically took place outside the prison and so required that I have two armed guards with me at all times while dressed in full irons--an unworkable situation.

I had a friend in the education department and another who was the Chaplain's clerk. On returning to my cellblock I'd get a "ticket" (permission slip) to visit one place or the other, and I'd hang out there. I was doing easy time.

For years I'd suffered from a rather severe hernia and decided to have it fixed on the government tab. I was transferred to the federal penitentiary at Leavenworth, Kansas where I did three months on my way to the Federal penal hospital in Springfield, Missouri.

After my operation I was sent back to The Hut. Because I was recuperating from surgery I had a doctor's order that I was not to lift anything over nine pounds. I was assigned to "food service" where I was given the job of preparing the menu boards above the three food lines in the cafeteria and keeping the salt and pepper shakers and sugar bowls full, an easy gig. Keeping the sugar bowls topped off was nearly a full time job. Cons would empty them into bread sacks every day and smuggle them out of the dining hall to be used for making prison hooch: alcohol.

On Thanksgiving, 1971, I was given the menu for the noon meal, which I was supposed to transfer to the menu boards. Printed at the top of the sheet was "Happy Thanksgiving," followed by the usual Thanksgiving fare: turkey, dressing, corn, cranberry sauce, pumpkin pie, etc.

I went to the head guard. "I ain't puttin' up nothin' that

says "Happy Thanksgiving! That's ridiculous," I protested.

"That menu comes directly from the Bureau of Prisons in Washington, D.C. You WILL put it up just as it is on the sheet," he insisted. "Bullshit," I said. "I ain't doin' it." Then he "shot" me, prison slang for writing me up and putting me on report. "Shots" are collected in one's file and used when going up for parole. This was the one infraction I was "shot" for during my stay in the federal system. I did not set the menu board up that day.

In December of 1971, The Rainbow People's Party produced, with the help of Pete Andrews, a local music promoter, and vast numbers of friends and supporters, "Ten For Two; The John Sinclair Freedom Rally." It was held in the 20,000-seat Crisler Arena at the University of Michigan, and was a showcase of progressive culture and politics.

Sinclair's appeal of his marijuana conviction, for which he was sentenced to nine and one half to ten years in prison, was then before the Michigan Supreme Court. Since Sinclair's sentencing in July of '69, there had been two years of organizing by the WPP and later the RPP; all of it came down to this hearing before the Michigan high court.

The Central Committee reasoned that a major public event, attended by 20,000 supporters, might catch the Court's eye and make it easier for them to make the difficult political decision to strike down Michigan's marijuana laws.

Allen Ginsberg, the gentle panda bear poet, performed, as did Bob Seger and Commander Cody and His Lost Planet Airmen. Stevie Wonder played, and so did two jazz gurus, saxophonist Archie Schepp and trombonist Rosland Rudd. Ed Sanders, the funky poet with class from the Lower East Side, read poems. Bobby Seale, Chairman of the BPP addressed the multitude. (Though I wasn't there, the highlight for me when I saw the film, several years later, were the 20,000 dope-smoking maniacs on their feet cheering Chairman Seale.) Jerry Rubin, Dave Dellinger, and Rennie Davis, nationally known anti-war activists and principles in the Chicago Seven trial, spoke eloquently. Sinclair's mom, Elsie, brought the crowd to its feet when, in her grandmotherly voice, fist in the air, she chanted, "I dig the music!" John Lennon and Yoko Ono headlined the show. Yoko sang a newly written song dedicated to the women of Ann

Arbor titled "Sister, Sister." Lennon performed a song written just for the occasion titled; John Sinclair--"It ain't fair John Sinclair--in the stir for breathin' air. ...what's a man to do? They got Pun Plamondon too."

The Ten for Two Rally was held on Friday night. The following Monday the Michigan Supreme Court ruled the Michigan marijuana laws were unconstitutional since weed was improperly classified as a narcotic, and sentencing under existing laws constituted "cruel and unusual punishment." Sinclair and twenty-six other prisoners were released later that day--a tremendous victory!

In early February of 1972, while I was in The Hut, I received a telegram from Buck. "Oral argument in Supreme Court February 24...Stop...Hold on...Stop...End of Message...Buck"

Chapter Sixteen

THE SUPREMES--1972

When it became known that the wiretap issue was being taken to the US Supreme Court--"The Supremes," as we referred to the High Court--the defense team enlisted the aid of Linda Huber and Bill Bender, associates at the Constitutional Litigation Clinic (CLC) at Rutgers Law School. It was their perseverance and persuasive arguments that led Arthur Kinoy, professor Emeritus at Rutgers Law and founder of the CLC, to agree to present the oral argument before the High Court[1].

[1] Author's Note: I was not there, the narrative for this chapter was gleaned from discussions with the principles involved, transcripts of the US Supreme Court argument held February 24, 1972, Arthur Kinoy's book, RIGHTS ON TRIAL and William Kunstler's book, MY LIFE AS A RADICAL LAWYER.

Just weeks before, Kinoy and others had finished writing a whopping 547-page appellate brief in the Chicago Seven case. Since the 1940's Kinoy had been a Guild member and "People's Lawyer's" and felt he needed a rest after the Chicago Seven appeal. He had also argued before The Supremes previously and was not eager to jump into the pressure-cooker atmosphere of research, analysis, dissection, and deadlines that a major constitutional appeal demands. He was not eager to take our case.

After listening to Huber's and Bender's presentation, Kinoy realized that what Nixon and his gang were really trying to do was create a legal precedent for the complete suspension of Constitutional Law. Kinoy reasoned that if "The Mitchell Doctrine" was accepted by the Court, and Fourth Amendment guarantees were suspended under the guise of "National Security," then other Constitutional safeguards could be terminated as well, using the same "National Security" argument. Due process of law, the right to vote, freedom to assemble and seek redress of grievances, freedom of the press--all were threatened by this frontal assault on the Constitution. Kinoy rose to the challenge. The power of the Northern Lights a year and a half earlier was undiminished.

> The Fourth Amendment to the US Constitution states:
> The right of the people to be secure in their persons, houses, papers, and effects, against unreasonable searches and seizures, shall not be violated, and no warrants shall issue, but upon probable cause, supported by oath or affirmation, and particularly describing the place to be searched, and the persons or things to be seized.

This protection, which Americans have enjoyed since 1791, is what Nixon and his band of crooks were attempting to dismantle.

Damon Keith, as the federal district judge for the Eastern District of Michigan, was also party to this litigation. Keith, Sinclair, Forest, and I were "respondents" in the matter before the High Court. The purpose of the government's appeal to The

Court of Appeals, and now to The Supremes, was to force Judge Keith to reverse himself--to make him declare that the warrantless wiretaps were legal.

Because of this, Keith had the right to be represented by an attorney of his choice. Keith asked the Michigan Bar Association to appoint a lawyer to represent him. The Bar chose one of its past presidents, William Gossett, who had since become general counsel for the Ford Motor Company and a ranking Republican in the Michigan power structure.

In prison in Terra Haute I trembled at the thought that our defense argument would be split, and by such a powerful Republican as Gossett. Could we count on this guy? Would he work with Kinoy? Would he try to steal the show? Would he undercut our argument--Gossett could screw everything up.

Our flesh-and-blood adversary in this battle was the Solicitor General, Erwin Griswold. He had represented the Johnson and now the Nixon administration before the High Court and had consistently argued restrictive, right-wing positions. On the morning of the oral argument, the Solicitor General was nowhere to be seen. This baffled Kinoy and the defense team since it was unlikely Griswold would assign an underling to such a landmark case.

Moments before the session was to begin Robert C. Mardian walked in with three Justice Department lawyers in dark suits, looking very much like mobsters, and took positions at the Petitioner's table. Mardian was wearing the long morning coat traditionally worn by the Solicitor General when arguing before the Big Court. This could only mean one thing: Mardian was going to argue on behalf of the President.

It was common knowledge that Mardian was a rabid right winger who, along with Rehnquist and Kleindienst, was part of the Goldwater Gang going back to 1964 in Phoenix. Mitchell brought Mardian to the Justice Department and made him head of the Internal Security Division with the goal of crushing all political dissent.

Years later it was learned that Mardian was one of the principle architects of the wretched Houston Plan, an ill-conceived operation which planned break-ins, kidnappings, mass arrests, and incarcerations, without charges, of Nixon's political opponents. The now infamous Counter Intelligence

Program (CoInTelPro) used during this time by the FBI had his stamp on it. But again, few knew of this at the time of the argument before The Supremes. Today a great deal more is known about Mardian. For instance, he was one of only a handful of creeps that were convicted for the Watergate break-in and the bugging of offices of the Democratic National Committee. But the Watergate caper was still four months in the future.

Since our first hearing in Detroit before Judge Keith, back in 1970, we had been reading the signature "William Rehnquist, Assistant Attorney General," at the bottom of briefs, motions, and legal memoranda advocating what I called at the time, "Yankee Doodle Fascism." My reaction to Richard Nixon's nomination of Rehnquist to fill a vacancy on the Supreme Court just months before the date of our oral argument could hardly have been a more cynical one. When the Senate spinelessly confirmed this neo-fascist to the nation's highest Court, the supposed protector and final interpreter of the Constitution, I could feel only stunned disbelief and utter contempt.

The Northern Lights came through again--Rehnquist was forced to recuse himself from participating in the wiretap ruling because he had developed the theory and prepared the arguments to be used by the Executive branch before the High Court while he was Assistant Attorney General.

Just before the Big Court was called to order, in walked Griswold. He seated himself in his special ornate chair, reserved only for the Solicitor General. According to those who were there, his presence seemed to say to the Court, "I'm not ill. I don't have a scheduling conflict, but I'm not going to argue this case. You will not hear this foul legal theory come out of my mouth."

Chief Justice Burger called the Court to order and gave Mardian the floor. Justice Marshall turned his chair and back to Mardian during most of his opening remarks, showing the Petitioner his contemptuous backside.

Mardian began by laying out the origin of the case and set out the chain of events leading up to this Supreme Court appearance. He was into his opening statement just thirty seconds when the Chief Judge asked Mardian to speak up. This isn't a big thing, but it did indicate an element of Mardian's timidity before the High Court, not a good sign for the Executive Branch.

Mardian argued that the wiretaps were legal:

> This 'in camera' [meaning only the Judge will see the document] submission would also show that the authorization of the Attorney General was for a limited period only, it described the premises where the installation surveillance was involved and indicated that the surveillance was subject to periodic review. Based upon this 'in camera' submission, the United States urged that the surveillance in question was lawful.

At this point, just three minutes into his argument, he was interrupted by one of the Judges; the transcript does not indicate whom.

The Court: "Periodic review by whom? The Attorney General or the Director of the FBI?"

Mardian responded, stammering, "Pardon me, sir, I didn't get that."

The Court: "You said it was subject to periodic review, and by whom?"

Mardian, getting a grip, replied, "By the Attorney General of the United States."

These interruptions, taken individually meant little. However, if they indicated a trend, it would be a long day for the Petitioners.

Each side was allotted an hour to make its case. We had to split our time between Gossett and Kinoy.

Mardian continued:

> While the constitutional issue is grave, and the stakes, as far as the government is concerned, are high, the issue before the Court can be easily framed. Stated negatively, the question is not whether electronic surveillance is a permissible governmental tool, for now we find that the question is whether in the limited areas of counter-intelligence activities the President of the United States

> may authorize electronic surveillance in the absence of a warrant by a member of the Judiciary of this nation.

He got that part of it right, but the issue was much broader. It came down to the issue of constitutional government or government by executive order.

The Petitioner went on:

> We suggest also that the constitutional authority of the President is not found in any one provision or any one article, but may be gleaned from the Constitution as a whole. And I speak now only of the constitutional authority of the President in the area of national security affairs.

At this point he was interrupted again. The Court: "Of course the Congress of the United States has a great deal of constitutional authority in the area of internal security and domestic affairs…" The unnamed Judge went on to ask Mardian if Congress could delegate an agent to do this investigative surveillance.

Mardian responded by stating, "Congress shall provide for the calling of the militia of the United States in the event of insurrection."

Aware Mardian was ducking the question the Judge continued: "Well, my question is directed to this: Is it your contention that only the President has this power…or would Congress not also have at least equivalent power in this area, if you are right?"

Mardian agreed, yet the Judge kept pestering him, using Mardian's precious time. "Why couldn't Congress equally do this investigating surveillance around the country through its designated agent?"

Mardian responded by saying this type of activity is peculiarly within the executive function.

They recessed for lunch at noon. Mardian would pick up his argument when they returned. He had been questioned twenty-eight times in the course of his half-hour presentation. This had to encourage the defense team for it meant that the

Petitioner's presentation did not address The Supreme's questions.

After lunch Mardian continued his feeble argument, at one point quoting The Privy Council of England. An unnamed Judge responded: "Of course The Privy Council isn't bound by the Fourth Amendment."

Mardian also argued that the amount of counter-intelligence information is too vast and too sensitive to be trusted to the more than six hundred federal judges in this country:

> And we would suggest that the interests of privacy of the American citizen is better protected in limiting this authority in the area of electronic surveillance in counter-intelligence cases to one man, the Attorney General acting for the President of the United States, rather than to proliferate it amongst all of the Federal sitting Judges in the United States.

Reading the above statement in the transcript several years later, I made a note in the margin: "According to Mardian, federal judges could not be trusted. Damn! This was the wrong crowd to make that argument to."

Next, Mardian made the argument that the wiretap information gathered on me was not used for a prosecutorial purpose, rather, *"the information obtained was totally unrelated to the crime for which these defendants were indicted."* In other words they wanted to know about my political activity, not criminal activity.

Mardian was getting close to the end of his allotted time; he seemed to be grasping at straws:

> I would like to point first to the Preamble to the Constitution. One of the primary stated purposes of the Preamble is to 'insure domestic tranquility.' I submit in this regard, that the protection of the Constitution...is not merely to protect the document itself, but to protect the principles under which the Constitution was adopted, and the rights guaranteed by that Constitution.

An unnamed Judge interrupted again: "Do you think

that argument helps you in this case?"

"Yes, sir," the Petitioner's lawyer went on, "I think I would hope to show that it does."

As Mardian continued to drone on, Justice Marshall, who had been listening to the argument with his back to the speaker, whirled in his chair and snapped, "What about--you keep ducking the Fourth Amendment. Are you going to get to it?"

Mardian, stammering, "I'm sorry, Your Honor?"

Justice Marshall: "The Fourth Amendment. Are you ever going to get to it?"

Mr. Mardian continued:

> We suggest in this regard that we are not asking for an exemption of the Fourth Amendment. We do not suggest the President is above the Fourth Amendment. We simply suggest that in the area in which he has limited and exclusive authority, the President of the United States may authorize an electronic surveillance, and in those cases it is reasonable. I would suggest in this regard that the Fourth Amendment does not prohibit all searches and seizures, but only those which are deemed unreason--

One of the judges cut Mardian off again: "And I understand your position that if the President decides it's necessary to bug John Doe's phone, that's it. There's nothing under the sun John Doe can do about it."

Mardian agreed with the Judge. With time running out Mardian closed his argument and reserved the rest of his time for rebuttal. He had been interrupted and questioned by the Court thirty-one times in the afternoon session alone.

Mr. Gossett rose on behalf of Judge Keith. At this time Gossett was still an unknown quantity to me. Had I been in court that day my fears would have vanished then and there. Within thirty seconds Gossett hit the nail on the head:

> Prior to this case, there has never been a serious challenge to the basic rule that ordinarily searches and seizures must be made pursuant to duly issued warrants. And if they're not, they're unreasonable.

> Indeed, the Executive seeks for all searches that the Attorney General may characterize or label as national security, an exemption from any meaningful judicial supervision, either before or after the search. Thus, the government, in effect, presents a startling proposition. It is that all so-called national security searches and seizures are non-justifiable. They simply are beyond the reach, beyond the competence of the courts. They are for the Attorney General, the Executive alone.
>
> The question before this Court is whether the Fourth Amendment is going to be protected, whether the protection of the Fourth Amendment is going to be respected, whether the people are going to be protected against arbitrary power of government.

Gossett gave a legal dissertation on the meaning of the word "reasonable" when applied to searches. He cited case law as established "in Katz," "in Burke," "In Camara." He recited the legislative history of wiretap law in America. He scolded the government for trying to muddy the waters by insinuating that "foreign intelligence" was somehow involved. He went through the government's briefs, page after page, pointing to inconsistencies, contradictions and omissions. He pointed out that the "inherent powers" argument, heard in the lower courts, was not mentioned in the brief to The Supremes. His was a tour de force explaining how wiretapping and the Fourth Amendment intersect. Though he was questioned thirty-one times in the course of his half-hour presentation, the Court's questions were information-seeking and less challenging than those posed to Mardian.

Then it was Kinoy's turn. His deeply held beliefs were apparent in his methodical, well-reasoned arguments; he pulled no punches. Using the Courts's own language and reasoning:

> Mister Chief Justice, and members of the Court. I rise before this Court to represent the three individual respondents: Sinclair, Plamondon and Forest. But, as the Court of Appeals has stated so powerfully in the opinion before this Court, the thrust of this case now goes far

beyond the rights and liberties of these three young men.

The government has seen fit to use this case as a vehicle for propelling a claim of executive power so ominous in its implications and sweeping in its dimensions that it has transformed this appeal into a case which, as this Court has said, touches the bedrock of our political system.

Mr. Mardian has seen fit this morning to call upon the authority of the great Chief Justice in Marbury. I would suggest to the Court that in the words of that Chief Justice this case has become one of those rare cases of peculiar delicacy, which call for the historic role of this Court as the ultimate interpreter of the Constitution. Now, the considerations, I suggest to the Court, are awesome and foreboding, which permeate the opinions of the District Court and the Court of Appeals, arose out of an openly expressed and frank attempt by the Executive to use this case to obtain the imprimatur of this Court for a program of domestic--and I stress that word--domestic espionage and surveillance of political opponents unprecedented in our history.

Now, as Mr. Gossett has pointed out, and in the words of Judge Edwards in the Court of appeals for the Sixth Circuit, this would, to place it bluntly, erase the Fourth Amendment from the domestic life of this country, the amendment which this Court has taught is the embodiment of fundamental principles of liberty.

I suggest to the Court that not since the days in 1761 when, before a Massachusetts court, James Otis pleaded a case, has a more classic general search ever come before this Court. Here you have a search of 14 months' duration, over 900 telephone calls involving, Lord knows how many thousands of people who, as Mr. Gossett said, dialed a number and unknowingly were victims of wiretapping.

The concept of the Court of Appeals that beyond doubt the First Amendment is the cornerstone of American freedom, and the Fourth Amendment stands as the guardian of the First. And this reflects the teaching of this Court.

Now the power which the Attorney General states here would legitimatize a widespread dragnet of a secret surveillance of domestic political opposition. Already the subjects of the Attorney General's suspicion fall on leaders of the Anti-war movement, black militants, Catholic activist pacifists, and advocates of youth culture.

As formulated here this morning and in the briefs submitted to this Court, that claim of executive power can include anyone who speaks out. Now, I put it bluntly to the Court, that this is not an exaggeration.

Unless this program, now loudly proclaimed by the Executive, of uncontrolled executive, warrantless, open-ended wiretapping of domestic political opponents, unless this is decisively repudiated, not sidestepped, and I urge deeply decisively repudiated by this Court, the inevitable effect will be, not to--and here I pause for a moment, I will not use the word, which I heard the Solicitor General two days ago before this Court say, was overworked in this Court; I will not say that the inevitable effect will be to "chill" the exercise of democratic rights. I would say the inevitable effect would be to "choke and stifle" the exercise of First Amendment rights by million of American citizens.

As Mr. Mardian said here this morning, this program of domestic political espionage is unrelated to any criminal investigative activity, but is merely an intelligence-gathering operation.

Mr. Mardian's argument is not with us. Mr.

> Mardian's argument is with those who wrote the Fourth Amendment. Mr. Mardian's argument, and the government's brief, reads as if, saying that, Oh, it's perfectly all right, we can do all these things because we're conducting investigative intelligence gathering, as if the Executive has limitless, uncontrolled powers in the area of political association, beliefs, and activities.
>
> I suggest that this Court should affirm the decision of the sixth Circuit, and in affirming the decision, this Court will be affirming the Fourth and First Amendments to the Constitution of the United States. Thank you.

Kinoy was not interrupted once! Not only that, but The Supremes let him speak a full five minutes longer than his allotted time. As he sat down Kinoy feared that he lost the case. Why hadn't they interrupted him with questions? Were they spellbound by his presentation, or indifferent to his remarks? Did he speak too much truth to power? Were their minds already made up?

Years later he told me that indeed, the lack of interruptions baffled him for years.

I've often wondered what Rehnquist thought and felt that day. Having recused himself, he had left the bench. Had he listened to the argument in his chambers--realizing that his neo-fascist legal theory was apparently, to us at least, being shot full of holes? It had to be a large lump to swallow as a Republican stalwart and corporate legal giant ran interference for a little white-haired, gnome-like lefty named Arthur Kinoy. And, I hope, an even larger lump formed as his peers picked at loose ends.

Chief Justice Burger thanked Kinoy and invited Mardian to take the floor. "You have 18 minutes, if you need it, we'll enlarge your time by a few minutes," the Judge said, trying to keep everything fair.

Mardian, rather than address the issues of Constitutional principles raised by Gossett and Kinoy, tried to obscure the issues by addressing the minutia of the case:

> I would suggest, in this regard, that while the warrant requirement, as it pertains to judicial proceedings, by and large are issued by members of the Federal Judiciary. There is a great body of statute in this country which permits not only warrantless searches, but warrants issued by persons other than judicial magistrates.

One of The Supremes interrupted: "Mr. Mardian, in all of these instances of other people issuing warrants, aren't they all subject to judicial testing--judicial review?"

Mardian, stammering again: "I--on a writ of habeas corpus, which I believe was the--"

The Court interrupted again: "I didn't say on any writ. They're subject to judicial testing, yes or no?"

Mardian, not wanting to answer, yet trying to appear in control, tried to duck the question. "Yes. They are subject to--"

Interrupted again, the Court was trying to pin Mardian down. "In your position, judicial test means an adversary proceeding with two parties; is that correct?"

Mardian: "The judicial review, I would say, based upon the warrant requirement in each case."

The Court: "And isn't that an adversary proceeding?"

Mardian: "Yes, sir."

The Court: "But in this case we don't have an adversary proceeding."

Mardian didn't address the Court's statement directly. Instead he mentioned Mr. Gossett and tried to steer the Court away from the issue of judicial review and oversight:

> Mr. Gossett represents the respondent court, and the respondent court certainly had in its possession, and that in camera exhibit should have been available, if it wasn't, to the attorney for the respondent court as distinguished from the respondent defendants.

The Court, interrupting again--"I understood that in camera means for the eyes of the judge and nobody else. Am I right or wrong?"

Again Mardian ducked the question: "I would assume

that at the time this matter came before the Circuit Court, at least, and before this Court, when Mr. Gossett became counsel of record, had there been any--"

The Court was getting somewhat short with Mr. Mardian. "Well, let me ask you now: Can Mr. Gossett see the in camera exhibit now?"

Mardian responded: "Yes sir. The contents, I presume, are known to--or should be known to Judge Keith, and we have no objection to Mr. Gossett's viewing the in camera exhibit."

The Court: "Can Mr. Kinoy--both of the lawyers?"

Mardian: "Mr. Gossett, who represents the respondent court, we certainly--"

The Court: "But the other lawyer can't see it? The lawyer representing the people involved can't see it?"

Mardian: Well, there's only one person involved. The only overhearing that we have is the overhearing of the defendant Plamondon."

The Court: "The one whose name is Plamondon--"

Mardian: "Plamondon, yes sir."

The Court: "--can his lawyer see it?"

Mardian: "No, the government's position which initiated--"

The Court: "Well, we wouldn't have an adversary proceeding, would we?"

Mardian:

> Well, we would not have an adversary proceeding in any instance where the overhearing involved matters relating to the national security. If there is a distinction between overhearing, in so-called foreign intelligence cases, as distinguished from national security cases, I have been unable, as objectively as I can, to distinguish between so-called domestic and foreign intelligence.

Toward the end of his allotted time Mardian made this statement: "Now, certainly, neither this President nor any prior President, to my knowledge, has authorized electronic surveillance to monitor the activities of an opposite political group."

This was an outright lie since Mardian knew the Attorney General had, just two weeks earlier, authorized wiretapping of another political party. Electronic bugs had already been placed in the Democratic National Headquarters in the Watergate complex.

He went on to say, a brief moment later: "But when we're talking about the on-going intelligence function of government, there is no probable cause in many cases, as that now is used in the criminal prosecutive sense." Finally, Mardian admitted the goal of the Executive Branch in bringing this to The Supremes. They want to wiretap anyone they choose without "probable cause."

Mardian was interrupted and questioned by the Court 34 times during his 18-minute rebuttal.

Whereupon, at 2:51 o'clock, p.m., the case was submitted for judgment.

* * *

Having heard the case in February, the Court was not expected to hand down its ruling until June. There was nothing to do now but wait. I continued to do easy time in The Hut. My policy for staying out of trouble was: don't gamble, don't do dope, and don't get involved with the queers. It worked for me.

During my time in the Wayne County Jail, back in 1970, while attending daily pre-trial hearings, I had on several occasions shared a holding cell in the Federal Building with Vito "Tony Jack" Giacalone, Don of the Detroit mob family. He was going to trial on loan-sharking and racketeering charges. Once he even shared his catered lunch with me (steamed lobster, shrimp in tomato sauce, and half a head of cauliflower smothered in cheese sauce). Usually, while in holding cells the menu was old bologna on stale white bread. I asked Mr. Giacalone how he got catered meals. "I have a note from a doctor saying I require a specialized diet," he said.

As it turned out we both ended up in prison in Terre Haute. I can't say we were friends, but we would nod to each other on the yard or in the dinning hall. One day I saw Mr. Giacalone (I always called him "Mister Giacalone") reading The New York Times. I approached him on the yard one day; his bodyguards and footmen stopped me as I approached. He shooed them away and motioned for me to come forward. I asked Mr. Giacalone if I could read his New York Times after he was through with it. Every day, for the duration of my stay in The Hut, when I returned to my cell for "count" after breakfast, there was a nice, crisp, New York Times, on my bed, still in the brown mailing sleeve.

In June, while I was reading The NY Times, a headline caught my eye, "5 Charged with Burglary at Democratic Headquarters." According to the article, on Saturday night, the 17th of June, five well-dressed men with electronic surveillance equipment were apprehended in the Democratic National Headquarters. Jesus Christ! I thought, Nixon is wiretapping the Democrats. The rhetorical speculation put forward by Kinoy at the argument before The Supremes in February had come to pass.

On Monday, the 19th of June, 1972, I received a telegram:

We won Supremes. Stop. Unanimous. Stop. Release imminent. Stop. Buck. End of Message.

Though I didn't know it at the time this Supreme Court decision and the Watergate break-in were connected. Years later it was explained to me.

It went down like this: The Justices decided the Supreme Court wiretap issue on Friday the 16th of June. According to Court rules the decision was to be kept secret until it was released by the Court, in this case, the following Monday. However, someone at the High Court, (Rehnquist, or his clerk?) notified the White House and informed them the wiretap issue had been lost.

This meant that any wiretaps installed by the Executive branch, or its agents, or Nixon's re-election committee, would be illegal on Monday, the 19th, when the ruling was made public. The Watergate burglars were sent in to the Democratic National Headquarters to retrieve the electronic listening devices on Saturday, the 18th of June, before the Monday release of the decision made warrentless wiretaps unconstitutional. The rest, as they say, sucks.

We will probably never know why my indictment was released to the press before I was taken into custody back in 1969. I think it was ineptitude. We do know the Nixon Administration brought charges against us in an effort to undermine the principles of Constitutional Law.

Another question also remains unanswered. Why didn't the government just turn over the wiretaps to us? At every step along the way--in District Court, the Court of Appeals, and the Supreme Court--the government, having lost its argument, could have given us the transcripts of the tapes and proceeded to trial. But they refused. Why? Prior to going underground in 1969, I, like everyone else in the White Panther Party, was working full time to get the Michigan marijuana laws overturned and Chairman Sinclair released from prison. One of my tasks was to make phone calls to powerful and influential people in an effort to gain their support. I called and talked to the Governor, our state and federal Senators, the Archbishops of Detroit and Grand Rapids, mayors and millionaires. I called Doctors, Lawyers, Indian Chiefs and a cast of a thousand others. This is why, I believe, the government could not afford to release the tapes. No one would mind if the government wiretapped dope-smoking, free love, communal communists and pinko hippies, but, wiretapping bishops, elected officials and representatives, educators, upstanding citizens in the community, this, Nixon feared, would not be tolerated by the electorate.

Or, perhaps they refused to release the tapes because there was exculpatory evidence on them. I don't remember this happening, but perhaps Valler called and congratulated me on picking the CIA target. Perhaps I told him I didn't know what the hell he was talking about. Perhaps I said, "I don't know you, don't bother me again."

I can only add that whoever bombed the CIA office in Ann Arbor in September of 1968 set in motion the planets that would ultimately collide, resulting in the Supreme Court decision which prompted the Watergate break-in. Whoever bombed the CIA indirectly brought down the Nixon administration, set back the right wing of the Republican Party ten years, and postponed neo-fascist designs on the Constitution until the year 2000 when the Republicans pulled off a right-wing coup.

Despite the favorable Supreme Court decision, my problems were not over. I still had a pot case in Traverse City. I still had the distributing obscene material to minors case in Ann Arbor. I still had weapons and pot charges in Chicago. I still had the hash case pending in Hackensack, New Jersey. And I still had a carrying a concealed weapons charge in St. Ignace stemming from my capture nearly three years earlier. Moreover, the Bureau of Prisons calculated my time to show I had another year and a half to serve on my thirty-month sentence for the possession of false selective service cards.

In a panic I contacted Buck. He contacted my numerous attorneys in the aforementioned cases and requested they file motions directing the prosecution to dismiss the charges against me based on the "speedy trial" provisions of the Constitution.

Apparently the local jurisdictions were waiting for me to finish my federal sentence before initiating legal proceedings against me in the local courts. This is unconstitutional and goes against volumes of case law. The Supreme Court had ruled that once a prisoner is in custody, as I was while in the penitentiary, the State courts must move in a timely fashion to bring outstanding charges to a conclusion, either through trial or dismissal. Since this was not done it took motions and judge's court orders to get my outstanding cases dismissed. Buck saw to it and it was done.

My issue with the Bureau of Prisons (BOP) concerning the calculation of my sentence was another matter.

The BOP argued that I had another fifteen months to serve in order to fulfill my minimum sentence; disregarding the fifteen months I'd served in county jails before I was sentenced on the draft card charges.

Buck was pressed with other cases and informed me I would have to handle this problem myself. Using the prison law library to do the research I filed a motion with Judge Fox in Grand Rapids arguing that I was a federal prisoner the entire time I was incarcerated, and that I must be credited with time served while in federal custody.

Six weeks after I filed my motion Judge Fox agreed and ordered my immediate release.

Chapter Seventeen

RELEASED FROM PRISON...JULY 1972

Just five days before my release from prison, The Prez and thirty-seven other anti-war activists were arrested for digging bomb craters on lawns around the U of M campus. "The 38-Special," as I referred to them at the time in a news article, had hit the main campus Diag, long a focal point for anti-war action, with multiple craters from four to thirty feet in diameter. Part of the national "Bring The War Home" campaign, this crater-digging action was intended to dramatize and so remind people of the death and destruction Nixon's war machine was inflicting on a poor, small nation of peaceful rice-growing farmers.

The first morning of the first day of my return to Ann Arbor, Party members and friends dug a large bomb crater in the front lawn of 1520 Hill. Grimshaw lettered a sign reminding people of the war's destruction and proclaiming that the sign and crater would remain until the war was over.

Two days after my return home, a public meeting was to be held to debate the strategy for the upcoming trials of "the .38 Special." Several hundred people were expected to attend. After a year underground and more than two years in prison, I was ready to rock n' roll. I looked forward to the meeting as an opportunity to re-engage with my community and show people what I had learned in my studies while absent. I wanted to re-establish myself as a leader in my community. I wanted to go in there and throw political punches, debate, get the dialectic revved up. I was excited and expected to kick some political butt.

However, with Sinclair's release from prison just eight months before, the Central Committee had learned to avoid various pitfalls in dealing with Party members coming out of prison or returning from the war. The CC was committed to seeing I didn't make the same mistakes Sinclair had, the main one being bodacious overextension. After being released from prison, Sinclair's eagerness to make up for lost time, coupled with his general enthusiasm and excitement at being on the streets again, compelled him to take on far too much. He joined committees, formed committees, dominated meetings, started business deals, and made commitments for himself and the Party that couldn't be kept.

This caused significant confusion, contradictions, and alienation in the community and Party. By the time I was released Sinclair had his feet firmly under him, had cleaned up his mess, mended fences, and focused his energy as he forged ahead.

The CC believed, and I concurred, that my own re-introduction into the community had to be "slow and easy." We all knew that with my propensity for militant rants there was no telling what I might say, encourage, endorse, advocate, or commit the Party to.

As part of the overall re-naming, reorganization, and demilitarization of the Party, I now had the title of Chief of Staff rather than Minister of Defense. The responsibilities of my new position included organizing and conducting political education classes for Central Staff, taking on the coordination of legal work to get Forest out of prison (Skippy had been cut loose on parole just prior to my release), and maintaining and remodeling our Hill Street houses. These were three areas of work I was skilled in, and all of them required that I spend most of my time at 1520, close to home.

With my participation and agreement, the CC developed a policy that called for me to attend community meetings in a "fact finding" capacity only. I was to make no commitments of either my time or the Party's. In addition, I was to attend all meetings in the company of another Party member who was to advise me and keep me under control. We even developed a code phrase that my Party escort was to say to me if I got long-winded or started making commitments or went on one of my radical rants. The escort was to say, "Pun, remember, you're suppose to call DS." This could be said from across the room, across a meeting table, or whispered in my ear; when I heard it I was to stop talking, immediately.

The Prez and I, along with several Party members, attended the big public meeting to plan the defense of "the 38 Special Forces Crater Digging Squad," another name I gave the group in a later news article. Nearly two hundred students, professors, activists, rascals, and militants of all stripes crowded into a large conference room in the Michigan Union.

The first order of business involved routine matters: how to secure bonds, find lawyers, and raise money for the legal defense; when and where to hold rallies and benefits; where to print leaflets and hold future meetings. This was easy. The progressive community in Ann Arbor had been dealing with these sorts of issues for years and had organized similar events hundreds of times.

I was so proud of myself as I sat there quietly, greeted by friends I had not seen since I went underground, patiently "fact-finding."

Soon the discussion turned to, What do we do next? Do we stop digging craters? Do we escalate the cratering to city property or make "incursions" into Ypsilanti or Detroit? Do we dig a swath of craters across the University golf course as a reminder of the carpet bombing of North Vietnam?

After listening for what seemed like hours, I rose to speak. I argued that we should continue to dig on University property, expand to city property, and then escalate to private property. I advocated digging up city sidewalks, cutting phone, electric, and water lines. I said we should disrupt the lives of citizens until the war is stopped. I encouraged digging on private property. "Bombs make no distinction," I argued.

The Prez banged her knee against mine. "Shut-up!" she said under her breath. "Sit down." I sat.

The discussion ebbed and flowed. The moderates among us argued that if we continued to dig we might antagonize and 'turn-off" students and liberals who support ending the war. They believed we would lose even more support if we dug on private property. The debate continued, back and forth.

I rose again, unaware that I was speaking in the learned dialect and mannerisms of prison. I was playing the role I knew best--militant ex-con.

With my arm outstretched and index finger pointed down, as if indicating a line in the sand, and with my head tilted back and lower jaw jutted-out, I began.

"Look here motherfucker, these god-damn honkies, in their safe little houses and safe little lives..." The Prez pinched the back of my leg, "Sit down," she hissed without moving her lips.

I kept talking. People started to mill about, a few left. "Check it out!" I yelled, still in my pontificating posture. "AIN'T NO MOTHERFUCKER LEAVIN' THIS MOTHERFUCKER 'TIL THIS MOTHERFUCKER IS SETTLED, MOTHERFUCKER!"

Audrey was sitting with several Party members across the room. At one point she spoke up while looking at her watch. "Pun, remember, you're supposed to call DS."

I didn't stop talking. I never stop when I should. Pacing with arms punching the air, I continued.

"We've got to disrupt this motherfucker! The American lifestyle and culture makes the war machine possible and necessary. We've got to attack the very culture, we've got to interrupt and inconvenience people's lives..."

The Prez grabbed me by the arm and hustled me out of there. In the hall she insisted I was breaking CC policy, that I was going over the top and must back off or risk unleashing the wrath of the Central Committee and the scorn of other community activists. I put up stiff resistance to this criticism, insisting our role was to lead the movement to greater and greater levels of militancy. She agreed in principle but argued that now was not the time and I was not the person to initiate this type of leadership.

At the next CC meeting everyone was pissed at me: the CC because I spoke publicly against direct policy, The Prez and other Party members because I resisted their instructions publicly and directly.

The Prez gave a full report. She said the worst part was when I called the women in the audience "middle-class chicks," and the liberal moderates who wanted to stop digging craters "a bunch of whimpering faggots."

The CC hammered me hard for disregarding a policy I had helped formulate and on which we had reached consensus. Not only were they upset about what I had said, they were pissed off that I had spoken at all.

I made a heartfelt defense of my actions, insisting, as if words were separate from action, that everything I said was correct, while admitting, with downcast eyes, that the manner in which I said it was incorrect.

"WRONG!" the entire Central Committee said in unison.

"It's the height of individualism," Sinclair said, "to establish a policy collectively and then to disregard that policy when you feel like it, with no commitment to collective decisions. Shame on you."

DS spoke up in a sarcastic tone, "And we don't call our sisters chicks. Did you ever hear of women's liberation? Did you ever hear of gay liberation?"

Leni chimed in. "We don't call gay people faggots, or queers, or any other disparaging names. And we don't call straight people those names as a way to put them down. No name-calling."

The Prez spoke up. "We've moved beyond shared daycare and cooking duties. You've been gone three years. A lot has changed. Those people at the meeting are the very people who have been supporting you while you were underground and in prison. They are the very people who supported Sinclair and helped change the marijuana laws. They generally support us now--and you called them a bunch of chicks and faggots."

Other CC members pointed out that my prison jargon and show-off style was out of place and looked ridiculous. People don't like being intimidated--you scared the hell out of some, I was told repeatedly.

With the realization that the criticism directed at me was essentially correct came a real feeling of embarrassment. I ceased my feeble defense and accepted the fact that I didn't have a very good read and feel of my community. What I thought would gain support for my position only served to alienate people. "Picking up a rock, only to drop on one's own foot," is how Mao put it.

Mao established the principle of criticism/self-criticism in the world revolutionary movement. The Black Panther Party utilized this theory and so did the Rainbow People's Party. The desire to become better revolutionaries and better men and women drove us to practice this principle vigorously. We would constantly review and critique each other's work. If our work were putting out the newspaper, we'd look at and collectively analyze the paper. If it were organizing an action or benefit concert, we'd debrief after, always focusing on the work, trying to make it better.

The criticism of me by the CC was not unusual or exclusive to me. Everyone's work, including Sinclair's, was constantly monitored and feedback commonly given at CC meetings.

I had understood and supported the "idea" of women's and gay liberation for several years, but now I had to incorporate these ideas and principles into my speech and everyday life. They had to go from my head to my heart.

I set about trying to fit in again, moderating my tone, trimming my politics to fit the current conditions, speaking with respect about groups of people. For more than three years I had been encouraging people to take the struggle to "the next level," a euphuism for more militant action. Yet, out of the joint for less than a week and I realized my "level" was considerably behind that of the people I wanted to organize. I needed to raise my political awareness several notches just to be average.

Soundly chastised, I stayed close to headquarters and

concentrated on my work, starting each day with a quart of beer.

*   *   *

I noticed immediately how changing our Party name and re-focusing our efforts on a local level paid off. Our political position in Ann Arbor had changed completely since 1969, the last time I was there.

We were no longer seen as outrageous hippies who smoked pot on TV and clambered for attention. Many in Tree Town saw us as astute political organizers with a disciplined and dedicated cadre of workers. The Party put major effort into building a united front organization that would establish and support progressive institutions built on an alternative economic and political base.

The united front, which relied on consensus building to reach decisions, was called Tribal Council (TC). (Utilizing Native American imagery, a staple in hippie culture since its inception.) Each CC member was charged with organizing the area within which he or she worked: Sinclair, who worked in the music community, organized musicians, promoters, and producers; DS, who worked in the economic sector, organized among hip capitalists, shop owners, and small businesses. The Prez was liaison between the Party and the city administration and certain community organizations. Skippy worked in the area of education and helped establish the first Children's Community Center. Other CC members organized food co-ops and educated citizens about nutrition and sustainable agriculture. Yet another CC member worked to help create a free health clinic, a drug help center, and programs for runaways. Some helped establish community radio.

I worked through the parks committee of Tribal Council to help organize and produce free music in Ann Arbor parks for a number of years. This was a huge undertaking with as many as ten thousand people in attendance at the Sunday free concerts held on a weekly basis during the summer months.

I also organized the Tribal Council Skilled Trades Committee, primarily an information directory and employment referral service for building trades and labor. I organized TC Legal Self Defense (LSD) as a financial and political support service for people busted on pot charges. I also organized The Michigan Committee For Prisoners' Rights as a voice for prisoners and an advocate for their human and constitutional rights.

In addition to Tribal Council, several Party members sat on the Community Center Coordinating Council (C-4), which organized, funded, and maintained a community center that included a 4,000 square foot concert/dance hall with a new hardwood floor installed by Party members and their chums. C-4 was designed to advocate for the "youth community" and administer funds allocated through disbursements of revenue-sharing funds. The Mayor even appointed DS to the new board of the local cablevision commission.

We didn't run or control all the committees we joined, though we were often accused of doing so. Generally we simply made our energy and skills available to build a better community, push our political agenda, and have some fun.

The editorial board of THE SUN, made up of both Party and non-Party members, decided to move THE SUN offices from our Hill Street address to offices across town, above The Blind Pig, a blues club in downtown Ann Arbor. This was done to strengthen the tie between the paper and the community, in part by weakening the RPP's influence over it.

Eventually, having minded my p's and q's, the restrictions on my speaking publicly had been rescinded.

Our alliance with the Human Rights Party (HRP) during this time, resulting in the election of two HRP members to Ann Arbor City Council, was the high point of our involvement with local electoral politics.

The HRP was a socialist-inspired party that believed a revolution could be achieved through the electoral process. They were Trotskyites essentially. We formed an alliance with them to gain political ground, to acquire experience, and to help prove or disprove the theory of electoral revolution.

Having won two seats in the citywide election, the RPP assumed the race for sheriff would be the next goal. When they informed us that they did not intend to run a candidate for sheriff in the upcoming fall elections, our hopes of developing a long-standing relationship with the HRP were seriously compromised. They didn't want to run a candidate for sheriff, they told us, for fear they might win! "The sheriff has to arrest people and evict people and put people in jail; we don't want that blood on our hands," as I remember them saying.

I remember as well, wanting to choke HRP leadership; yet their view prevailed. The RPP tried to maintain an alliance with the Human Rights Party, but it was pointless if they didn't want to seize political power. Our position was, as the popular saying of the time went, "Political power grows out of the barrel of a gun." If the HRP won the sheriff's race, they would control the guns in the county, that's political power.

* * *

On the economic front things should have been better for the RPP than they were before I went underground and to prison; instead, the Party was on the verge of going under from month to month.

Sinclair's book, GUITAR ARMY, had been released but the distribution was screwed up; anticipated income never materialized. A movie of the now infamous 10 for 2--John Sinclair Freedom Rally, held in December of '71 and produced by John Lennon and Yoko Ono, was due for release and we expected some residuals. But Yoko wanted proceeds to go to her charities while we wanted the money to come to us or at least to some of our charities. Yoko held up the movie, which to this day has never been released, though a pirated copy exists and is shown from time to time in outlaw locations.

Sinclair and other business cronies set up Rainbow Multi-Media, an umbrella holding company for a number of Rainbow enterprises. Rainbow Trucking was a distribution company of hippie artifacts: tee shirts, bongs, rolling papers, books, newspapers, records etc. Rainbow Press was a printing company and Rainbow Graphics, a design company. Rainbow Management managed and booked bands and clubs. These businesses sustained themselves briefly but never caught on enough to become financially stable.

Rainbow Multi-Media produced the first Ann Arbor Blues and Jazz Festivals, certainly the high-water mark for artistic content, yet a financial disaster. We had expected the Festival to stimulate significant cash flow. It didn't. I came to believe that Sinclair was suffering under some kind of retribution Karma, bayou voodoo curse, or witching hex that precluded him from making money from any financial enterprise he entered into.

DS, the RPP chief financial officer, kept rolling over loans on the promise of a big pay-off on any number of upcoming events. He juggled books and cash, floated checks, and signed promissory notes, while his hair grew whiter trying to keep our rather large operation going and our collective noses above water.

Chapter Eighteen

IT ALL STARTED INNOCENTLY ENOUGH…1973

It all started innocently enough. Cheeseburger was a member in good standing in the Rainbow People's Party. He worked in the economic sector, you might say, as the Party's weed broker. Only occasionally, when good deals came along, he bought and sold kilos to other dealers who broke it down into lighter weights.

Eight months after my release from prison, Cheeseburger, The Burger for short, and I were arrested and charged with armed robbery, extortion, conspiracy to extort, criminal usury, and conspiracy to commit criminal usury.

Michigan's Attorney General (AG) took the case away from local prosecutors and assumed direct control, an unusual move. Moreover, the AG issued a press release, rare in a criminal matter, and circulated the seldom-used "long form" indictment that contained every outlandish and outrageous charge the so-called victim made against us. This set off alarm bells in our heads. It seemed that the State, at the highest level, was committed to the destruction of us as individuals and by extension our political organization, even if it meant fabricating a case.

As was common with good customers, The Burger fronted fifteen kilos of mid-grade reefer to Uwe Wagner, a hippie with connections throughout northern Lower Michigan. Uwe promised to pay $3,000 in thirty days. He didn't pay, or else this story would never have happened.

I should make clear that reefer transactions generally were not conducted at our Hill Street houses. The smoke was never stored there and rarely was the money since it was deposited as soon as it was made. Only one CC member (not me), along with The Burger, conducted the business and knew the details of the various deals going on at any one time.

Burger, in order to insure his own good health, since other dealers had fronted the kilos to him, saw it as his professional responsibility to collect the debt from Uwe.

Friends in northern Michigan found Uwe, the villain, in Honor, a small town just west of Traverse City. He was holed up in Whispering Waters Cabins and Motel, kitchenettes available by day or week.

I saw Burger just as he was about to leave in the Volvo wagon to pay Uwe a visit; he told me of his plan. "Hell, I'll go with ya, maybe we'll meet some hippie girls in Traverse City," I said as I ran inside to sign out with the Officer of the Day. "You shouldn't be doing this by yourself anyway--better to have someone with you," I told him as I jumped in and we peeled-out, throwing gravel into the bomb crater.

Three hours, a six-pack of St. Paulie Girl, and numerous

joints later, as we neared Honor, I asked The Burger, "So what's the fucking plan? I mean we go in this guy's house and ask him for our three grand, right?"

The Burger nodded in the affirmative while keeping his eyes on the icy January roads.

"What if he don't want us to come in?" I ask.

"We ain't askin' if we can come in." The Burger answered.

"What if he has a gun?" I wondered.

"He don't have no gun. He's an 18-year-old punk. He's a little squirrelly, pimply-faced, greasy bastard with low self-esteem--he don't have a gun, he's a punk," The Burger snapped.

"What if he don't have the money or the reefer? I asked, trying to think this through.

"Then the son of a bitch will have to make arrangements. I ain't comin up here again," The Burger growled.

After thinking for a moment, Burger continued: "If he don't have the money I think he will offer us all his earthly belongings as a good faith gesture until he pays the dough, kinda like collateral."

"OK, let's do it…we're not going to fuck him up, right?"

"Right," Burger answered as he skidded the Volvo up the two frozen ruts that led to Uwe's cabin.

We parked in front. There was nothing surreptitious about our conduct, as far as we were concerned; we were going to a business meeting. The Burger tried the door; it was open so we went in.

Uwe was there with his friend Bruce, a 17-year-old hippie vagabond.

They were startled to see us and sat peacefully on the couch in the tiny living room of the small cabin as we looked for pot or money. We found various quantities of opiates, which we flushed down the toilet. The RPP had a firm and stern position on hard drugs; we did not tolerate them in any manner. Party members did not use and we destroyed all we ever found.

As I expected, Uwe didn't have the money or weed so we took his stereo, records, hookah pipe, bongs, and clothes, along with other worthless hippie knick-knacks.

We took photos of Uwe and promised to expose him as a hard drug dealer if he didn't come up with the money. We left

Bruce alone since he seemed to simply be in the wrong place at the wrong time.

We returned to Ann Arbor and placed Uwe's stuff in storage without giving the incident much further thought.

A month later The Burger and I were arrested on the aforementioned charges. When added up we were facing; if convicted, life plus 65 years, with maximum sentences that would run consecutively, which we expected to happen if we were found guilty.

"Damn! How did I let this happen?" I asked myself again and again.

The Attorney General sent two assistant AGs. The lead, Wilson, was an experienced "hack" with a shiny seat on his frayed suit. The other was a clean-cut, right-wing Republican, whiz-bang, just out of law school. He wanted our heads on his mantle. A Michigan State Police (MSP) Red Squad investigator ably assisted them. It was clear the State saw this as no ordinary criminal case.

At arraignment the Judge set our bond at $100,000 each--ransom really. Having once been a Federal Ten-Most-Wanted fugitive who had fled prosecution in the past, my credibility, when I promised to return for trial, was somewhat strained. We sat in jail unable to post our bonds for more than a month.

At the preliminary exam, where the State shows a crime has been committed and shows probable cause that the defendants (The Burger and I) committed the crime, the State's case began to unravel.

Remember Bruce, the 17-year-old innocent bystander? As the only eyewitness, the AG obviously needed his testimony. But Bruce, after Burger and I left Uwe's, had split for Boston and laid low, we later learned. A subpoena was issued, and the Michigan State Police (MSP) tracked him down and contacted the Boston Police to serve the subpoena. The Boston Police paid Bruce a visit at his new pad, found a three-foot pot plant growing on the windowsill, and placed him under arrest.

MSP detectives then traveled to Boston and brokered a deal whereby the Boston pot charges would be held in abeyance until Bruce successfully testified in our trial back in Michigan. If Bruce did a good job in Michigan the Boston Police would drop the charges. All were agreed.

The MSP purchased an airline ticket for Bruce and gave him instructions to be in Cadillac, Michigan, on a particular date to meet with the AG and go over testimony.

Bruce cashed-in the ticket, bought some pot, and ignored the subpoena.

The MSP, with the help of the Boston Police, tracked him down again and placed him under some kind of extra-legal witness protection arrest before escorting him by plane back to Traverse City. There they deposited him in a local motel and "ordered" him to remain incognito.

We knew none of this at the time of course, since The Burger and I were still in jail; only later did we hear the story.

At the very same time that the MSP were depositing Bruce in a Traverse City motel, Buck and DS were in Traverse City investigating Uwe's hard drug dealings and other sleazy transactions.

They found out that for the past year Uwe had been dealing in heroine, morphine, speed, pot, and even pieces of broken-up asphalt floor tiles, which he wrapped in aluminum foil and sold to kids as hashish. We had to wonder why the MSP had no interest in Uwe's crimes.

Through Buck's somewhat shady network of connections, he found the location of the motel where Bruce was being held. He reasoned that the defense team had a legal right to interview the eyewitness before the preliminary exam, so DS and Buck paid Bruce a visit.

The way DS remembers it, they found Bruce with his motel room door open, sitting on the bed, eating a bowl of cold cereal. They invited him to dinner. Bruce agreed and they went to the very public Big Boy Restaurant.

Buck asked Bruce straightforward questions: "Did you see a gun or any other weapons?"

"No."

"Did Pun or The Burger threaten you or Uwe with bodily harm then or some time in the future?"

"No."

"Did they break anything?"

"No."

"Did they steal Uwe's stuff?"

"No."

"Did Uwe offer his stuff as collateral?"

"Yes."

"Is what you told me true, and will this be your testimony at the preliminary examination?"

"Yes."

*   *   *

At the preliminary exam the State's case was all but blown out of the water. Bruce's testimony was unrehearsed and quite believable, rooted as it was in the truth. Even Wilson's intimidating cross-examination did not shake Bruce from the fundamental truth.

After seeing how weak the State's case was, the Judge dropped the armed robbery charge and lowered my bond to $10,000 and The Burger's to $5,000.

At our first meeting upon being released on bond, Buck ranted and raved and called me stupid names for getting anywhere near a dope deal.

"Don't you ever learn? Don't you think?" He wanted to know. "You're about the hottest guy in the state, you cannot be involved in anything illegal."

"What's criminal usury?" I wanted to know. "It sounds like some kind of slavery or sex for hire crime."

Buck paused long enough to ignore me and continued his scolding: "You've got to think about the ramifications of your actions, this sucks."

I never think about the ramifications of my actions. Throughout my young life I focused on the "now." Am I happy now? Or sad, or bored, or angry? My life was focused on the present. Remembering the past and the consequences of past actions never seemed to figure into my calculations. Likewise, planning for the future, or saving for the future, or denying desire now, in order to have a better future--this was not part of my thought process. "No past, no future, only now," could have been my mantra.

I knew, for instance, at age 14, that when I stayed out all night with my older friends I would be punished when I got home. But the attraction of the moment had a magnetic pull on me greater than the promise of fun in the future or fear of the punishment I would get when I got home.

Buck was fuming: "Pun, don't ever, EVER, ask me to defend you on another pot charge. I'm gonna take this case because they are politically motivated charges, initiated by the State to silence you. As I said before, this sucks. Incidentally," he went on, "criminal usury is charging too much interest on a loan."

Buck's anger was a manifestation of the principle of criticism/self criticism and did not represent a split in our friendship, which endures today; but rather it was a forceful, articulate analysis of objective conditions at the time.

Once again we had to rev-up our legal defense team and "go to the mattresses" in a fight for our lives. Even though the armed robbery charge had been dropped, many people remembered the headline "Plamondon charged with armed robbery," but did not hear of the dismissal. Furthermore, we were still facing 65 years if convicted.

There was a broader political principle at stake as well. If the State were successful with the politically motivated prosecution against us, then they would use it against other political groups they found objectionable.

* * *

I love a good court fight the way a mountain climber loves the danger of climbing, or the way a bullfighter loves the intensity of the match between man and beast. In both instances the cutting edge is sharp, mistakes can be fatal, preparation is everything. But with numerous successfully fought legal battles behind us, most notably the Sinclair pot case that ended in changing the Michigan marijuana laws and the CIA bombing/Supreme Court litigation, putting together a defense and media team to face the onslaught of the State legal machine was second nature to us.

Buck, DS, and I were the center of the team, with Buck in charge and DS acting as coordinator. Sinclair was our senior consultant with Fenton and Kelley running the media campaign.

Justice depended on us getting our version and interpretation of the facts to the public and informing them of the shenanigans of the State. Fenton was the man for the job.

Sinclair had recruited him away from Liberation News Service, a news subscription service not unlike United Press International (UPI) and the Associated Press (AP). A New York-bred media genius, Fenton was well- known as an outstanding photojournalist with a published book of photographs documenting the anti-war and counter-culture movement titled, SHOTS. He had been connected with the Underground Press Syndicate and was functioning at the time as editor of *THE SUN*. Without a doubt, Fenton was the man for the job.

As was done in our CIA/Supreme Court case, DS and Buck assembled a group of lawyers who would work for free and each took on an aspect of the case and prepared legal briefs and supporting memoranda. One lawyer prepared a brief seeking separate trials for Burger and me. Another wrote a brief challenging the legality of wiretaps the State had made of Uwe calling me. Yet another researched extortion law. Law students at the U of M brought together information on jury selection and evidentiary challenges.

Buck assigned me the responsibility of preparing two major motions. One was a motion seeking dismissal of all the charges based on the argument that the entire case was politically motivated and brought primarily to silence me and discredit the Rainbow People's Party. (See appendix).

This was a ballsy move. It let the prosecutor know that we were not going to challenge the facts of the case--just the interpretation of the facts. We knew the Judge would not grant this motion, but it allowed us to educate His Honor on the maneuvers and mechanizations of the FBI, the Michigan Attorney General's office, and the MSP in bringing this case.

The second was a motion arguing for the right to act as my own attorney, in addition to Buck. This would allow me to cross-examine Uwe and might give us a psychological edge.

* * *

My time in county jails and prison was not just spent reading Mao and Lenin and Burroughs and Kesey and Fanon and Marcuse and Castenada and Che and Snyder and Debs, among others; I also studied law. Specifically, I studied those laws that the government was using to put me away and keep me locked-up.

I had written successful motions while in Federal prison to force my release soon after the Supreme Court decision prompted the Government to drop their prosecution of me in the CIA case. In addition I had typed most of the other motions filed thus far in this case. I was familiar with legal proceedings, jargon, protocol and proper filing form. So in assigning me these two motions, Buck was not totally off the wall. He checked my work and countersigned below my signature.

The Burger and I, now out of jail, wanted more time to prepare our case and to breathe free air. Buck filed a motion for a postponement or continuance of the trial because he, too, needed more time, as he was preparing for a trial in Phoenix at the time. The State resisted this vigorously, as it did every motion we filed.

Our Judge denied Buck's postponement motion but changed the venue of the trial, per another motion we'd filed, to Cadillac, the county seat. With the new venue, the Judge reasoned, we only had a three-hour drive rather then a three-and-a-half hour drive. The Judge also granted our motion to have a local attorney appointed to assist us and make available office space, Xerox machine, law library and the like. Likewise, the Judge also granted my motion allowing me to defend myself as Buck's co-council.

Still, we desperately needed more time before trial. In another gutsy move, fully supported by the defense team, Buck refiled the motion for postponement, or, in the alternative, a motion to withdraw from the case. Buck's threat, couched in legal jargon, meant, "Give us more time, or I'm dropping out."

The Judge could have easily denied our continuance motion and granted Buck's motion to withdraw. That would have left us at the mercy of the Court and our future in the hands of whomever the Judge appointed to defend us. Yet we knew the Judge was eager to get this case over with and Buck's withdrawal would set the process back several months. In addition, the Judge was aware that we were trying to build a record for appeal.

Buck prevailed, the Judge granted our motion for postponement. With our legal victory in hand, we began in earnest to prepare for trial. About this time I began drinking heavily. It was difficult to sustain the breakneck pace of the constant legal meetings, Party meetings, and political meetings, the researching and preparation of briefs, the mad dashes to get papers filed on time and in the proper form, and the binges of methamphetamine use, all while maintaining the image of a self-sacrificing revolutionary. Alcohol became a way to unwind--a refuge in the storm.

* * *

The fundraising campaign for our defense jumped into high gear. Rock bands performed at benefit concerts held in various bars and clubs around town on a weekly basis. Benefit film showings were hosted by film co-ops on campus. Several people in Detroit hosted expensive cocktail parties where liberal folks, who liked to hob-nob with the radicals, could discuss the case with the party's celebrities: Party members and local attorneys.

The Prez gave interviews to various media several times a week. When big news happened, like the armed robbery charges being dropped or the stunning testimony of the eyewitness, Bruce, a press conference would be called at which Sinclair and Buck would join The Prez to analyze the developments. At other times The Prez would solicit various progressive businesses and friends for financial support, while DS made his way across campus soliciting funds from sympathetic professors and from others in his subterranean world of connections.

* * *

We rented a house in Cadillac that slept ten and moved essential personnel in. The trial was expected to take two weeks. Skippy and I went up a week before everyone else to set up the house and do jury pool investigation. We had a copy of the jury pool list, which is a public document since the names on it are chosen from the county voter registration list.

Every day for a week, with a 12-pack of Bud beside me on the seat, I drove around Wexford County checking out names and addresses of potential jurors. I would drive by the address, notice the type of neighborhood, and note how many cars in the drive. Were there any bumper stickers? I made a note if they had kids, particularly teenagers, and also if they had a motorcycle or hippie van--anything that may give us a clue as to the political thinking and culture of the potential juror.

Skippy ran the trial house; he was house captain. He did the cooking and cleaning, answered the phone, printed press releases on the mimeograph machine we brought with us and kept order during hectic times.

Fenton came up to run the media and PR operation. He set up interviews, issued press releases, wrote news stories, held mini-press conferences, and generally spun events in our favor. He also set up live feeds to WABX radio in Detroit that ran several times a week. With his little cassette recorder he would interview lawyers or witnesses or trial spectators, or narrate a straight newscast into the recorder. Then he would remove the mouthpiece from the phone, connect two alligator clips to terminals in the mouthpiece, push the button, and the tape would play "live" on the air in Detroit.

Sometimes the station would "interrupt regularly scheduled programming to bring you this special report." Other times the station would run the tape with their regular hourly news. Often, Air Aces, as the gang of prominent WABX air personalities were known, would play the tapes during their shows and editorialize in our favor. Fenton is a genius.

Just days before the trial was to begin I met lovely Marci, a local girl working in a country club restaurant. We struck up a friendship that developed into a love affair.

In the course of our intimacy Marci told me that up until recently she had been the Judge's mistress. THE JUDGE'S MISTRESS! I told Buck immediately. Buck, Marci and I got together to talk this new information through. We met at the picnic table outside the trial house, where we held all-important meetings to avoid being electronically wiretapped.

Marci was an attractive young woman in her early twenties and had been born and raised in Cadillac. On the surface she appeared to be a straight, middle-class woman with a proper bra and upbringing. I came to know her as a more experiential and liberated woman than her demeanor revealed.

She talked to us on the condition that we in no way use

the information to harm the Judge personally. We agreed.

As usual Buck's questions were direct and to the point.

"How long was the affair with the Judge?"

"About three years," she answered.

"Who broke it off?"

"He did, we did."

"Where did you carry on this affair?"

"At motels--sometimes we went out of town. Sometimes at the Court House.

"Did you ever make love in his chambers?"

"Yes, quite often."

"Did you ever do it in the court room, on the bench?"

"Yes--sometimes he'd have me wear his robes."

Having seen her naked, my mind wandered.

"I knew it!" Buck screeched, slamming his palm to the table. "I knew it! Those goddamn Judges get it all."

We went on to query her about the Judge's likes and dislikes, his pet peeves, his hobbies, his political affiliations and leanings (moderate Republican).

"One thing," Marci reminded us several times, "he doesn't like being lied to, if he catches you in a lie he'll hang you."

We took note of this. Everything we were saying in Court was true, though some truths were stretched tighter than others.

* * *

For two days we tried to pick a jury. On the third we informed the Judge we felt we could not get an impartial jury of our peers and wished to dismiss the jury and go to trial before the Judge.

Again, this was a nervy move, but we had little choice. During our voir dire we found the overwhelming majority of the jury pool to be ardent Nixon supporters despite the fact the administration, as a result of the Watergate scandal, had been coming apart at the seams since April. As early as May the Senate Watergate hearings were underway and a shit storm was headed toward Nixon.

Most jury pool members also felt that marijuana was a

dangerous drug like heroin, and that longhaired people should get haircuts and find jobs. Exercising free speech during wartime, they felt, was absolutely unpatriotic and everything would be fine if hippies just quit rocking the boat. No, these were not our peers.

On the opening day of trial we were all standing on the steps of the Courthouse waiting for the doors to open when young Bruce showed up. Buck introduced me and we chatted as we exchanged pleasantries. I asked Bruce where he was staying. At a local motel, with arrangements made by the MSP, he said. I told him we had plenty of room and that he could stay with us if he wished. Perhaps, I suggested, he could collect the money for the motel and put it in his pocket. This sounded like a good idea to Bruce, so he moved in with us. We gave him his own room and treated him like a team member. Every morning he rode to court with us and every evening he'd return.

Wilson, the lead prosecutor, had a fit, but to no avail. Everything we did was quite legal. Neither The Burger nor I discussed testimony or the facts in the case with Bruce. Jesus, we had the State's star witness living with us, what more could we ask for?

During trial the State overplayed and overstated their case on every occasion. This tactic may have played well to a jury, but to the Judge these were unnecessary theatrics. The State, for example, arranged to have the foremost "voiceprint expert in the world" flown in from MIT to testify, with graphs and massive computer printouts. The expert testified that beyond a shadow of a doubt my voice was on the tapes that had been submitted as evidence.

When it was our turn to cross-examine the expert, Buck simply rose and stated that the defense would stipulate that it was my voice on the tape. After all, under direction of the MSP, Uwe had called ME. Of course my voice was on the tape. We believed the wiretaps supported our case. If the prosecution would only have asked, Buck told the Judge, we would have stipulated such, saving the Court time and expense. The Judge gave a sigh of exasperation directed at the prosecutor for overplaying his hand.

Around town we were polite and courteous with the locals; some even came to like us. The whole defense team and our supporters ate lunch every day in a downtown Swedish Smorgasbord restaurant. We became regulars and were treated deferentially by the staff that we came to know by name.

One day, Wilson, the hack, was dragging a four-foot by eight-foot piece of corkboard into the courtroom on which he had affixed fifteen 8x10 photographs. He was having trouble maneuvering the corkboard and holding open the swinging gate in the baluster that separated the spectators from the well of the Court. I jumped up and hoisted one end of the panel and held the gate open for Wilson to walk through. Together we placed the board on an easel in the front of the courtroom. My action was a courteous gesture that put the Judge and Court personnel at ease and made everyone smile.

The exhibit was related to a meeting between Uwe and me. The last time Uwe called our headquarters I took the call. Uwe said he had the money and would meet me in the mall parking lot, in section "P," in a red Ford pick-up with a camper on the back. I drove through the mall parking lot looking for anything suspicious, suspecting an ambush. After ten minutes of observation I approached Uwe's vehicle. He was with an older, rather scruffy dude, maybe a biker-type.

Uwe had a wad of bills and tried to give me the money there. I said no, and told him to follow me to the storage shed in the student ghetto and to do the exchange there.

On the four-by-eight foot panel were several aerial photographs of the mall parking lot with my vehicle circled and Uwe's marked with a red "X." They had photos of my ride in various sections of the lot as I reconnoitered the area. Wilson called the pilot and MSP photographer to testify that one flew the chopper and the other took the photos nailed to the board.

Again, when our turn came to cross-examine the witnesses, we stipulated that the MSP took the photos and they appeared to be accurate. I did meet Uwe in the parking lot and would have stipulated to this early on to save the Court's time and expense if the prosecution had only asked. Buck used the opportunity to remind the Judge of the dangerous Gestapo tactics used to arrest me while I was driving on busy Packard Avenue and the threat to innocent civilians as police officers careened recklessly with guns sprouting from a dozen cop cars.

Again the Judge sighed, rolled his eyes at the

prosecution and asked Wilson to continue and to please be thrifty with the Court's time. Another point for our team.

I felt sure Bruce had cinched the victory for us. He contradicted Uwe's testimony directly and convincingly and refuted the State's charges one by one.

The Judge found us innocent of all charges save one; Extortion by Threat of Accusation. The Judge explained that when we took photos of Uwe and threatened to expose him as a hard drug dealer and rip-off artist unless he paid us, we were committing extortion by threat of accusation. You can't do that he told us. You can't threaten to expose someone, even if it is true, in order to pressure them to pay a debt. We were guilty.

The Judge set sentencing for three weeks hence.

Chapter Nineteen

THREE WEEKS HENCE…JULY 19, 1973

I was certain I was going to prison. I figured The Burger would get one to five and I'd get five to ten. A bummer to be sure, but with "good time" The Burger would be out in nine months and I'd be out in something over three years.

And we had the right to appeal. If we were to be sentenced to time in prison, an appeal was certain. We felt the judge would grant us appeal bonds, so the likelihood of us leaving for prison the day of sentencing was slim, or so we believed.

Nevertheless, Sinclair had been denied appeal bond in his famous weed case in a situation similar to the present circumstances. Anything could happen.

The night before sentencing someone threw a big party on a farm near Ann Arbor. Buck, The Burger and I, as well as the entire defense team, overindulged in pot, alcohol, nitrous oxide, and speed.

We awoke late, foggy-headed and hung over. Buck, The Burger and I made a reckless dash to Cadillac, with only one stop to pick up a dozen Heineken. We arrived bleary eyed and smelling of beer and reefer. The Prez, DS, and several Party members and supporters left after us, yet arrived with plenty of time to spare.

The Judge was a kindly older gentleman with white hair and an air of confident control. Upon taking the bench, he called Wilson, Buck, and me to the bench (I was still acting co-council).

His Honor asked if any of us had seen the pre-sentence report prepared by the State parole and probation department? (See Appendix A).

Wilson had seen the report but neither Buck nor I had. The Judge ordered a two-hour lunch recess so we could review the document.

We learned much later, after comparing the pre-sentence report with other files secured from the government under the Freedom of Information Act, that the bulk of the information in the 22-page, single-spaced report, was prepared by the Behavioral Science Division of the FBI in 1970, while I was 10 Most Wanted. It was a psychological profile that I was sure was designed to show me as a dark and unrepentant habitual criminal.

A state probation officer had interviewed me, changed the captioning on the FBI report, added some pertinent new information, and filed a very wordy study of my young outlaw life.

We made two copies of the report, retired to a conference room in the Courthouse, sent out for sandwiches, and frantically scanned the report looking for any statement we needed to challenge or rebut.

"Christ they have my entire police record--from '62 through '72--20 arrests, that don't look good." I muttered as I tried to eat egg salad on rye, my stomach churning and head pounding.

"Did you see this?" Buck asked, sliding his copy across the table. Buck had bracketed a section on page four:

> Note: records reveal Defendant born 4-27-45 during time when his natural Parents were both patients at Traverse City State Hospital. Mother a mixed blood Indian and Father half-blood Ottawa Indian. Parental rights were terminated by the Court in 1946. Defendant did not tell writer about his adoption by the Plamondon's, although subsequent verification information indicates that he has been aware of this fact for years. It does not indicate, however, that he possesses the complete factual story in terms of the history of his natural parents.

This was new information, the first time I'd heard of my birth in the State Hospital and the race of my mother and my father's Tribe. But I couldn't relish or even ponder for long this new information. I went back to rapidly scanning the report, looking for the one sentence or statement that the Judge could use to justify sending me away.

Buck highlighted several more paragraphs on page 14 and called my attention to them:

> Biological Father: Born 2-16-1886 in Newaygo, Mich. Half blood Ottawa Indian. He completed 7th grade. Worked as logger, railroad fireman and farm hand. Entered military service on 3-9-1914 and after injury was honorably discharged 8-10-1916. He was admitted to Traverse City Regional Psychiatric Hospital (TCPH) 6-1-43 suffering from chronic alcoholism. He died on July 21, 1954 at TCPH. Cause of death: Cerebral hemorrhage and myocarditis.
>
> This was followed by the following entry:
>
> Biological Mother: Very little is in the record regarding the mother. Born in 1906 in Canada. Her family was Indian and moved to the US in 1909 and became naturalized citizens. She received a high school education. She worked as a telephone operator. She was admitted to TCPH of 2-14-44 suffering from syphilis.

More new information. My mom was 39 and my dad was 58 when I was born. This was all interesting, but would not send me to or keep me out of prison. I moved on looking for the damning statement. But overall the report didn't look too bad. There were no glaring contradictions or misrepresentations that we needed to challenge. It was time to go, our two hours were up, and our moment of reckoning was at hand.

The July humidity made the red sandstone Courthouse like a pressure cooker as we stood before the Judge waiting to be sentenced. Images of a cartoon Courthouse under pressure, the walls ballooned out, hissing steam from doors and windows, filled my head. I wasn't sure which would blow first, the Courthouse or me as we stood waiting to hear our sentences.

The Judge began slowly, fiddling with a sheaf of papers on his desk. "For many years I've had a love affair…" he paused and jogged his papers. I felt my heart go to my throat as my knees weakened. *Damn!* I thought, *He knows I've been getting it on with Marci, this is a bad sign.*

With my heart pounding, and my eyes stinging from perspiration, he continued "…with the Michigan State Police. But this case has soured that relationship like no other…"

Goddamn! This is great. I thought as the Judge went on to spank the MSP and the Attorney's Office for what seemed like twenty minutes. He said that when they heard my name mentioned they set out to bend rules, cut corners, overreact and ignore more significant crime in order to put me in prison.

Eventually he stopped his harangue against the State and turned his attention to us. With no lecture or scolding he sentenced The Burger to three years probation. In a flash I re-evaluated the situation. Since he had given The Burger three years "paper" it was likely he'd give me 1 to 5, or so I thought.

The Judge turned to me and gave me five years probation. I stood as if thunderstruck. Buck leaned over and whispered, "Close your mouth."

Chapter Twenty

A BLUES & JAZZ DIRGE FOR RAINBOW PEOPLE'S PARTY--1973-'75

The State had tried hard and gone to great lengths to put me in prison; anything less was a defeat for them. For us, probation was a victory, since it showed the Judge's total rejection of the State's extravagant lie and foiled their goal of putting me away and throwing away the key. This legal victory had a particularly sweet taste since I had had a front line position in developing the legal and media strategy used to defeat the State's extra-legal onslaught.

Around this time I began drinking excessively nearly every night, yet functioning every day. The Cadillac court case is the last clear and continuous memory I have until September 1976, when I started driving semi-trucks for the rock group KISS on their national Dressed To Kill tour.

The glow of our Cadillac victory soon faded as the struggle for daily financial and political survival dominated our lives. During the time I had been preparing for trial, Sinclair and others had been organizing the 1973 Ann Arbor Blues & Jazz Festival. I jumped in where I could and was given the task of organizing a crew to sell festival programs. I gathered a squad of runaways and street people to hawk the program, for which they earned a decent wage. My crew sold every last program and accounted for all the money. We were probably the only segment of the festival that could make that statement.

Additionally, I was "on call" to help deal with any political agitation stirred up by "anarchists" or other undisciplined elements who commonly frequented large outdoor festivals specifically for the purpose of leading a crowd to crash the gate. Throughout the summer, several groups of such people traveled from festival to festival doing this.

On the Saturday of the festival, my network of street people informed me that a group of surly anarchist were going to cause a commotion and attempt to get the crowd to rush the gates so everyone could get in free. Fortunately, most festival goers had purchased their tickets in advance and were not likely to be interested in helping a bunch of rowdies rush anything. A good number of others fully expected to pay the measly sixteen dollars for a weekend of music. The would-be gatecrashers were far outnumbered. Still, from a public safety point of view, an organizer cannot take a chance that a small group of sorry-sorts might create a ruckus and turn a crowd into a mob. So, like a hippie Batman, I swung into action. I got some wristbands that allowed free admission and collected my pal "the fireman," a Native American activist and employee of the Ann Arbor fire department. Then I rounded up Eugene, the president of an Ypsilanti motorcycle club that had been contracted to provide security around the festival grounds' perimeter fence.

When the festival gates opened, tickets were being taken, and music lovers began flooding the infield in front of the stage, Eugene, the fireman and I went to mingle in the crowd outside, looking for agitators. We found them just as they began chanting "Free Music! Free Music!" We calmed down the ringleaders long enough to advise them that their plan was ill-conceived. For one thing, I explained, the bikers hired to do fence security had been tipped off and were itching for a fight. For another, the would-be gatecrashers didn't have the numbers to pull off such a bold move; at most, there were twenty in their group. I handed out the bracelets to a handful of the most vocal instigators, instructing them to attach the bracelets loosely so they could be removed and re-used by others in their group. I figured they'd be smart enough to take the offer, which they did.

The idea that the festival music should be available to everyone cost-free is based on standard anarchist thinking, of course; but it may also have been related in this case to the complaints of local ultra-leftists and self-proclaimed radicals who had been attacking the RPP in the underground press, charging that its members were nothing more than bourgeois capitalists exploiting the youth culture and getting rich. They were idiots. They made no distinction between the Party, a non-profit political/cultural organization, and Rainbow Multi-Media, a for-profit corporation and producer of the B&J Festival.

Moreover, despite its legal status as a for-profit corporation, Rainbow Multi-Media had made every effort to include the community in the planning and preparations for the festival. The local food co-op sold steaming bowls of organic gruel and various sandwiches with the texture and flavor of straw. The Free Medical Clinic provided on-site medical care, The Children's Community Center provided a supervised child care/play area. Other groups sold juice or tee-shirts or candy bars to raise money. Several organizations had set up information tables in a massive effort to reach out to and interact with the various communities they served.

Even security inside the festival grounds was a community endeavor. For several years, The Prez had been organizing local youth to serve as peacekeepers at large gatherings. We knew from past experience that music, reefer, large groups of young people, and police didn't mix well. So The Prez, with the support of the Party, organized the Psychedelic Rangers to keep order at large events. The Rangers had the support of the entire community, even the police department. Many times the Rangers had defused tense situations that the police only would have made worse. Having the Rangers patrol inside the grounds, while the bikers patrolled the perimeter, meant that the police were essentially relegated to directing traffic.

*　　　　*　　　　*

Ten minutes after I'd handed out the free admission bracelets, the same group of hooligans began chanting "Free Music! Free Music!" again; a crowd was starting to gather. I fetched the fireman and a few of his guys, then Eugene and some of his lieutenants, and headed for the front gates. As we walked we made a plan. Each of us was to single out a vocal agitator, engage them in dialogue, and walk them away from the fracas. "Each one take one and get him out of there," is how I put it at the time.

My posse of ten rounded the corner and immediately engaged the rabble. "Why are you doing this?" I demanded of the ringleader. "This is a community-supported event. Why are you doing this?" I was right in his face.

The derelict hoard, most of whom would doubtless be returning to their private schools and universities in the fall, shouted: "Music should be free!"

"Count Basie don't play for free--the electricity ain't free--the airlines and buses ain't free and neither are the hotels!" I hollered back with as much machismo as I could muster, which is considerable. Their magic was broken. Quickly the bikers grabbed four guys and gave them the bum's rush to the road.

In the meantime, the fireman and his guys were doing a fine job defusing the situation they'd been handling until one of the gate-crashers said five car loads of AIM (American Indian Movement) members were coming to join his band of anti-social ruffians--an obvious lie. This clearly angered the fireman, a member of Michigan AIM. He and his crew quickly grabbed the interlopers and put them in hammerlocks, headlocks, wristlocks, arm-twists, and hair grabs as they hustled them out. I grabbed my guy by the wrist and upper arm, steering him forward at a fast pace; all the while he kept saying, "Okay, okay. I'm goin'.

I'm goin'." When we got to the edge of the festival grounds, I gave him a shove and kicked him in the ass, yelling, "and stay out!" I'd always wanted to do that. In my heart, though, I knew that in different circumstances one of those agitators might easily have been me.

Oh, but the music! Freddy King, Count Basie, John Lee Hooker, and Yusef Lateef. That was just Friday night and Saturday afternoon. Saturday night it was Ray Charles, Charles Mingus, Jimmy Reed, and Big Walter Horton. Whew! The Sunday afternoon line-up included Ornette Colman, Victoria Spivey, Sippie Wallace, a young and vivacious Bonnie Raitt, Joe Willie Wilkins & the King Biscuit Boys, featuring Houston Stackhouse, and then Luther Allison. On Sunday night Sun Ra played, followed by Homesick James, mighty Joe Young, and Hound Dog Taylor and The House Rockers.

Although it was an artistic triumph, the festival lost money, big time. I never knew the details, or wanted to know them, but many hopes, plans and promises went down the drain with that financial flop.

The Prez and I drifted apart, each consumed with our own work and different sets of friends. I started hanging at The Blind Pig, a city landmark today, but then a new blues club in an antique Ann Arbor building. It had the first cappuccino machine in town.

Pretty soon I met Nadine, a barmaid at the Blind Pig--the Pig, for short--and a dropout from the music school at the University. I began spending more time with Nadine and her friends and going home less. Meanwhile, the Prez would sometimes not come home for several nights in a row. We sometimes went a week or more without seeing each other, which was fine with me; avoiding personal or marital problems was one of my principles.

* * *

During the winter of 1973-74, Republicans and reactionary Democrats on the City Council united to pass an ordinance which prohibited Rainbow Multi-Media from producing the 1974 Blues & Jazz Festival in Ann Arbor. The festival was driven into exile, and would now take place on a small college campus across the Detroit River in Windsor, Ontario. As at past Festivals The Burger was the stage manager. This year I was the site manager, responsible for making sure that such things as port-a-johns, ticket booths, a first aid tent, site lighting, and food booths were set up, and that chain link and snow fence for crowd control and traffic flow as well as a system for trash handling were in place.

The Burger and I went to Canada a week early to build the stage and prepare the site. I hired Eugene and ten or so of his biker friends as a construction crew and as loyal muscle. I hired some Canadian guys too, eh, and set to work.

Friday morning, before the festival started, a flatbed semi pulled onto the grounds loaded with several dozen portable toilets. I showed the driver a sketch of the site and indicated that six potties would go here, and six here, and six here, and so on.

The driver said that it had been all over the news that many people were getting arrested or turned back at the border because of drugs. TV and print media were speculating that the turnout would be small, and even had a news clip of a hippie saying, "Nah man, I ain't goin'. I ain't gonna let no Canadian look up my butt hole," or so it was reported to me.

The driver said his boss wanted him to get a check before delivering the toilets. He wanted $1,500 up front, or he would not drop his load. "Out of the question!" I exclaimed, and sent someone to find Eugene. In a matter of hours we were expecting ten thousand maniacs, I said, trying to reason with the dude. I told him we had signed contracts. I said no one was on site that could write checks. I said this was a bullshit way of doing business.

Eugene and three of his leather-vested, bare-chested brothers walked up. I pulled Eugene aside and said, "Look man, the health inspector is coming in an hour to give us a final inspection, we have to have those shitters in place, they cannot leave this site. Period."

I didn't know how, but I knew Eugene would not let the truck leave with the outhouses on board; Eugene would do whatever it took to get the job done.

I continued arguing with the driver, pointing out that we had done many festivals in the past and that everyone had gotten paid. The driver held his ground and insisted he was only following his boss's order and that the matter was quite out of his hands.

Just then Eugene called us over to the dude's truck, which was leaning forlornly like an old workhorse resting a tired leg. "You've got a flat tire here," Eugene said. Just then a forklift came over from the stage area and guys swarmed over the flatbed loosening straps and sliding the blue plastic carcasses around.

The front tire was flat. Someone had cut off the valve stem, easy enough to fix, but a pain in the ass. "You better let us get some weight off this rig before the other one goes flat," Eugene said, walking to the other side of the tractor and bending down near the front tire, holding a pair of side-cutters used to snip the valve stem.

Slow as he was, the driver got the picture. We unloaded the toilets and moved on. I don't know if he ever got paid, though I do remember a service truck repairing his tire.

Saturday morning, just hours before the gates were to open, in the middle of dealing with the fact that there was no power in the dressing rooms, no power to the concession stands, and that a thousand feet of snow fence was needed in the parking lot, The Burger and I were arrested by the Dudley Do-Rights of the Royal Canadian Mounted Police.

It seems that on Friday evening, as Sinclair had attempted to enter Canada to attend the Festival, he was stopped at the border and refused entry, being a man of less than stellar reputation, according to Canadian Immigration. We later learned that the FBI contacted the Canadians and encouraged them to refuse Sinclair entry.

Sinclair was panicked and enraged. This was his festival, he felt. He and Andrews had organized and financed it. The Canadians, however, paid no heed to Sinclair's protestations.

Sinclair called a press conference in Detroit and ranted and raved on TV about the pigs conspiring to make the festival a failure. During his rage against the machine, Sinclair pointed out, "They let Plamondon and Burger in, hell, they're both felons; why won't they let me in?" That's all it took. Sinclair had inadvertently sicced the Mounties on us.

We were arrested as undesirable aliens and for failure to

report previous felony convictions upon entry. We were taken away in handcuffs and transported to a magistrate who released us to return to the festival since we were essential personnel. Our release was contingent on our being deported the following Monday.

I don't remember much of the festival, only James Brown holding up the show for two hours until Andrews could produce $10,000 cash or certified check.

Monday, after we broke the place down, and cleaned up, and loaded our fence, great spools of wire with light bulbs fastened every ten feet, ladders, shovels, and miscellaneous gear into a Ryder rental truck, we drove to Canadian Immigration at the Ambassador Bridge. We signed some papers; they assigned RCMP cars to follow us over to the American side. That's how we were deported from Canada, I haven't been back since.

The B&J Festival was an economic catastrophe. Our personal, Party, and corporate finances had been exhausted, and left in shambles, as if ransacked, after the debacle in Canada.

As in a family, money woes brought to the fore resentments and animosities, and led to questions about the personal commitment of individual Party members. I could see the writing on the wall: It was all falling apart, the commune, the Party, my marriage, Rainbow Multi-Media; it was all circling the drain.

Gratefully I don't remember the details, only a heavy atmosphere in the Hill Street houses, an atmosphere of guilt (what could I have done better?) and resentment of others' failures (so and so could have worked harder).

Sinclair tells me, though I don't remember it, that we had a big Party meeting in late '74 where it was decided that Sinclair and Leni and the kids, The Prez, Fenton, and others would move THE SUN to Detroit and carry on the fight. The option was left open: I could re-commit to the struggle and move to Detroit, or go my own way. I chose the later and didn't look back. That for me was the end of the Rainbow People's Party.

The history of the Detroit Artists Workshop, Trans-Love Energies, The White Panther Party, and the Rainbow People's Party is yet to be written. This account should not be seen as even a feeble scratching of the surface in an attempt to tell those stories.

My love, respect and gratitude go out to those who supported me and the various organizations I was in over the years. Highest honors are due those young people, kids really, who gave the full measure of their dedication and devotion to the effort of bringing down the government and giving birth to a new political and cultural order.

DS in his fine poem sums up my feelings precisely:

A MEMO FROM THE CHIEF OF STAFF
(for former members of the Rainbow People's Party)

There was the necessary essence of contrary,
to play what fool was simply

otherwise, as against the fool roles
long writ out for us
in advance.

There was nothing to be gained
and much to be risked
in the effort.

There was a flower of folly there,
fit perhaps for laughter;
but it was fearful what it took to fertilize;
and still less funny, what it took
to pluck it.

There is grace from it, to have seen one's ego
stark naked in the harsh light
of its demands,

stretched out like an unshed snakeskin
on the beautiful table,
with such a flower as the centerpiece.

There went my outsized heart, for one, utterly
spent:

not so important, indeed; but still,
not a seemly subject for any second
guesses
but our own.

--DS, Fall 1980--Spring 1988

Chapter Twenty-one

"WHAT'S A PO' BOY TO DO, 'CEPT JOIN A ROCK ROLL BAND?"--1975

--Rolling Stones

I moved out of 1520 Hill Street so as to avoid any discomfort or unpleasantness during the Party's collapse and the break-up of my marriage.

Nadine and I rented a small house on Jewett, off Packard, and I got a job with The Good Time Film Co-op, a student organization at the University that booked, promoted, and presented films at multiple venues on campus.

As a student organization they had free office space in the Michigan Union, a grand old building in the center of campus. Because the printing and posting of fliers is essential to promoting films, or anything else on campus, the film co-op started its own print company called The Good Time Print Co-op, and set it up in their fourth floor offices.

My new job was to run the printing operation and expand the business by soliciting the multitude of political groups that were forever printing posters, leaflets, flyers, and the like. I expanded the business ten-fold. I hired two poster artists, one full-time and one part-time, bought new stock and equipment, and organized a crew of "professional" street people and "townies" to post flyers around campus, town, and even at the campus of Eastern Michigan University in Ypsilanti, some eight miles to the east.

Our printing fees were thirty percent less than those of our competition. Of course, we paid no taxes, rent, utilities, or insurance, and we bought most of our stock through University Catalogues, paying below wholesale prices. It was not my business acumen that made the business grow, but, simply our ability to take advantage of loopholes and opportunities afforded student organizations at the University. Neither The Good Time Film Co-op nor the Good Time Print Co-op were even "co-ops," strictly speaking. Students signed the appropriate papers and assumed the position of officers, but there were never any meetings and rarely did we even see the student officers. I was left to my own conspiracies.

Despite the fact that The Good Time Film Co-op and its print shop subsidiary were making money hand over fist, the film co-op was not paying the film distributors. I began receiving angry registered letters and phone calls from irate attorneys and collection agencies in California demanding payment. Legal action was threatened, as was confiscation of the cooperative's property and the placement of liens against the University. "Criminal charges could be sought," I was told in a phone call.

I met with the co-op officers and informed them that creditors were at the door like mad dogs. The principle officers were already well aware of the situation. They were into the film distributors to the tune of forty thousand dollars. They'd run this scam for nearly three years and were about to skip town. They were undecided as to whether they were going to join the liberation struggle in Eritrea or the guerillas in El Salvador; either way, they were taking the money with them.

They said I could have the print co-op business if I could isolate it from The Good Time Film Co-op and advised me to do the necessary paperwork to protect the print shop equipment from confiscation. I found new student officers and changed the name of the offices with the University to simply "The Print Co-op," and we survived the whirlpool when the film co-op went under.

It was during this time, with Nadine prompting me, I made contact with my family in Kalamazoo. The family had moved in 1965, when I was working for the union. Accompanied by Nadine, I spent Christmas, Mother's Day, and other holidays with my family for the first time in ten years.

But it was also about this time that my drinking problem took a turn for the worse. Binges came more often, as did "blackouts," that peculiar phenomenon common to alcoholics. During blackouts I functioned, sometimes for twelve hours or more, in a trance. I could have been driving, or having multiple conversations while doing errands around town, or talking to a whole group of people at a party; I might even have been the life of the party. But upon "waking" I'd have no memory of those hours. I've known men who say they have functioned for days and weeks on end in a blackout.

Blackouts and me go way back. Like the time, back in 1962, when I came to while sitting on a couch in a New York City apartment, surrounded by people having a party. I didn't know how I got there or even who the people were. Or the time in 1963, when I woke up in my apartment in Pennsylvania, my clothes covered in blood not my own. I had no idea whose blood it was or how it got there. I had bruises on my neck too, with no clue as to their origin.

Despite the drinking, I was still able to work. In early 1976 The Burger called me to see if I wanted a job. He had been working for the rock group KISS as a truck driver, but a new tour was being organized and he was to become a soundman. I could have a job driving semis for KISS if I wanted it. I told the student officers at The Print Co-op that I was moving on. They had no interest in keeping the print shop running so I put the business, equipment, stock, offices and name up for sale. Some anarchist gave me two thousand dollars and I walked away.

The trucking company with the KISS contract was called SHOWMOTION. It was owned by JB, the former president of a Detroit gangster motorcycle club, and Car-One, a syndicate out of Chicago. Car-One had stage lighting systems on tour not only with KISS, but also with the likes of Pink Floyd and Foreigner.

The KISS tour lasted nine months. I kept renting the house in Ann Arbor with Nadine, who was upset that I'd gone on the road. So regularly, whenever we had a few days off in a nice town, I would fly her out to visit me in Seattle, New York, New Orleans, Philly, Washington, DC, and other cities. This helped diminish her resentment. When the KISS tour was over I returned to Nadine full time and got part-time work as a "will call" union stagehand at University events.

In 1977, Bob Seger and the Silver Bullet Band, who had opened for KISS during the 1976 tour, went on tour headlining their own show with the release of Stranger in Town. Since SHOWMOTION also had a contract for trucks and drivers with Seger; I went with his tour as a driver of one of three semis.

The Seger tour was a great success. He broke attendance records in Michigan, up and down the east coast, and across the south. I kept my drinking in check enough to put up a professional façade.

However once back in Treetown I was not so successful; my drinking was beyond the pale. Nadine fired me--I'd pissed the bed once too often.

I moved to Joliet, Illinois, and in with Juliet, a girlfriend I kept on the side during the latter part of my relationship with Nadine. I then went out on a second Seger tour, when the Hollywood Nights album came out in the winter of '78.

During that tour a Boston snowplow ripped the bumper off of my parked rig. Because Car-One had issued a new company policy, all drivers were now responsible for the first $1,000 insurance deductible for damage done to the rented trucks.

"Bullshit!" I said. "If I'm responsible for the deductible, then you have to pay me more money." At that time I was making $550 a week, plus $35 per diem (all green money, no taxes), most of which went up my nose in the form of cocaine.

Hotels were paid for.

I refused to pay the deductible, so Car-One fired me on the spot and flew another driver out to take my rig. I told Seger I'd been fired and would be going home. He suggested I hire on to his crew as bodyguard/security director. I was responsible for Seger's and the band's personal protection while at concerts. I'd interact with hotel security, coordinate limousines, bellhops, and make sure luggage was secure and delivered to the proper rooms or flights. I would work with police or security at the venue, secure the dressing rooms, and tag along on most public outings as a bodyguard. I jumped at the chance, even though it meant my pay was cut in half. Now I was riding on jets and limos, going to good restaurants and cool clubs, and hanging with Seger and the band from time to time.

One of the job's perks was the ready availability of alcohol and cocaine. As security director I more or less controlled access to Seger and the band while at the show. It seemed that at every gig local radio personalities, junior record executives, and journalists would ply me with grams of cocaine in an effort to gain access to Seger or to get backstage passes. In addition, each venue was supplied with several cases of beer and assorted hard liquor and wine. By show time I had stuffed my nose with coke many times and sucked down five or six beers. When the show was over, and Seger was safely back in his hotel room, I'd pick up where I left off.

Occasionally Seger and the Silver Bullets would fly home between gigs. I would stay on the road with the crew, whoring around, doing cocaine and drinking. But it would be wrong to give the impression that all roadies had a character or inclination similar to mine. Some occasionally overindulged in various vices during a tour, but not consistently the way I did. By and large they were professionals who took great pride in their work. I was an example of self-will run riot.

For company in this life in the fast lane, I flew Juliet of Joliet to Las Vegas, LA, San Francisco, Boston, Miami, Detroit and other cities on the tour. Often however, I spent time with the local ladies. Though, I must say I spent more time alone than rolling in some sweet girl's arms. The road is a lonesome life. The boisterous, over-the-top lifestyle was usually only a mask to hide the loneliness and fill the void.

My near constant quest for women, driven by lust, fueled by cocaine, and made clumsy by alcohol, was a measure of my isolation. I didn't really have relationships with women. I had sex with women, and women had sex with me because I had cocaine. Sex became a measure of my worth; I felt like I was somebody, I felt validated, only when I had seduced a girl. Naturally, the dance of seduction and sex became a game rather than an expression of love. As I explored the very frontiers of sexual experimentation, tender, loving sex became alien to me, which unavoidably led to problems later in my life.

* * *

When I was on duty with Seger I carried a leather wrapped blackjack, sometimes called a sap, which was about 18 inches long with two ounces of led sewn into the end, about the size and shape of a horse cock run over and flattened on the highway.

Usually I kept the weapon in one of the road cases. At the afternoon sound-check I'd retrieve the sap and carry it while on duty. I would stuff it down my Levi's in the small of my back. I used it once to smash the hands of a gang of bikers in Tempe, Arizona, when they tried to storm Seger's dressing room. Each time they grabbed the edge of the door to pull it open, I'd rap their fingers a sharp blow. I kept them at bay long enough for the rent-a-cops to clear the hallway. Another time I smashed a cat in the Adams apple with it when he grabbed my hair and wouldn't let go as I escorted Seger and the band to limos after a gig in Buffalo.

One night in Boston I returned to the hotel with Seger, the sap stashed in the small of my back. With Seger safely tucked in for the night I took some Quaaludes and went to the rooftop bar. Later, in the lobby, I tipped over the cigarette machine because it ate my money. This led to an argument with the hotel manager, who kept hassling me, his face inches from mine. When he grabbed my arm and spun me around I threatened him with the blackjack. The clerk called the cops. I made a dash for the elevator but was arrested while waiting for the door to close. On the way to lock-up one of the Boston cops asked me if I was the infamous Pun Plamondon, the White Panther. I told him

"No, I'm Larry, Pun's my older brother." "Where is he now?" the cop wanted to know. "He works on a dude ranch in Colorado," I said.

Gordy, the road manager, got me a lawyer. It cost me $2,000, I got out of jail in the morning and all the charges were dropped. Nevertheless, Seger let me know this was unacceptable. I continued with the tour but walked as if on eggshells scattered on thin ice.

A short time after the Boston gig we were playing the Maryweather Post Pavilion, an open air, park-like venue outside Washington, DC. Jimmy Carter was president at the time.

As usual I arrived early to check the dressing rooms to make sure the deli-trays, fruit bowls, liquor, and beer were present as per the contract rider. I also checked with the security team at the facility, since they did hundreds of shows a year in the same venue and knew what they were doing; I only had to review their set-up. I got the will-call list to the ticket window, handed out backstage passes to roadies' girlfriends, local celebrities, and various special guests, and generally "hung-out backstage."

At the appropriate time I went to the backstage entrance, to meet Seger and the band (count them, 9 total) as they exited the five limos along with wives and girlfriends, the accountant and the tour manager. I escorted them to the dressing rooms, made sure they had everything they needed, and returned to the stage door to drink a beer and smoke a cigarette.

Just then five unmarked police cars pulled into the backstage parking area. Each with small hubcaps and little wire antennas poking from the roof. The cops were packed four to a car. Some were dressed as bikers wearing Levi jackets with the sleeves crudely cut off. Others were dressed as preppy college students, with pastel sweaters tied loosely around their necks. Some looked like suburban hippies with leather headbands. Still others were dressed in the style of Sears. One guy looked like my old high school football coach, with a green nylon windbreaker zipped up tight, khakis, and a baseball cap. All wore earpieces. Many dissolved into the gathering crowd, others filtered to the backstage area.

Christ, we're being raided! I thought as I ran to warn The Burger. "We're being raided," I whispered excitedly into

Burger's ear as he sat at a console conducting a sound check. He put on his headphones and spoke into the mouthpiece. Immediately the sound crew and lighting crew knew the cops were in the joint, and coke and weed was hidden in special compartments built into road cases.

The Burger turned back to me. "Stop them," he said.

I found the promoter backstage and got right after him. "What is the meaning of this?" I demanded. "What are all these narcs doin' here? We're not a druggie band; we don't promote drugs and are not noted for using them. We're a professional operation. These pigs got to go. This is going to piss off my band. It will upset our guests--Seger might even cancel the show--get these guys out of here! At least out from backstage," I insisted.

The promoter escorted me to the fella who looked like my old football coach. "I'd like you to meet Secret Service Agent Truck," he said, "Dump Truck." We shook hands. Agent Truck showed me his credentials; I gave him my business card saying I was security director for this outfit.

He told me that Chip Carter, the president's son, was attending the concert and what I saw was his security detail. He informed me they were not present to make arrests, only to insure Chip's safety. "Well goddamn," I said, "that's pretty cool."

"Would you like to meet Chip?" Agent Truck asked. "Damn straight," I answered.

Chip was over by the grand piano, which was getting a last minute tuning. (A piano tuned in the warm afternoon will be out of tune in the cool of the evening.) I was introduced, and we chatted. I asked if he wanted to meet Seger and the band? "Oh yes!" he said, and was very excited, like any fan about to meet an idol.

I checked with Seger in the dressing room to make sure it was cool, then brought Chip and Dump back and introduced them around to the guys and the female back-up singers. I alerted The Burger, and he and several other responsible roadies stopped in for introductions, drinks, and a round of photographs. Not liking to be photographed, I ducked out.

The agent stationed outside the dressing room door pulled me aside and said, "We are here to protect Chip's body from any outside threat. If he wants to do drugs, we won't stop him or arrest anyone, that's not what we're here for." "Yeah, Riigghhtt," I laughed. "Are you hitting on me for drugs?" I jokingly asked him.

A short time later Chip and Dump left the dressing room and took up their positions stage left, behind the curtains, where they watched the whole show from the wings.

After the show, Chip went back to see Seger again, attended by another agent Truck had assigned to Chip. The Agent Truck shook my hand, "Nice working with you; everyone was very cooperative. This sure beats working for "the old man." I told him I appreciated the compliment and said that generally, if we are treated in a professional manner, with a certain level of respect, we respond in kind.

"By the way," he said, "there used to be a guy named Plamondon that was from Ann Arbor. Are you the same?"

"No," I answered. "I'm Larry as it says on my card. Pun is my younger brother. He's managing an avocado farm in Florida."

"Let's trade T-shirts," Truck suggested. I went to a road case, grabbed a handful and followed Dump to his car. From the trunk he took a red, white, and blue jersey with "DEA" (Drug Enforcement Agency) silk-screened on the back in eight-inch letters and a logo depicting Inter-Agency cooperation on the front, and gave it to me; I still have it.

I finished the tour with Seger, then picked-up some small tours, driving trucks for Dire Straits, Alice Cooper, Styx and others. However, word on the grapevine was that "Pun can't keep it together. His drinking is getting out of hand; he's an accident waiting to happen and 'wwd' [weird when drunk]." I knew this was true. When the third Seger tour went out, I was not asked back.

*   *   *

I picked-up some stagehand work at the University and hustled jobs as a carpenter, under the influence of alcohol most of the time.

In 1979 I made a trip to Traverse City to visit my quadriplegic cousin Bill. In the course of the visit I ran into my first girlfriend and love, Wiseacre. While visiting and catching-up, I told her that I had found out about my biological mother and father a few years earlier when I was being sentenced on the thirty-pound reefer deal. I mentioned my conception in the TC state hospital.

She told me Roger's younger brother was the current director of the state hospital. Roger had been a childhood playmate, one of the old neighborhood gang of chums. Like most younger brothers, we ignored Roger's and kept him out of our activities, so I had no longstanding relationship with him. Now he was a PhD and director and of the Regional Psychiatric Hospital.

I called Roger's brother and told him I was interested in any files or records the hospital might have regarding my biological parents. A few days later he called to say that if I came by his office I could look at the files. I met with him, and after pleasantries were exchanged he gave me a six-inch thick file on my father and a somewhat smaller one on my mother. He said I could take the files home but had to promise to return them since he was breaking numerous laws and regulations by giving them to me and could be fired if found out.

The files contained daily ward notes on faded and brittle paper, monthly doctor and social worker reports, as well as physical and mental assessments of both my parents. I found the paper where my dad acknowledged paternity and another when the court terminated parental rights. I found a receipt for twenty dollars my dad had put into an account set up for me. I believe it was his attempt at support.

I found two photos of my dad; one was a front and profile view taken at Jackson Prison; wearing the prison number 48892-J across his chest, he looked like John the Pillager. In those days, if a person was arrested for public drunkenness three or more times in one year, they were sent to prison for a year. The other photo was another front and profile view taken much later than the first by the state hospital. Like my own, his hair was wavy, graying, and coarse. His dark eyebrows and eyes were identical to mine, though my eyes don't yet carry the look of a man defeated--the sad and tired eyes of the man in the picture.

I found notes of telephone conversations between the hospital social worker and members of my dad's family. Apparently the hospital had been trying to place me with one of them. One aunt was ill and could barely maintain her existing family. Another aunt was not at all interested in taking me under any circumstances. She was quoted as saying, "No good will come of this union." I don't recall any mention of my uncles. I found my father's death certificate stating that he had died at the hospital in 1954 and was buried in Newaygo.

My memory of my mother's file is very sketchy. There was no photo, and just medical reports using a lot of big words. They identified her as five-foot two and 110 pounds. The files mentioned a baby carried to term. There was mention in the files of my mother's syphilitic condition and her great shame. I realize now that I have not put effort into tracing my mother's life and family. I tried once, but since the records are all in Canada I easily put it off.

Overall, the files did nothing to build my self-esteem. The general picture of my father was of a drunk whom the family had taken in time after time over the years, until they were pretty much at the end of their rope. Very few good things were written in the record about my father.

I picture my mother as a pretty woman, yet sad and full of shame.

Chapter Twenty-two

BLACKOUTS AND LIGHT BULBS--1981

An alcoholic like me must keep on the move. On first meeting, people liked me. But as they got to know me better, as they saw me in various stages of drunkenness, and as they witnessed more and more outrageous behavior, they liked me less. Inevitably I would pull some dastardly deed that would expose me as a drunken lout and I'd have to leave the area in response to the weight of pure embarrassment--or worse.

A friend of mine, who was in the business of importing and distributing weed, was building a fine home in the Irish Hills of Michigan, about an hour's drive from Ann Arbor. His business required that he travel a great deal. Until the house was finished, his wife and young son lived in Ann Arbor.

Electricity and gas utilities had already been hooked up, the master bedroom and several other rooms on the second floor were completely finished and painted, and carpeting had been laid. Since the house had no furniture yet, My Friend kept a cot in the master bedroom and would stay over while working on the house in his spare time. He suggested I place a pallet on the floor in one of the finished rooms and stay there while working on the house.

This was a good plan. I had no real place to stay since Nadine had thrown me out and Juliet of Joliet, who was getting mighty tired of my antics, had made it clear that she'd be pleased when I finally left for good. I'd also worn out my welcome with Ann Arbor friends who were tired of me crashing on their couches, eating their groceries, and causing drunken scenes from time to time.

It was a pleasant fall; the weather was mild for late September. I spent my day spackling and sanding drywall or installing wood casing to windows and doors, easy but detailed work. I worked at a leisurely pace, smoking "the product," as My Friend called his weed. In the afternoon I drank beer and ate venison steaks for dinner. I worked enough to make slow progress over several months.

Occasionally, when My Friend was out of town, My Friend's Wife would stop in to visit and check on progress. She was a petite and vigorous twenty-five-year old who had given birth to My Friend's son two years earlier. Once she came by with a bottle of wine and a gram of cocaine. We lolled away the afternoon tooting the 'cain, smoking the product, drinking wine, and talking.

Since the birth of their son, she told me, her husband no longer thought she was attractive: "He says my boobs sag and my pussy is stretched-out. Having sex with me was like screwing a feed sack, he said. He never does me anymore...He does those teenyboppers though." She went on to tell me she was bisexual and would sometimes spend nights with her lesbian friends on campus. We spent the night on the new blue carpet in one of the upstairs bedrooms.

Other times she stopped by with beer and toots, and maybe had time for a "quickie" while her son slept in the car. On a few occasions, tooted up on cocaine, awash in alcohol, and stoned on product, we played sex games, like "tie me up and make me," or "wear this, I'll take your picture," or "Talk dirty to me," mildly kinky stuff, stimulating and quite harmless.

This went on for several weeks. I knew from past experience that doing a guy's wife is one thing; doing a guy's wife in the guy's home is another--risky, though it added a level of animal excitement, like the randy ram breeding in a rival's harem. Nevertheless, I took a room in a private motel only three miles from the house. My Friend's Wife spent a few nights with me when she could get the grandmother to take her son.

One weekend My Friend, just back from an extended trip to Colombia, informed me that his friends, the Yoopers, who were from Watersmeet in the far reaches of the Upper Peninsula, were coming for a visit. We could expect to do some heavy partying.

When the Yoopers arrived about ten in the morning, we started snorting toots and drinking beer. After a while, we made a run to the country deli and picked up some steaks, a pint of whiskey each, and several cases of beer. We drank and snorted coke and toked joints and played ping-pong in the unpainted living room throughout the afternoon. We forgot about the steaks, but it didn't matter because we took out the pistols and shot the empty pints and beer cans. I remember being staggeringly drunk.

After that I have only brief glimpses of memory, like frames from a black and white film randomly edited, with large portions of blank, black screen.

...It was dark outside. I don't know if thirty minutes or three hours had passed since my last clear memory. I "came to" standing in the harsh light of the laundry room, stupefied as My Friend hit me over the head again and again with a metal-handled dust mop, and My Friend's Wife screamed, "Get Out! Get Out! Get Out!"

...Then I was standing in darkness, outside on the gravel driveway. The Yoopers stood there too, mouths agape as My Friend systematically smashed all the windows out of my 1970 Audi with a baseball bat.

Brief states of consciousness came in flashes as if illuminated by a mental strobe light; its bright illuminations were as startling as the blackness between the images were frightening.

At one point I remember lurching forward, hugging My Friend and crying, "Why are you doing this? Why are you doing this? I love you, man!"

He pushed me away screaming, "Get out of here, get off my property!"

I pleaded with arms outstretched: "Why are you doing this? You are my friend, I love you, man."

"YOU TRIED TO RAPE MY WIFE YOU SON-OF-A-BITCH! GET OUT OF HERE BEFORE I KILL YA!"

"Man, I didn't do that! I wouldn't do that, I love you, man, you and your wife are my friends, I wouldn't do that!" I repeated over and over.

"You assaulted my wife! Get off my property--I'm getting my pistol!" he raged as he threw the bat at me and stalked inside; the Yoopers followed.

I came to a bit. Like a horror movie, when a flash of lightening reveals the monster for the first time, I saw in a glimpse of memory my leather belt wrapped around the neck of My Friend's Wife as I tried to force her to give me a blowjob, reminiscent of the sex games we had sometimes played. I quaked and wanted to vomit. I shook my head to rid myself of the nightmarish vision.

It could not be true, I thought. *I would not do such a thing, not to friends. Impossible!* Yet the scantest memory remained to tell me it was true, a memory that makes me shudder in shame even today.

I have but a few regrets in my life; that night is one. If I could take it back, if I could erase the terrible memory and trauma of it from the minds of My Friend and My Friend's Wife, I would do it in a heartbeat. I would go anywhere, meet any reasonable requirement, if I could help heal the pain and damage I inflicted that October evening.

* * *

I loaded my fear and guilt and remorse and disbelief into my windowless Audi and limped, broken and hung over, to the west side of the state, driving at night to avoid notice by the police. My brother let me stay in his basement while I licked my wounds and scraped some money together to get the Audi fixed.

As soon as the hangover passed I started drinking again. I now know that it is natural for alcoholics to drink to deaden the pain and dull the memory of past atrocities, and that it is essential for the alcoholic to keep drinking in order to avoid coming face to face with the degradation and destruction our actions have caused.

I spent my time drinking beer and watching daytime television behind shaded windows. Shortly I got work with some illegal Mexicans finishing concrete on a federal job. I made pretty good money for a couple of weeks and got the glass replaced in the Audi.

My brother told me of a co-operatively-owned conference and recreation center and summer camp for kids located in the area. They were looking to hire qualified staff. The camp is located in the rural forests of southwest Michigan and has an impressive history with origins in the "folk school" and early labor and socialists movements. In fact, the White Panther Party held its one and only National Congress there in 1970 while I was underground. I hired on as a maintenance man--firewood cutter--at the camp/conference center. A practicing alcoholic like me (though I didn't call myself that at the time) tries to maintain an image, a front, as if we are in control and on top of the action. Though our spiritual, moral, physical and mental health is in turmoil, we project confidence, as if everything is okay. I'd been acting like someone else all my life--this was easy.

At thirty-four, I was the oldest on a staff of eleven. With my worldly, devil-may-care, take-charge attitude, my "let's party" enthusiasm, and my self-inflated image as an organizer, I soon became a big man on campus, ingratiating myself with the others.

Still trembling and guilt ridden from my last blackout and attack on My friend's Wife, I kept my drinking in check, drinking heavily at night in the quiet of my cabin.

One of the first people I felt drawn to at the camp was Carly, a seventeen-year old who was mature in body, mind and spirit beyond her meager years. She was at camp because she couldn't live at home for one reason or another and had been kicked out of public and private schools. She had run away from home and hitch-hiked to the west coast and back, all before age seventeen. Designated as "student/staff," she worked like the rest of us (the camp provided fall and winter recreational and conference programming, so there was lots to do), but was simultaneously a student being tutored by the camp directors in preparation for her GED test.

Carly was a free spirit who liked to smoke dope, drink beer, and listen to music. I was experienced in all three areas, and we soon became allies, then lovers. Over time we grew quite fond of each other. That a seventeen-year-old fox would find me, a man twice her age, attractive and sexual made me feel virile. I made it through the winter working and hanging with Carly while keeping my drinking within bounds, more or less.

When spring came we began to prepare the facility for summer camp. As was customary in this co-op, members pitched in during work bees to help maintain the place. It was at the spring work bee that I met Patricia. Pat was petite and lean with the tanned muscles of a canoeist or backpacker. Her boyish haircut made her seem sleek and quick. Though not deaf, she is fluent in American Sign Language and had taught staff and children the rudiments of signing at the previous summer camp. She was a poet and glowed with energy--and--she was my age.

On this work bee weekend, Patricia taught the whole dining hall a few signs to translate the Eagle's song "Peaceful, Easy Feeling," and everybody sang along while signing as she and a handful of her former students led the group accompanied by guitar.

It brought tears to my eyes to hear the little voices, singing so innocently and with such conviction along with their parents. The whole dining room was swaying in unison and signing, giving image and motion to the words, "I've got a peaceful easy feeling." It became more than I could bear. I wept, and fell in love with Patricia. I quickly left the dining room hiding my tears.

My emotions were boiling. Rattled to my core, I sat on a bench outside where I could still hear the singing, the children's voices and the more timid ones of the adults, creating a harmony led by children. In anguish, I blurted great heaving sobs.

All that I longed for my entire life was in that dining hall. Peace, acceptance, tolerance, harmony, and tranquility. I had never known such feelings. It was just yards away, yet I could not participate, could not be part of it; I crumbled in the presence of such emotions. It was heart-wrenching. I wanted to experience those feelings, to live in those emotions. Why couldn't I? My life was completely at odds with what I so desired, it was the opposite, in fact. I was in turmoil and filled with guilt, remorse, shame, anger, and fear. I was nearly dead inside.

This didn't just happen to me overnight. I'd been dragging around this sort of baggage since I was fourteen. How many times had I promised myself I wouldn't drink to the point of blacking out? How many times had I sincerely promised that to a loved one or a friend or boss? Countless.

I would tick off my many blackouts, remembering what I could of past mental voids. Once, when I was sixteen I woke up in my '49 Ford which was parked on a residential street in TC with its headlight broken, antenna snapped off, and the door handle ripped clean off. I had no memory of how I got there or what had happened to my ride. I promised myself then that I wouldn't drink so much.

Another time, I remember waking up as a strange woman in hair curlers, clutching a housecoat at the neck, a young girl by her side, was saying, "shshsh, he's waking-up," followed immediately by a man's voice hollering, "I'll kill the bastard!" Three steps and I'd hit the door, made it to my Ford, and laid rubber for half a block as a man who looked like Homer Simpson stood in his jockey shorts pointing his shotgun after me. Apparently, although I have no memory of it, I had gone to visit my high school sweetheart in the wee hours of the morning. She lived in tract housing, a new phenomena in Traverse City in the fifties. All the houses were identical except for the paint jobs. Clearly I had gone into the wrong house and passed out on the wrong couch. I promised myself again, I wouldn't drink so much.

I had promised Wiseacker, The Prez, Nadine, Juliette of Joliet, to say nothing of my high school sweetheart and my present partner, Patricia; countless promises.

Like luck, when it came to promises, I used more than my share.

* * *

I set about to win Patricia's attention and then her affection, keeping my drinking heavy rather than excessive, if there can be a distinction.

My first instinct was to establish a relationship with Patricia and keep Carly on the side. Patricia lived in Chicago where she had worked for seventeen years counseling heroin addicts who were trying to kick the habit. Carly lived at camp; this just might work. But it became immediately clear that Patricia would brook no bullshit of that nature, nor would Carly for that matter.

Patricia was clearly special and deserved a level of respect I had not shown other women. I knew I would have to manage my drinking or lose whatever chance I had with her. And I knew I would have to tell Carly I would not be seeing her anymore, which I did. It was the first time I'd been this honest and straightforward in many years. Usually I just quit seeing the woman, without explanation. I assumed, since neither of us had made a commitment to the other, that this would be an easy break-up with a minimum of hassle.

Carly informed me she was pregnant.

I avoided the situation altogether. Carly took her GED and passed, of course. Two weeks later her mother informed me that Carly would be having an abortion in Chicago without further delay.

I drove Carly to the train station in Kalamazoo, making lighthearted and jovial comments on the way. She answered in monosyllables, obviously depressed. At the train station I hugged her, wished her luck, said, "It's been real," and left thinking I had gotten out of that without too much hassle.

This is another situation I wish I could reverse. My treatment of Carly at this difficult time was incredibly cruel and insensitive. My selfishness was inexcusable. I saw Carly some fifteen years after the abortion and did my best at making amends. I told her I was a very sick man in those days, I was better now and tremendously sorry for the pain and suffering I'd caused.

She hauled off and hugged me. With tears in her eyes she said, "I've been waiting fifteen years to hear something like that from you. Thank you."

"By the way," she said, "I'm a friend of Bill's," which is a code phrase used to indicate that the speaker is a member of a certain 12-step program for alcoholics who wish to remain anonymous.

"I am too!" I blurted, and we hugged again.

Today, Carly, who has been sober many years, is a professional editor and graduate student at a prestigious midwestern university. Everyone who knows her is proud of and impressed by her.

* * *

When Patricia heard about the abortion, she was rather disappointed. Had she been informed, she would have suggested Carly have the baby and she, Patricia, raise it. Nearing forty she knew that her biological moon was ticking, and the prospect of my getting sober in time to be effective was looking mighty slim.

I often wonder what the baby would have looked like, Carly being a beautiful dark-skinned girl with Black and Native blood and black curly hair. What a spirit we might have given form to.

Patricia took the job as Summer Camp Director and I stayed on as Work Projects Coordinator, a position that required me to organize and supervise campers and their counselors in various maintenance projects around camp, such as digging out a tree stump or building a sidewalk, painting a cabin, or work in the garden.

By then, Patricia and I were in love. She quit her job in Chicago and moved, furniture and all, into a camp cabin with me.

I approached the first session of summer camp thinking this would be a piece of cake. After all, I reasoned, I had organized White Panthers and Rainbow People with some measure of success. How hard could summer camp be? During the first two-week session I presented myself as joyful and easygoing, though every night I drank twelve beers and in the morning went to work only slightly bleary-eyed, grumpy and smelling of stale beer.

By the second session of camp I was generally too hung-over for breakfast, though I made morning announcements with a puffy face and a coarse voice wafting beer and sweat. Or I would go to my cabin and drink three or four beers in my cabin at lunchtime, go back to work in the afternoon, and return for another dozen beers at night. This was not everyday behavior, but it happened too frequently to go unnoticed.

This state of affairs did not suit Patricia at all. She made it clear, right from the start, in no uncertain terms, that she would not tolerate, under any conditions, my excessive drinking. There was no wiggle room, no accommodation, no giving in. Her demand was incessant, her tolerance zero. She stayed on me constantly, making my drinking life miserable. I'd stop for a couple of days, until the heat was off, the hangover gone, and I could keep down solid food. Then I'd do it again.

By the last session of camp I was hiding several quarts of beer around camp; in the shop, the well pit, the basement, I'd slobber down slugs of beer throughout the day and another dozen at night. I'd go to work late the next morning a mess, reeking the fumes of hell.

It's hard to accurately describe the downward spiral. A third of the time I spent drunk, a third hung-over, and a third dry, trying to reassure Pat, gain friends and neighbors' trust and clinging to the last threads of self-respect. When I was sober I could be charming, and in tune with the kids, being someone they liked and wanted to spend time with. Still, my last weeks at camp were a personal disaster, and I'm grateful that no children or anyone else was injured due to my functioning in an alcoholic haze. When camp was over, my drinking only increased. It felt like my soul was dying, and only alcohol kept me going.

I tried various methods of controlled drinking: I tried not drinking on an empty stomach, but the food only made my vomit chunky. I tried just drinking wine. I tried not drinking before noon, then six o'clock, then I tried drinking stuff I didn't even like, such as sloe gin, thinking I'd drink less; it just made me puke in colors. I tried drinking just on weekends, then just on Saturday, then just on Sunday. I tried stopping completely. None of it worked. Finally, Patricia's incessant demands and reasoning with me convinced me to seek treatment for alcoholism. The treatment center was ineffective. Another honest attempt resulting in failure.

*　　　　　*　　　　　*

It was winter then, and we'd moved away from camp and into a windy farmhouse heated with a sorry wood burner. Certainly this was the coldest winter of Patricia's discontent. Drunk, I had run the Audi into a ditch and ripped the muffler and tail pipe off, flattening two tires, and was arrested for drunk driving. I junked the car to pay the towing and impound fee.

Several months later I totaled Patricia's car when I missed a curve in a blackout and wrapped her Escort around a telephone pole. I was unhurt, not even a scratch--God's own drunk.

I desperately and sincerely wanted to quit drinking, and did, hundreds of times. I just couldn't stay quit. I'd stop for a week or two, then go on a bender, each one worse than the last.

These repeated failures and broken promises collected like old dented refrigerators, broken stoves and the rusting hulks of Pontiacs scattered around the yard, I took them with me wherever I went.

I was going regularly to meetings for alcoholics which seemed like the last hope. One evening I took Patricia's 18-speed bicycle with the intention of riding the seven miles to town to attend a meeting. On the way I changed my mind and visited a country roadhouse tavern.

Falling several times while trying to return home, I somehow bent the front wheel so it wouldn't turn, twisted the handle-bars out of whack, and broke off a pedal. I had not blacked out, but was just drunk, out of control. Unable to push the bike, I threw it in the ditch and crawled off into the woods to sleep. In the dark I raked leaves over myself in an attempt to stay warm. In the morning I found I had slept in a patch of poison ivy.

There was no sympathy from Patricia as the itching poison covered my body. At the next meeting of alcoholics, with my eyes swollen shut from the blisters, ears blocked, and body completely covered in pustules, I cried, blurted and blathered with great gobs of snot running from my grotesquely swollen nose.

"I'll never get it," I sobbed. "I'll never get sober and find the serenity you all have."

"I accept the first step of this program," I said. "'I am powerless over alcohol and my life has become unmanageable.'"

"But I can't relate to the second step," I told them. "'Came to believe that a power greater than myself could restore me to sanity.'"

"I don't believe in a higher power," I went on, "other than the coercive power of the State and the revolutionary power of the people. Neither of these 'powers' kept me from drinking."

I knew God wasn't going to help me. I didn't even like God. My friends in the alcoholics club advised me repeatedly, "You must find a spiritual basis for your life, God or a higher power or the wind or electricity--something that is greater than you which can remove the obsession to drink."

"God damnit! How the hell is the wind going to keep me sober?" I demanded.

I stayed sober two months once. Then I borrowed my buddy's pick-up--I told him I had a job and needed to move lumber--a lie. I got drunk, burned the starter out of his ride, and didn't come home for two days. Another refrigerator strewn in the yard of failures.

I had a job roofing a neighbor's house. He was gone and I found two bottles of Mogen David wine and drank both. I awoke the next morning to yet another failure rusting in the yard.

Nothing was working, I tried every conceivable cure. The program for alcoholics wasn't working, I just couldn't get it. Their focus on God or "a higher power" as they like to say, and their practice of ending each meeting with The Lord's Prayer seemed like out- and-out Christianity to me. I had an attitude, and didn't want to change it.

I was at the end of the line. I did not believe I would ever stop drinking and knew that if I kept on I would kill myself or some innocent person on the highway. Alcohol had kicked my ass. Suicide seemed a reasonable solution.

* * *

As a boy I had sometimes hung out with the sheriff's son, back in the days when the sheriff lived at the county jail. We'd do sleepovers and such. Once a deputy showed us a file containing black and white photos of all the suicides in the county over the past umpteen years. Most were of men with a shotgun blast to the head, typically having sucked the barrel as they pulled the trigger. Brains, blood, hair, and bone were everywhere in the photos: on the Frigidaire, on the dishes draining in the wire rack in the sink. Pieces of skull, like broken teacups, littered the countertops; brains, the viscosity of melting Jell-O, dripped from the ceiling and vertical surfaces.

It's notable the number of photos that showed a whiskey bottle or empty beer cans littering the table in front of a corpse with the top of its head blown away. Before placing the file back in the cabinet, the deputy pointed to a photo with the stumps of his first two fingers (lost in the war): "He couldn't face life with the bottle and he couldn't face death without the bottle."

This was great fun for us twelve-year-olds. We never tired of looking at "the pictures," as we came to refer to them. I suggested my friend take the file to school so we could show our friends. Sister Janet caught us passing the pictures during catechism class and Catholic shit hit the fan. I wasn't allowed to play with the sheriff's son anymore.

I decided not to blow my head off; the mess seemed unnecessarily traumatic.

Patricia and me were living on a lake with access to our neighbor's canoe. I decided to make one more attempt to stop drinking. Just one more. If I failed, I'd simply take the canoe out into the center of the lake, tangle my legs and arms in ropes and capsize, solving the problem and giving Patricia the plausible explanation that I'd "drowned in a boating accident."

At this point I was completely shattered. I had no moral, mental, or spiritual strength. I was beaten, there seemed to be no fight left in me. My soul was dead.

The most devastating revelation I had about my situation was that I had no defenses at all against drinking. If the idea came into my head, I did it. There was no internal struggle, no mental debate. There was a devil on one shoulder saying, "Go ahead, drink, you're a grown man. If you want to drink, you have the right." But there was no angel on the other shoulder saying, "Don't drink, you have so much to live for and so much to lose." This realization that I lacked any power to resist picking up the bottle was the final blow; my defeat, was now complete and absolute. *How could I win if I couldn't even fight?* I wondered. I felt completely hopeless.

However I continued going to meetings for alcoholics because they repeatedly said, "Keep coming back" and "Fake it 'til you make it." I was "white knuckling it," as they say in the group. Holding on for dear life, grinding it out inch by inch. The thought of a long life sober, in constant battle with my demons, looked less appealing than a short life drunk.

Around this time I got a call from a woman I knew from my days in Ann Arbor. Crystal had been a member of The Felch Street Gang. By the time the Weathermen were located in the Felch Street house, Crystal had had a baby and was left behind when the Weatherpeople went underground. Now, fifteen years later, she was a features writer for the Sunday Detroit News, and wanted to do a human-interest story titled: "Famous Radicals, 15 Years Later, Where Are They Now?" She wanted me to be the principle personality in the piece. Would I be interested? Would I come to Traverse City for an extensive interview?

I'd been sober for a couple of weeks and had started thinking about this book. I felt a good long interview might stimulate and inspire me to remain sober and concentrate on writing. Besides, a trip would allow Patricia and I to spend some time together away from home in neutral territory.

Crystal lived north of Traverse City, near Sutton's Bay and the reservation of the Grand Traverse Band of Ottawa. She lived in a well-kept house up a long drive off the state road with her husband and their daughter.

The interview itself was uneventful, though grueling. I told stories and anecdotes for eight hours straight, while this book took form in my head.

Late in the day, Crystal's husband arrived. He was a huge man, a full-blood Indian with a chest that seemed the size of a 55-gallon barrel. He seemed to fill the entire kitchen door as she introduced us.

"This is my husband, Louis Sawaquat," she said as we shook hands.

He looked to be more than sixty, but I was never good at

judging age, perhaps he was fifty. Either way he was considerably older than his wife who was somewhat younger than I. *The old fart is doing okay for himself,* I mused at the time.

He was dressed in a white tennis outfit: white tennis shoes, white socks to the knee, white shorts and a white shirt with a green alligator over the left breast; he was holding a tennis racket. His long, jet-black hair hung to his mid-back. Not the image that first comes to mind when thinking about traditional Indians.

He seemed huge to me. I don't know why. His head seemed the size of a five-gallon bucket. "Are you Indian?" I asked, always eager to point out the obvious. "Yes, I'm Anishnabee," he responded.

"What does that mean, Anishnabee?" I asked.

"First People or First Nations. We were never Indians, India is way on the other side of the world," he answered.

"What Tribe are you?" I asked.

"Odawa. In English it's Ottawa."

"I'm part Ottawa. I got some court papers years ago that said my dad was part Ottawa and my mom was part Ojibway."

"Humm," he said while rubbing his massive chin, which looked to be the size of kerosene lantern. "Which part?" he finally asked.

"Excuse me?"

"Which part?"

"I'm sorry, I don't understand."

"Which part of you is Ottawa? You said you were part Ottawa. Which part of you is Ottawa?"

"I don't know, a half or quarter I guess."

"Which half? Does it run horizontally, at your waist, or vertically, down the center of your chest?"

I laughed uneasily and said I never thought about it like that, while wondering why he seemed so large and why he was busting my chops.

After some lighter banter Louis excused himself, and Crystal and I finished up the interview. As we were taking coffee cups to the sink and clearing the table, Louis stuck his head in and said, "I'm going to smoke this pipe." In his massive hands he held a bundle the size of a small baby wrapped in an Indian blanket. "Do you want to join me?"

"Sure," I said, excited about participating in an authentic Indian pipe ceremony.

Sitting on the floor in the living room, still in his tennis outfit, Louis unwrapped his bundle and placed the objects in a special order. There was an eagle wing fan and the pipestone bowl and wooden stem. There was a copper container, seven small round stones, shells, herbs and feathers and even some salt, among other items. Louis still seemed larger than life as he put the pipe together, spun it around and pointed it to the four directions as he loaded it with "a-say-ma" as he called tobacco.

He spoke in English and Anishnabeemowin, the language of The First People. He asked the spirits to come and join us, the spirits of our ancestors, the spirits of animals and birds, and the spirits of turtles. On and on he spoke, spinning the pipe and pointing it to the four directions. Calling the spirits of grandmothers and grandfathers, the spirits of cousins, nieces and granduncles, and calling the spirit of bears and wind, long since gone from this world.

Once he pointed the pipe toward the window and said, "We invite all our tall brothers who stand around us and don't move, to join us in this circle."

I knew he was talking about the trees and a great chill and shudder came over me. I thought I was going to faint or lose balance and tip over. The hair on my arms and the back of my neck stood on end and I was seized by something,

Louis lit the pipe and passed it to me several times, sometimes chatting in between.

Soon the discussion got around to my alcoholism as we continued to smoke. I explained to Louis my inability to stop drinking. I repeated the advice given me by my friends in the alcoholic's association, that I must find a higher power, God or some such, and find a spiritual center to my life if I was ever to recover from alcoholism. I explained that I didn't believe in God or any of the religions with their narrow-minded, intolerant philosophies and exclusionary doctrines.

"A higher power?" he said quizzically, rubbing his gigantic chin again. "They must mean, The Great Mystery. Gitchi Manidoo. Great Mystery. Some say it means Great Spirit, but our people always say, 'Great Mystery.'"

There was no fanfare, no drum roll or clap of thunder.

Just a bright light somewhere near my heart, an opening, enlightenment.

"A mystery?" I stammered, incredulous and flabbergasted. "A fucking mystery? All this grief is about a fucking mystery?"

"It's always been a mystery," Louis answered, "Since the Anishnabee were first placed here, it's been a mystery."

He seemed normal size now: 6'2" or so, 220 pounds. I continued to shake my head, incredulous.

"You mean to tell me that to be spiritual I don't have to believe in God the Father, the Son and the Holy Ghost? I don't have to believe in Allah or Buddha or the virgin birth or the rapture or the fucking saints or any of it? All I got to do is believe in a mystery? That a mystery is a power greater than myself? Fuck! I can do that. I can do that! A fucking mystery," I muttered, shaking my head and grinning.

Chapter Twenty-three

THIS AIN'T NO HOLLYWOOD STORY--1982

If this were a Hollywood story I could wrap it up in a nice little package right now. The pipe ceremony and discussion with Louis sparked the beginnings of a spiritual awakening. The smallest ember smoldered as if I possessed a new spirit. The idea that my spirituality could be based on acceptance of a Great Mystery was new and unfamiliar to me.

Long ago I had questioned the validity of Catholicism/religion/spirituality. In the second grade, when Sister Casper was preparing us for our First Communion, she explained the concept of limbo, that place set aside by God as a repository for the souls of very young children who died having committed no wrong, but yet are stained with Original Sin, the sin of Adam and Eve. These pagan babies are not being punished in limbo, Sister Casper explained, but they can never see the Glory of God because they died before the stain of Original Sin was washed away by baptism.

Poor pagan babies. To me it seemed like they were being punished. This seemed blatantly wrong and an affront to my sense of fairness, even as a seven year old. After all, those souls did not ask to be born.

As a young boy, when I was arguing with my mother, being harangued and brow-beaten, she'd yell: "We took you in, gave you a home, clothes, food…and this is how you treat us?" I'd scream back, like a soul of limbo: "I didn't ask to be born--or adopted." Certainly the most hurtful thing an adoptive parent will ever hear.

Later, in the fifth grade, when I heard about the atrocities of the Inquisition, I had to wonder why a Catholic God would be so vicious and close-minded. My questioning gradually lead to an rejection of all things spiritual.

I was in high school when any faith I still had collapsed completely. The Pope and other big shots of the Church had just held a grand meeting in Rome--The Second Vatican Council--and decided to change Church doctrine and some of the rules--before this time, eating meat on Friday was a mortal sin. If a person died after eating meat on Friday without having confessed this sin and performed penance, he or she would have gone straight to hell for all eternity. But then, after the big meeting, the Church fathers changed the rule. Now you could eat meat on Friday and not burn in hell for ever and ever. I could barely believe it. Souls had been condemned to hell for eating meat on Friday for more than nineteen hundred years, or so I'd been told to believe. Now, all of a sudden, it was okay.

I came to believe it was all a marketing ploy by the Church. Like double "green stamps" at the grocery store, or a manufacturer's rebate. The new rule was designed to attract customers to the product. The Pope and his cronies wanted membership, which ultimately meant money and power. I turned away and never looked back.

Falling away from the Catholic God of my adoptive parents, I turned away from all Gods. I had read some Zen Buddhism, of course, and looked into Yoga and other forms of meditation, I'd read Black Elk Speaks, too, trying to find a form of spirituality that made sense to me. Nothing clicked. The Great Mystery, to which Louis had introduced me, was still too new. Fearing that it might just be bullshit, despite its ring of truth, I approached it tentatively, unsure and wary. It would make a better story, I know, to be able to say that I quit drinking immediately after my conversation with Louis, to say that my mind and heart instantaneously opened to the "Om" of the universe, and that "we lived happily ever after."

* * *

But this ain't no Hollywood story. In reality, my recovery has been slow and gradual. I had a few more drunken episodes, none worth recounting--just the usual pain, degradation, disgust, and remorse. I kept going to meetings of anonymous alcoholics still very unsure about the whole "higher power" business. But I was beginning to believe that it was the Great Mystery that made the geese fly south in the winter, the monarchs return to Mexico, sparrows to Capistrano and vultures to Hinckley. The more I said it, the more I came to believe it.

Before I left his house, I had asked Louis what I could do to find out more about my Ottawa heritage. He gave me the phone number of Juanita Dominic, a former President of the Northern Ottawa and Chippewa Association of Michigan. When the federal government violated treaties and abolished the Tribes of Michigan, The Northern Ottawa and Chippewa Association was the principle native organization carrying on the fight for treaty rights and reaffirmation of sovereignty for the First Nations of Michigan.

Once back home with Patricia I rooted out the pre-sentence report from my Cadillac pot case seven years earlier. I found the name of my father and mother and called Juanita Dominic. She had no information on my mother since my mom was from Canada. When I told her my father's family name she responded immediately. "Oh yes, Aiken, let me see..." I could hear her turning the heavy pages of what I later found out was a large ledger. "Yes, here it is; you come from the Maple River Band of Ottawa. At treaty time their villages were over at St. John's, north of Lansing. Your treaty-signing chief was *Wabagekgek* (literally, White Tail Hawk--in dialect, Marsh Hawk). Your grandfather's name was Thomas. You're Turtle Clan. You have three uncles; Bud, Larry, and Bird. You have two aunties; Gladys and Genevieve."

I didn't know what to say. One minute I was nobody, a person without a history, with no known origin--a no brand kid. The next I was somebody, a person with a family history, blood relatives and a place of beginning. I fumbled around looking for something relevant to say, I was stunned.

I asked Mrs. Dominic if I could come to Petoskey to see my father's name on the page. I don't know why, but it seemed important to actually see it for myself. I guess I felt that would make it real.

We visited Mrs. Dominic in Petoskey, Pat and I. Louis Aiken--the name was written in fine Indian agent longhand in a massive government census ledger bound in heavy canvas with a leather spine and corners. It was real--government certified; I was somebody.

Several weeks later Patricia contacted The Michigan Inter-Tribal Council where she talked to an Ottawa by the name of *Spirit Man*. Patricia passed on the information we'd gotten from Mrs. Dominic and was told that this was enough data to apply to the Bureau of Indian Affairs for an Indian card and to make an application to the Grand River Bands of Ottawa for Tribal membership.

The Grand River Bands of Ottawa is comprised of nineteen separate Bands, including the Maple River Band, that inhabit the greater Grand River watershed. Since the 1855 Treaty of Detroit, these nineteen Bands have been united into one political entity known as The Grand River Bands.

In the early part of August, 1982, I had my last drink. I didn't know it was my last at the time, but it worked out that way. I had asked the Great Mystery to remove my obsession to drink. Without fanfare or even my noticing, the obsession was lifted. When the thought of a drink entered my mind I now had the ability to reason with myself and think, I get in trouble when I drink, I better not, at least today.

Doing this one day at a time led to a week sober, then weeks, then months. I continued to go to the meetings of alcoholics. I began to listen rather than debate silently what others were saying. I quit thinking of witty retorts and focused on the truth of what was being said and how it applied to my life. I began to take the advice given by others who were struggling with the same problem. I made a point of speaking at every meeting about how I was doing, my ups and downs. As my time in sobriety grew so did my self-esteem and confidence, tempered with a small measure of humility.

One of the recommendations made by my group of alcoholic friends was to find a sponsor, a person I could confide in, someone to help guide me on the path of sobriety, someone with experience living life sober.

Jingle was the dude. He was older, twenty years my senior Jingle was a former Marine Corps welterweight boxing champ, biker, beatnik artist, and wino from the old days of canned heat and hobo jungles. He is a charismatic man, the salt of the earth, respected and loved by most.

For several months before asking him to be my sponsor I had listened to his remarkable story of wives, families, homes, and businesses lost; fame and fortune pissed on or punched in the nose at the most inappropriate time--and yet he was sober and happy. He told his story with humility, honesty, and humor. At one meeting he was going on and on about something, I don't remember what, and he said, "I ain't no goddamn Christian...," then continued his rant.

Jesus Christ, I'd never heard anyone say that before! *Well, I ain't no goddamn Christian either.* I thought, *I'm going to ask him to be my sponsor.*

After the meeting we went to his house, a standard, Midwest farmhouse, eighty some years old, tidy and in good repair. As he walked in the door his three-year-old daughter dashed across the floor, arms up-stretched, screeching "Daddy! Daddy!" I wanted that. Not the child necessarily, but I wanted someone, Patricia, to be glad I was home. Instead, she waited in fear and trepidation that I might come home drunk, or dead, or not at all. Even though I wasn't drinking at the time, she often tiptoed around me, careful not to upset me, trying to make sure I got my way lest I go into a "dry drunk" and bump around like the loud, unreasonable, arrogant male I frequently was. I wanted Patricia to wait for me with joyful expectation, like that child had for her father.

Jingle agreed to be my sponsor and has been ever since.

Having been sober for a year and firmly committed to attending meetings of alcoholics, Patricia and I decided to get married. I very much wanted to become more Ottawa, and part of that meant marrying Patricia in a traditional Ottawa wedding ceremony, which Louis agreed to perform.

Louis also suggested I go to some pow-wows, sweat lodges, and ghost-suppers. He encouraged me to make the traditional four day fast of the Ottawa.

*　　　　　　*　　　　　　*

The pow-wow grounds were out the Dam Road, past the Tribal campgrounds, near the old boarding school, down by the river, where the cottonwoods grow. Never having been to one before, I was ambivalent about going. One minute I was very excited, hoping to get closer to my culture. The next, cynically hesitant, fearing this all may be bullshit. I had only been identifying myself as an "Indian" for six months.

The hand-painted cardboard sign and arrow pointed the way to the pow-wow grounds. Hundreds of vehicles filled the dusty, corn-stubble field-turned parking lot. I felt disappointment at first. Most of the people looked white. Maybe this was nothing but a Chamber of Commerce, tourist extravaganza, Mickey Mouse pow-wow.

Once inside the pow-wow grounds I got the full picture. Hundreds of Indian camps were set up around the perimeter of the field; there were store-bought tents, four- walled military style tents, a handful of teepees, pup tents, a yurt, motor homes, pop-up campers, house trailers, and one overloaded Winnebago.

The dance arena was a large circle, maybe fifty yards in diameter, set up in the center of the field. Rope and 2 x 10 planks on plastic milk crates formed the circle. Around it, on the outside, were traders selling everything from beads and herbs to furs and deer antlers, and from jewelry, face painting, fine art, and sculpture to bumper stickers, cotton candy and fry bread.

In the very center of the dance arena was the drum arbor made of cedar poles, with the top covered in boughs. Ten or more large drums were set up, each had four to ten male singers. It was crowded with fifty or more singers milling around, visiting, joking, and eating fry bread, while one changed his young son's diaper.

One of the drums started. Thump, thump, thump, thump. The sound wasn't filling my ear and head so much as my chest, a rhythm giving my heart a new beat.

Then the singers began, their high-pitched wails creating a path, higher and higher straight to the heavens. *Wow!* I thought, *this is gonna be good.*

I stood on the west side of the arena, outside the dance circle with the other spectators. "Dancers! Line up at the eastern door! All rise please! Gentlemen remove your hats; Grand Entry is about to begin!" The announcer spoke through a crackling, tin-horned PA system. "Grand Entry reminds us of the time, after the Great Flood, when the Anishnabek and all the animals re-populated the earth," he continued.

The pace picked up. Dancers hurried to the east side of the arena. Grandmothers quickly finished tying feathers and bells on their grandchildren. Schoolgirls took time for one last coat of hair spray. Thump, thump, thump, thump.

By looking through the arbor, I could see across the arena to the eastern door, where the dancers enter the circle. Since most of the singers were standing I only had a partial view, brief glimpses as the dancers came into the arena...a wolf head bobbing...an up-stretched arm holding a staff of eagle feathers...a turtle shell painted in a special way...a fish and lightening bolt on a shield...a flurry of fringe...the blur of a big, beautiful, blue/black beaded belt.

The volume rose as the dancers kept beat with their feet. Drum, singers, bells, jingles, rattles, all in time, creating a center, a focal point, a common unity--community.

Thump, thump, thump, thump. The ancient wail of the singers was taking me higher and higher.

I must have looked away. When I looked back, suddenly the dancers were there, right in front of me, looking ten feet tall. Out from behind the arbor they came, a rank of dancers coming right at me, solid, like a wall, larger than life. Anishnabee warriors, dancing hard, feathers and fringe flying. Teenager girls dancing with shawls, like iridescent butterflies shimmering. Old men and women, dancing slowly, their steps stately if unsteady.

They seemed to be coming for me.

My chin dropped. The crowd had dissolved in white light: I could see only dancers. The dust from their feet made them appear as if floating. Thump, thump, thump, thump.

They kept coming, dancing to the beat. Men and women

in traditional dress, earth tone colors. Teenagers in purple and silver feathers and fringe. Children dressed in colors of the rainbow. Thump, thump, thump, thump.

Pressure built in my chest; it seemed I might explode. Thump, thump, thump, thump.

"OOHHAA!" A great involuntary moan-yell burst from my throat. In a flash I was shot through with emotion; first a sad arrow pierced my heart as all that I'd missed sparkled in front of me. "AHHHH!" From deep inside my voice exploded again, for just as quickly I felt the glow of a hot, sweet pride in knowing I belonged to something that was timeless yet present. I felt connected, for the first time in my life, to something that was bigger than I was--Something complete, whole. My past was behind me; my future was with these people.

Then, in less than a drumbeat, I was filled with anger toward those who took me from all this while I was just an infant. "ARRGGHHG!" I raged again, bent over now, hands on my knees; sobbing. *My life might have been different,* I speculated.

This was too much for me. My emotions were raw. In my thirty-five years I never experienced such emotion. I had to leave.

The spectators had all backed off a step or two during my outbursts. I was standing alone in the crowd. Grand Entry was still in progress but the dancers and music seemed spectral, ghost-like.

Just as I was leaving I noticed an overweight, middle-aged man dressed in yellow shorts and shirt, with a camera around his neck. He leaned over, cocked his head toward me and said under his breath, into his wife's ear, "He's a medicine man."

A medicine man! A medicine man! Did that son-of-a-bitch call me a medicine man?

The familiar voice of rage was building in my head. *I ought to kick his ass; I ought to stomp his nuts,* I fumed.

Then another, sarcastic, thought interjected: *just keep judging people, keep grinding that axe of anger, that'll keep you sober.*

I retreated to my pick-up. Something very painful, yet joyful and fulfilling, was happening to me. I felt like I was being born into Ottawa culture, seeing the world in a bright new light. I had found something I didn't know I was missing, something I could identify with and belong to, something definitely larger than myself.

*   *   *

Unfortunately the dawning of my spiritual enlightenment did not resolve other personal problems. Though I was not drinking, I had a lifetime of alcoholic thinking and habits to overcome.

For instance, I lied a lot. About big things, like how much money I'd run up on my credit card, or little things, like leaving the light on in the barn all night. I lied out of habit, without thinking, trying to avoid a harsh word, a judgmental scowl, or punishment, just as I had done as a child.

I was still impatient, arrogant, and controlling, too. And I was still very much a verbal bully. Seeing the world and every contradiction as black or white, I tended to judge people as either with me or against me, as either right or wrong depending on whether or not they accepted my definition of reality.

On the other hand, I wasn't drinking, or running around with women, or looking for a fight, or running any semi-legal scams. I was making progress. I cherished a new serenity. I worked, went to meetings of alcoholics, and tried to put into practice the dozen steps which are the foundation of the group, and helpful hints I heard at meetings.

Step ten was the most useful to me: "Continued to take personal inventory and when we were wrong promptly admitted it." This step was very close to the principle of "criticism/self-criticism" as practiced by the White Panther and Rainbow People's Parties years before. Both practices were designed to make the practitioner a better person; this was understandable to me. It allowed me to step back and critique myself, and when I was wrong, promptly admit it. Times were hard and I was difficult to live with, the tenth step made me less so.

*   *   *

When I asked Louis what my next step was in becoming Ottawa, he answered: "Your name and your Fast."

Patricia and I had begun regularly attending pow wows and participated in several sweat lodge ceremonies in preparation for our wedding. We had hunted and gathered magic plants and animal parts and Patricia spent months making gifts for our wedding day give-away.

Louis had tutored us in the custom of giving and receiving gifts, of using tobacco as a sacred offering or as a gift to a person. He said the entire creation is a gift from the Great Mystery and that we Ottawa are part of the Mystery and are therefore gifts to each other and to creation. A nice thought.

The "Fast" is an ancient tradition among the Ottawa and our "big brother" the Ojibway, and our "little brother," the Potawatomi. They call it a "vision quest" in the Hollywood movies, but this ain't no Hollywood story. Louis explained that the Fast is a doorway that opens to new understanding. In pre-contact times, Louis explained, the Fast was traditionally done in one's youth. But since native families and culture have been scattered and under attack for five-hundred years, many Ottawa come to their culture as adults and carry on as best they can.

Louis said that while fasting I would be visited by spirits in many forms and, instructed me to remember how my spirit visitors arrived. From this, he said, he would find my name.

Louis put me out to fast on north Manitou (Mystery/Spirit) Island, the island which had been formed when a little baby bear drowned on its swim across Lake Michigan with its mother. It lies nineteen miles out from the Great Sleeping Bear, in the little finger area of the Michigan mitten. My four days alone without food or water, while sleep deprived, brought many spirits to my camp.

On each morning of my Fast two hawks--Red Tails--visited my spot, soaring on updrafts, twenty-five feet overhead as the wind hit the bluff. One was older and larger, and had flight feathers missing from each wing and tail, which made it appear somewhat tattered and worn: The Elder.

The Elder flew above and somewhat behind the younger and smaller hawk, which had the sleek shape of a fish in flight. The Elder, the only one talking, screeched out instructions and encouragement to the younger, less experienced bird of prey.

"Keep your tips up! Tips up, tips up, tips up!" the Elder squawked. I could see the youngster concentrating, his tips up.

What would it be like, I wondered, to be watched over by elders who shouted instructions and encouragements?

After I told Louis of the hawks and various sightings of animals and spirits while fasting, he only nodded and said the spirits were checking on me, though I didn't see all of them by any means. By the way, he said, "I have your name."

I would have to make preparations, Louis informed me, for my naming ceremony. I would need to find four sponsors and prepare a feast and give-away--until then he would keep my name to himself. In the meantime, I began an undisciplined study of Anishnabeemowin, the language of the first people. At one time in our history the Anishnabee were one people and spoke one language, Anishnabeemowin. A thousand years ago we migrated from the east coast of North America to our present location in the woodlands of the Great Lakes and beyond. Over the centuries the Anishnabee grew into three great nations: Potawatomie (Bodawatomie), Ottawa (Odawa) and Chippewa (Ojibway). Collectively the Anishnabee are known as, The People of The Three Fires.

* * *

By 1984 I had made many friends in the Anishnabee community of Michigan. At the invitation of my new friend from the Intertribal Council, *Spirit Man,* I joined an Ottawa drum group called TWO HAWKS and spent several years traveling the midwest, often with dancers, presenting programs at universities and public schools. Throughout the summers we drummed and sang at pow-wows around the Great Lakes states.

I gave the traditional gift, a small cloth bundle of tobacco (asayma) to *Spirit Man,* a military veteran and Pipe carrier, and asked him to be one of my sponsors for my naming. He agreed.

I had decided when choosing my sponsors, to pick the first four traditional Anishnabee Pipe carriers the Mystery put in my life-- at least one would need to be a woman of course, in order to maintain that "balance" I was learning about and striving for.

Pipe carriers are the very spiritual heart of the traditional Anishnabee. They carry the Pipes for the Anishnabee and are required to present the Pipe and perform appropriate ceremonies when asked: At funerals, birthings, weddings, naming ceremonies, to council a family in strife, at graduations and celebrations, in prisons and hospitals and when the young go off to war.

Some are better at it than others. The Mystery put the best in my life.

Through *Spirit Man* I met *White Pigeon*, a Potawatomie Vietnam veteran, a Pipe carrier, and traditional leader. He introduced me to his mother, Virginia, a respected grandmother and Elder who carried a Pipe and is an encyclopedia of the ways and customs of our people. They both agreed to be my sponsors at my upcoming naming ceremony.

My fourth sponsor was *Leader Cloud*, an Ottawa from the Little Traverse Bay Band up near Petoskey. Several years younger than me, he was a college graduate and an electrical engineer working for General Motors in Lansing. He is a traditional Pipe Man who traces his name back to before there was English. His family origins go deep, to Garden Island in the big lake.

Sponsors serve as helpers, much the way "godparents" do in Judea-Christian beliefs. They can be called on for support, advice, or service, though they rarely are anymore. People are so busy and the dominant culture promotes isolation and individualism so successfully, that it's hard to hold onto old ways whether Judea-Christian or Native.

* * *

Patricia and I bought the Mosquito Ranch in the mid-1980's: Forty acres of swamp and woods at the end of a mile-long driveway with rudimentary buildings and no electricity or running water. Soon enough we had electricity and water and a phone and mortgage payments. I felt I was no longer free, tied as I was to the bank. But it was a reasonable trade-off for the feeling of stability, serenity and connection to place I had so seldom known.

At this time (1984) my traditional Anishnabee friends, those following the old ways, were often looking for a place to hold ceremonies and other gatherings. The Mosquito Ranch was perfect for such events. We began holding traditional ceremonies at the Ranch twice a year (spring and fall), and still do.

Four years after my Fast, when Louis had first known my name, I was ready for my naming ceremony. I felt I had been fully accepted into the Native community of Michigan. I was a drummer and singer with the TWO HAWKS drum group, a traditional dancer, and a budding storyteller.

The ceremony took place in our longhouse, which is made of bent saplings covered with canvas tarps. It is approximately forty feet long, twelve feet wide and seven feet high. (Some are much larger.) More than a hundred people attended my naming ceremony. All my native friends came, as did many I didn't know. Many of my non-native neighbors and friends attended as well.

When all were assembled, Louis gathered my sponsors and me in the center of the longhouse (Kenwassowigwam), surrounded by my community. Quietly he told my sponsors and me my name, Neech Gigek (Two Hawks). He had me face the four directions, one after the other. Speaking in Anishnabeemowin, so the native spirits would understand him, he introduced me to the spirits that live in those directions while fanning my name to each of them with his eagle wing. One of my sponsors led me around the assembled people introducing me to everyone by my new name.

At a naming ceremony it is customary for the sponsors to say a few words of support for the one who received their name. *White Pigeon* rose to speak. A Vietnam veteran and former "grunt"--combat infantry--with a division they call the Electric Strawberry, he told of a battle he was in against Viet Cong guerillas.

White Pigeon's squad had been ambushed in a rubber plantation. Outnumbered and caught in crossfire, the squad laid down a blanket of fire as they made a tactical withdrawal. He said the enemy was close, so close he could hear them hollering, cursing the American dogs as they were chased through the plantation, bullets whizzing.

A dirt road bisected the rubber farm. Built higher than the surrounding terrain, the road was ditched on each side. He blasted away so his comrades could flee. Then they let loose a torrent of rounds so he could catch up. At one point, his squad made it to the far side of the road and pumped out covering fire for *White Pigeon*. He turned to run with the enemy shooting from behind rubber trees just seventy-five yards away.

While running through the ditch and up the bank, he fell as the enemy closed in, bullets, like bees, swarmed around him. *White Pigeon* said an American grabbed him under the arm and pulled him to his feet; together they made it up the bank and across the road to where the Americans regrouped under cover. Air strikes were called in, the enemy scattered, and the danger passed, at least temporarily.

When his squad gathered and all were accounted for, he asked who helped him up the bank. No one from the squad had. Everyone said he was the last one over the road and came alone, without aid.

In the longhouse that day *White Pigeon* said he believed that I was the American who helped him up that ditch, way back in Vietnam.

I was lucky to be sitting on a blanket on the ground. I felt like I'd been hit in the chest with a shovel. I wanted to grow smaller and smaller, until I was invisible. I felt I did not deserve the honor *White Pigeon* had bestowed on me. I hadn't work hard enough to end the war. I hadn't made enough speeches, written enough articles, or thrown enough monkey wrenches in the machinery of war. I hadn't sacrificed enough. I hung my head. Later, I took great comfort in knowing that at least one Vietnam veteran understood that by opposing the war I was trying to help him up the bank, I was trying to save his life.

The giveaway was next, followed by the feast. I was back on cloud nine.

I felt I had completed the circle begun at my birth. I was back with my people, I had my name, I knew my clan, and I was studying our language. I had the respect of my community and people I loved. Every day I was learning something new, a different way to look at the world and relate to this creation.

It was at my naming ceremony that I met *Standing In the Sound of Thunder,* a former Marine and Vietnam combat veteran, a traditional Pipe Man, and Thunder Clan member, and his wife, *Woman of Dawn*. We became the best of friends and spent a year traveling to pow-wows, spiritual conferences, and meetings with elders. He told me my name was an ancient Anishnabee warrior name, and that with such a name came significant responsibility.

I was told that it was my mission to find out about that name and about the warriors who carried it before me. According to *Standing In the Sound of Thunder*, I would learn these things through dreams and by listening to elders and children.

From him I learned respect for life. In the Christian tradition the first principle of belief or faith is love: "God is Love," "Love thy neighbor," "Love your enemy," "Love the sinner, hate the sin," Love, love, love. Even as a child it was apparent to me that this love philosophy had a significant weakness. I found it impossible, for instance, to love an adult who, I believed, did not love me. It was hard to believe that someone loved me when they were slapping the shit out of me all the time. As I grew older, it became clear the Christian world in general did not practice its own first principle. Love Hitler? Love the Japs? Love the commies? Love niggers? Love the fags? No one was doing what they were preaching. I myself saw no reason to love Richard Nixon, J. Edger Hoover, or any of the exploiting, undemocratic capitalists who were raping and heaping havoc upon this planet and its impoverished people.

According to *Standing In the Sound of Thunder*, respect rather than love is the first principle of spirituality of the Anishnabee. In the Anishnabee way, all life is sacred, all life is beautiful, all life is part of the Great Mystery, and it must be respected. There is no command to love. One must respect, or one is not living the Anishnabee way. This made sense to me.

* * *

At the St. Ignace pow-wow in the Upper Peninsula, I met another Vietnam veteran, Donny Dude, a Potawatomie and Pipe man who lives on the Hannaville Indian Reservation. He is part of a network of Traditional Anishnabee I've been blessed to be associated with over the years. A rather small and wiry man for a Potawatomie, Donny is tremendously respected as a leader in traditional communities across North America. For years he has helped hundreds of native men quit drinking and drugs using the red path and the teachings of our ancestors. He is a renowned healer using herbs, drums and magic songs.

Donny had set up his large tee-pee. Upon our late night return from the casino a group of us decided the men would sleep together in the tee-pee and the women would sleep in our various camps around the pow-wow grounds, those who wanted, of course.

We spent the night laughing, lying, and telling stories. Toward morning, after most of the others had fallen asleep, Donny and I were still talking. I told him of the rocky road I had traveled to get to where I was--sober five years. I told him of my fateful first meeting with Louis Sawaquat. I told him how the introduction to The Great Mystery put me on the red path and road to recovery.

I explained as well as I could, how Louis had looked so large during that first meeting, how his head, jaw, chest, and hands had all seemed several times larger than life. I'd wondered about this for some six years, ever since it happened, but could not explain it.

Donny explained that alcohol has a spirit. That's why hard liquor is called "spirits," he said. According to him, the spirit of alcohol had completely taken over my body, driving out my native spirit even my human ghost. My alcoholic spirit was mean and quite vicious and scared off any benevolent ones that approached me.

Louis's manitou knew this, Donny said, so it grew bigger and bigger in order to show his power and intimidate the spirit of alcohol.

Donny said that when Louis brought out the pipe and called the spirits of my ancestors and relatives, when he called the spirits of animals, it was as if he were calling warriors to battle. When he called the spirits of trees, "those tall brothers who stand all around us and don't move," the battle was joined, and as quickly the battle was over, the spirit of alcohol had fled, frightened by the power of Louis's ghost and those gathered around us.

"No shit?" was all I could say.

"No shit," Donny answered, and fell asleep.

Chapter Twenty-four

HOME TO THE OTTAWA--1984-2000

My adopted dad died in October of 1988 while fishing with my younger brother. I mark his passing as the time when I joined the human family. Over the years I'd attended funerals, wakes, and memorial services, and had close friends and loved ones die unexpectedly; however, I had never experienced a sense of loss or grief other than what I had faked to fit in with the other mourners. I never knew those emotions until my adoptive father passed. My grief and sense of loss wasn't staggering or overwhelming in any way. But it was real. It was new. With it came empathy for my whole adoptive family-- mom, sisters and brother; I had never felt closer to them. It was a small step from empathy for family to empathy for the world.

In the past my solidarity with poor and suffering people was based on a sense of justice and fairness--politics. This was different. Now I knew, on a personal level, the sour taste of grief, sorrow, and loss. When I see pictures of a Palestinian mother holding a child murdered by occupation forces, I know something, just something, of what she is going through. When I see the families of Israelis mourning their student daughter, killed by a bomb as she rode to school, I too weep for the family, and the needless loss. Or in Colombia, where the drug war is really a war on native people. I identify on a personal level with their suffering. I now feel connected to the rest of the world on a human level.

* * *

With the help of *Spirit Man*, I applied to the Bureau of Indian Affairs in Sault Sainte Marie for my Indian card. I felt the revulsion many native people do when having to ask the government to certify who they are; it's degrading. Six months after receiving my card, I applied to The Grand River Bands of Ottawa for Tribal membership. Two years later I received my Tribal membership card and genealogy going back to the 1836 Treaty of Washington.

The extensive travel with the Two Hawks drum group became cost and time prohibitive so I quit and started dancing at local pow-wows with the other traditional dancers.

In my travels and studies of Ottawa culture I heard many stories that gave me a spiritual center and moral compass. The stories explained and reinforced ancient teachings and traditions as they passed on morals and values that have held the First Nations together all of these centuries. I began repeating the stories, at first, just to friends, then whenever friends gathered. Soon I was telling stories at pow-wows, potlucks and meetings.

I liked talking and telling stories. People told me I was good at it--not something I'd heard very often in the past. As I kept telling stories, the praise continued. Soon others began giving me stories: elders, children, WWII, Korean and Vietnam veterans, native historians and genealogists. I received my first Eagle Feather in recognition of my traditional storytelling.

About this time I was given the traditional gift of tobacco and asked to be the Master of Ceremonies at various traditional pow-wows around the state. Then I was appointed to the Grand River Bands Tribal Council. I served for two years before my methods of thinking and style of work clashed with the majority on the council.

Even though I'd made progress in toning down my arrogance, my desire to be involved and to control situations, and to push, push, push for faster action, had a direct bearing on my inability to get along with Tribal Council. I wanted our fight for treaty rights to be a high profile campaign with an energetic strategy designed to keep the case of the Grand River Bands on the front page and front burner. The Council and its leadership felt otherwise. I resigned when it became clear I was a hindrance to the tepid, sedate functioning of the Council.

My alcoholic friends with many years of sobriety behind them say that we alkies need to "Let go and let God," or, in my case; "Let go and let the Mystery." We don't need to be in charge of everything, we don't need to have an answer for everything. We can let go and let others run the show; we are not the end all and be all of knowledge and right thinking. Letting go is hard for me to do.

Around this time I was contacted by the local cooperatively-owned recreation center and summer camp for kids I previously mentioned. They had been contacted by a white guy, a "New Age" charlatan, who was running weekend seminars giving out Indian and clan names, arranging vision quests, conducting sweat lodge ceremonies, and giving out drum-making kits and instructions for people who paid big money. The New Age Indians wanted to rent the camp for a weekend seminar.

The camp director, who had misgivings about the request, showed me the brochure and asked for my opinion about this group of wannabees. The brochure stated the leader had spent six months living with the Sioux. For $600 you could come to the gathering for a weekend "of native culture, wisdom, and magic," and receive your "spirit drum" to take home. At the $700 level you could receive your spirit drum and your Indian name. For $800 you got your spirit drum, your Indian name, and your clan name. At the one thousand dollar level you received your spirit drum, your Indian name, and clan name, and your vision quest with the sweat lodge thrown in free.

I flipped my lid. I expected the brochure to read, "Operators are standing by; if you call in the next ten minutes we will include the ginsu knife and hair in a can." I was incredulous. How dare this white guy manipulate and exploit our culture and spirituality for such tacky personal gain?

From time to time throughout the year Pat and I host sweat lodges at the Mosquito Ranch. We had one scheduled for the weekend after I had heard about the charlatan's seminar. As we Anishnabee were preparing the lodge, building the fire, heating the rocks, and cooking the medicine, I raised the issue of the wannabees and the exploitation of our spiritual heritage. I wanted to know what to do. I felt we should do a raid on their camp, count coup, and maybe steal their women and cars since they didn't have horses.

None of the others felt as strongly as I did. "Who cares what the Anglos do? Fuck 'em." seemed to be the predominant sentiment.

"But this seems wrong to me, these people playing with our culture. Shouldn't we do something? Punch them in the nose at least?" I said.

Leader Cloud is a wise man. He explained that the wannabees were spiritual tourists, flitting from one form of spirituality to the next, sampling some here and some there. Last year, *Leader Cloud* said, they were probably Buddhists, the time before that they were probably Hindus, or Druids or Wiccans and before that they were probably Baptists, Methodists or Episcopalians.

There was no need to concern ourselves with these people, *Leader Cloud* said. No good will come from their playing Indian. They are not a threat to our culture or us. We've been in this place four thousand years, following these teachings. Our people and culture will outlast them all.

The fire sizzled, the rocks were white hot, almost transparent. *Old Man*, a WWII vet chimed in: "Our responsibility is to learn the traditions and ceremonies of our people and pass them on to the children."

What a huge load had been taken from my shoulders: I am not responsible for what others do. I am responsible only for myself. What a relief. I don't have to be in charge.

I realized this applied in my daily life as well. I didn't have to insist my wife do the garden my way; she was quite capable of doing it her way. I didn't have to inject myself into every minor and major issue, I didn't have to give my opinion on every subject or offer advice when it was not needed or wanted. I didn't have to act like a dominant white male. This was a big change for me--how nice it was.

* * *

Grand Rapids has been called "Grand Rapids" for just over three hundred years. For a thousand years before that it had always been called *Owashtanong,* or "place where the river does a big turn." For centuries the Ottawa have lived on the west side of the river, and that is still so today. After Detroit, Grand Rapids has the largest urban native population in the State.

The Grand River is one of the longest in Michigan. It begins in the center of the state, north of the capital, Lansing, and meanders westward collecting the Flat, the Maple, the Thornapple, the Looking Glass and other rivers as it heads to the big lake, Gitchi Gummi.

Near the town of Ada the river makes a hard turn to the north running about fifteen miles before it turns back to the west for about five miles. Then it goes south for about ten miles through the city of Grand Rapids where the actual rapids are, then west again to *Gitchi Gummi.* This horseshoe turn, the largest on the entire river, is some thirty miles from start to finish.

US 131 is the main north/south corridor across Grand Rapids. Where it crosses the river there is a great sweeping bridge, several miles long, in the shape of a giant "S." Hence the name, "the S-curve bridge."

In late 1998 a section of the S-curve Bridge sank eleven inches. It seems the foundation of one of the great pillars, anchored to gypsum below the riverbed, had eroded, causing the pillar to sink nearly a foot. Huge slabs of concrete roadway, like tectonic plates, became misaligned. As a result, the Michigan Department of Transportation (MDOT) and the Federal Highway Administration declared the bridge "a clear and present danger," and a rush was on to repair the bridge before it settled any more or collapsed completely.

Because federal road building funds were to be used, the law required an environmental impact study. In the course of the study it was discovered that directly under the bridge was an undisturbed Odawa village, covered with fill dirt, dating to the 1800's. The law required that the area to be disturbed in the building of new foundations must be treated as historic archeological sites--a full archaeological "dig" was ordered.

There are hundreds of known native village sites across the state. Over the years farmers have plowed over most of them, or they were destroyed in the construction of housing developments, or otherwise disturbed in the process of road building or burying utilities. This site was unique in that it was undisturbed, protected as it was under eight feet of fill dirt. Through testing, the archeologists knew this village site was located atop even older villages. The archaeologists could barely contain their excitement.

MDOT met with the Grand River Bands Tribal Council to solicit our support for the impending archaeological dig. I was not a Tribal Council member at the time, having resigned the year before. However, I was active with our tribal Graves Protection and Repatriation Committee and was invited to attend the meeting.

The fact of the matter was that the bridge was going to be repaired, with or without our support. Likewise, the archaeological dig was going to happen, with or without the Tribe's acquiescence. MDOT wanted our blessing and support so the project would run smoothly without resistance from local Indians wanting to protect the village site. They had only nine weeks, in the dead of the Michigan winter, to finish the dig. Road builders were eager to get started.

Our Tribal leadership reasoned that by cooperating rather than resisting we could have more influence. The Tribal Council negotiated a pre-dig agreement with the state that spelled out the conditions for our cooperation. First, any human body parts found would be returned to the Tribe for proper reinternment. Since this was a village and not a burial site, however, this was not likely to be an issue. Second, burial objects or objects of cultural patrimony would be repatriated to the Tribe. Third, Tribal monitors would have free and complete access to the site for purposes of monitoring work and insuring that the state was living up to the agreement.

I was appointed a Tribal monitor. For a week I watched as 'dozers scraped away the eight feet of backfill. Then thirty-five archaeologists from all over the country swarmed onto the site. This was a big deal. I watched as they laid out a grid pattern, using string. They set up a transit, global positioning devices, laser levels, and cameras.

They rented two mammoth circus tents that covered the entire dig area. Gas heaters were installed to keep the workers warm and to keep the ground from freezing. Electric generators were set up, and miles of extension cords were laid to feed the two halogen lights used by each archeologist.

They began digging, scraping the earth away a centimeter at a time, taking pains to record all details of any artifact found. They put their scrapings through quarter-inch screen, careful not to miss a thing. At first they found mostly historic stuff, debris left during the transition period of native/white contact: clay pipes, shirt buttons, handblown glass bottles, flakes of flint from tool making, and a few stone arrow points.

Meanwhile I was going broke, my credit card having taken a significant hit since I'd accepted the position as an unpaid Tribal monitor. I asked the foreman, a young man with a PhD in stone tools, if I could hire on as a common laborer. Having worked in the construction trades most of my life, bulldozers, backhoes, holes in the ground, and outside work were all familiar to me.

Fortunately, they needed a "logistics engineer," someone to keep the heaters and generators running, the lights burning, and the work site safe. They also wanted someone to serve as a cultural interpreter to tell what they knew about artifacts found. I hired on to fill both positions.

Most of the archaeologists on the job were rather young, in their late twenties and thirties, and all had degrees of one kind or another. These were not the "loot and scoot" grave robber archaeologists that native people have come to distrust and dislike, but a new generation of diggers with respect for the culture and people they were studying. Multicultural education and training had paid off in the respectful conduct of these young professionals.

As they dug centimeter by centimeter into the "paleosol" --the old dirt--more ancient artifacts from my ancestors' lives and culture were unearthed. Thousands upon thousands of flint flakes no bigger than a fingernail were found, demonstrating that flint tool making was a never-ending project. In one instance a digger uncovered a rock the size of a football. He dug around the rock and, without disturbing it, removed the dirt from around its base until finally the rock stood on a pedestal of dirt like an ancient organic football trophy.

The PhD and several others gathered at the pit as the digger removed the large rock. Beneath it were several dozen arrow and spear points in various stages of manufacture, an ancient stash left by a man perhaps five hundred years ago and untouched since.

They also uncovered several small holes in the earth, each about the size of a coffee can; in these were found burnt corncobs that had been used as smudge pots at various locations around the village in an effort to keep the bugs and mosquitoes at bay. The archeologists loved finding the corncobs since they could do accurate carbon dating on them.

The discovery of several fire pits was also important. By studying the debris left around the fire the diggers could determine whether the site was a temporary camp or a permanent village. At a fire pit in a temporary camp you could expect to find flint flakes on one side of the fire and sewing awls and seeds from food preparation on the other, showing that men and women had worked together.

In a permanent village, only flint flakes are found around certain fire pits, indicating that men had gathered there. At others only seeds and other remnants of women's activities remained, showing that men and women had worked separately. (These gender role distinctions were much like they are today at the Mosquito Ranch during ceremony time. The men gather together to sharpen knives, fix chain saws, or tell stories. The women work together too, cooking, doing bead and quill-work, or making reed mats for the longhouse, while, like the men, they visit and share stories).

The archaeologists dug and dug; I was told every three centimeters was going back a hundred years. Cooter, a young man from Virginia and the only digger on the job without a degree, was working on a pit at the far end of the site. He and his daddy and his daddy's daddy had all been coal miners. He had gotten into archaeology because his girlfriend, a sweet young woman from the University of Ohio, was forever traveling off to various digs around the country. On this dig she was a crew leader. He reasoned that to keep her he would have to join her. Because of his experience in the mines he was a natural, and although he had no degree, he was unsurpassed in "data recovery," as digging is called.

At one point, Cooter called me over to his pit. "Check this out," he said. I looked into his pit, about a meter deep, and was startled to see it glowing, as if a fluorescent light were burning at the bottom. He had uncovered a large bear canine tooth nearly five centimeters long. Amazingly, that tooth seemed to be filling the pit with light as it glimmered at the bottom.

Upon close examination we found a tiny hole on the root end of the tooth, which someone had obviously drilled in order to affix a string so it could be worn as a necklace. I was mesmerized; even in my hand it seemed to emit light and vibrate. I told the PhD foreman, "You'd better keep an eye on this. I haven't wanted to take anything from this site, but given half a chance I'd steal that. It would look good on my dance outfit." Quickly the foreman placed the tooth in a baggie, recorded the data, and squirreled it away. It will eventually be returned to the Tribe as an artifact of cultural patrimony.

At a later time another digger called me over to his pit. "Look at this," he said. In his hand he held a small metal cone, made of copper. "It's ornamentation," he told me.

"Oh wow! A jingle cone!" I blurted. "Well, yeah…ornamentation," he repeated.

"It's quite a bit more than ornamentation," I responded. "That's a jingle cone, from a Jingle Dress."

"Yes, it's ornamentation often worn on dresses," he insisted.

"Do you know the story of the Jingle Dress?" I asked.

He did not. After he climbed out of the pit I told him the Jingle Dress story.

In the roar and drone of the generators and kerosene heaters, the air hung damp and low to the cold earth in the massive green and white-striped circus tent.

The many versions of this story differ as to location and family, but all remain true to its magic. I began.

Quite some time ago, the story goes, there was a band of Anishnabee whose village was located on the shore of what we now call Lake Manitoba. Many people in the village were sick, some say even the animals and Mother Earth herself were sick. The Healers, Medicine People, and Dreamers had all said the prayers, sang the songs, and made medicine just as they had learned from their Elders, who had learned from the Elders before them. The Clans had conducted the appropriate ceremonies as handed down with the Original Instructions. Nothing worked. The people and animals and earth continued to die of the sickness.

During this terrible time there was a girl who had a dream. In her dream she saw herself dancing. She saw herself wearing a dress like no one had ever seen before. It was made of fine doeskin with hundreds of small copper cones sewn to it.

In the dream she was dancing steps no one had ever seen before. While she danced, she carried an Eagle Wing Fan. Whenever the drummers hit four strong Honor Beats she would wave the fan to the four directions.

The girl told her grandmother of the dream. The grandmother set out to make just such a dress. It took a full year. Each day the grandmother would make a copper cone and sew it onto the dress. As she made the cone, folding and hammering it around a pointed stick, she said a prayer. In so doing she placed a prayer in each one of the three- hundred-and-sixty-five cones, one for each day of the year.

At the next gathering the girl wore the dress and danced the steps just as she remembered from her dream. As she danced the cones jingled together releasing the grandmother's prayers. When the drummers hit the honor beats the girl fanned the prayers to the four directions.

Soon the people in the village, the animals, and the earth itself were healed.

Today women and girls still dance the Jingle Dress. Grandmothers still say prayers as they sew the cones to the dress. Often Jingle Dress Dancers are given the traditional gift of tobacco and asked to dance for someone who is sick or in prison or suffering from drug or alcohol addiction.

In Anishnabeemowin the Jingle Dress Dance is called Miskiikii Akii Ziigawin or "earth medicine dance."

As I finished the story I noticed that about twenty-five archaeologists had surrounded me, mouths open like a bunch of goldfish. Even with all their multicultural sensitivity these professionals too often failed to connect the object with the people. A person made the jingle cone, perhaps my great, great, great, great grandma. A person burnt the corncobs, and fashioned the arrow point. A person made the bear's tooth into a necklace.

The archaeologists knew the culture that produced the object; they knew the time period too, and even the technique. But they didn't know the person who made the object.

I know the person, or the person's relatives, their cousins, their relations; I see them every day. I dance with them, go to hockey games with them, and attend potlucks with them. Endless potlucks.

When I handled the old, tarnished jingle cone, or the bear's tooth, or the burnt corncobs, or arrow points, I didn't feel as though I was handling "artifacts." I felt I was touching my grandmother's heirlooms, real connections to my ancestral past. I believe these objects are the witness to history and carry the story of my ancestors in this place.

I gathered a bucket of the old dirt, the ground my ancestors had lived and died on. I carried it home and put some in each of my wife's houseplants. I ate a pinch of it; I wanted to connect physically, in a concrete way, with my ancestors from that ancient time; the rest I spread on the garden.

The dig was nearing completion. 'Dozers and cranes belched smoke and stood by waiting for orders to begin the roadwork. I called *Standing In the Sound of Thunder* and invited him to come down and conduct a pipe ceremony to put the Spirits at ease before the site was backfilled with dirt, but he was on his way to Washington. He assured me, however, that a pipe ceremony would not be necessary. Instead I should smudge the area with sage and sweet-grass, place tobacco and cedar in the area, and speak what I knew of the language so the Spirits would know they were among friends. I should thank them, he said, for all the gifts they left us and all the new knowledge they brought to us. "You are quite qualified to pray," he said. "You do it."

I never felt closer to my people than at that time or more connected to place.

My circle was complete.

EPILOGUE--August--2004

Every year the Little River Band of Odawa holds a Language and Cultural Preservation Camp on Tribal grounds across from the casino in Manistee, Michigan. The Little River Band is the nearest tribal neighbor of the Grand River Bands; many of them are our cousins.

For many years I've presented storytelling workshops at the annual camp. In 2002 an Odawa who makes his home in San Francisco approached me after one of my storytelling sessions and introduced himself. His last name was Aiken, the same as my biological father's. "What was your father's first name?" he wanted to know. "Louis," I answered.

"Your dad was my great-uncle. We're related," he said beaming.

"We're blood relatives?" I wondered aloud.

"Yes. My great grandpa was your granddad's brother. We're cousins of some sort."

I was taken aback. For some reason it never occurred to me that I would have living relatives.

"You've got all sorts of relatives around Newaygo. Etienne De Lamorandiere was French and the first white guy to settle in what is now Newaygo County. He married an Anishnabee named *Woman of Falling Snow*. That was the beginning of our family tree in America," Aiken continued.

I had to sit down.

Aiken knew the genealogy of our family inside-out. Excited, he continued: Etienne De Lamorandiere opened his trading post in Newaygo in 1790. Though French, he had sided with the Indians and British against the Americans in the War of 1812. He was arrested by the Americans as an Indian sympathizer and detained in Detroit for several months before they let him go. After the war he moved to Drummond Island and opened a trading post, but he was promptly burned out by American competitors in retaliation for his support of the Indians in the war. So he moved again, this time to the north shore of Georgian Bay, just above Manitoulin Island, to a little settlement called Killarney in English-speaking Canada, where he died, Aiken paused, then began again, like a waterfall, spilling out family history.

"We should go to Newaygo," he said. "I can introduce you to all of your cousins. Oh, here's my daughter, let me introduce you." Within moments he resumed his recitation of the family tree: "There were three sons, Robert, Tom and Jake, your grandpa is Tom, I came from Jake's line--Tom and Jake married two sisters, Eva, your grandma, and Libby, my great grandma."

He could see my head was spinning. Slowing his pace, he went on: "Eva and Libby were sisters from Indiana. They married Tom, your grandpa, and Jake, my great grandpa."

Though encouraged by Aiken's excitement, I had some apprehension about meeting my long lost family. From what I remembered reading in the state hospital files some twenty years before, my father had not been held in the highest regard. I didn't know what kind of reception I would receive. I put Aiken off, at least temporarily.

* * *

One of the good things about being adopted is that it allowed me to create my own family from the native people I met and admired. I could pick and choose from the best of the Odawa Nation. There were a number of people I called cousin, and even more whom I called nieces and nephews and many Ottawa men and women I called brother and sister. There were a few Elders to whom I gave the traditional gift of tobacco asking if I could call them grandma and grandpa, Nokomis/Mishomis. Even though this family existed only in my head, it gave me great comfort.

* * *

In 2003 I saw Aiken and his daughter, Katrina, at Little River language camp again. When camp was over they visited the Mosquito Ranch. Aiken was still insistent and excited about taking me to Newaygo to meet my relatives.

"You've got to meet *Flower*, she's your first cousin. Her name actually means *Pumpkin Flower*. Your dad was her uncle. They lived on the farm together," he went on in his usual enthusiastic way.

"Aiken, you must understand," I said, "my father was not the favorite son of the family, or anything close." I handed him an 8x10 photo of my dad--front and profile, holding his prison number just below his chin--taken fifty years ago, in Jackson Prison. "Also," I went on, "I carry a lot of baggage with me too, like this," I said, handing him a dog-eared copy of my FBI most-wanted poster.

"I'm not sure these people will want to welcome an ex-con, commie bastard, hippie-turned-Indian, alcoholic heathen into the family. My greatest fear is that someone will run me off at the point of a shotgun." As I made the statement and I realized how unlikely this was, my fear and apprehension vanished.

Aiken himself seemed completely unphased by these revelations. He was much more interested in linking me up with *Flower.* "You've got to meet her. She's elderly and rather frail--she's 85. But her mind is sharp and she has a tremendous memory of the old days--she's your nearest living relative. She's just the sweetest little thing," he insisted. "I've already called her, she's expecting us tomorrow at two o'clock. You meet me at the motel and I'll take you over there. She is expecting us.

* * *

Newaygo is a small village notched into the side of a steep hill where Penoyer Creek joins the Muskegon River about an hour and a half north of the Mosquito Ranch. Flower lives with her husband in a well-kept farmhouse more than a hundred years old on the original Lamorandiere homestead. For nearly a mile, on both sides of the gravel road, Aiken pointed out the family's former property.

"There's an Aiken. There's a Lamorandiere. There's an Aiken. Lamorandiere. Aiken. Lamorandiere."

"How come we're Aiken and not Lamorandiere?" I asked.

"Etienne had three sons Alexis, Jake and Aiken Lamorandiere. At some point Aiken Lamorandiere dropped his last name and took his first name as his last. That's how we're Aiken," he answered.

He rattled off the history in a torrent: Indians were not much liked in those days. When Etienne married one, he was called an Indian lover, and worse. Then, too, Etienne was not much loved by the Americans since he supported the Brits and Indians during the War of 1812. Sometimes members of the family used the name Aiken to throw people off the name Lamorandiere, for instance if government contracts were involved. As we pulled into the driveway, he said, "I think Aiken is the Indian pronunciation and spelling of Etienne. We could be Aiken or Lamorandiere, they're interchangeable."

Flower welcomed us into her tidy home and greeted us warmly. I was introduced to her across the kitchen table. As I leaned over to shake her hand, she took mine in both of hers and held on tightly while looking me over.

"Oh, you're a handsome man. You look very much like Uncle Bub, especially around the eyes, and your hair," she said still squeezing my hand.

"Did you know my dad?" I asked.

"Oh yes, Uncle Bub was around while I was growing up. He sometimes lived with us and worked on the farm. I always liked him." She was still holding my hand in both of hers, rubbing my skin over and over. "Come, I've got pictures to show you."

We sat on the couch in the living room, *Flower* holding my hand, the wall covered with pictures of children and grandchildren in graduation gowns and Marine Corps dress blues with white caps. There were pictures of *Flower's* mother and father, my auntie and uncle. There were photos of cousins, uncles, and aunties. She also had several shoeboxes and photo albums full of pictures, and from a little cardboard jewelry box, no bigger than a pack of cigarettes, she pulled out a tintype, one and a half by three inches, showing three Ottawa men. "Here's a picture of your grandpa and his two brothers," she told me. Thomas, my grandpa, perhaps twenty-five, was on the left--leather boots to the knee, one leg pointed south. A big, strapping man, he stood with his chest out in his coarse woolen trousers, held up by stout suspenders. He wore a heavy woolen shirt and what looked like a dark bone breastplate, or perhaps beadwork, at the neck. A short, square-bottomed tie covers this. His round Ottawa face, with square bangs across the forehead, stared back at me.

Jake stood on the right, in the counter-pose of my gramps, left leg pointed north. He was dressed in the same leather boots, coarse trousers, and short, square-bottomed tie over a dark, double-breasted shirt with two buttons per side. He appeared to be the youngest of the three, a powerful man with the same round Ottawa face and bangs as his brother.

Robert was seated on a stool between the two with his legs crossed at the knees. He had a long, thin face, like a Sioux or Cheyenne, and was not as barrel-chested as his younger brothers. He wore boots laced to the knee and the same dark, heavy pants. His shirt was double-breasted, cavalry-style, with six shiny buttons. Four white ribbons hung down the front of each side of the dark vest he wore. On his wrist were what looked to be deer-toe bracelets, or perhaps jingle bells--big, bulky things.

The three look to be full-bloods, their dark, shiny faces expressionless as they posed in front of a backdrop of a Grecian garden with an archway and urns. I silently gave a sigh of relief to see the dark complexion of my progenitors. I wish I were dark like that.

Later I had the tintype enlarged. On the bottom of Robert's boot, cleats are clearly visible. The little spikes helped their wearers to walk on logs: these men were lumberjacks. They were probably dressed in their best, which would explain the breastplate and bracelets. No doubt an itinerant photographer had visited their lumber camp or shot the thing when the three had visited a Michigan lumbering town.

Flower continued to hold my hand and rummage in a shoebox. "Here's a picture of your dad taken in Chicago before he joined the army in 1908; he was 22." The 4x8 black and white photo had been printed on cardboard and had a nice gray frame. The photo showed a handsome man in a light-colored, three-piece suit with a white shirt and bow tie sitting on a stool in front of a curtain. He was staring back at the camera with a slight cocky smirk on his lips. With his black hair slicked back, he looked quite dapper.

"Here's one of your grandpa and your dad," she said, handing me another 4x8. In this photo, my dad was just an infant being held lovingly by my grandpa. On the back someone had written in pencil; "Tom and Louis, 1886."

"Here's a tin-type of your dad's auntie." This one showed a dark-skinned Ottawa woman with the customary round face and big cheeks, like those of any number of Ottawa women I know today. On the back of the picture was masking tape, and in pencil: Rose Lamorandiere, 1885.

"Here's a snapshot of your dad with some of his cousins," she said. They all appeared to be in their teens, standing close together in the fall of the year, looking like Bonny and Clyde and the Barrow Gang. On the back was written in ink: "Archie, Louis, Delise and Susie." Diagonally, in dull pencil, someone had scrawled; "Skinny, Lou, Babe and me."

"Here's one of your dad in the army." It was an 8x10 in a cardboard frame. He was at attention in his "Smokey Bear" hat, wool tunic, and jodhpurs tucked into tall leather boots. I noticed two holes in the frame and thumbtack indentations; someone had had this picture on their wall. Looking closely at the tack marks, I could see rust stains. This picture had hung on a wall for a long time, long enough for the Michigan humidity to rust the tintacks. Someone had been proud of this picture and of my dad.

"Here's some postcards your dad sent while he was in the Army. What a beautiful hand he had," she said, admiring the perfect flowing penmanship.

Flower continued to show me pictures, and in them I saw a part of my dad and his life I had never imagined. Here he is in one taken at a picnic; he, and everyone else is smiling. Here he is in front of a large pile of oyster shells. Here he is with cousins, standing in front of a black sedan, his leg jauntily placed on the running board. Here he is in front of a small wooden church with nearly twenty family members, all of whose names had been listed on the back.

No longer was he the one-dimensional drunk that everyone was angry and short-tempered with. Now he appeared loved and part of a family.

"They all had a problem with alcohol," cousin *Flower* said, rubbing the top of my hand again. "Your grandpa and his brothers, your dad and his brothers; they all had big problems."

I picked up one of the pictures I'd laid aside. "Oyster shells?" I wondered aloud.

"Grandpa and your dad used to harvest oyster shells out of the river," *Flower* remembered. "Then they sold them by the wagonload to the button factory over in Freemont. I've got several pieces of jewelry made with river pearls."

She found a shoebox and put pictures by the handful in it for me. There were tin-types of my grandma, Eva Mundy, and her sisters and brothers, and of as my grandpa and his brothers. There were Kodak snapshots of my dad and his siblings, my aunties and uncles. It was wonderful. Then it was time to go; I could tell the visit had tired my elderly cousin. I promised to visit again.

My drive home was filled with emotion. My circle is truly complete, I'm back with my Tribe, I'm connected to this place by blood and family. But a moment of sadness struck me when I asked myself: *To whom will I pass these photos and stories? I have no children.*

* * *

I've gone back to visit cousin *Flower* several times. On one visit I asked if she knew anything about my mother. She only knew that I was conceived in a cherry orchard on Old Mission Peninsula. It seems the State Hospital would rent out patients to local cherry farmers during the harvest. *Flower's* mother had told her that my dad and mom snuck away from the picking to be intimate.

On another visit *Flower* took me to my father's grave. The grave marker is an old metal one, gray and weather-stained. It's in the shape of a cross with fluted floral columns and filigrees. The engraved panel reads: "Mary Rose--May, 1862-July 1865."
Below it was another entry: "Baby--April 19-April 21, 1889."

"Your dad is buried in this grave," my cousin said, pointing to the marker. "He was buried on top of those children; that wasn't uncommon in those days."

"I should get a marker for my dad's grave," I mused. "I could mount it right below the monument on the stone base."

"Yes, you should," cousin responded. "Come on, I'll take you."

"Now?" I asked.

"Why not? Are you in a hurry?"

We drove to the small local monument shop, and I helped *Flower* inside. The showroom was empty. She began opening doors to small offices, then a door that went to the back shop. "Where's Martin?" she asked the startled young man in the back.

He looked at her with a rather quizzical smile. "Martin?"

"Yes. Martin Postma. We used to belong to the same church. I bought the headstone for my first husband from him," she went on authoritatively.

"Grandpa retired twenty years ago. He lives in Kalamazoo," the young man responded.

"Well, that would be right. I buried my first husband twenty-four years ago. Where's Dale, his son?" my cousin asked.

"Dale's my dad. He's at the Kalamazoo store. I'm Dick. What can I do for you?

"We want to buy a bronze plaque to mark a grave." She paused, looked at me and asked, "What do you want it to say, Larry?"

"It should read: LOUIS AIKEN--FATHER-VETERAN. February 16, 1886--July 21, 1956."

- Sinclair is a working poet and bandleader living in The Netherlands, he tours regularly.
- DS is a poet and hides his poems in Florida where he works in a bookstore.
- Leni Sinclair is a grandmother and photo journalist/ archivist living in Detroit.
- Forest is a working class poet and teamster living in Indianapolis.
- Skippy is living in California where he owns an alternative promotion/distribution company.
- Buck Davis is lawyering and fighting the good fight in Detroit.
- Len Weinglass is a legal warrior living on a farm in New Jersey.
- Arthur Kinoy passed from this earth in October of 2003.
- Fenton lives in New York and owns a communications and promotion company.
- Kelley lives and writes in San Francisco.
- Bill Kunstler passed into the spirit world in September of 1995.
- The Prez lives in Detroit where she teaches Tai Chi.
- Emil lives in California where he practices photography.
- Kramer makes music and lives in LA.
- Red Haired Audrey is a massage therapist living in Ann Arbor.
- Werbe is a public affairs director for a radio group in Detroit.
- Cheeseburger is a production manager for rock-n-roll acts on tour. He lives in Ann Arbor.
- Grimshaw is a poster and design artist living in midtown Detroit.
- Louis Sawaquat lives on the rez in northern Michigan.

APPENDIX A

SOURCE OF REFERRAL: On 7/27/73 case referred to the Probation & Parole Agent for presentence investigation and report by District Court, Cadillac, Mich. AEA[1]

[1] Prior to sentencing on extortion charges in 1974, the Judge released the following presentence report. The bulk of the information was gathered by the Behavioral Science Division of the Federal Bureau of Investigation in 1969 and 1970, while I was on the Ten Most Wanted list. Their report was captioned: CHAOS--Lawrence Robert "Pun" Plamondon. Although there are spelling, punctuation and grammatical errors, I left it largely unedited so as to not alter the quality of the report.

PREVIOUS TROUBLE: The following information is a composite obtained from Grand Traverse Probate Court, Grand Traverse Sheriff's Dept., 86th District Court, a FBI Behavioral Science report, a previous presentence report and State Police fingerprint and voiceprint returns under Bureau Identification #567712. Quotes indicate that the material comes verbatim, either as a result of agent Manor's Traverse City investigation or from the Federal presentence of several years ago compiled by agent Anderson:

Juvenile History: 7/1/60 petition filed by the parents under Chapter 712A, Compiled Laws 48, Section 2(a) (m), being disobedient to the reasonable and lawful commands of parents and school authorities. In conjunction with this petition a report was received from Mrs. Margaret Keith, county welfare agent, also dated 7/1/60: 'Larry is an adopted child. He was expelled from St. Francis High School this spring and because of behavior difficulties--staying out very late without permission--being insolent and disobedient, it was referred to the Catholic Service Bureau for study and recommendation.' The Catholic Service Bureau recommendation is 'a placement away from the home environment, preferably a group setting such as offered by the Father Gibault School for Boys in Indiana.' Also included in the Probate record are reports dated 9/21/46 written by Mary J. Clark, executive secretary, Michigan Children's' Aid Society, outlining the Defendant's parents' background. (Note: records reveal Defendant born 4/27/45 during a time when his natural parents were both patients at Traverse City State Hospital. The mother had been committed in 1941 and the father the following year. Parental rights were terminated by the Court in 1946. Defendant did not tell writer his adoption by the Plamondons, although subsequent verification information indicates that he has been aware of this fact for years. It does not indicate, however, that he possesses the complete factual story in terms of the history of his natural parents (AEA). I believe you also have copies of the psychological report written by Mr. Jim Woodrow, then employed at the Northwestern Michigan Child Guidance Clinic, dated 7/28/59, which shows that upon testing the Defendant had a verbal scale I.Q. of 93, a performance scale I.Q. of 91, for a full-scale I.Q. of 92. (Note: report described him as one 'who tests in the range of average intelligence on the Wechsler-Bellevue scale form II.' It further describes him as an 'introversive personality with good phantasy life. He may react to environmental stimulation with inadequate controls. He is sensitive and in contact with reality. He seems to have made normal role identification of the sexes" AEA). In a report written by Catholic Service Bureau, prior to Defendant's appearance in court, it was indicated that Mr. George Plamondon, Defendant's adoptive father, appeared before the Catholic Service Bureau on 5/11/60. He advised the following: 'Larry refused to accept any kind of authority either from parents or from school. His refusal to study (had to repeat most subjects in 9th grade), his insolence which frequently results in his leaving home and not returning until anywhere between 3 and 5 am. Mr. Plamondon expressed real concern that his son's behavior will ultimately lead him to court and he wanted to prevent this if possible. He cited several occasions where Larry had stolen the key to the grocery store (the family business, AEA) and has taken beer and wine to be shared with his friends. Mr. Plamondon related there has been difficulty with Larry which began shortly after their daughter was born. They have become more intense in the past three years. He felt part of the problem was due to no consistency regarding discipline and the fact that Larry is repeatedly threatened by his mother that he will be sent to reform school and that if he continues his acting out behavior, he will end up in the State Hospital as he is mentally sick. Apparently Mrs. Plamondon is constantly nagging him and as a result, Larry stays away from home as much as possible.' The report later continues, stating that a great deal of fighting between the parents was noted by Mr. Plamondon. His major concern is to make a plan for Larry and then leave because he cannot live under these circumstances. He believes another important aspect is Larry's adoption, which is constantly thrown up to him. He believes Larry should know more about his adoption, but doesn't know how to tell him in view of the fact that both of Larry's parents are committed to the State Hospital and he was conceived in the hospital.'

The report from Catholic Service Bureau later continues with Larry dated 5/16/60. 'He did indicate some concern about being expelled from St. Francis as he indirectly admitted he has encouraged this action.' The report goes on to say that Larry did state that he wanted to go to Traverse City High School as most of his friends and associates attended there.

The Probate records, as a result of this hearing on 7/1/60, show that Larry was enrolled in the Father Gibault School for Boys in Terre Haute, Indiana, on 7/6/60, and was finally released from the home on 7/8/61. The records end at that point and discharge was affected from the Court on 6/15/62. The summary from Father Gibault's School, following release, offers further information under 'General Adjustment Rating,' which was described as poor to fair. The following comments are made:

'Larry's peer relationship wasn't too good; he tended to be a bully; he associated mainly with those whose size he respected. He liked to be highly regarded by others. Little improvement was shown during his stay.'

The report a bit further on states: 'His philosophy seems to be that an action is right or wrong, depending on whether you get caught or not.' He was described as having a pleasant exterior, but regarded as sly. Further comment made, 'He works all possible angles to his advantage.' Under a heading entitled 'General Remarks,' comments are made indicating good physical and mental abilities but a certain lethargy in using same. A considerable amount of guidance and encouragement were suggested but caution was offered, 'He's a diplomat, very clever. Anyone attempting to counsel him should be wary. The boy must be made to choose the proper avenues. He has no desire for self-discipline. He can be likeable. In summation, his stay here has been very erratic.'

Chief U.S. Probation Officer Richard Anderson in his presentence makes some interesting observations, 'Plamondon seems to be a rather classic case of a rejected, adopted boy who very much needed recognition. He found himself in a home where the adoption was thrown up to him, there was fighting between the parents and when Defendant was 5 or 6 years old another child was born to the parents. The foster mother then repeatedly threatened the Defendant that he would be sent to reform school if he continued his acting out behavior. As a result of her constant nagging, Defendant stayed away from home as much as possible, apparently going to such extremes that when Larry would either run away from home or be kicked out of the home by the mother, the local sheriff would befriend him and take him into his home for brief periods of time.' (Note: the sheriff Mr. Anderson refers to is Sheriff Richard Weiler of Grand Traverse County, whose feelings about this phase of Mr. Plamondon's life are pretty much the same as those expressed above. AEA)

Mr. Anderson goes on to comment, 'Defendant now considers himself a revolutionary who admits his revolutionary endeavors at first were crazy and that he is now reaping what was sowed when the White panther party was first formed and involved in. He seems to be indulging in a great deal of self-study and seems to be a dedicated, strong-willed individual who is seeking some of the recognition he has always wanted by attacking a system which largely because of personal reasons has not given him the things he has wanted out of life.'

<u>ADULT HISTORY:</u> 3/31/62, appeared in Traverse City Municipal Court. Placed on probation for 30 days. Appeared before justice Edward Schumer for heckling a group of Coast Guard at the A & W Restaurant. Later beating a Coast Guardsman. To make written report of activities each Friday to City Police Dept. To stay away from A & W Restaurant.

9/22/62, Traverse City Police Dept. Minor consuming vodka. Appeared in District Court on the same date and received a sentence of $100 fine, $7 cost, or 30 days. Committed to the Grand Traverse County Sheriff's Office and was released on September 24, 1962, upon payment of costs.

1/19/63, Traverse City Police Dept. Leaving the scene of a property damage accident. Appeared in court on the same day. Received a $100 fine, $4.30 court costs, or 35 days. Committed to the grand Traverse County Sheriff's Office and was released on

1/21/63.

8/1/63, arrested by Grand Traverse County Sheriff's Office on a charge of assault and battery. Appeared in Municipal Court on 8/2/63 and received 45 days in the county jail, $50 fine, $11.50 costs or 20 additional days. He was released from jail on 9/15/63.

8/25/64, arrested on a charge of malicious destruction of property. Appeared in Municipal Court on 8/28/64 and received a $25 fine, $4.30 court costs or 5 days and was released 8/28/64.

12/19/64, arrested as a disorderly person--creating a disturbance--minor consuming and resisting arrest by the Traverse City Police Dept. Pleaded guilty to disorderly person, received 20 days suspended. Defendant released 1/2/65.

6/3/65, arrested for expired operator's license and double parking by Traverse City Police Dept. Appeared in Municipal Court on 7/1/65, receiving $1 fine and $2 costs.

7/1/66, arrested for drunkenness by the Grand Traverse County Sheriff's Office. Appeared in court the same day. Received $25 fine, $9.50 court costs or 7 days. Released from jail on 7/7/66.

7/1/66, arrested for drunkenness. Appeared in Municipal Court 7/11/66 and received a $35 fine, $12.50 court costs or 10 days and was released from jail on 7/20/66.

9/7/66, arrested at Ithaca, Michigan for D & D and paid $50 fine, $5.15 costs.

12/11/66, arrested at Manistee for disorderly person. Assessed $20 fine, $9.70 costs or 7 days.

11/3/67, arrested by Traverse City Police Dept. for speeding, no operator's license on person. Appeared in Municipal Court on 11/6/67 on the no operator's license. Received a $15 fine, $4.30 court costs or 5 days. This was paid. 12/1/67 appeared in court for speeding. Received an $18 fine, $7 costs or 5 days and this was paid.

6/18/68, arrested for violation of state Narcotics Law. Appeared in district court on same date and demanded an exam which was set for 6/19/68 and bond was set at $20,000. Appeared in court on 6/19/68 at which time he waived examination, was bound over to Circuit Court. The case was later remanded to District Court for a preliminary examination. Such was held on 3/1/69, at which time he was again bound over to Circuit Court. This case was dismissed by the Grand Traverse County Prosecuting attorney's Office. On 5/3/72.

4/15/69, Police Dept., Ann Arbor, Mich., distribution of obscene, lewd material to persons under 18 years of age. Dismissed.

8/1/69, Police Dept., Ann Arbor, Mich., indecent exposure. Defendant urinating in an alley. Case dismissed.

8/19/69, Sheriff's Office, Hackensack, N.J., possession of narcotic drugs; possession of prescription legion drugs. No disposition indicated. Defendant advises this was dismissed.

9/21/69, Police Dept., Chicago, Ill. UUW and possession of narcotics--no disposition. U.S. Attorney's file reflects bond default. Warrants issued for failure to appear. Defendant advises cases have been dismissed.

7/23/70, State Police, St. Ignace, Mich., carrying a concealed weapon. Released to federal Government on the charge following. Case dismissed.

7/25/70, U.S. District Court, Detroit, Mich.--conspiracy charging destruction of government property. Subsequently a U.S. Supreme Court decision held that the government must make available to defendant its wiretap evidence. They declined to do so and case dismissed.

4/16/71, False Federal identification (possession of two falsely made Selective Service certificates). He entered a plea of guilty* before U.S. District Judge Noel P. Fox, Grand Rapids, Mich., 10/18/71 to Count I of the indictment that had been filed and at the same time count II was dismissed.

*Sentenced to 28 months with service of sentence at Terre Haute, Leavenworth and Springfield. Received 15 months credit for time in Kent County Jail, Grand Rapids, leaving only about one year on the Federal sentence. During jail confinement he was charged with conspiracy to possess marijuana and hashish and on 11/25/71 a six-month jail sentence was imposed to run concurrently with the Federal disposition.

To more properly understand how this case developed, one has to back up in time to October 1969 when Mr. Plamondon learned that he was sought for conspiracy to bomb the C.I.A. Building in Ann Arbor. He went underground, writer understands, for the next 10 months, traveled extensively in the United States and in Europe until his arrest on July 23, 1970, in Michigan. Mr. Anderson's presentence report points out, "on July 23, 1970, a Michigan State Police Trooper stopped a Volkswagen bus near Riggsville, Michigan, for throwing beer cans out of the window. The driver identified himself as Milton Edward Taube, and produced a vehicle registration indicating the vehicle belonged to a friend. The Trooper admonished Taube and allowed the vehicle to proceed. As a result of the Trooper putting the information into the LEIN system (Law Enforcement Information Network, author), a Michigan State Police radio broadcast ordered the Volkswagen to be stopped to see if the Defendant, who was a Federal fugitive, was in the vehicle.

As a result of the broadcast a deputy sheriff stopped the Volkswagen near Engadine, Michigan, and with the assistance of a Michigan State Police Trooper had the three occupants exit from the vehicle. One of the occupants using the name of William George Taft was found to have a two shot loaded .38 caliber gun with him. The officers then placed all three occupants of the Volkswagen under arrest for carrying a concealed weapon.

William George Taft was later identified as the

Defendant and his companions were Milton Edward Taube and John Waterhouse Forrest. As a result of search warrants, State Police located in the Volkswagen bus two loaded shotguns, one unloaded .30 caliber carbine with ammunition, a box containing 22-2″ x 16″ sticks of gelodyn explosives and 15 sticks of 60% Austin dynamite in a black plastic sack.

In Plamondon's wallet, the arresting Michigan State Trooper found Selective Service registration certificates and a Social Security card indicating that he was one William George Taft, 1809 N. Halstead, Chicago, Ill. The report goes on to say, 'A later check with the Chicago North Branch Selective Service System, Chicago, Ill., advised that no William George Taft was registered there and that the cards in the possession of the Defendant appeared valid, but were not. There was no such address as the one listed on the certificates.'

Mr. Mannor, during the course of his investigation in the Traverse City area, talked at length to Mr. David Downer, who is a contemporary of Mr. Plamondon, but, more than that, a childhood friend and neighbor. His comments are informative, coming as they do from this particular perspective:

"It should be noted that the following information was received from Mr. Downer regarding the defendant's early history which is by all other records incorrect. I included this only to give you some indication as to what the community's understanding of Larry's background was. Mr. Downer reported that, 'Pun's natural mother was a sister of Alice Plamondon, the adopted mother.' He reports that the defendant's natural father was believed to be a Puerto Rican who was working on the boats that came into Traverse City. His information continued that after Larry's birth he was given to Alice Plamondon who was then married. Mr. Downer describes the defendant's father as a very passive, dependent sort of guy who was well liked in the community and got along well with everybody. He states that the defendant's mother was, 'The dominant disciplinarian in the family. She was kind of cold and a rejecting sort of woman and no one in the neighborhood got to know her very well. She used corporal punishment frequently particularly concerning the defendant up to age eight or ten. She was always screaming at him for any infraction of the house rules and hitting him.'"

"Mr. Downer reports that, 'Larry was always running around with older crowds from two to five years older than himself. He strived very hard to keep up with them physically and be as good in sports, baseball, football and the like as they were.' He went on to state that this group that Larry ran around with, which included Mr. Downer's older brother, as well as some other young men, was kind of a wild group but one that did not seem to use alcohol until they were at least of legal age. The group was described as kind of wild in a prankish sort of way and Larry seemed to enjoy this group.

"Mr. Downer described the neighborhood at that time as a small, close knit group of people who worked very well together in doing things for the children of the neighborhood. He described one situation where they bought two lots in the neighborhood, put up electric lights and drove a well so that the kids could have an ice skating rink during the winter. Mr. Downer also stated that the neighborhood was made up of various groups of children separate from the others.

"In describing Mr. Plamondon, Mr. Downer stated, 'In spite of the family situation he (Larry) seemed light-hearted, entertaining, kind of prankish, but a likeable person. Everyone knew he had the devil in him, but he was likeable.'

"In relating to his school activities, Mr. Downer stated that Larry or Pun was expelled several times from school. He excelled athletically, but would quit or get kicked off. He seemed to have no self-discipline and didn't like or handle authority very well.

"During what would have been the last couple of years of school, Pun changed crowds from the neighborhood crowd to a rather more aggressive crowd. This group was frequently involved in fights and Mr. Downer indicates that Larry became very combative, began picking fights, most of which he provoked. In this regard Mr. Downer stated that Pun always picked on either someone bigger than himself or two or more people and he apparently began drinking quite heavily.

"Mr. Downer reports that approximately the time that the neighborhood group of young men graduated from high school and that Larry should have graduated, he went out east, believed to be in Greenwich Village in New York, where he stayed approximately a year. While there he learned to make sandals and yippie-beatnik sort of jewelry. Mr. Downer reports that Pun then returned home and had done a complete 'flip flop' and was now very passive, where most of the time he wore extremely long hair and a beard and seemed to be withdrawn and soft spoken and refused to fight anyone. He reports that defendant's old friends would try to draw him into fights and he would walk away. He seemed very protective of the young people who were drawn to him because of his philosophy at that time. Mr. Downer reports that Pun did become very philosophical at this time and seemed to attract somewhat of a local following.

"Mr. Downer in summarizing his feelings indicated that in the later years of Pun he always seemed to have an attitude of 'I am all right--you are all wrong' kind of attitude which he feels is symbolic of a battered child. He stated that throughout Larry's early years he seemed to be particularly reckless in all of his activities, be it sports, bike riding, fights or what have you. He would be very challenging to others and would always have to go one step beyond them. Pun seemed to be a young man who had a great need for personal recognition. He would associate with persons who were more allies than friends and Mr. Downer continues this by stating that he felt his present relationship with the Rainbow People's Party is pretty much the same. Mr. Downer went on to state that he felt that the defendant's wife, Genie, was more of an ally than a lover."

OFFENDER'S PERSONAL HISTORY:

Biological Father: Born 2/16/1886 in Newaygo, Mich. Half blood Ottawa Indian. He completed 7th grade. Worked as logger, railroad fireman and farm hand. Entered military service on 3/9/1914 and after injury was honorably discharged 8/10/1916. He was admitted to Traverse City Regional Psychiatric Hospital (TCPH) 6/1/43 suffering from chronic alcoholism. He died on July 21, 1954 at TCPH. Cause of death:" Cerebral hemorrhage and myocarditis.

Biological Mother: Very little is in the record regarding the mother. Born 1906 in Canada. Her family was Indian and moved to the US in 1909 and became naturalized citizens. She received a high school education. She worked as a telephone operator. She was admitted to TCPH on 2/14/44 suffering from syphilis.

Adoptive Father: 54 years of age (d/o/b 10/31/18). Residence in Kalamazoo, Mich. Defendant understands that his present source of income is welfare and Social Security. He suffers from back injury, believed to be a slipped disc, and his condition is deteriorating. Prior to being disabled was employed at Western Michigan University for approximately 7 or 8 years. He graduated from high school, worked a year on construction work, sailed on the Great Lakes for approximately five seasons. Followed that by working with a brother at a co-operative in Leelanau County. Family then moved to Traverse City where for some years they operated a store at the point where Three Mile Road intersects 31 North. Ultimately the business failed due to a combination of factors. He went to work for Golden-Fowler Furniture Co. of Traverse City as a truck driver. He stayed with this employment until he secured work at W.M.U. in their maintenance department.

Adoptive Mother: 59 years of age (d/o/b 5/12/14). Defendant advises that she currently is disabled as a result of a stroke occurring a year ago. Apparently there is paralysis on the left side and she has frequent dizzy spells. Her situation is described as worsening. He states that other than employment as a housewife she also worked in the family store and, in recent years, as a domestic.

The mother's history as available to the writer offers some revealing insights. She was 4 ½ years old when her mother died of influenza during the 1918 epidemic. In fact, it appears that she was admitted to a hospital for treatment at the same time her deceased mother was leaving. Her mother was pregnant at the time of her death and the five children were then cared for by various relatives for an extended time. Her father disappeared from the picture when his plans for a second marriage fell through. Ultimately she was placed with an aunt who was unable to keep her. So transfer was made to an orphanage when she was six years of age. At eight she was placed for adoption, which apparently never worked out well. Reports available to the Probation Agent indicate she stated of her foster parents, "They should never been allowed to adopt a child." It seems that her foster father drank heavily and that the foster mother had adopted her simply for the purpose of trying to save the father's situation. She graduated from high school and ultimately returned to the aunt with whom she had lived as a child. She worked as a domestic at this time. On one occasion she met her foster father and apparently kept touch with them occasionally through the years. She said to a caseworker once with tears in her eyes of her foster parents, "They meant more to me than I did to them."

Brothers & Sisters: It is to be noted here that at the time Defendant was adopted there were no children. Subsequently they had three (two girls, one boy, ages 22, 20 and 17) and we know of their current situation only from what Defendant tells us. Defendant says that he has a good relationship with his sisters and brother.

EARLY LIFE: Lawrence Robert Plamondon was born in Traverse City 4/27/45. I have already given some information alluding to Mr. Plamondon's adoption. While we do not have a specific date this occurred, it apparently was either late in 1946 or early 1947. As we have already indicated, he did not tell the writer about the adoption, perhaps feeling it was unimportant or, on the other hand, for reasons he felt too personal to discuss. Describes his situation with the Plamondons as generally rough. Said that his relationship with the father was always good and that it improved markedly with his mother after his prison experience. Generally he was relieved and happy that the situation had improved somewhat. He says that he is now picking up some of the things he missed in his early years. He lived at home for the most part until about age 18, other than the time spent at the Boys School in Indiana.

EDUCATION: Tells the writer that he attended Traverse City St. Francis High School through the 9th grade, then to Father Gibault's School in Indiana for a year. Points out that arrangements were made through the Catholic Service Bureau and the step was taken because he had been rowdy, had poor marks in school and really did not make any progress. He describes his Indiana experience as "not bad." He finished the 10th grade and returned to stay with his parents. Started the 11th grade and about that time was arrested for minor in possession. St. Francis put him on probation and stated that he would not be able to play football. Shortly thereafter he skipped a day, and, as he put it, "They asked why and where and I gave a flippant answer and was expelled." He liked all kinds of math, didn't care for English and history, but says now his feelings are just reversed. Admits frankly that he did not apply himself. Said that the regimentation at the school was hard to take. Most of his friends, he reports, attended Traverse City Central High School. He feels he might have done better at that facility, but his parents strongly resisted change. Says that his academic record is essentially C's and D's.

Mr. Mannor's Traverse City investigation, and specifically contact with St. Francis High School, resulted in the following information: "Records at St. Francis indicate that the Defendant entered from St. Francis Elementary School on September 7, 1959, as a ninth grade student. He continued in school until May 7, 1960, at which time he was dismissed because of his antagonistic attitude, willful destruction of property (he ripped apart a history book rented from the school and broke some windows) and because of his breaking of all the rules. Records reflect that the school officials found Larry to be 'dishonest and untrustworthy.'

"School records reflect that a transcript was sent to the Father Gibault School and that Larry attended Father Gibault from September of 1960 until the end of the school year. He re-enrolled at St. Francis in September of 1961 and for that school year there is almost nothing in the records.

"Larry re-enrolled again in September of 1962 as a probationary student, at which time he was given some very stringent rules as to behavior in the classroom and on school grounds by which he had to abide. He failed to do this and was subsequently dismissed from school in October 1962.

"School records reflect that [in] Larry's 9th year at school he received low to failing grades, with only one C reported and believed to be in Glee Club. His second year at school the grades increased appreciably and then he received C's primarily, but all within the average range.

"While school records are very sketchy as to other activities, it was noted that he was in Glee Club. School records are also incomplete for grades and the reason for this was not known. There is no reflection anywhere in the school records as to his attendance record, though this also remains a blank area. The final thing in the school records is that a transcript of his grades was sent to the Adult Education Office of the Traverse City Public Schools in January of 1965." Mr. Mannor also checked Traverse City Senior High School and they have no records of any kind on Mr. Plamondon.

EMPLOYMENT: While still in school he was employed by Frank Paulos Oldsmobile Sales for about 8 months. He left home and went on his own, proceeded to Grand Rapids with friends, stayed briefly and then returned to the Traverse City area where he worked on tree farms and dormitory construction at the Interlochen Music Camp. Stayed in the area for the summer and then to New Jersey for a year during 1964 and '65, working on building construction. He returned to Michigan thereafter. With a girl he met a Frank Paulos's, went to Florida and worked on a survey team for 7 to 8 months. He broke up with the girl and was on the road, as he puts it, for 9 to 10 months, mostly the east coast. Then returned to New Jersey and his job with the survey company for another 6 or 7 months. He recalls he was about 20 years of age when he returned to Michigan and got employment as an organizer for the AFL-CIO in terms of organizing harvest laborers on the Michigan to Florida route. Apparently stayed with this a few months before coming back to Traverse City. He worked at odd jobs until he went to Flint where, with several partners, he operated a TV antenna installation service for a brief period of time in 1967. Shortly thereafter he moved to the Detroit area, secured a job as a sandal maker in a boutique and within a short time met David and John Sinclair and has maintained his associations with them since. Rainbow People's Party, he points out, had its origins in Detroit and the so-called Artists Workshop. Subsequently this became Trans Love Energies, then the White Panther party until 1971 when reorganization took place and the Rainbow People's Party came into being.

In talking about his association with Rainbow People's Party he feels now that their designation as the White Panther Party was a poor choice and gave them a posture and image that was wrong. He states they had no idea how to be a revolutionary and felt that you had to be an agitator and rabble-rouser. "What we are doing now is a science--a political science. Essentially before we were trying to destroy and now it is building. We're trying to concretely organize people to achieve goals. We have a vision of what things ought to be (in this connection gave as an example the drug crises center the food co-operative program). In summation he commented, "If you do right, you move ahead. We are as critical of ourselves as other people are of us."

Mr. Larry Haefeli, Probation Agent, Ann Arbor, who made investigative contacts in that area for the writer, reports on Defendant's situation as follows: "Pun Plamondon is currently the chief of staff of the Rainbow People's Party and is in charge of maintaining the two households which that organization occupies on Hill Street in Ann Arbor. Upon his release from prison Pun was assigned this duty by John Sinclair. Since his release Pun has been very active in community affairs and according to all persons contacted is a definite benefit to the community.

"Rev. Robert Hauert of the University of Michigan's Religious Affairs Office indicated that he first met Pun when he officiated at Pun's marriage. The Reverend stated that the Rainbow People's Party is quite different from other aspects of the community, however, it is a very stable force here in Ann Arbor. On religious holidays, the Reverend observed that more traditional American values are upheld in this community than in the community as a whole. The Reverend feels that the Party and other affiliated organizations act as an integral part of the community and help stabilize and bring into the community those individuals who would not ordinarily be included. Basically, the Party endeavors to employ and train "street people" and is active in organizing community affairs such as free concerts, food co-operatives and other activities.

John and Leni Sinclair have known Pun Plamondon since 1967. At that time Pun came to Detroit to join the Artist Guild which was created by John Sinclair and his brother at the Wayne State University campus. At that time Pun was militant and exhibited very radical tendencies. However, John Sinclair indicated that he feels Pun has changed drastically since that time. The Artist Guild is a group of people brought together to share ideas and talents. Pun at that time was a leather worker and was quite talented in that field.

Dr. Richard Mann, a psychology professor at the University of Michigan has known Pun for several years. Dr. Mann indicated that he has warm and respectful feelings towards Pun and feels that he is a definite asset to the Ann Arbor community. Pun works very closely with young people and the Doctor indicated that he treats them in a positive manner. Dr. Mann admits, though, that Pun was not always this way and that at one time was quite a different individual.

Pun's primary tasks include working with Rainbow Trucking which makes silk screen T shirts, distributes drug education material and makes other articles. There is another division, Rainbow Multi-Media, which is run by John Sinclair. This branch of the organization promotes concerts and other public activities. Recently they sponsored the Ann Arbor Jazz &

Blues Festival which attracted well over 30,000 people in three days."

MARITAL HISTORY: Defendant met Genie Johnson, now 26, in Detroit in the spring of 1967 shortly after his move to that city. They lived together for a period of time and were legally married November 25, 1968, at Ann Arbor, Michigan. He describes their marriage as a good one, pointing out that her politics, attitude, thinking and philosophy parallel his own. He points out that in many ways, particularly patience and concern, she is better than he. "She is of much help to me, critical and free with her knowledge." He spoke of her early life, pointing out that her father is a retired Air Force colonel and both parents presently reside in Atlanta, Ga. He states that there wasn't any place for her in the home in terms of her early life, which was characterized by a great deal of insecurity.

They have not had any children, although Mrs. Plamondon was at one time pregnant and suffered a miscarriage enroute back to Michigan from the Woodstock Festival. He points out that it is his feeling that the miscarriage was precipitated by their arrest and confinement in New Jersey at that time for possession of marijuana.

Speaking about the possibility of children, he indicated that they are not in the picture for several years as both he and Genie wish to be more settled. He points out that he is having trouble putting things together after two years in prison (released 7/72), and then the current deal.

Mrs. Plamondon has been most active in the Rainbow People's Party over a period of years and has been strongly involved in a number of their community oriented programs. We note a comment in the Federal presentence to the effect that "Defendant stated his wife is very much a revolutionary; that she has traveled all over, been to North Viet Nam and Sweden and that both of their lives are dedicated to a revolutionary movement which will bring power to the people.

ECONOMIC SITUATION: He has been a participating member

of what he at one point during the interviews termed "a community living experience" with his total needs being met by Rainbow People's Party. Neither he or other members of the Party have, as a result, any assets or liabilities.

HEALTH & HABITS: Generally speaking health is good. Eyes, ears and teeth are problem free. Has had his collar bone fractured on two occasions, but no disability as a result. Has had two hernia operations. Smokes approximately five packs of cigarettes a week. Describes himself as a "social drinker." As far as intoxicants, frankly admits that he had problems years ago, but these are now solved.

RELIGION: Writer neglected to discuss this with Defendant. There is information in the Federal presentence of 1971 that may reflect his present beliefs and we are quoting it for such value as it may have: "Defendant was reared in a strict Catholic home. At the present time he considers Christianity in the United States irrelevant and unnecessary. He does not know as he believes in God. States he is reading the Bible, but strictly to obtain historical perspective and he does not attend Church anywhere."

EVALUATION OF DEFENDANT BY RICHARD L. MANNOR: Interspersed throughout the presentence report has been a considerable amount of information gathered by Mr. Mannor in the Traverse City area. Basically this covers a period of his life from 1945 to about 1967. Mr. Mannor, in my judgment, is a dedicated, understanding and concerned agent whose assessments of people show great insight. Realizing that he would develop a feeling about Mr. Plamondon based on the information he was gathering, we asked that he evaluate it for the period noted above:

"It appears we have a product partially of a home environment where a passive father and an aggressive mother compounded the fact that Larry was adopted and came from rather inauspicious beginnings. Apparently things went well until the Plamondons were able to have their own child, at which time Mrs. Plamondon no longer needed Pun because she had one of her own flesh and blood. As a result she became very aggressive toward him, showed little understanding of his wants and needs and almost totally rejected him. Larry, to make up for this lack, became the neighborhood prankster and dare-devil and by this method was able to receive a lot of community recognition and even sympathy. He continued in this vein through elementary school, junior high school and high school, and it appears that he became more aggressive as time went by in an effort to maintain his identity and to keep the kind of attention that he apparently needed. He has been described as aggressive in athletics as well as his personal behavior, but it should be noted that in athletics, which indicate a rather positive thing, that he was not able to affect the necessary discipline to do as well as some of his classmates and peers. The record will back up, I think, that Larry at that time turned to anti-social activities almost exclusively for the fulfillment of these needs. One needs only to look at the school records where he was a constant source of trouble, the court records where he was continuously involved in drinking, fighting, destructive kinds of things.

Because Larry was able to receive a great deal of recognition from his neighborhood, later his school authorities, various social agencies with which he was involved, as well as the court, he probably lost a sense of social responsibility and, in effect, became a young man without a great deal of conscience. It is believed that many of his friends, neighborhood associates and the community at large probably over-rated Larry's natural abilities and mental capabilities. He may well have realized this and this forced him to even greater anti-social acts to meet in some way the expectations of those aforementioned people. Unfortunately, through all of this, he received a great deal of support and I feel that this has carried over into his adult life. I believe that Mr. Downer probably put his finger on it when he stated that Pun has a great many allies, but probably very few close personal friends."

Respectfully submitted,
Arthur E. Albright
Probation & Parole Agent

AEA:dnr

APPENDIX B

Testimony of Sergeant Clifford A. Murray, special investigation unit, Intelligence Section, Michigan State Police, before the United States Senate Internal Security subcommittee, September 25, 1970.

"I would like to say at this time that is the opinion of myself and that of my department that the White Panther Party is working toward obtaining control of large masses of young people for the primary purpose of causing revolution in this country.

"The methods used to recruit these people is based upon a complete dropout of our society and the adoption of a system involving 'rock' music and the free use of drugs and sex in a setting of commune living.

"It is apparent that every attempt is being made to break down the moral relationship between the youth and his or her parents along with a complete disregard for law and order.

"It is also apparent that much of the material used in writings published by this organization come directly from the 'Red Book' of quotations by Mao Tse-tung. While Mao relates to the 'masses' as the workers, this organization relates to the 'masses' as young people...

"Gentlemen, based on the information that we have obtained through other normal police functions, we would have to consider the White Panther Party as an organization bent on total destruction of the present Government of the United States and detrimental to the welfare of this country.

"Thank you.

APPENDIX C

STATE OF MICHIGAN
IN THE CIRCUIT COURT FOR THE 28TH JUDICIAL CIRCUIT

PEOPLE OF THE STATE OF MICHIGAN,
Plaintiff

File No. 716

-vs.-

LAWRENCE "PUN" PLAMONDON and

_______________(Cheeseburger).
Defendants

MOTION TO DISMISS INFORMATION

Defendants, by and through their attorney Hugh M. Davis Jr., move this honorable court to dismiss the information filed herein and show as follows:

1. The instant prosecution is a bad faith, malicious and unlawful criminal action brought discriminatorily by the attorney General of the state of Michigan at the behest of the Michigan State Police and various other federal and local police

agencies.

2. The instant prosecution deprives defendants of the rights, privileges, and immunities granted them under the Michigan Constitution and the First, Fourth, Fifth, and Ninth Amendments to the U.S. Constitution.

3. The instant prosecution is being brought for the purpose of staining defendants with the taint of criminality, thereby announcing to the public at large that they should be shunned, silenced, and avoided.

4. The instant prosecution is being brought in order to chill and deter the political activity of defendants and the political organization to which they belong.

5. The instant prosecution is being brought discriminatorily, with an evil eye and an unequal hand, for the purposes of harassing, intimidating, and silencing the political activity and free association of defendants, their friends, neighbor, fellow community residents, peers, and political associates, thereby depriving them of the equal protection of the laws and infringing on protected rights of free speech and association.

6. The instant prosecution is one in a long chain of abuses initiated by the Michigan Attorney General and the Michigan State Police and suffered by the defendants, their compatriots, and the political organizations to which they belong.

7. The instant prosecution is brought by the Attorney General without hope of ultimate success or in the legitimate interests of criminal justice, but for the purposes of stifling and chilling massive public, legal, political action of progressive and rainbow people throughout the state of Michigan.

8. Separately and in addition thereto, the totality of the circumstances in this case offends a sense of justice, thus depriving defendants of due process of law, contrary to the

United States and Michigan Constitutions.

9. In support of the above averments, defendants show as follows:

A. Both defendants are members of the Rainbow People's Party.

B. The Rainbow People's Party and its predecessor organizations, the White Panther Party, Trans-Love Energies, and the Artists Workshop/Detroit, and the members thereof, have for the past nine years been the victims of a vicious vendetta by the government of the state of Michigan through the agencies of the Attorney General, the Michigan state Police, and various local and federal police agencies.

C. In pursuance of this vendetta, the Attorney General, acting alone and in concert with various local and federal government agencies, has caused the arrest of Rainbow People's Party members on no less than 22 separate occasions.

D. No less than 15 of the prosecutions were dismissed by the court, dropped by the prosecution, or reversed on appeal.

D. No contested case has ever resulted in a conviction which has been upheld.

F. This shows a pattern of discriminatory prosecution brought in bad faith.

G. The main motivations for this vendetta have been the Rainbow People's Party's belief that drastic changes are needed in American society, its advocacy of the legalization of marijuana (coupled with its opposition to so-called "hard drugs"), and its sponsorship of various "youth culture" programs.

H. Under the attack of such bad faith, malicious, discriminatory prosecution, the Rainbow People's Party and its members have waged many legal battles resulting in several landmark decisions, among them People v Sinclair, 387 Mich 91 (1972), overturning the state's felony marijuana law; United States v United States District Court, 407 US 297,324 (1972), outlawing domestic "national security" wiretapping; and an action which resulted in the correcting of inhumane conditions in the Wayne County Jail.

I. The Rainbow People's Party and its members

are currently involved in other litigation of far-reaching consequences, including an action against the University of Michigan for discriminatory denial of student facilities and an action against various United States officials for denial of civil rights and violation of the wiretapping laws.

J. The attitude of the state of Michigan and its Attorney General toward the Rainbow People's Party is set out clearly in briefs filed by the Attorney General in support of a motion to dismiss a civil action brought by John Sinclair against various state prison officials. These briefs demonstrate that this group is deeply feared by the Attorney General--and at the same time ridiculed in a manner supposedly beneath the dignity of legal counsel.

K. The Rainbow People's Party and its members are and have been under constant surveillance, by electronic and other means, by the Michigan State Police and other police agencies, and have been labeled "subversive:" The partial story of this surveillance is told in a printed extract from the 1970 hearings on alleged subversion in the "new Left" held by the United States Senate subcommittee. (A copy of extract appears in this book as appendix B).

L. While incarcerated, Rainbow People's Party members suffered special hardships inflicted only upon those of "political prisoner" status.

M. The actions of the Attorney General in this action show a pattern of discrimination and a totality of circumstances which offend a sense of justice, among them:

(1) The failure to prosecute the complainant for his admitted multiple transactions and business involving hard drugs.

(2) (OMITTED IN ORIGINAL)

(3) The request by the Attorney General for exorbitant $100,000 bond for both defendants Plamondon and Cheese Burger, despite the fact that Burger's only prior conviction was for illegal possession of alcohol.

(4) The injection of the issue of a marijuana

transaction into the case without bringing the same before the court for it to be resolved.

(5) The prejudicing of defendants, presuming their guilt, by claiming that the complainant and his family feared for their welfare without offering any proof of the same.

(6) The issuance of a rare press release by the Attorney General on the topic of the $100,000 bond and the detailed nature of the case.

(7) The military-type raid on the offices of the Rainbow People's Party during the arrest of defendant Burger and the Gestapo tactics of the on-the-highway arrest of defendant Plamondon, despite the fact that he is a well-known community leader and would have been available at any time at his office.

(8) The attempt to entrap defendant Plamondon (but not defendant Burger) into incriminating telephone conversations.

(9) The filing of a very unusual "long form complaint" at the District Court, which was very suitable for release to the press.

(10) The bringing of what can only be termed speculative and dubious charges--such as "criminal usury"--on the sole word of a complainant lacking in credibility.

WHEREFORE, defendants pray that this honorable Court dismiss the information filed herein against them, and that they be discharged.

Respectfully submitted,

Lawrence "Pun" Plamondon--Defendant

Cheese "The Burger" Burger--Defendant

Hugh M. Davis Jr.--Attorney for defendants

Dated: June 20, 1973